THE WORLD ATLAS OF
BEER

THE WORLD ATLAS OF
BEER

TIM WEBB & STEPHEN BEAUMONT

MITCHELL BEAZLEY

Dedication
For Maggie and Siri-Ann, the loving and supportive ladies in our lives.

The World Atlas of Beer
by Tim Webb & Stephen Beaumont

First published in Great Britain in 2012 by Mitchell Beazley,
an imprint of Octopus Publishing Group Limited, Endeavour House,
189 Shaftesbury Avenue, London WC2H 8JY
www.octopusbooks.co.uk

An Hachette UK Company
www.hachette.co.uk

ISBN: 978 1 84533 633 2

A CIP record for this book is available from the British Library.

Set in Garamond and Futura.

Printed and bound in Hong Kong.

Head of Editorial Tracey Smith
Senior Editor Leanne Bryan
Copy Editor Jo Richardson
Proofreader Jamie Ambrose
Indexer Cathy Heath
Art Director Jonathan Christie
Executive Art Editor Juliette Norsworthy
Designer Jeremy Tilston
Picture Research Manager Giulia Hetherington
Picture Researcher Maria Gibbs
Beer Label Researcher Michael Gill
Production Manager Peter Hunt

Consultant Editor
Joanna Copestick is an author, a book publisher and a member of
the British Guild of Beer Writers. She spent several years working
for CAMRA (Campaign for Real Ale) as Head of Publications. She has
been a beer judge, worked as assistant editor of the *Good Beer Guide*,
and was on the judging panel for the British Beer Writer of the Year
Award in 2011.

Cartography
Digital mapping by Encompass Graphics Ltd,
Hove, UK, www.encompass-graphics.co.uk

A Note About Alcohol Content

The authors believe in the importance of knowing the strength of the beer you drink and have thus listed the alcohol contents for each beer reviewed. Readers should be aware, however, that the allowable margin for error in different countries varies such that the strength listed on the label and that measurable in a lab can vary up to one percent and, occasionally, even more.

Confusing matters further, breweries sometimes change the strength of a beer, both in terms of general production and from country to country. So a beer well known as a 6% alcohol by volume pale ale, for example, can unexpectedly morph into a 5.5% or 6.5% brew, or be produced at 6% in its home country but rise to 7.5% for export.

As a result, while the alcohol contents listed in this book were, to the best of the authors' knowledge, accurate at the time of going to press, they may not remain consistent with every consumer's experience.

Contents

Foreword	6
Introduction	8
How the Book Works	10
What is Beer?	11

THE NATURE OF BEER — 12

THE ORIGINS OF BEER	14
HOW BEER IS MADE	16
Malt & Other Grains	17
Hops	18
Yeast	20
Brewing & Fermenting	22
WORLD BEER PRODUCTION & HOP CULTIVATION	24
CRAFT BREWING	26
HIGH-VOLUME BREWING & CONVENIENCE BEERS	30
BEER STYLES	34
BUYING BEER	35
STORING BEER	36
SERVING BEER	37
POURING BEER	38
TASTING BEER	40
BEER & FOOD	42
Food Affinity Chart	44

THE WORLD OF BEER — 46

EUROPE	48
BELGIUM	52
Trappist & Abbey Ales	54
Oak-aged Ales	58
Lambic Beers	62
Saison Beers	68
Spiced Wheat Beers	72
The British Influence	74
Regional Beers	76
GERMANY	80
Helles & Other Pale Lagered Beers	82
The Beers of Franconia	84
The Altbiers of North Rhine Westphalia	86
Kölsch	88
German Wheat Beers	90
Dark Beers & Bock	92
AUSTRIA	94
CZECH REPUBLIC	98
Pale Lagers	100
Darker Lagers & Other Czech Beers	104
GREAT BRITAIN & IRELAND	108
Pale Ale & Bitter Beers	110
Porters & Stouts	116
Brown Ale & Dark Mild	120
Stronger British Ales	122

Local Heroes & New Beginnings	124
FRANCE	128
Bière de Garde	130
Bière de Blé Noir & Other Local Specialities	132
NETHERLANDS	136
Bok & Meibok	138
Other Dutch Beers	140
SCANDINAVIA & THE BALTIC	142
Denmark	145
Norway	148
Sweden	150
Finland	152
The Baltic States	154
ITALY	158
Italian Breweries	160
REST OF EUROPE	166
Collaboration Beers	172
THE AMERICAS	174
THE USA	178
California	180
Pacific Northwest, Alaska & Hawaii	184
Rocky Mountains	188
Midwest & Great Lakes	190
Northeast	196
South	200
THE CARIBBEAN	203
Extreme Beers	204
CANADA	206
Québec & the East	208
Ontario & the Prairies	210
Alberta, British Columbia & the North	212
LATIN AMERICA	216
Mexico & Central America	218
Brazil	220
Argentina & the Rest of South America	224
AUSTRALIA, NEW ZEALAND & THE FAR EAST	226
AUSTRALIA	228
NEW ZEALAND	230
THE FAR EAST	232
Japan	234
Vietnam	238
Thailand	239
REST OF THE WORLD	240
Emerging Markets	244
Beer Festivals	246
International Beer Festivals Calendar	247
Glossary	248
Index	250
Picture Credits	255
Bibliography & Acknowledgements	256

Foreword

Wine may accompany dinner and fine whisky a good book, but beer always seems to go better with life. Yet as with any companion, it should be chosen well and properly understood.

For 10,000 years beer has, in turns, been consumed as an intoxicating foodstuff, promoted as a protector of public health, used as a means of placating a workforce, become a lucrative source of taxation, and seen as a suitable focus for global business. It is perhaps only in recent years and since we nearly lost it altogether, thanks to wars, industrialization, and prohibition in several forms, that it has become a drink to be enjoyed and explored in its own right.

Our aim in this first edition of *The World Atlas of Beer* is to provide the uninitiated with an introduction to the best of modern brewing against a backdrop of its history and provenance, and to offer more seasoned beer travellers an opportunity to take stock after an eventful period of renaissance for the world's favourite alcoholic drink.

I began to take beer seriously in 1974, when I signed up to my lifetime membership of CAMRA (the Campaign for Real Ale), founded three years earlier by young journalists intent on vociferously defending some of Britain's older styles of ale. Success seemed unlikely, but youth knows no boundaries.

At that time we thought we were alone, having no idea that a few wishful thinkers in other countries had, since the mid-1960s, been buying small breweries in which to make examples of their traditional local brews, or that, as I discovered years later, groups of American home brewers, used to making old-fashioned beers in ways unknown to the post-Prohibition brewing corporations, had begun agitating to be allowed to produce them commercially.

For four decades I have been watching a quiet, unlikely revolution unfold that has revived beer's fortunes in ways that even my most zealous contemporaries could not have predicted.

When the greatest beer writer of all, the late Michael Jackson, first penned his *The World*

Above: Prohibition in the USA 1920–1933: A barrel of confiscated illegal beer being poured down a drain.

Left: In Britain, brewers responded to Temperance Movement concerns by creating light, sweet stouts.

Guide to Beer in 1977, he was describing a devastated landscape in which few areas remained unscathed. He recorded the robust living beer cultures of West Germany and Czechoslovakia, saw potential in the threatened and declining ones of Britain and Belgium, and went on to describe past glories in a dozen other countries where well-crafted beer had become virtually moribund.

Although its author was not to know it at the time, the first *World Guide* eloquently defined the story of beer at the moment of its lowest ebb. Our challenge, in contrast, has been to map the steady victories of an unexpected survivor, at a time when it has regained its confidence and a new *Zeitgeist* exists, filled with optimism and innovation.

Researching this book in the second decade of the twenty-first century, we were amazed to discover new craft breweries in no fewer than 74 different countries, all intent on producing flavoursome beers on a human scale.

What follows, we hope, is a fair and realistic global review of fine beer, as it cascades through new and exciting times.

Cheers!

Tim Webb
Cambridge, UK

Above: A tray of plenty. Such is the profusion of beer styles today that many bars offer "tasters", which allow patrons to sample several beers in small portions.

Introduction

Were there ever to be the right time for a book such as this, it is now.

The world has never before seen such an enormous range of brewing activity across all continents, with home brewing even taking place at research stations in the Antarctic. And neither would our ancestors have borne witness to such an astounding diversity of beer styles, from pilsners to porters and red rice ales to inspired re-creations of archaeological brews, nor had such ease of access to the fine ales and lagers of faraway lands.

To underline just how widespread brewing has become, we estimate that the twenty-first century may boast over 10,000 breweries worldwide, producing in excess of 60,000 regularly made beers. By any standard, those are phenomenal totals.

Perhaps unsurprisingly, this state of affairs has resulted in a growing gulf between breweries large and lumbering and those small and nimble. Yet rather than the big guns smothering smaller interests, we have found that it is the smaller craft brewers who have taken the lead, guiding the industry – including, in many cases, the multinationals – forwards in ingenious and often iconoclastic ways.

Indeed, such is the success of small-scale, artisanal brewing today that the world of beer has become an amorphous entity, and defining it is now a task akin to drawing a picture of a fast-moving train. Even as Tim and I sit respectively in Cambridge, UK, and Toronto, Canada, having completed the bulk of our research and tasting for this book, the burgeoning craft beer movement continues to charge stubbornly ahead, delighting our sensibilities and palates while frustrating our efforts to pin it down.

Almost anywhere you turn there is locally brewed beer. Sure, the same familiar names will most frequently appear on store shelves and bar or pub beer lists, but for the individual willing to commit the time to research and investigation, the reward is often an out-of-the-way IPA or unexpectedly characterful stout or pilsner. It is our hope that this book will provide both tools and inspiration for such present or potential beer explorers.

So long as we retain a suitable degree of historical perspective, the way forward for craft beer and its enjoyment and appreciation is overflowing with possibilities. Our youngest legal drinkers have grown up with the existence of craft breweries and their brands, whereas for Tim and especially myself, such beers were once but early anomalies. Increasingly, even the youth drink for the occasion rather than out of slavish devotion to a specific marketing campaign, ordering from one set of brands when drinking with friends at a bar or pub, another while cheering on the local sports team, and yet another when entertaining at home.

Today, there is virtually no aspect of social life from which beer is excluded, and seldom must the beer drinker endure the scorn of the surrounding wine tipplers. Beer is exciting, beer is gastronomic, beer is as social as it has ever been – and beer is worth talking, and reading, about.

Welcome to our world of beer. We hope you enjoy it.

Stephen Beaumont
Toronto, Canada

Above: Even naturally cloudy beers are enjoying a renaissance.

Right: Traditional Pilsner beers in iconic glasses at *U Zlatého Tygra* (The Golden Tiger) in Prague.

Above: "Hands on" is more than a mere catchphrase at many craft breweries, where small production runs and tight budgets make manual labour a necessity.

How the Book Works

Beer is the world's favourite alcoholic beverage, consumed in one form or another everywhere it is not specifically prohibited, and in many districts where it is. As such, documenting its place in the world is a complex task, made all the harder by its stubbornly evolving and expanding nature. The following pages, arranged geographically by country and region, constitute our attempt to put this changeable picture in order, uncovering beer's past, documenting its present, and doing our best to foretell the future. To accomplish this, we have employed several devices.

National & Regional Profiles

With brewing's reach now stretching around the globe, we have had to make difficult decisions on where best to apportion our pages, ones that some readers will no doubt disagree with. We apologize in advance to any beer aficionados who feel that their country of birth or beer of preference receives short shrift.

Within each entry, further divisions have been made. In relation to many older brewing lands, we have singled out specific styles this way, while most New World entries have been organized geographically and, in some instances, a combination of the two approaches has been used. Beer as a subject matter is amorphous, and no single approach will serve all occasions.

Tasting Notes

In most cases, we have illustrated the variations on beers, breweries, and national tastes with examples of beers that in some way epitomize what is going on. These are not "the best beers in the world" – an odd concept in so wide a field and not one that plagues those who relax into fine wines. See them instead as above-average examples of a particular statement.

With very few exceptions, notably Belgium's Trappist and lambic brewers, we have not allowed more than one beer to be included per brewery. Thus some of the most prodigious talents in the industry are confined to a single mention, while a few rogues trading off the fame of a beer created by their forefathers have equal billing in our inadvertent hall of fame.

The World's Brewing Giants

In general, little mention has been made of the world's most popular beers. Sadly, within the world of beer, fame is rarely achieved or sustained through maintaining distinctive features, but rather is accrued by association with different forms of celebrity, or popular interest, in turn bought through sponsorship.

As it would be the height of foolishness to ignore completely the Goliaths among our host of worthy Davids, however, we have included in each entry a list of "Local Labels" highlighting the big-selling beers unique or primarily limited to their national markets. The parent company of each of these brands is identified in parentheses following the beer name.

Maps

In a world as densely populated and, it must be repeated, as changeable as that of beer, it is nigh on impossible to plot the breweries of every nation on a map. We have, therefore, adopted a variety of approaches in our attempts to provide geographic context to the book. Again, we apologize for any omissions, intentional or otherwise.

Terminology

Like most foodstuffs, beer comes with its own lexicon of sometimes baffling terminology. We have attempted to avoid such jargon as much as we are able, and have provided a Glossary (see pp.248–9) for reference when such efforts have failed.

Left: Depending on the location, maps may feature statistical information, historic brewing trends, metropolitan regions and their breweries, or beer-traveller highlights.

Right: Tasting notes feature beer and brewery names, alcohol content, brewery location and website, and, where available, label illustration.

NÄRKE KULTURBRYGGERI
- med anor från allra första början -

Kaggen!
STORMAKTS
PORTER 2008

Kraftig och värmande Imperial Stout bryggd med ljunghonung från Närke och lagrad på ekfat i 2,5 månader. Serveras med fördel i små kupor vid lägst 14°C. Den bryggdes i december 2008 och går bra att lagra i många år.

OG 1.112   Öl är Konst!   ABV 9,5%

KAGGEN! STORMAKTS PORTER (9.5%)
Närke Kulturbryggeri, Örebro (Örebro)
Sweden's most challenging brewery, founded in 2003, creates several versions of this imperial stout. This example presents one of the most impressive taste sensations of any beer in this book or elsewhere.
www.kulturbryggeri.se

What is Beer?

The legal definition of beer varies around the world in both its precise specifications and its purpose. In countries such as Norway and Japan, for example, if a drink is defined as a beer, it will attract a higher rate of tax than other alcoholic beverages of the same strength. In France, the opposite applies, although in part because wine is already heavily subsidized by the European Union for being an agricultural by-product, while beer is considered manufactured. In Texas, where beer itself is admittedly fairly well defined, any brand over 5% ABV must legally be billed as either ale or malt liquor, regardless of how it has been fermented or conditioned. And so on.

What is clear is that beer is the product of grain, whereas wine is derived from fruit (other than apples and pears, which yield, respectively, cider and perry), and mead is fermented from honey. So sake, beverage alcohol pedants will tell you, is therefore a kind of beer, although we counsel not to try explaining this to a Japanese sake enthusiast.

Beyond the grain requirement – itself rather broadly interpreted by certain brewing companies – and whatever legal constricts may exist from jurisdiction to jurisdiction, beer is a rather nebulous entity. Unlike wine, which is regulated through both appellation controls and convention, restrictions as to what a beer may or may not contain, or how it might be described, are few.

This has created the rather absurd situation whereby the consumer is awarded minimal information as to what he or she is buying. So while no one would expect a Chardonnay wine to boast any flavour profile other than that of a wine made from Chardonnay grapes, an IPA in Britain might be dryly malty and below four per cent alcohol, while one in California could be aggressively bitter and above seven per cent in strength, and yet another in eastern Canada similar in appearance, aroma, and taste to a mainstream lager.

As frustrating as this situation may be at times, especially for the beer novice, it is also responsible for one of beer's foremost strengths: diversity of styles, ingredients, and characters. The same creativity that results in a strong ale in one country being comparable to a "session" beer in another also permits brewers the use of unconventional ingredients and techniques, which in turn result in beer's constantly evolving and expanding palate of flavours.

So, to return to the matter at hand, if you ask for a definition of beer, the short answer is a moderately alcoholic beverage created by the fermentation of sugars that are derived in largest part from the boiling of particular specified grains, most prominently malted barley, with seasoning provided by hops (*see* pp.18–19).

In a more practical, functional sense, however, beer is anything a brewer can conspire to create, beginning with grain, usually with added hops, and always fermented by some form of yeast but also potentially incorporating any and all manner of ingredients, from

Above: Whole hops are added to the boil at McMullen's brewery in Hertford, UK.

berries to legumes, coriander to tobacco leaf, and conditioned or aged in any of a multitude of ways, including in stainless-steel tanks, large stoppered bottles, or used whisky barrels (*see* p.22–9).

Many German brewers may still find solace in the *Reinheitsgebot* or "Purity Order" (*see* p.80), but for much of the rest of the brewing world, and the vast majority of the craft brewing fraternity, such restrictions no longer apply. The rulebook has been thrown away – let creative anarchy reign, wisely or otherwise.

THE NATURE OF BEER

Policy-makers in the EU make a small, innocent-looking yet remarkably important distinction between wine and beer. The first, they declare, is "an agricultural product", while the second is "manufactured". This differentiation may seem pedantic but it costs beer drinkers billions of euros annually, since winemakers benefit from an agricultural subsidy denied to brewers – even those who still brew on the farm.

It is not just politicians who see beer as a product of manufacturing industry. Over the centuries, as the specialist cooks who were the first brewers became artisans paid to turn grain into a social lubricant, fortunes were made in trading these commodities. Some built their reputations on distinctive and enjoyable beers, whereas others sold ones that, although no more than a degree or two above acceptable, were more affordable and had greater potential for profit.

The brewing business is in constant flux, its dynamics driven by the age-old tensions between the craftsman brewer intent on making the best-tasting product, and a vendor intent on supplying customers often more taken with intoxication than subtler pleasures.

The turning of barley into beer is at one and the same time simple and immensely complex. A home brewer might make something acceptably challenging from a store-bought kit using extracts, while a modern master brewer might have added a doctorate to his degree before being allowed to design a drink intended for necking effortlessly from a can.

Such are the complications behind a beverage of multiple personalities – the bringer of warmth and liquid replenishment, of conviviality and menace, the fount of all indolence and a perfect accompaniment to cheese – that we call beer.

Opposite: At the small-scale, non-automated level, brewing remains an often intensely physical activity. Here, Bill Batten of California's AleSmith Brewing Company rakes out the spent grain after the mashing process.

THE ORIGINS OF BEER

We infer from the pattern of crops planted by the early inhabitants of Mesopotamia and the Fertile Crescent that they were probably brewing a form of beer by 9000 BC, although the earliest direct evidence comes from residues on pottery fragments found in the Hunan province of China dating from 2,000 years later.

By 3000 BC, it seems Egyptian brewers had determined that barley was the best grain for brewing and had developed crude forms of malting. We also know that the Celts were brewing with barley, wheat, and oats by 2000 BC.

Beer making was originally a domestic pursuit, frequently carried out by "ale wives" alongside baking. Even the early "common" or town brewers often employed women to oversee the recipes and the brewing.

The curse of ancient brewers was oxidation. Contact with air rapidly turns the alcohol in sweet, heady fermented grain extracts into nauseating aldehydes and sour organic acids. Beer makers sought for centuries to delay this process by using herbal mixtures called *grut* (also *gruit* and *gruut*). Some purveyors, such as those in medieval Bruges, became immensely rich, including those claiming health-giving or aphrodisiac effects for their patent recipes, despite the limited usefulness of their products.

Hops had been used by apothecaries for centuries to add scented bitterness to ancient medicines and may have been used in brewing, too. They contain antioxidants that slow acidification and antiseptics that reduce fungal and other infections, so became the ideal brewers' remedy, their use spreading across Europe from Bohemia between the eleventh and fourteenth centuries.

Before it was understood to be a living microorganism, yeast, captured in a runny suspension, thick paste, or as dried granules, was revered as a gift from God that made bread dough rise before baking and turned thin porridge into intoxicating ale.

Although beer had always varied in strength and composition through local circumstances and traditions, from the seventeenth century brewers began to emulate particular styles and fashions. The new coke ovens allowed lightly cooked malts to be made, from which pale ale could be brewed. Eighteenth-century London saw the creation of first porter and then stout. In 1842, a blond, ice-stored beer was made for the first time in the southern Bohemian town of Pilsen.

The Industrial Revolution made it possible to brew in ever-larger quantities, while the age of steam brought speedier transportation on land and at sea, enabling the same beer to be available over vast areas, including overseas.

In 1862, French microbiologist Louis Pasteur and colleagues invented a process that allowed brewers to kill off the tiny creatures that both created and ruined the flavours of beer, driving beer makers away from vinous oak-aged ales to concentrate on making sweeter dead ones.

By 1900, brewery companies the world over had the capacity to create and sell a wider range of beers than had ever before been possible. Who knows how things would have been by now had 50 years of carnage, economic recession, and Prohibitionist politics not begun in 1914?

Come 1965, only four countries – Great Britain, Germany, Czechoslovakia, and Belgium – could claim to have much of their culture of quality craft brewing remaining, and even those were struggling. The game was almost up for beer.

Nobody foresaw what happened next.

Above: Modern brewers' control over fermentation owes much to the work of brewing scientists of the 19th and early 20th centuries, such as those pictured here at the Carlsberg laboratories in Copenhagen.

Opposite: Egyptian pharoah King Intef II offers milk and beer to the gods Ra and Hathor at Thebes, ca. 2100 BC.

HOW BEER IS MADE

Beer is a deliberate drink. The vagaries of terroir or harvest, barrique or cork need rarely be endured by the brewer. Instead, they get to choose the colour, clarity, and intensity of their beers, the extent and nature of their bitterness, and most of the immediate or lasting flavours and aromas held within them. They decide the amount of alcohol they will eventually contain and even the size, tint, and consistency of their heads.

At every stage, they balance the competing demands of cost and excellence, of individuality and conformity, of consistency and flair. At the same time, they must obsess about doing no harm, ensuring that rogue microbes do not infect the yeast or any of their equipment, including the containers in which the beer will be stored for sale.

When a beer goes wrong, the fault can usually be traced to human error rather than an act of God. Whether a beer entertains with its perfect balance and imaginative edges or simply bubbles from a can with nothing to say beyond its brand name, it is the product of thoughtful deliberation.

If the beer you are drinking is dull, perhaps its makers are telling you something.

Right: Brewers and beer enthusiasts alike know that aroma is every bit as important as taste in the appreciation of a beer.

Above: You can never be too careful. Sampling wort from the lauter tun in one of Bavaria's older breweries.

Malt & Other Grains

The heart of any beer is its malted barley. Harvested cereal is threshed and the grains kept warm and damp in order to germinate and become seeds in neat, broad, tended piles at a maltings. The action of enzymes in their cell walls changes starch into sugars suitable for fermentation into alcohol. To capture this at its optimum, the maltster kills off the enzymes by a sharp burst of heat.

Types of barley vary in their sugar content and their mix of background flavours, but also in their yield per hectare. British brewers often favour Maris Otter, a tasty yet relatively low-yielding variety grown mainly in East Anglia. Their Czech counterparts swear by the Haná varieties from South Moravia, while German colleagues prefer the appropriately named Malz.

Malted barley can be made to a wide variety of specifications, for beer brewers and others. While a whisky distiller may specify that a kiln be peat-fired, the brewer will be more concerned about the duration and temperature of the roast.

At the lighter end, pilsner malt is barely toasted and has not browned, allowing its use in the creation of light, blond beers. Pale ale malt introduces an amber tone, with slightly darker crystal malt typically adding toffee character. Vienna malt brings in ruddy brown, as does the darker *Münchener* (or Munich). At the roasted end of the spectrum, chocolate malts look and taste caramelized, turning a beer black and acrid when less than ten per cent is added to the mash.

Although barley is the undisputed king of the brewing grains, wheat and oats have just as long a pedigree. These can be malted or used plain, bringing a heavy sweetness to young beer – oats more so than wheat – but greater astringency when their sugars are fully fermented. They bring practical challenges, too, producing a milky protein haze that can be difficult to clear and, if making up much over a third of the mash, clogging up brewing vessels like soggy pasta.

A few craft brewers have revived the use of older grains such as spelt, buckwheat, rye, and others, while experiments with sorghum and millet in the developed world smack more of cost-cutting. These cereals do appear in beers in sub-Saharan Africa, in some instances by political imperative, as in Nigeria, where the use of local sorghum is mandated as an economic measure.

Adjunctive grains like maize and rice or simpler saccharides such as starch, syrup, or crystalline sugar thin out the flavour of beer. This can make a heavy beer more approachable, a 9% ABV beer readily withstanding the replacement of 15 per cent of its sugars without suffering. In lighter beers, they serve mainly to keep costs down or simplify further the taste of an already thin brew.

Above: Traditional floor malting of barley requires that the grain be turned manually so as to ensure even kiln-drying.

Hops

The common hop (*Humulus lupulus*) is crucial to the smell and taste of a beer. Farmed hops existed in central Europe as early as the seventh century and were probably used in brewing long before the king of Bohemia taxed them in 1089. By the fourteenth century, they were a routine ingredient of most European beers.

Hop flowers or cones contain a variety of naturally occurring chemicals that reduce fungal and other infections and slow oxidation, while their oils provide floral and herbal aromas and citrus flavours. Bitterness in varying degrees is liberated as alpha acids, which are activated on boiling (*see* p.22) and measured on a scale of International Bitterness Units (IBU).

Sour and bitter tastes trigger in-built warning signs in humans that help us spot poisonous foods and liquids. These become more acute in pregnant women and nursing mothers, and may account in part for beer's greater popularity with men, although social conditioning probably plays a stronger role. Recent years have seen substantial changes in the acceptability of bitter beers, led by trends in the USA.

Hops are little used beyond brewing, so hop growers must follow the trends of an industry that, until recently, was moving in the direction of ever less-assertive beers. The consequent fall in hop acreage saw hop growing disappear altogether from some regions: for example, Ireland.

The emerging popularity of styles such as American pale ale and Belgian *saison* along with the increasingly imaginative use of the flavour properties of some hop varieties are now impacting on hop farmers. Hop yards are no longer confined to the European heartlands of brewing, and growers in North America, New Zealand, China, and even Argentina have joined a reviving international trade.

Over 200 types of hops are currently used by commercial brewers, many being recent hybrids. Each has its own profile of antiseptic properties, flavours, aromas, and bitterness. Picking the right hop recipe for a beer is like choosing the herbs, spices, and vegetables to make a stew.

As a rule, single varieties work less well than a carefully concocted mix, but some newer strains are good enough all-round performers to make successful single-hop beers, and even conservative growers are looking to create more.

Better-known British varieties include Fuggles, Northern Brewer, Bullion, various Goldings, and the relative newcomer Challenger. German brewers prefer the so-called noble hops like Tettnang, Spalt, the variants of Hallertau, and the Czech staple Saaz.

Although US growers arrived fairly late to the party, they have caught up with winning varieties such as Amarillo, Cascade, Willamette, Columbus (aka Tomahawk), Chinook, and others. More recently, New Zealand has made its presence felt with oddly fragrant varieties such as Nelson Sauvin, Pacifica, and Motueka.

While the mix of hops is crucial, the form in which they are used is important, too. Whole hops come compressed in bulky and cumbersome sacks, but provided they are fresh they should be considered the gold standard. The alternatives are pellets, jam-like extract, and oils.

Brewers can argue long into the night over the relative merits of these various forms of hops. Condensing a contentious debate into a few simple points, the use of hop pellets is indistinguishable from that of whole pressed hops, provided they have been crushed when deep-frozen from a fresh state. Many are not, but those that are will actually stay in that fresh state for a longer period of time than will pressed hops.

Extracts and oils struggle to do more than the needful, and where better brewers use them, it tends to be in combination with whole-leaf hops.

BOY HOPS & GIRL HOPS

Only female hops are used in brewing, since male hops taste bad. As propagation is vegetative, males are weeded out of hop farms. Even when growing some distance away, they can distract the females, ruining their taste and potency by making them, as one grower put it, "stop work and party". Cultivated males only survive because they are necessary to create new varieties.

Above: "Hop Vine", from *The Young Landsman*, hand-coloured lithograph published in Vienna, 1845.

Opposite: The growth of hop-centric beer styles, such as pale ale and IPA, and the expansion of both craft and convenience brewing in emerging markets such as Brazil and China, has the potential to place strain on the world's hop supply.

Yeast

Yeast is the microscopic miracle that shapes a beer, creating its alcohol and directing its character. These tiny, single-cell fungi feed on the sugar in wort (the sugar-rich liquid extracted from the mashed grains – *see* p.22), producing alcohol and carbon dioxide as waste products in the process of fermentation. While there are dozens of grain possibilities and hundreds of hops to choose from, the number of strains of yeast available to a brewer is measured in thousands.

By convention, yeast are referred to in the plural. Those that ferment ales are known collectively as *Saccharomyces cerevisiae*. Working at room temperature, they rise initially to the top of the wort – hence ales are often termed "top-fermented". *Saccharomyces uvarum* are better suited to work at lower temperatures, congregating towards the bottom. These beers traditionally went on to be stored (or "lagered") at low temperatures and so "lagers" are termed "bottom-fermented".

In modern brewing practice, the distinction between ale and lager has blurred beyond recognition. Some brewers push lager yeast to ferment beers at room temperature and above in a couple of days.

It can take a lifetime of beer tasting to appreciate how much the right (or wrong) yeast can manoeuvre a beer. To take a short cut, seek out one of the Bavarian wheat beers that use *Hefeweizen* ale yeast to create an intense banana and clove presence (*see* pp.90–1). Then swap to a Belgian ale that has attained its distinctive spicy character from a specialist yeast strain rather than the addition of hard-to-regulate spice powders (*see* pp.72–3).

Brewers of old often said that yeast imposed their brewery's thumbprint and used a favourite strain to ferment beers of different styles with a shared backtaste. This was usually dictated by practicality, as yeast permeated everywhere in the brewery and would alight on open fermenting tanks come what may.

Brewers used to source yeast by skimming it off the last batch of beer. This left a lot to be desired because rogue microorganisms of all sorts, not least wild yeast, can contact and infect the yeast source. Since most fermentation now makes use of sealed

Above: Skimming yeast off a top-fermented beer.

systems that can easily be sterilized between brews, modern-day brewers can choose different yeast for each brand, although yeast sourcing remains critical and can be a logistical headache.

The aim should be to have a reliable supply of the same active yeast, free from impurity, every time the same beer is brewed. Larger breweries employ microbiologists to manage their own yeast bank on site. Those who cannot afford such a luxury can sometimes rely on an independent yeast bank to maintain supplies of fresh yeast, while others use dried yeast, bought in as needed.

Any division of opinion between brewers about the use of hop pellets is as nothing compared to the diversity of views around dried yeast. We know a couple of excellent small breweries that appear to ferment their beers reliably and consistently with dried yeast, but far more report or else display a problem whereby their beers acquire a background taste of cardboard or stagnant pond water.

The issue is so critical that some smaller European brewers have taken to importing live yeast from US suppliers every time they brew. One who tried to reduce costs by shipping in bulk and keeping unused yeast in refrigerated, tightly sealed containers found so much cross-contamination within a few months that he declared, "Yeast are more promiscuous than sports stars."

Right: Stainless-steel conical fermenters are now the norm in breweries both large and small.

Brewing & Fermenting

All great beers are the products of careful design. Whether the idea for them originated from the creative brilliance of an individual, or the methodically collated preferences of the less inspired, all beers are the result of intention.

Some of the brewer's design decisions involve having access to particular equipment, although more relate to options of timing, method, and ingredients. Different factors will weigh more or less heavily, depending on the type of beer involved but, whichever it is, the final product is the result of a series of key decisions common to all.

1 PREPARING THE GRAIN

The malted barley and other grains are run into a hopper before crushing and grinding in a mill to produce grist. The resulting mix is sometimes called the grain bill.

Brewer's key decisions:
Which type of malted barley to use? Sourced from where? In what proportions? And in what quantities? What other grains, grain derivatives, or additional sugars to use, if any?

2 MASHING

The brewing water (or liquor) is adjusted to the right alkalinity or mineral content before being delivered into the mash tun, where the grist is mixed into it and agitated with a mechanical rake or paddle system. The temperature of the boil in its different phases will determine the form and extent of the sugars that are extracted. Higher temperatures mean a greater proportion of complex sugars that sweeten the beer and enhance its body but reduce its alcohol. Typical temperatures are between 60°C (140°F) and 80°C (176°F), usually taking between one and two hours. A simple boil is called infusion mashing. Where liquid is run off into a separate kettle, heated, and run back into the mash tun, once, twice, or three times, this is called single-, double-, or triple-decoction mashing.

Brewer's key decisions:
What ratio of grist to water? Containing what minerals? How long to mash? At one temperature or in different phases? Using only infusion, or with decoction, too? If so, how many times?

3 SPARGING

At the end of mashing, the sugar-rich liquid, now known as sweet wort, is run off while the residual grain and chaff are held back, classically in a separate vessel known as a lauter tun, where it is sparged with hot water to release more sugar. Excessive sparging will release unwanted chemicals from the husks.

Brewer's key decisions:
Sparging to reach what final concentration? Filtering directly or using a lauter tun?

4 BOILING

The sweet wort is channelled to a brewing kettle, or copper, where hops are added. The mixture is brought to the boil for between one and three hours, which sterilizes the mix, stops all enzyme action, and releases bittering alpha acids from the hops. Some brewers add herbs and spices at this point, while others add additional hops late in the boil for freshness and aroma.

Brewer's key decisions:
Which type(s) of hop to use? In what forms? Sourced from where? Added how often during and after the boil? At what points? In what quantities? How long to boil? And at what temperature? Under any pressure?

Above left: All beers begin with grains of malted barley being crushed in a mill.

5 PREPARING THE HOPPED WORT

After the boil, hops are separated from the mixture, sometimes through a separate container called a whirlpool and/or through a sealed unit called a hopback. The hopped wort is then usually fed through a heat exchanger to cool it before it reaches the fermenting vessel. These measures filter out the solids at the same time as retaining the maximum amount of volatile, aromatic taste components.

Brewer's key decisions:
What equipment should be used? To reach what temperature and clarity?

6 FERMENTATION

Whether designed to produce an ale, a lager, or a lambic, primary fermentation is vigorous. Flatter, open vessels are more vulnerable to infection, while taller, sealed fermenters can physically stress the yeast. The hotter the temperature, the more volatile the production of flavoured esters – chemical compounds contributing to fragrance and flavour, generally perceived as fruitiness. Lower temperatures lead to greater sulphuring.

Brewer's key decisions:
When and how to prepare and aerate the yeast? Using which strain(s)? How much yeast to add? Pitched how quickly? What size, shape, geometry, and construction of fermenting vessel or vessels? What starting temperature? Rising to what maximum? Controlled how? How to separate and recycle spent yeast?

7 CONDITIONING & PREPARING FOR SALE

Secondary fermentation and/or conditioning add considerably to the quality of a beer. The simplest form, popular in the UK, involves the transfer (by racking) of beer into casks, where it will continue conditioning for up to three weeks, the addition of finings helping to clear its residue. Other beers are filtered and run into conditioning tanks for cold storage (lagering) or, occasionally, wooden casks for ageing. Bottle-conditioned beers are typically filtered or even pasteurized before being bottled with fresh yeast and, sometimes, liquid sugar to spark refermentation. The top lagers are cold-conditioned for about 12 weeks, some receiving a late addition of freshly fermented wort, known as krausening. Fresh hops are added to some ales during conditioning, a process known as dry hopping.

Brewer's key decisions:
For how long? In how many phases? At what temperature(s)? What size and shape of vessels? In metal or wood? What refermentation (e.g. krausening or adding fresh yeast), if any? When to rack, bottle, or can? Coarse, fine or sterile filtration? With or without centrifuging? Any blending? Or doctoring by dilution, colouring, flavouring, or sweetening? Pasteurized or not? By flash, tunnel or membrane method? Reseeding the cask, keg, or bottle with fresh yeast? With warm chambering? What are the best bottles or barrels? What glasses, dispensers, and words serve the beer best?

And throughout: how is everything kept super-clean and free of contamination?

Above: Hot wort at the end of a boil.

Yet after all this careful deliberation, the brewer must be resigned to the fact that, ultimately, variables outside his or her control – including age, storage, condition of draught lines, temperature, and even the style and cleanliness of the glass itself – will impact just as much on how the beer presents in the glass.

WORLD BEER PRODUCTION & HOP CULTIVATION

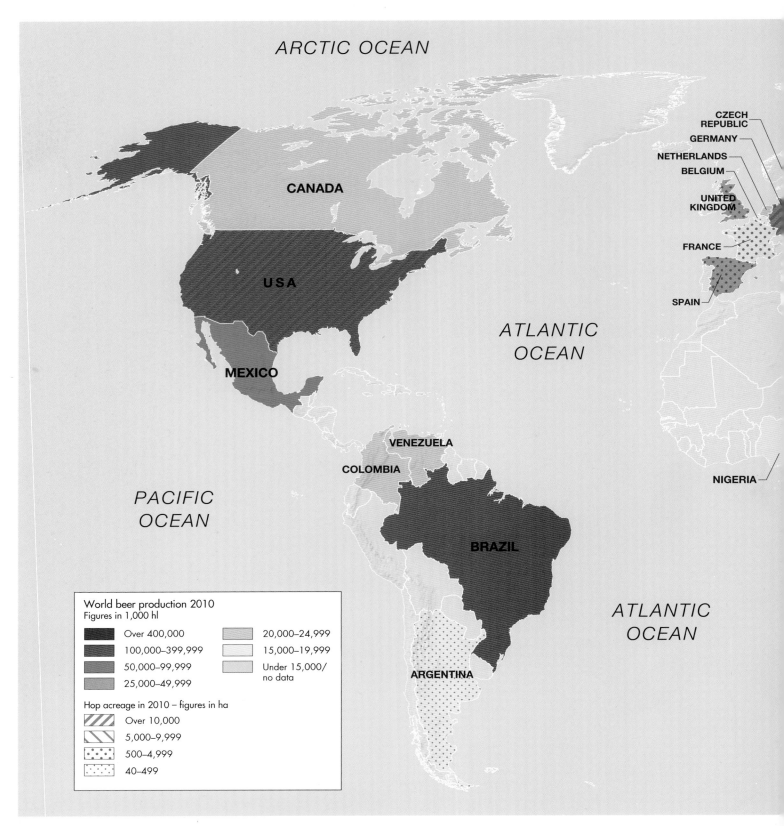

ARCTIC OCEAN

CZECH REPUBLIC
GERMANY
NETHERLANDS
BELGIUM
UNITED KINGDOM

FRANCE

SPAIN

CANADA

USA

MEXICO

ATLANTIC OCEAN

VENEZUELA

COLOMBIA

NIGERIA

PACIFIC OCEAN

BRAZIL

ATLANTIC OCEAN

ARGENTINA

World beer production 2010
Figures in 1,000 hl

■ Over 400,000	▨ 20,000–24,999
■ 100,000–399,999	▨ 15,000–19,999
■ 50,000–99,999	Under 15,000/ no data
■ 25,000–49,999	

Hop acreage in 2010 – figures in ha

▨	Over 10,000
▨	5,000–9,999
▨	500–4,999
▨	40–499

As brewing has spread across the world, so, too, has the cultivation of hops, although there are now worries that the former might soon outpace the latter.

DATA SOURCE: BARTH-HAAS GROUP

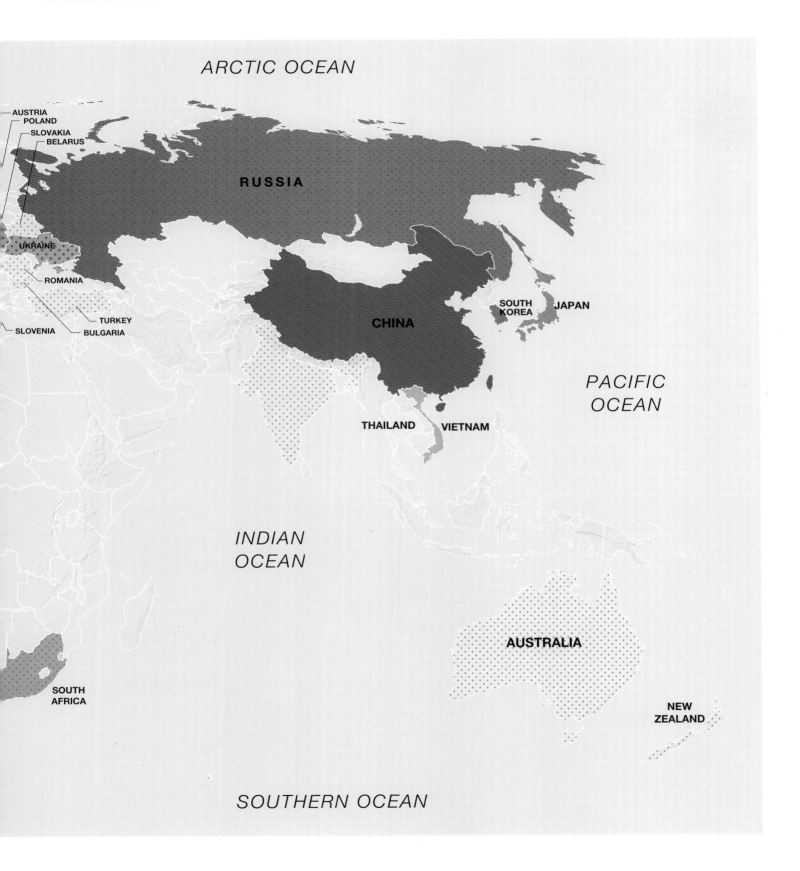

CRAFT BREWING

In the last four decades, there has been a global reaction against the simplification of beer that, while largely spontaneous, recognized early the importance of keywords. UK's CAMRA, the Campaign for Real Ale (originally the Campaign for the Revitalisation of Ale), was swift to pounce on "real" as the best adjective to define its ales of choice (*see* p.110), while Belgium's first consumer group picked "artisan".

In North America, the early days saw "microbrewing". It was a simple enough task to define what it was and was not. Small scale was good; large scale was bad. Big brewery beers had multimillion-dollar advertising campaigns; microbrews were sold in person, often by the brewery owner. Microbrew came from down the block; "macrobrew" from somewhere anonymous.

Time proved the problematic nature of this word, however. To begin with, some small brewery brands were simply not at all good, ranging in fault from lack of balance and confusion of flavour to infected or otherwise technically flawed character. Then so-called "stealth" beers arose – brands made to seem "micro" when they were in fact the products of large breweries or business concerns established purely to capitalize on the popularity of the growing microbrew trend.

The final nail in the coffin of "microbrewing" arrived when some of the pioneering breweries grew too large to be described in such diminutive terms. So North America adopted a new term – "craft brewing" – and with it a new need to define what it was and, perhaps more importantly, what it was not.

While the romance persists of beer lovingly crafted by hand, rather than forged by sophisticated machinery, the truth is that many craft breweries today rely on state-of-the-art equipment and computerization to produce their brands, and it is exactly this technology that allows such operations to grow in size and maintain consistency and character as they do so.

So if it is not size or technological advancement, what does separate the craft brewery from the beer factory?

First of all, and perhaps pivotally, craft brewers do not employ high-gravity brewing (*see* p.30), or rather it is the overwhelming convention that they do not.

The use of brewing adjuncts is another area in which craft breweries and the larger-scale industrial concerns generally differ. To lighten the body of their brands, and in some cases reduce costs, many of the world's larger breweries employ alternative sources

CAMPAIGN FOR REAL ALE

Above: The original consumer backlash against convenience beers celebrated its 40th anniversary in 2011 with more than 125,000 members.

Left: Sorting grain at the Lagunitas Brewing Company, Petaluma, California. Craft breweries like Lagunitas have spearheaded a revolution in the way North Americans drink beer.

Above: Wooden casks with internal linings, such as these in a brewery warehouse in Traunstein, Bavaria, grace many a bar counter in various parts of Germany.

Left: Cascade, the strongly aromatic American hop that has come to typify numerous American beer styles, most notably the American pale ale.

Below: All in this together: across North America and much of Europe, small breweries provide more jobs than their industrial counterparts.

of fermentable sugars such as maize, rice, starch, or, in some instances, pure liquid sugar. These adjuncts in some cases amount to a full one-third of the sugars available during fermentation.

Craft brewers may also employ alternative sugars during the creation of some beers, although usually in much smaller concentrations and, since craft beer is known for its robust flavours, rarely in an attempt to lighten the character of an ale or lager. Such practices would include the addition of flaked maize to certain British best bitters, the use of candy sugar in the brewing of Trappist ales (*see* pp.54–7), and the employment

of wheat or wheat flour as an agent for increased head retention.

But enough about what craft breweries do not do. Let us turn our attention to what is it they do that makes them "craft".

Probably the most important aspect of craft brewing is the ability and willingness of its adherents to innovate. Since the late 1970s, almost every significant taste innovation in brewing – as opposed to technological innovation, at which the big breweries excel, or market-orientated innovations such as unusual bottle shapes – has come directly from craft breweries.

This includes everything from the popularization of American hops to the ageing of beers in various sorts of wooden barrels; the use of wild yeasts and other microflora during fermentation to sherry production-inspired, *solera*-style conditioning.

Then there is the addition of a massive array of flavouring ingredients, including whole oranges and other citrus fruits, wild flowers, spices of almost every conceivable description, and even tobacco leaf.

Variety is another hallmark of craft brewing, but by no means is it a universal one. Whereas most of the world's largest breweries boast very broad brand portfolios consisting of, at best, only a handful of flavour profiles, craft breweries tend to offer a much greater breadth of taste experiences even with their generally smaller collections of brands. Thus, craft brewing has provided, and continues to provide, the fuel for the unprecedented variety of beer that we enjoy today.

In innumerable ways, craft breweries have become the tail that wags the proverbial dog. Although great in number, they remain relatively "micro" in terms of the total volume of their output, accounting for no more than

a few percentage points of market share in some nations and far, far less in others. Yet their influence cannot be overstated.

If craft breweries have success with American-style pale ales, even the world's largest brewing company will give it a shot. If ales aged in old bourbon barrels develop niche appeal, at least a multinational or two will try the technique, even if their need for volume requires putting the broken-down barrels into the beer, rather than vice versa. And if the smaller brewery cannot be emulated, it might instead be purchased.

This strikes at the heart of what is perhaps key to the best definition of craft brewing, which is to be experimental, innovative, and against the status quo – in other words, a leader rather than a follower.

Above: Jean Van Roy hosts a tasting at Brasserie Cantillon in Brussels – producer of fabulously original beers using the oldest of methods.

Right: Beer sampled directly from the tank at the Bekeerde Suster brewery in Amsterdam.

HIGH-VOLUME BREWING & CONVENIENCE BEERS

Opposite: Massive, high-speed bottling lines, such as this one at the Carlsberg-owned Feldschloesschen brewery in Switzerland, package more beer in a few minutes than most craft breweries do in a day, and with far fewer employees.

A recent report sponsored by the European Union described the largest brewery company in Europe as "bankers who make beer". It was a concise observation, but was it fair? Perusing the mission statements of the world's six largest brewery companies, one could be forgiven for thinking it was.

Above: High-gravity brewing saves on space during the production process, gaining volume by adding water to the beer at the time of packaging.

Each company focuses on the need to grow, drive costs down, improve business processes, and make higher profits for shareholders. Not one mentions improving their products, which is odd given that in almost all their traditional markets they are experiencing declining sales, in contrast to their smaller competitors.

In the latter half of the twentieth century, large brewing companies concluded, with some justification, that their customers lacked discrimination beyond knowing a familiar product when they saw one. Several generations of consumer had been content to absorb a rising proportion of both water and non-malt sugars in their beers, so why should a producer intent on keeping costs down not oblige them?

High-gravity brewing allows a company to make more fluid in less space. A beer brewed and fermented to, say, 7.5% ABV can be diluted to 5% ABV by adding 50 per cent water shortly before canning, thus cutting by one-third the expensive storage space it takes up at the brewery.

The posh end of the market moved its allegiance to wine, but the greater mass continued to follow wherever the big brewers led, smiling at the adverts and living the part of a happy, if docile, flock.

No beer was too simple. Substituting the maximum-allowable amount of simpler sugars for those derived from malted barley removed only one-third of the beer's body, which was not enough for some. So-called "light" beers had to be supplemented by "ice" beers, from which residual flavour particles were cold-filtered and centrifuged away, leaving a veneer beer consisting mainly of alcohol, sugar, and bubbles. A colourless, "clear" beer was even tried at one point.

The mass market was expressing distaste for taste, playing perfectly to production methods that reduced fermentation and conditioning times to the minimum required to create a palatable alcohol delivery device that was still legally beer.

Idiot-proof dispense became a non-issue once the can was accepted as a normal receptacle for what used to be a living product. The unpleasant tastes caused by short-cut methods can be hidden provided people can be persuaded to drink their beer super-chilled.

In the history of beer, the journey from ale wives stirring cauldrons in their kitchens to bankers counting cans off a production line took over a thousand years, although the last part was taken at a sprint.

Large producers are now searching for a big idea to counter falling sales in their core markets, but hope to buy time by appealing to new consumers in China and India, the newness of whose wealth will, they hope, render them as incapable of discrimination as their Western role models.

Their optimism may be misplaced.

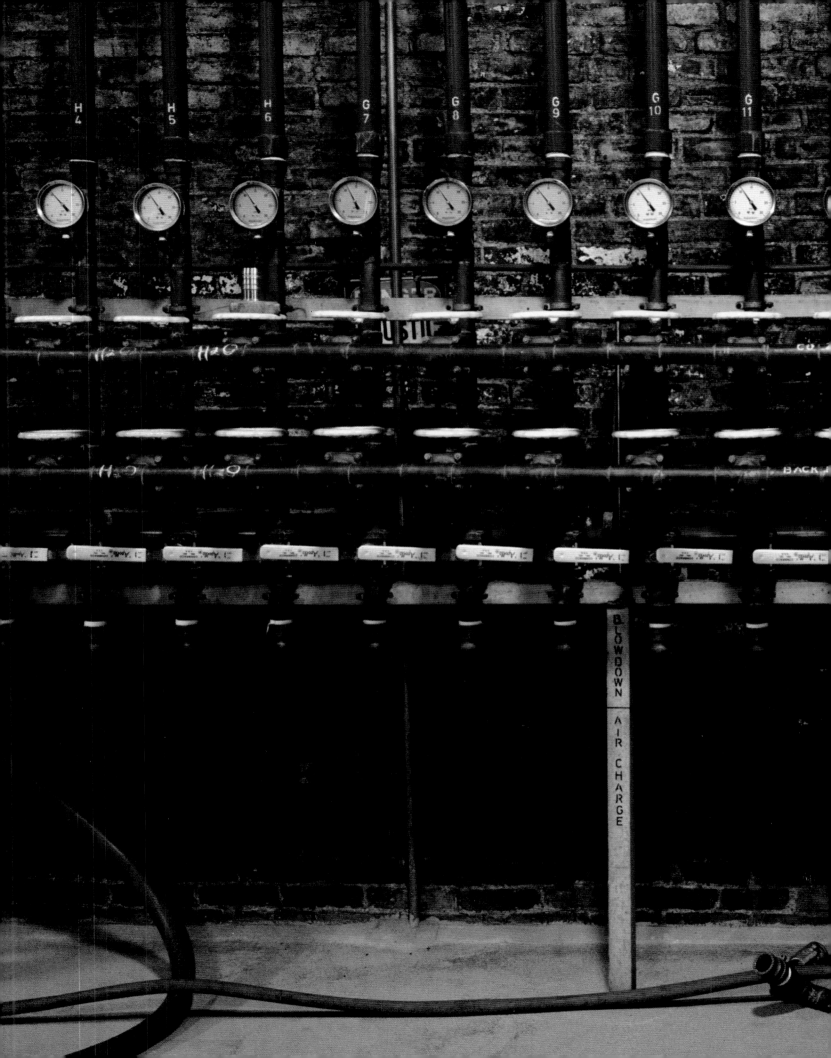

BEER STYLES

The first attempt to create a popular catalogue of the beers of the world by style was by the late beer-writing pioneer Michael Jackson in his 1977 book, *The World Guide to Beer*. His intent at the time was to clarify and elucidate often obscure and regional beers for an audience that had largely never before encountered them.

Unfortunately, this approach has evolved into a morass of confusion and obfuscation, with it seeming at times as if every new beer is awarded its own unique style descriptor.

Much of this style expansionism is rooted in the USA, where a broadly experimental school of brewing has resulted in no fewer than 83 categories being judged annually at the Great American Beer Festival and dozens more recognized by the Brewers Association's official guidelines. Dark American-Belgo Style Ale, anyone?

The stated, traditional style categories of the kind that Michael Jackson defined still possess some meaning, and so these are what we have chosen principally to focus upon in this book. Readers should be aware, however, that virtually every beer type in the world, from Burton-upon-Trent's pale ales (*see* pp.110–3) to the lambics of Belgium's Payottenland (*see* pp.62–5) and Finland's *sahtis* (*see* pp.152–3), are subject to multiple interpretations, revisions, and oft-dramatic variations.

Further muddying the waters are the ways in which different nations view their beers. The French, for instance, focus primarily on colour as a defining factor, whereas the Italians add strength and cultural inspiration to their system of classification and Americans apply terms like "double", "triple", or "imperial" to high-strength and/ or highly hopped versions of almost any existing style, even going so far as to label some beers "imperial mild" – tongue firmly planted in cheek, we hope.

Our intention is not to diminish any of the beers falling into the new categories and classes noted above, some of which, as observed in the pages following, are excellent. Rather, until such time as a simplified system of categorization for the fruits of the global craft beer renaissance arises, we recommend readers simply to note what might be written on the label, in books, or online, and above all else maintain an open and unprejudiced palate.

Right: Different beer styles may become distinguished from each other by colour, strength, ingredients, method of production, place of origin, or, in some cases, wistful marketing.

Previous page: Brewing is both craft and science. Having a healthy understanding of mechanics doesn't hurt, either.

BUYING BEER

All beers have enemies, chief among them light, heat, and, for the great majority of mainstream beers, age. Which is why the greatest damage inflicted upon the beer you buy is likely to take place before you even purchase it, making your choice of retailer all the more important.

When shopping for beer, look to buy from a source where stock turnover is apt to be high and where individual bottles are not left exposed under fluorescent lights. The best will have refrigerated coolers or a beer storage area maintained consistently at something approaching cellar temperature (14°C/58°F) with staff who are beer savvy and willing to share their knowledge when asked. Purchases that reveal themselves to be "off" in some fashion should be happily refunded or replaced, since with some beer prices approaching the range typically occupied by fine wines, quality assurance should be as good as that found in better wine shops.

Below: Utobeer, in London's Borough Market, stocks at any time some 700 international beers culled from a portfolio of brands numbering in excess of 2,000.

STORING BEER

Most beer purchases will be brought home, chilled, and then consumed, which is an approach we cheerfully endorse. Pay heed, however, to those bottle-conditioned beers that require at least a couple of days for their live yeast content to settle and ensure that those beers – mostly ales – intended to be enjoyed at cellar temperature (around 14°C/58°F) are not served ice-cold.

For longer-term storage, avoid placing bottles in areas exposed to bright light or extremes of heat and cold, as these are sorely detrimental to beer. Exposure to strong odours can also be an issue, but only if you plan to cellar the beer for the longer term.

Certain beers will develop enhanced character if allowed to age undisturbed for months or even years, and for these the most preferable conditions are provided by a cool, dark corner protected from light, smells, vibrations, and dramatic shifts in temperature. Better a warmer spot that stays at a constant temperature than a cooler one that becomes periodically warm, and best of all is a place that is consistently and moderately cool rather than arctic in nature. Optimally, the long-term cellaring of beer should take place at a temperature somewhere between 8°C and 14°C (46°F and 57°F),

although most beer should survive shorter periods of storage perfectly well at temperatures between 1°C and 24°C (34°F and 75°F).

If you intend to build over time a sizeable collection of vintage beers, whether at home or at a licensed premises, we recommend investing in a wine refrigerator or a professionally designed cellar space.

All bottled beer is best stored upright to avoid prolonged contact with the closure. This is also true of most cork-finished bottles, since the generally lower-grade corks used by brewers, as opposed to Bordeaux vintners, are more prone to imparting cork taint to the beer.

Below: Matt VandenBerghe, of Seattle, Washington's Brouwer's Cafe and Bottleworks beer store, transformed a root cellar in his home into an elegant space for storing his considerable beer collection.

SERVING BEER | THE NATURE OF BEER | 37

SERVING BEER

Bottled beer requires little specialized equipment to serve it. In most cases, a bottle opener and glass will do the trick, while even the most involved service will only necessitate the addition of a corkscrew to your arsenal. Decanters and aerating funnels need not apply.

Certain glass shapes and sizes are designed specifically to enhance the tasting experience of the beers that they serve. For example, the oversize tulip for Duvel (*see* p.76) allows necessary foaming; the statuesque, vase-like *Weissbier* glass aids the even distribution of suspended particles; the diminutive cylindrical *Stange* for *Kölsch* helps retain gas before swift dispatch; and the chalice used for stronger abbey beers enables warming of the beer in the palms. Others, though, are employed primarily for the sake of tradition or aesthetics, as with the varieties of British pint glass, German steins, or thistle-shaped glasses for Scotch ale.

Most bottled beers show well and can be enjoyed from stemmed, tulip-shaped or chalice glasses, or even large, balloon-like wine glasses. For optimal enjoyment and presentation, however, we recommend building at minimum a stock of variously sized stemmed glasses for higher-strength, aromatic ales, pint glasses for larger-format "session" beers, and *Weissbier* glasses for beers of that style.

Duvel Moortgat of Antwerp have made the ballooned *tulip* glass its own.

The *nonic* British pint glass has bulging sides to assist stacking.

German ceramic *Humpen* mugs alter a beer's taste by hiding its appearance.

A broad-bowled *chalice* allows stronger ales to be warmed in the palm.

The pinch-topped, stemmed *snifter* works as well for barley wine as for brandy.

Czech lagers glint best in a heavily faceted, thick-walled, half-litre *pull*.

Lagered ales in Köln and Düsseldorf appear in a narrow cylindrical *Stange*.

Unlike its Champagne equivalent, a beer *flute* can often be straight-sided.

Helles beer from Munich demands a *Maß* – the ultimate super-sized jug.

The *shaker* is synonymous with draught beer in the US and western Canada.

A foggy Bavarian wheat beer only reaches full pomp in a puffed-out *Weizen* glass.

A stemmed *wine glass* with a broad bowl is the simplest way to present many styles of beer.

POURING BEER

THE BELGIAN POUR

Many stronger ales, especially those associated with Belgium, are bottle-fermented, meaning that a sediment is present. Although nutritious, these dead yeast cells can be visually unappealing and will alter the taste of the beer, so careful decanting is necessary. (The sediment can be consumed on its own as a sort of brewer's multivitamin.)

Begin with the glass held at a 45-degree angle and start pouring the beer slowly down the side.

While continuing to pour, slowly straighten the glass, making sure not too much of a head is allowed to form.

THE HEFEWEIZEN POUR

Unlike most stronger ales, wheat beers are generally intended to be enjoyed in a cloudy state, with the yeast from their bottle-fermentation included in the glass. In the case of the German *hefeweizen* beer style, this involves a somewhat ritualistic pour into a very specific, almost vase-like beer glass.

Start pouring slowly with the glass held at a fairly steep angle, otherwise the beer will immediately generate prodigious amounts of foam.

As the pour progresses, carefully straighten the glass and allow the head to form. If too much foam is generated, slow the pour and increase the angle of the glass, but don't stop pouring altogether.

THE STANDARD BEER POUR

The pouring of a beer into a glass should be one of the simplest actions in the world of food and drink, but it is all too often conducted carelessly or with undue speed, resulting in either a foamy mess or a too-bubbly brew with no head. With a little attention to detail, however, a picture-perfect beer is within easy reach.

A clean glass and a steady hand are key to the perfect pour. Start off by holding the glass at roughly a 45-degree angle and slowly begin to pour the beer.

Keep pouring the beer down the side of the glass, never towards the middle. If the foam is not rising quickly enough, simply straighten the glass a bit.

Keep pouring in one continuous motion, otherwise the yeast will become mixed with the beer. If too much foam is forming, simply tilt the glass more towards the diagonal.

As the pour is coming to an end, watch for any sediment rising to the neck of the bottle. The goal is to stop pouring just before the yeast escapes.

An expertly decanted beer will boast a rather dense collar of foam atop bright and unclouded beer. The chalice glass is an allusion to monastic brewing traditions – and an elegant one at that.

When about three-quarters of the beer has been poured, stop and gently swirl the remaining beer so that any residual yeast clinging to the bottom of the bottle might be picked up. Don't swirl too aggressively or you'll end up with a bottle of foam.

The beer should become cloudier when you add the final few ounces of beer and yeast to the glass. The goal here is a thick layer of dense foam atop the cloudy beer.

No doubt one of the most visually appetizing beers, a well-poured *Hefeweizen* is truly a thing of beauty; no wedge of lemon required!

Pour slowly in a single motion. Part of the enjoyment of a beer is the anticipation of that first sip, so there is no reason to hurry.

As the glass fills with beer, gently straighten it so that a decent-sized head forms. Now you can stop pouring down the side of the glass and begin pouring more towards the centre.

When complete, a collar of foam roughly an inch or two in depth should allow for all of the beer's aromatic qualities to present themselves.

TASTING BEER

To appreciate a beer properly, you should always enjoy it from a glass and never swig it from the bottle or can, since doing so deletes the contribution made to flavour by aroma and appearance. A fine beer is deserving of a more thoughtful approach.

1 Observe

This might seem elemental, but brewers go to great lengths to give their beers just the right appearance, and besides, if you look closely enough, your beer could be telling you something. Clouding can be deliberate or not, excessive or incidental foaming could be a sign of infection or old age, and if the colour has a brassy tinge to it, oxidization may be an issue.

3 Taste

Take your time to discern the tastes within your beer, thinking about what is in your glass and your mouth. Sip slowly, allowing it to roll over your tongue and around your palate, appreciating the tones before you swallow. Then, before returning for another sip, consider the aftertaste – is it bitter or malty, sharp or warming, short or lingering? Creating a personal catalogue of the flavours you find in beer takes time, but it becomes easier with experience. Above all, trying to absorb what it is that you have just tasted will lead to a better appreciation not only of the beer just finished but also of all subsequent beers.

2 Smell

Sniffing your beer can draw odd looks in a bar, but appreciating the aroma is essential. We humans can discern hundreds if not thousands of smells, yet only a handful of tastes, so when our brain aggregates the two to create flavour, it is the nose that brings the subtleties. In an ale, try to detect fruity aromas; in a lager, look for notes of straw, hay, or fresh-cut grass; in a malty beer such as *Bock*, hints of toffee or caramel; in hoppy beers, herbal, spicy, or citrusy notes; and in lambics, musty farmyard scents.

4 Consider

Seldom will your first impression of a beer remain unchanged to the end of the glass. Nor may it be carved in stone by just one sampling. In the way that a song or piece of music at first dismissed can, over time, grow on you and become a favourite, so it is that some beers, unimpressive at first, may after full consideration become part of your regular repertoire.

BEER & FOOD

As more flavourful ales and lagers have found their place on the world stage,
it is perhaps only natural that in the 1990s many beer aficionados began to turn
their attention to where wine has long ruled – the dining table. Good thing, too,
because as it turns out, beer is probably the most versatile beverage there is
for pairing with food.

The utility of beer as a dining companion begins with the wealth of flavour possibilities it presents, a result of the almost unlimited number of ingredients and seasonings it may contain, from malted grain, hops, water, and yeast to a panoply of spices, fruits and vegetables, herbs and edible flowers, chocolate, coffee, and even specific, flavour-enhancing varieties of sugar.

As with any other beverage, however, the successful harmonizing of beer with food is largely dependent upon the skills of the person making the pairing. Fortunately, with the assistance of a few handy pointers, the basics are fairly simple to absorb. The rest will come with practice.

WEIGH UP THE DISH

Most people at all serious about food and drink will be familiar with the notion of lighter and heavier dishes, such as salads as opposed to stews or grilled red snapper compared to roast beef. Extending this principle to the beverages we drink with our meals, we can conclude that ales, with their bigger, rounder, and fruitier bodies, pair better with heavier flavours such as red meats, while generally crisper and cleaner lagers better complement lighter flavours such as seafood and poultry.

MIND THE SPICE, SALT & FAT

Few aspects of food try the vibrancy of a palate more than spicy heat, serious saltiness, and fattiness arising from cream or deep-frying. Beer, however, happens to possess two elements that combine to combat the deleterious impact of these factors: carbonation and hoppiness. The effect of each of these is to wipe away lingering fat, salt, and spice, readying the mouth for another bite of the dish, rather than allowing multiple mouthfuls to accumulate like layers of ice, ultimately obscuring the original taste of the food.

COMPLEMENT OR CONTRAST

The cornerstone of any food and beverage partnering exercise is the search for complementary or elegantly contrasting flavours, the former being always much easier to find than the latter. In the case of beer complements, focus on the robust flavours where such are found in the dish, like imposing, malty ales with sweet, long-cooked meats or *Märzens* with roasted vegetables. For contrast, consider flavours that cut or somehow counter the nature of the food, as a dry and roasty oatmeal stout might do when combined with a soft and odoriferous cheese, or as a thinly malty pilsner could affect a plate of *fettuccine Alfredo*.

CONSIDER SWEETNESS

Unlike wine, beer offers a world of possibilities when the time comes for dessert, providing that, except in the case of chocolate, the beer selected is sweeter than the dessert. The reason for this is that, in the same way as the residue from sweet, minty toothpaste will make fruit eaten afterwards seem tart, a dish sweeter than the beer served with it will cause the beer to seem flat in flavour, or even sour.

Where chocolate is concerned, food and drink fall into similar categories, since chocolate, like beer, will almost always have a degree of pleasing bitterness to it. With such a common ground in taste, it becomes a simple matter of playing with flavours – usually those resulting from the use of dark malts, such as roastiness, liquorice, stewed fruit, and, yes, chocolate – without needing to be overly concerned with sweetness.

Left: A pie and a pint is a long-standing pub favourite...

Opposite: ...but beer also has the versatility to partner almost any food, including herring and onions.

Food Affinity Chart

Food	Key Flavours	Beer	What Makes It Work
Oysters	Delicate, briny	Dry stout, *méthode champenoise* beer	The boldness of a stout provides cleansing contrast, while the Champagne-style beers offer salt-cleansing bubbles and gentle flavours
Charcuterie	Meaty, spicy, fatty	Best bitter, non-assertive pale ale, Flemish oak-aged ale, *Altbier*	Fruity flavours to complement the cured meat, with some hoppiness or acidity (oak ages ales) to counter the spice and fat
Foie gras	Unctuous texture, rich	Belgian-style strong golden ale	The high effervescence will cut through the fattiness of the foie, while the spicy fruitiness of the beer will complement the rich flavours
Globe artichoke	Sweetens the perceived taste of whatever is served with it	Best bitter, pale ale	The sweetening effect of the artichoke will be absorbed by the hoppiness, allowing the malty qualities of the ale to shine through
Cream soups	Rich creaminess	Bohemian or German-style pilsner	Crisp hoppiness to cleanse the palate of the fat and refresh the taste buds between spoonfuls
French onion soup	Beefy, sweet onion, fatty cheese	Hoppy brown ale, *Altbier*, lower-strength barley wine	Sweet malt for the onions, roasty, earthy flavours for the beef, and some hoppiness to balance the fat of the cheese
Green salad, vinaigrette	Crisp greens and acidic dressing	*Helles*, German-style pilsner, lambic	Fresh malt flavours to complement the greens, with hops or acidity to counter or complement the vinaigrette
Green salad with fruit	Sweetness from the fruit, regardless of type	*Hefeweizen*, Belgian-style wheat beer	Either style of wheat beer will complement well the fruity sweetness, with their light bodies not overwhelming the flavours of the greens
Ceviche	Tart, acidic from the citrus juices used to "cook" the fish, salty	*Saison*, dry *Helles*	As tempting as it might be to match acidity with acidity, such as a lambic, better to provide a hoppy foil supported by a firmly malty base
Oily fish such as salmon, sardines, or herrings	Oily nature combined with assertive fish flavour	Stout, dry brown ale, dry *Dunkel*, *Dunkel Weisse*	Dark and earthy malt flavours to complement the fish, plus some degree of hoppiness or spiciness (*Dunkel Weisse*) to counter the oils
Delicately flavoured fish such as red snapper, black cod, and plaice	Light fish – not too much in the way of fatty oils	*Helles*, *Kölsch*, *Weissbier*, Belgian-style wheat beers	Soft and gentle flavours will harmonize well without overwhelming the flavour of the fish
Fish and chips	Deep-fried batter, potato	Pilsner, mildly hoppy golden ale, best bitter	A crisp hoppiness will meet the fatty fried batter on its own terms, without the flavour of the beer becoming overbearing
Hamburger	Fatty beef topped with multiple garnishes	Assertive pilsner, pale ale, IPA	Strong flavours and fattiness require equal presence from the beer, plus a fair degree of hoppiness
Pizza	Tomato sauce, multiple topping variations	Vienna lager, *Bock*	The light sweetness of a Vienna or *Bock* will match the sweetness of the sauce, while the drier yet not bitter finish will cleanse the palate
Roast beef, cooked to medium-rare	Sweet taste of beef accentuated by caramelization of the outside "crust" of the roast	Brown ale, best bitter, abbey-style *dubbel*	The key is sweet, fruity flavour from the malt without too much hop bitterness, which any of these styles, sagely selected, will provide
Game meats and birds	Slightly gamey flavours, less fat than beef	*Brettanomyces*-affected brown ales, Flemish oak-aged ale	The mild gaminess of the flesh will be nicely balanced by the tartness from the *Brettanomyces*

Food	Key Flavours	Beer	What Makes It Work
Fried chicken	Deep-fried batter	Hoppy *Märzen*, golden bitter	Some hoppiness is desired because of the fried nature of the dish, but a firm, gently sweet maltiness will benefit the bird
Roasted or grilled poultry	Rich poultry, gravy	Pale *Bock*, fruit beer	Relatively simple sweetness is needed to complement the diverse flavours in the dish
French soft cheeses such as Camembert or Brie de Meaux	Ample creaminess with a touch of acidity from the rind	Oatmeal stout, porter, robust brown ale	The acidity will be well met by the roastiness, while the creaminess of the cheese will accent the richness of the beer
Firm, aged cheeses like Cheddar or manchego	Sharp, fruity and nutty	British pale ale, best bitter, dry brown ale	Fruity malt and nutty or spicy hop complements similar flavours in the cheese
Dark, high cocoa-content chocolate (70 per cent or higher)	Intense, often fruity or nutty, some bitterness	Almost anything dark and rich: imperial stout, barley wine, strong Trappist and abbey-style ales	Similarly robust and comforting flavours, with modest to mild amounts of bitterness matching that same quality in the chocolate

Above: Even sommeliers will admit that beer pairs better with a selection of cheeses than does wine.

Above: Often called "liquid bread", a pint of porter is a pleasant companion to hunks of thickly buttered fresh bread.

THE WORLD OF BEER

It is sometimes said that countries divide by their consumption habits into wine drinking, spirits drinking, beer drinking, and abstinence. If that was ever true, it is certainly no longer the case. Beer is universal.

Of the top 40 beer-producing nations, three are in North America, six in South America, eight in Asia, three in Africa, and – with the exception of Australia – the rest in Europe. They include numerous countries traditionally thought of as wine drinking, such as France, Italy, Spain, Portugal, Hungary, Chile, and Argentina.

The global spread of beer brewing owes its origins to European colonial expansion in the eighteenth century and mass emigration to the Americas in the nineteenth. Wherever they ended up, colonists and émigrés tended to take with them the brewing preferences of their countries of origin, by importation initially but followed in due course by the building of breweries in their adopted home countries to re-create the beers of the old.

More recently, beer's growth has been driven and shaped by the ambitions of expanding corporations, keen to harmonize and exploit international drinking habits, often associating their brands with the trappings of a desirable, wealthy Western lifestyle.

Before 1914, local variations on brewing practice within and between countries were limitless, the only discernible trends being towards cleaner methods, larger production facilities, and the use of more reliable ingredients. However, by 1975, for reasons outlined elsewhere, while the world was drinking ever more beer, the variety available had shrunk considerably.

Four decades on, there are two distinct maps of beer brewing in the world. One that concentrates on ownership will show an ever-smaller number of large producers holding over 90 per cent of world beer production, relationships between the companies becoming increasingly complex and blurred. These players jockey for position in a few potentially huge markets where the volume of beer drunk has been restrained, such as China and India, while sales in virtually all their traditional markets are in decline, sometimes alarmingly so.

On the other hand, for those more inclined to following the fate of interesting and entertaining beers, a parallel world view shows craft brewing in different forms re-emerging strongly across each of the traditional brewing nations, and in dozens of others that had not previously enjoyed such a tradition.

Although sourcing reliable data is virtually impossible, it is likely that during 2010, in each and every country where beer production was falling, the proportion made by craft producers was rising, and that in those countries where overall production was rising, craft beer sales were rising, too.

Consumers the world over appear to be giving a clear message that they appreciate interesting beers and will keep buying them, whereas industrial brands are starting to lose their appeal.

What follows is a snapshot of where quality beer lies at the start of the second decade of the twenty-first century, beginning with those countries of the Old World whose traditions have most influenced the craft brewing revival to date and proceeding to those nations in the New World whose efforts will most likely shape future changes.

Opposite: A barley field at dawn near Gubbio, Umbria, Italy.

EUROPE

The battered remains of several millennia of commercial beer brewing around the world were, by the 1970s, found mainly in four parts of northern and central Europe – mainland Britain, the western halves of Germany and Czechoslovakia, and Belgium. Here were variously found cask- and bottle-conditioned ales, cloudy wheat beers, strong ales aged in oak, plus blond and other lagers that had been cold-stored over months as their originators had intended. Provided you knew where to look.

The inhabitants of other parts of the Continent, such as northern France, the Netherlands, Austria, Switzerland, northern Italy, and the countries of Scandinavia and the Baltic rim, remained keen consumers of beer. But they had, like consumers in the rest of the developed world, taken to accepting increasingly industrialized beers made in a narrow range of styles that many in the corporate brewing world seemed to hope would become single and universal.

The story of beer's revival in Europe mirrored the revival of interest in other consumer staples such as quality breads, cheeses, and other local specialities, and may indeed have been slightly ahead of the trend.

The flow and content of the increasing interest has varied from one country to another, but there is currently no European nation in which the number of breweries or the variety of locally made beers is in decline. In Britain, France, Denmark, Germany, and Italy, the number of commercial breweries that have opened since 1990 and are still operating is measured in three figures, with Austria, Switzerland, Sweden, Norway, Belgium, and the Netherlands all boasting dozens.

Previous page: Rolled hay harvested from a field of barley in Karst, Slovenia.

Above: Time and again, beer proves itself to be the most sociable of beverages.

Above: Old traditions meet modern times: friends toast in Alpine dress in a Bavarian *Bierhaus*.

At the same time, there has been a considerable expansion in the number of different styles of beer found in most countries. No longer is pale ale the principal preserve of British brewers, nor stout the speciality of Ireland. Even the Belgians, whose secret treasure trove of local beer styles provided the seeds from which much of the interest in craft beers grew, must accept that most of their finest beers have impressive imitators elsewhere.

Germany's obsession with pure, precise, and predictable beers, sometimes cartooned as "a thousand subtle variations on the same drink", has been around for five centuries, but even there, younger drinkers are experimenting with styles of beer far distant from their borders. Meanwhile, in Britain, the children of the original "real ale generation" are starting to move beyond their parents' confines. The growth of "special beers" has occurred largely at the expense of bigger-brand blond beers, although many of the best-quality lagers have been affected, too, damned by their association with Everyman's world beer. Europe's most impressive bottom-fermented beers achieve excellence through use of the best ingredients, careful brewing, and three-months' cold storage, all of which cost more. The willingness of brewery owners, investors, and customers to support that will be critical to their future.

Nonetheless, European beer has entered the twenty-first century in better shape than it has been for a long while, and nobody is taking bets on it going anywhere else but up.

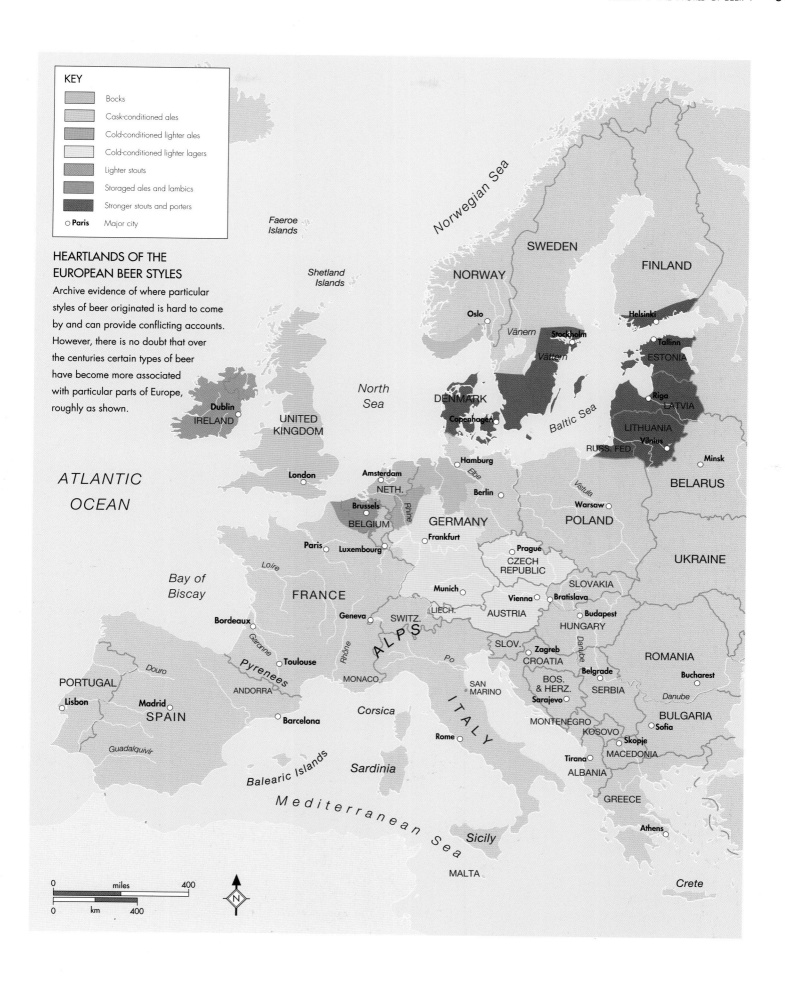

KEY

- Bocks
- Cask-conditioned ales
- Cold-conditioned lighter ales
- Cold-conditioned lighter lagers
- Lighter stouts
- Storaged ales and lambics
- Stronger stouts and porters

○ **Paris** Major city

HEARTLANDS OF THE EUROPEAN BEER STYLES

Archive evidence of where particular styles of beer originated is hard to come by and can provide conflicting accounts. However, there is no doubt that over the centuries certain types of beer have become more associated with particular parts of Europe, roughly as shown.

BELGIUM

Belgium is to beer what France is to wine or the Scottish Highlands to whisky. It is the mother ship of craft brewing. If you understand the variations on beer making concocted here on the north coast of continental Europe, you will be over halfway to appreciating the immense range of tastes and forms that beer can assume.

The Confederation of Belgian Brewers claims that the country's brewers produce over 400 discernibly different styles of beer. Some contain virtually no alcohol, while others over 12 per cent, their characters ranging from sickly sweet to frankly acidic and accessibility from love at first sip to a lifetime of gradual understanding.

Where other nations' brewers seek perfect presentation, the Belgians have mastered variety. The theory goes that as a legacy of over 30 invasions and occupations by foreign armies in the last millennium, including two in the twentieth century, the Belgians developed a parochial mentality that encouraged the retention of local practices, in beer making and much else.

This may be so, though Flemish brown ales and the taverns that served them already enjoyed a reputation for excellence among the merchants of the Hanseatic League back in medieval times, when the *gruut* barons of Bruges were among that world's top commodity traders (*see* p.15).

By 1980, the ragbag of small-town Belgian breweries that refused to conform to the global vision of familiar, shiny, white-foamed, easy-drinking lagers stood out above the flood waters, preserving the skills, imagination, and awkwardness that enabled the world's next generation of brewers to question why only industrial beers should be considered "normal".

From barely a mention in economic texts of the 1960s, beer has become one of Belgium's best-known exports. Over 60 per cent of the beer brewed here is now sent for export across Europe and to North America, Australasia, and the Far East.

Above: *Fin-de-siècle* style meets *oude gueuze* at the café À la Mort Subite in Brussels.

BEST-SELLING LOCAL LABELS

Affligem	(Heineken)
Alken	(Heineken)
Grimbergen	(Heineken)
Hoegaarden	(Anheuser-Busch InBev)
Jupiler	(Anheuser-Busch InBev)
Leffe	(Anheuser-Busch InBev)
Maes	(Heineken)
Palm	(National)

Left: Ghent in east Flanders, one of a dozen top
city-break destinations for beer-lovers.

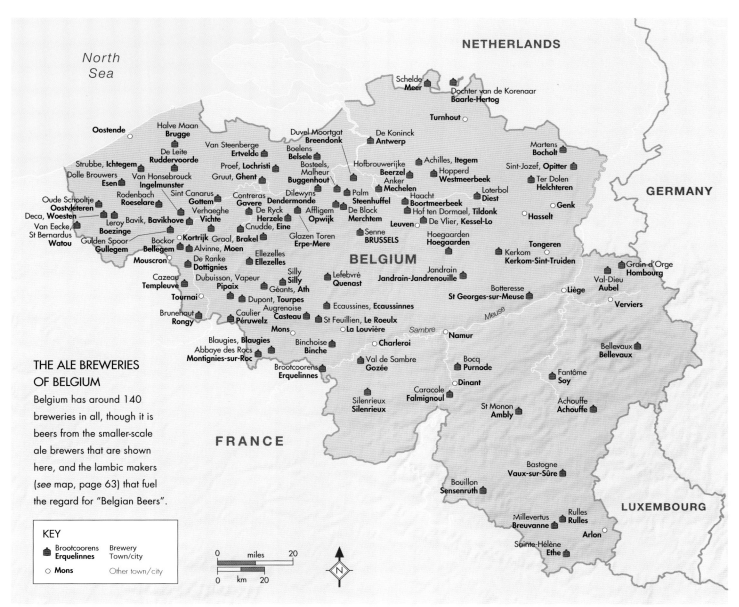

THE ALE BREWERIES OF BELGIUM

Belgium has around 140
breweries in all, though it is
beers from the smaller-scale
ale brewers that are shown
here, and the lambic makers
(see map, page 63) that fuel
the regard for "Belgian Beers".

KEY

Brootcoorens **Erquelinnes**	Brewery Town/city
○ **Mons**	Other town/city

Trappist & Abbey Ales

Perhaps the most well known of Belgian beer types are those brewed by monks. Abbeys in northern Europe have been brewing for well over a thousand years.

Above: The logo that denotes a beer of genuine Trappist origin.

The Rule of St Benedict, the sixth-century text that underpins the traditions of Christian monasticism, allows the daily consumption of alcohol by those in holy orders, suggesting "one hemina of wine" – most likely half an imperial pint (28cl). It encourages productive labour, too, and the creation of "liquid bread" from cereals harvested from the abbey farm plays well with the Benedictine tenets of peace, prayer, and work. In centuries past, it was also the healthy alternative to water.

Abbey brewing additionally provided an opportunity for excellent public relations. The taverns and inns found near the gates of ancient abbeys were popular with the business traveller of old for their simple but wholesome food, fine home-brewed ales, and better-informed guests.

French abbeys were stripped of wealth and influence by Napoleon Bonaparte in 1793 and several moved to the relative safety of the then Southern Netherlands. It was not until the 1830s, after the creation of the kingdom of Belgium, that a few recommenced brewing, initially on a tiny scale.

THE TRAPPIST BREWERIES ▶

The six established Trappist abbey breweries were joined in 1999 by a seventh, newly constructed at the Cloister in Achel. Two more are being developed and hope to brew by 2015, just over Belgium's borders with north-east France and the southern Netherlands.

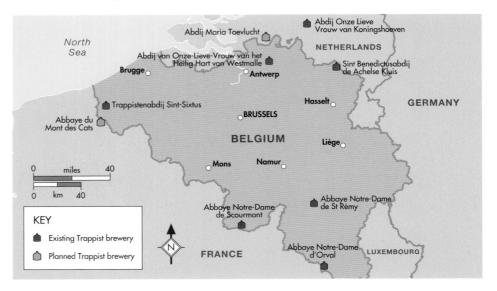

KEY

🏠 Existing Trappist brewery

🏠 Planned Trappist brewery

BEER SELECTION

CHIMAY TRIPLE (8%)
Chimay, Scourmont (Hainaut)
Space restrictions and increased production at Scourmont saw tall fermenters installed, with bottling and conditioning taken off site. Its strong blond ale, Cinq Cents, is smoother on draught and more bitter, sold in 75cl (26.4fl oz) bottles.
www.chimay.com

KAPITTEL PRIOR (9%)
Van Eecke, Watou (West Flanders)
This heavyweight, dark *tripel*, more typical of the older tradition that never disappeared on the Belgian coast, reaches its best after about five years in a 75cl (26.4fl oz) bottle, becoming heady with pear drops.
www.brouwerijvaneecke.tk

ORVAL (6.2%)
Orval, Villers-devant-Orval (Luxembourg)
Orval's main beer is an orange-amber pale ale that is dry hopped during conditioning (*see* p.22) and has *Brettanomyces* added to the bottle (*see* p.65). It should pour rocky-headed and have a pungent edge, its flavour surreptitiously enhanced by its iconic bottle.
www.orval.be

The Vatican allows commercial beer making at seven abbeys, all run by the Cistercian Order of the Strict Observance, or Trappists. While one, Koningshoeven (trading as La Trappe), is in Dutch North Brabant, the rest are found in Belgium. These are St Benedictus (Achel), St Sixtus (Westvleteren), and the abbeys of Our Lady of Scourmont (Chimay), Saint-Rémy (Rochefort), Orval (Orval), and the Holy Heart of Westmalle (Westmalle) (*see* pp.56–7).

There is no Trappist beer style as such, though all must be brewed within the walls of an abbey, by or under the supervision of members of the order, and all income must be used to benefit the monastic community or else to support charitable work.

Koningshoeven produced only lager in the 1970s, but all current Trappist beers are ales. The majority are dark, ranging from 6.5 to 11.2 per cent alcohol, although there are also two memorable pale ales and several strong blonds. Most are found only in the bottle.

The ancient quality marks of XX and XXX are roughly equivalent to the more modern Dutch terms *dubbel* and *tripel*, which although now used increasingly by craft brewers elsewhere are seen as having monastic origins. They originally inferred that a beer had double or triple the amount of malt in its mash. The term *quadrupel*, invented for a new La Trappe brand in 1990, has no historical precedent.

Above: The brewing room at the Abbaye Notre Dame de Saint-Rémy, near Rochefort.

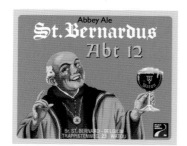

ST BERNARDUS ABT 12 (10.5%)
St Bernard, Watou (West Flanders)
The brewery was founded in 1946 solely to brew imitation Westvleteren beers, but since 1992 it has gone its own way, producing an improved range that includes this fruity, golden brown barley wine, which ages well for at least five years.
www.sintbernardus.be

TRAPPIST ACHEL EXTRA BRUIN (9.5%)
Achel, Hamont-Achel (Limburg)
St Benedict's cloister began brewing light beers for its refectory in 1999, progressing to stronger, bottled ones, including this huge brown ale with nutty undertones that seems to keep forever.
www.achelsekluis.org

In recent years, the annual output of Chimay and Westmalle has risen to over 125,000 hectolitres a year. Earlier in the twentieth century, a few commercial breweries were licensed by the order, with varying degrees of formality, to produce imitations of Trappist beers on a larger scale. Other brewers followed suit without invitation, using images and words associated with monks to market beers entirely for commercial gain.

Arrangements became more confused when various orders signed up to deals licensing the use of a particular abbey's name or location as a brand name. Sadly, the link between the image and any authenticity was often an early casualty.

Some of these so-called "abbey beers" are undoubtedly accomplished brews, some more so than the Trappist originals. Others, however, are dull and sweet, with little to recommend them beyond an allusion to godliness.

The badge "authentic Trappist product" may only appear on a beer made at a Trappist abbey. Attempts to confine further the term "abbey beer" to brands supported by a monastic order are difficult to justify from a consumer viewpoint, as the best of these often have no such link, while the less interesting can be highly lucrative.

BEER SELECTION

TRAPPISTES ROCHEFORT 6 (7.5%)
TRAPPISTES ROCHEFORT 8 (9.2%)
TRAPPISTES ROCHEFORT 10 (11.3%)
Rochefort, Rochefort (Namur)
Currently the most accomplished range of Trappist beers comes from the Abbaye Notre-Dame de Saint-Remy near Rochefort, where three dark bottled ales are created which, in rising order of strength, might respectively be called rustic, noble, and majestic. The two stronger beers are among the finest examples of beer to be found anywhere.
www.abbaye-rochefort.be

TRAPPIST WESTVLETEREN BLOND (5.8%)
TRAPPIST WESTVLETEREN 12 (10.2%)
Westvleteren, Westvleteren (West Flanders)
The brewery at St Sixtus's abbey retains open fermenters. These help to create a delicate, aromatic "local" blond ale made with whole hops and best drunk at the café by the abbey gates. The heavier, light brown ales, 12 and the lesser 8, possess but do not enjoy cult status and may disappoint unless aged in the cellar for two years.
www.sintsixtus.be

Opposite: Upkeep of the 20th-century abbey at Villers-devant-Orval is funded largely by the production of its brewery, to the right of the picture.

BROTHERS WHO BREW

Growing awareness of its brewing tradition may yet attract more young men into the Trappist Order, but for now, most of its involvement is supervisory. The senior overseers are largely self-taught, but the wisdom of some is highly regarded by other brewers.

At Chimay (see p.54) and La Trappe, professional brewing teams see themselves as running a smallish brewery in a special place, with ethical and governance oversight.

At Westmalle, Orval, Rochefort, and Achel (see pp.56–7), the collaboration is more complex. For example, the efficient yet environmentally sensitive brewery extension on abbey-owned farmland at Westmalle is a fine example of technology shaped by wisdom.

Only at Westvleteren (see p.56) do members of the order carry out much of the day-to-day activity, made possible in part by its "small country living" dimensions.

Monks and lay staff at all the brewing abbeys are allowed beer, but are a sober lot. At Rochefort, the daily ration is 33cl (11.6fl oz) of 8, but consumption is largely confined to the festivals of Christmas and Easter. At Chimay, Westmalle, and Orval, lower-alcohol beers are brewed for community members.

Right: Overseeing beer production at the abbey breweries requires a keen eye and a steady hand.

TRIPEL KARMELIET (8%)
Brouwerij Bosteels, Buggenhout (East Flanders)
The most overtly sumptuous and spicy variation on blond *tripel* is brewed from a three-grain mash including oats, making it sweeter, softer, and grainier. A great comfort beer.
www.bestbelgianspecialbeers.be

ST FEUILLIEN TRIPLE (9%)
Brasserie St Feuillien, Le Roeulx (Hainaut)
Full-on, malt-laden triple with more aromatic hopping than most. The old family brewery that makes it sometimes bottles it in oversize Champagne bottles (1.5–9 litres/0.3–2 gallons) to improve the yeast action.
www.st-feuillien.com

WESTMALLE DUBBEL (7%)
WESTMALLE TRIPEL (9.5%)
Westmalle, Westmalle (Antwerp)
At Westmalle, they produce the beers that could claim to define the terms *dubbel* and *tripel* in their modern usage. This includes a rule that has held since the mid-1950s that *tripel* should be blond. If well stored, the Dubbel should develop chocolate nuances, while the Tripel becomes honeyed.
www.trappistwestmalle.be/en/Page/
leveninarbeid.aspx

WITKAP PATER DUBBEL (7%)
Slaghmuylder, Ninove (East Flanders)
Created by a former Westmalle brewer in the 1920s and taken on by this small family brewery in 1979. A classic *dubbel*, which is caramel-laced and malt-driven, with an appealing tang.
www.witkap.be

Oak-aged Ales

There are few more extraordinary sights in the world of beer than the temple rooms at the Rodenbach brewery in Roeselare, north of Kortrijk (*see* photo, opposite). Nearly 300 straight-sided oak tuns, most carrying around 180 hectolitres of beer, sit upended on plinths a metre (three feet) or so above floor level. Most are filled with the same gently maturing brown ale, some coming ripe in 18 months, while others need two years and more to reach acidity equivalent to a typical Sauvignon Blanc.

Twenty kilometres (12½ miles) southeast of here, the Verhaeghe brothers make a range of beers to a similar principle at their higgledy-piggledy, nineteenth-century family-owned brewery and wholesale drink business (*see* below). Halfway between the two, the commercially successful Bavik brewery matures a pale ale on oak, to the same ends.

Storing beers in oak casks was the norm until the arrival of cheaper metal alloys. How long some have been deliberately aged in oak is less clear, though it is known that when the porter makers of early eighteenth-century London began to do this, they were building on a longer history of "stock ale" production in many countries.

The flavour effects of ageing in oak come not from the wood itself but from the microflora that live between its fibres – *pediococci* that produce lactic acid, which sharpens a beer but is otherwise largely tasteless and odourless. But used as a counterpoint to the sweetness of caramelized brown ale, it creates some pretty sophisticated flavour mixes.

Anxious to conform to more conventional tastes, producers had in recent decades shied away from releasing these beers in their undiluted forms, preferring to use them as a blending agent, typically adding 20–25 per cent of aged beer into freshly made ale of the same type. With the return of interest in craft brewing, it is the "neat" products that are attracting attention once more.

Right: Oak-aged Rodenbach Grand Cru – perhaps the most striking brown ale in the world.

BEER SELECTION

DUCHESSE DE BOURGOGNE (6.2%)
ECHT KRIEKENBIER (6.8%)
Brouwerij Verhaeghe, Vichte
(West Flanders)
This excellent, small family brewery produces gritty, light Vichtenaar (*see* above) as well as the smooth and buttery Duchesse, the most elegant of a dark and tangy range. Echt Kriekenbier is uniquely made by steeping whole fruit in oak-aged ale, ending deceptively strong.
www.brouwerijverhaeghe.be

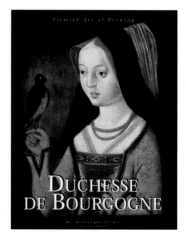

MELCHIOR (10–11%)
Brouwerij Alvinne, Moen
(West Flanders)
At the experimental edge of small-scale cask ageing and other techniques, the brothers-in-law of Alvinne create one-off variants of six strong ales in a remarkable range of beers.
www.alvinne.be

Next page: Beers from different vintages aging at a lambic cave, somewhere in Payottenland.

In a world grown used to the idea that sour beer is "off", the likes of Rodenbach Grand Cru or Verhaeghe's Vichtenaar can repel beer drinkers at first taste, although those who like aged red wines, particularly a Cabernet Sauvignon, can pick up the drift more swiftly.

Forty kilometres (25 miles) east of Kortrijk, around the market town of Oudenaarde, brewers had until the 1980s aged wort derived from stewed brown ales – brewed overly long to make more caramel – in smaller-sized oak casks. Sadly, today's producers "age" their beers with enzymes in steel containers.

Interest in oak ageing is increasing and new beers are likely to be created as surviving producers enjoy success. Experimentation with beers that are stronger, paler, or have whole fruit steeped in them has already begun.

Some brewers are also experimenting with ageing beers in brandy, whisky, port, and wine casks, though it may be some while before the subtle advantages derived from using microflora adapted to surviving the cask's last occupant can be teased out from the effect of spiking a brew with several pints of Cognac or single malt!

Above: Before blending, the individual character of each and every tun of ripened ale is tested in the laboratory and by experts' palates.

OERBIER RESERVA (9%)
De Dolle Brouwers, Esen (West Flanders)
Kris Herteleer, 1980s' Belgian beer revival pioneer, stays young by exploring the use of spirits casks to mature various vintages of his excellent, lactic-edged, dark, and convoluted *Oerbier*.
www.dedollebrouwers.be

PETRUS AGED PALE (7.3%)
Bavik, Bavikhove (West Flanders)
Originally made for the USA, as suggested by the Anglicized name, this overtly oak-aged blond ale is so unusually dry that it has since been released at home, too.
www.bavik.be

RODENBACH GRAND CRU (6%)
Rodenbach, Roeselare (West Flanders)
Dark and lightly acidic, this carefully matured and instantly striking drink is confident in its eccentricity. Served from an ice bucket in summer, it is a unique restorative.
www.rodenbach.be

Lambic Beers

Lambics are the only types of beer that Belgium can still claim entirely as its own. The most refined of the traditional versions of these beers are among the finest and most unusual drinks on the planet, although few ordinary drinkers would consider that they have flavours anywhere close to beer.

The 12 companies that make lambic beers are all based within 16 kilometres (10 miles) of Brussels' southwestern boundary. While all makers of oak-aged ales use the vintner's ways with barrelling, lambic brewers take a further step towards winemaking by adding no yeast to their beer, relying on nature to do it for them.

Lambic is the collective name for a clan of beers, distinguished from ales or lagers by the method of their fermentation. The common ingredient of all lambic beers is a basic brew that is itself also called lambic.

This base beer derives from the wheat beer tradition of central Europe (*see* pp.72–3) and is mashed with 30–40 per cent unmalted wheat. It differs from most other wheat beers in that it is high in hops, but the clash of bitter and sweet flavours is avoided by using cones (flowers) that are usually at least three years old. These are low in bitterness and floweriness yet still high in natural preservatives, to fight off spoiling.

Above: Lambic ages patiently in the cellars at Brouwerij Boon in Lembeek.

BEER SELECTION

3F VINTAGE OUDE GEUZE (6.5%)
3F SCHAARBEEKSE OUDE KRIEK (6%)
Drie Fonteinen, Beersel (Flemish Brabant)
Armand Debelder blends and steeps lambics from other brewers to sell on draught at his brother's café-restaurant in the village square. Vintage Oude Geuze bottles spend at least three years in the cellar, allowing it to develop great complexity, maximizing the aromas and backtastes of *Brettanomyces* fermentation (*see* p.65). Schaarbeekse Oude Kriek uses the historically preferred but rare, locally grown Schaarbeek cherries to re-create the quintessential *kriek* taste.
www.3fonteinen.be

BOON OUDE KRIEK (6%)
BOON OUDE GEUZE MARIAGE PARFAIT (8%)
Brouwerij Boon, Lembeek (Flemish Brabant)
While others campaigned passionately to preserve lambic, Frank Boon carefully planned to revive it. Now the largest producer of traditional lambic, his Oude Kriek has more fruit than most, from cherries sourced in Eastern Europe. Mariage Parfait is the stronger of two traditional *gueuzes*, blended from higher-gravity lambics that have more character but with restrained acidity.
www.boon.be

THE LAMBIC MAKERS OF BRUSSELS AND PAYOTTENLAND

Production of the world's most unusual and sophisticated lighter beers is largely confined to the Payottenland area of Flemish Brabant, south and west of Brussels, where a dozen producers borrow winemakers' methods to coax extraordinary flavours from simple wheat beers.

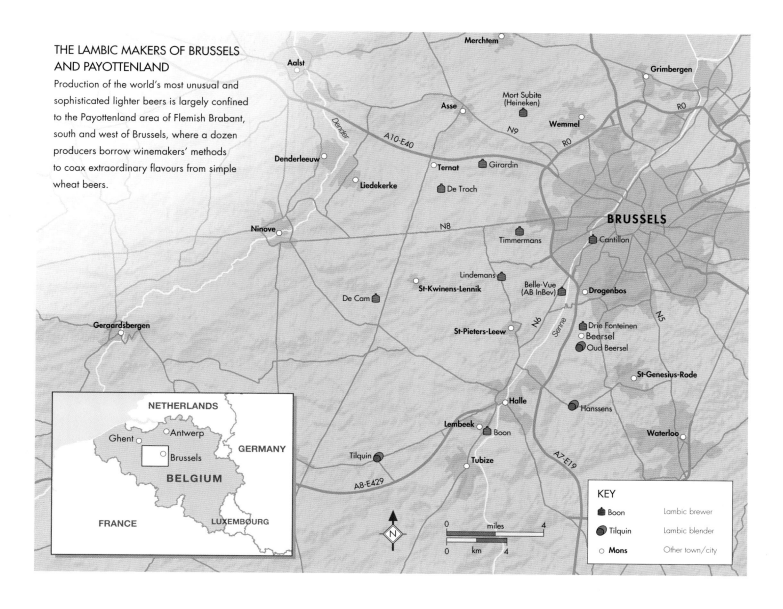

KEY
- Boon — Lambic brewer
- Tilquin — Lambic blender
- Mons — Other town/city

CANTILLON BROUCSELLA GRAND CRU (5%)
CANTILLON IRIS (6%)
CANTILLON ROSÉ DE GAMBRINUS (5%)
Cantillon, Brussels
The last lambic maker in Brussels is a centre of excellence, an official museum, and a one-issue campaign all under one roof. Visitors will find up to a dozen of Jean Van Roy's world-class beers available. Grand Cru is, unusually, a fully matured bottled old lambic, so should be nearly flat. Iris is not legally lambic or *gueuze*, as it is deliberately produced from 100 per cent malt to make a point. Rosé de Gambrinus is a rare example of *framboise* – a delicate, aromatic, and spritzy raspberry lambic.
www.cantillon.be

DE CAM OUDE GEUZE (6.5%)
Geuzestekerij De Cam, Gooik
(Flemish Brabant)
To relax at weekends, commercial brewer Karel Goddeau runs this lambic "cave" in a folk museum complex, making several impressive beers that include this top-rate traditional *gueuze*.
http://users.belgacom.net/gc762821/NL/brouwers/decam/decam.htm

Above: Detail from Pieter Brueghel the Younger's *Fair with a Theatrical Performance* (1562). Hermitage, St Petersburg.

BEER SELECTION

GIRARDIN LAMBIC (5%)
GUEUZE GIRARDIN 1882
(BLACK LABEL) (5%)
Brouwerij Girardin, St-Ulriks-Kapelle
(Flemish Brabant)
Most of the draught lambic found
in Payottenland cafés originates at
this publicity-shy farm brewery. The
oude version of its Gueuze Girardin,
distinguished from a simpler version
only by its black label, is considered
by several other lambic makers to be
the best *gueuze* of all.
www.geuzeinfo.com/index.php/
girardin

HANSSENS ARTISANAAL OUDE
GUEUZE (6%)
HANSSENS ARTISANAAL
OUDBEITJE (6%)
Hanssens Artisanaal, Dworp
(Flemish Brabant)
The old farm buildings at the back of
John Matthys' and Sidi Hanssens' home
contain marshalled rows of casks in which
lambics mature with a distinctive Hanssens'
thumbprint. There is woodsmoke amid
the citrus splinters in their Oude Gueuze.
Oudbeitje is the only traditionally made
strawberry lambic, retaining distinct fruit
presence long after colour and sweetness
have disappeared.
www.geuzeinfo.com/index.php/
Hanssens-Artisanaal

After brewing, the filtered wort (*see* p.22) is decanted into a cooling vessel (or *koelschip*), like a large paddling pool, where by tradition it cools "under an open roof beneath the night sky" in order to introduce airborne yeast. In reality, most brewers blow air over the top that is coarsely filtered to keep out insects, giving them some semblance of control.

However, where other brewers pitch a measure of carefully cultured, pure-strain *Saccharomyces* yeast into their beers to spark fermentation (*see* p.20), lambic makers rely on "wild" or naturally occurring yeast to perform "spontaneous fermentation".

The extent to which the fermenting microflora come from the atmosphere, night sky or otherwise, from the brewery rafters, or from the walls of the wooden casks into which the contents of the *koelschip* are poured is a matter of much debate in lambic circles. It is most likely that all three sources contribute something.

Wherever they come from, sufficient *Saccharomyces* arrive to fuel a primary fermentation that is fairly vigorous for two weeks before meandering for another three or four. As with oak-aged ales, *pediococci* then work to produce lactic fermentation (*see* p.58), responsible in part for bringing a variety of citrus flavours.

Where lambics enter a world apart is in their third phase of fermentation, which becomes more apparent in the second and third year in oak. Slow-fermenting yeast strains called *Brettanomyces*, adapted to live frugally off cellulose in the wood fibres of each cask or tun, help the beer develop add-on characteristics conjured up in descriptions such as "old bookshop", "horse blanket", and "hay barn".

You can still find "raw" draught lambic in some local bars in Brussels and Payottenland, sold from plastic containers because local health inspectors mistrust wood. Served six to 12 months from barrelling, it is termed *jong* and tastes of mushroom and ale, while after two or three years on oak it becomes *oud* (old) and tends to be flat and vinous.

Before 1950, most lambic ended up as *faro*, a draught beer to which sugar had been added so as to spark lightly fizzy refermentation and soften acidity. This can still be found in a few cafés, such as De Rare Vos at Schepdaal in the heart of Payottenland, due west of Brussels.

Nowadays, most traditionally made lambic is used mainly to create bottled beers, such as *oude g(u)euze* (*see* below) and *oude kriek*.

Belgian law currently defines lambic beer in a way that includes some with only a passing connection to the authentic version described above. Thankfully, the European Union has stepped in with some formal designations that can only be used to describe lambics made in the traditional way, involving the Dutch and French words for "old".

Traditional *gueuze* – *geuze* in some local dialects – has a base of young lambic into which is blended a quantity of older lambic, before bottling with a drop of liquid sugar. The young provides the body, the old brings the character, and the sugar creates the sparkle. Generally, the greater the proportion of three-year-old lambic, the more characterful the *gueuze* will be.

Traditional *kriek* is made by steeping cherries (*krieken* in old Flemish) in a cask of lambic for six months or so. Though occasionally encountered on draught, most is bottled. It is best to use fruits that are hard, dry, and slightly bitter, with their stones intact to add a little almond into a delightful mix of fruity, sharp, and musty flavours.

Steeping raspberries creates the equally traditional but nowadays rare *framboise*. Successful experimentation with steeping grapes, apricots, strawberries, and other fruits has yet to become sufficiently established to earn a title.

As well as those producers shown below, some traditional *gueuze* and *kriek* is made by family-run De Troch, Mort Subite (Heineken), and Timmermans, a subsidiary of a larger drinks group. The largest official lambic brewer, Belle-Vue (Anheuser-Busch InBev) makes no traditional products.

Next page: A rack of organic *gueuze* maturing in bottles at the Brasserie Cantillon in Brussels.

LINDEMANS CUVÉE RENÉ OUDE GUEUZE (5%)
Brouwerij Lindemans, Vlezenbeek (Flemish Brabant)
Renowned brewers of delicate, lemony lambics much prized by blenders, Lindemans spent two decades making mostly sweet fruit beers before their Cuvée René brands marked a return to traditional lambics with a lighter touch.
www.lindemans.be

OUD BEERSEL OUDE KRIEK (6.5%)
Oud Beersel BVBA, Beersel (Flemish Brabant)
Gert Christiaens saved the idiosyncratic Vandervelden brewery in 2007, as a place to mature, blend, and steep lambics. Drive, luck, and local support have helped regrow some sophisticated beers, including this dark, dryish *kriek*.
www.oudbeersel.com

TILQUIN GUEUZE À L'ANCIENNE (6.4%)
Gueuzerie Tilquin, Bierghes (Wallonian Brabant)
Pierre Tilquin bought in his first lambic in March 2009 and sold his first *gueuze* in summer 2011 – illustrating the financial commitment required of a new lambic maker. His early beers are encouragingly fine.
www.gueuzerietilquin.be

Saison Beers

In Wallonia, the French-speaking southern region of Belgium, the self-respect of many craft brewers has returned with interest in a type of beer called *saison*, dubbed "farmhouse ale" by some proponents, though its revival may inadvertently have amalgamated several unrelated versions of "seasonal" beer to create something new.

In centuries past, farmers often brewed in the winter for extra income, adding value to some of their grain harvest. In summer, they would not brew, as there were other priorities. Additionally, open vessels in overheated fermenting rooms were vulnerable to insect attack and other types of spoiling, so they would brew extra beer to tide them over the summer months.

The story goes that such beers would be stronger and hoppier than regular beer, and therefore they would keep better. While this has the essential ingredient of a good theory, in that it is plausible, it lacks a reliable historical record and the ability to withstand some basic questions. For example, what would make someone working in the hot sun want to drink a 6.5 per cent alcohol beer?

A more likely theory, supported by what production records survive, suggests that Wallonian summer beers, made mainly

for farm labourers in rural areas and miners and steel-workers in the industrial towns springing up along the Meuse, Sambre, and Canal du Centre, featured mainly water for rehydration and sugar for energy.

It is known that light and sweet ales appeared around Liège and the industrial areas, in some ways similar to the lighter mild ales of the North of England and the English Midlands. There were ultra-light and hoppy beers, too, more associated with rural areas and possibly sharing a heritage with lighter forms of lambic called *meerts* or *maerts* that were still used in blending by lambic makers like Boon (*see* p.62) and Tilquin.

A third form may also have existed that was heavier and hoppier, but if so, it is likely that this would have been reserved for celebrations around harvest time.

It is possible that that all three forms were termed *saison*, but whatever the history, the type that has risen to fame

BEER SELECTION

IV SAISON (6.5%)
Brasserie de Jandrain-Jandrenouille, Jandrain (Wallonian Brabant)
Superb, delicate yet vibrant, perfectly hopped, pale *blonde* new-style *saison* that arrived almost fully formed from this newly constructed brewery, housed on an old farm.
www.novabirra.com/pages/ivsaison.html

SAISON CAZEAU (5%)
Brasserie de Cazeau, Templeuve (Hainaut)
Light *blonde* ale that looks the part despite liberties having been taken with any defined style, thanks to elderflowers being added, showing off its hops and bringing a distinctive summery twist.
www.brasseriedecazeau.be

in the last two decades is an aromatically bitter, grainy pale ale that owes its revival to the understandable success of Saison Dupont in North America, a beer that helped fuel the American enthusiasm for testing just how far hopping can go.

All the forms of *saison* survive with varying degrees of success, but it is the new-style *saison* beers that have found their moment, appealing in particular to those who like prominent aromatic hop presence without stinging bitterness. As well as those mentioned, St Feuillien Saison and De Ranke's Saison de Dottignies are worth finding.

Above: Wooded hills and meandering rivers epitomize the Ardennes, southern Belgium's forgotten quarter.

Opposite: Brewer Jean-Louis Dits at his open mash tun at the steam-powered Brasserie à Vapeur in Pipaix.

Next page: The hop harvest, near Poperinge in West Flanders.

SAISON DE PIPAIX (6%)

Brasserie à Vapeur, Pipaix-Leuze (Hainaut)
Jean-Louis Dits assures all that this distinctive, dry spiced beer is from an ancient brewer's recipe found at the unique steam-powered village brewery he saved from closure in 1985.
www.vapeur.com

SAISON DUPONT (6.5%)

Brasserie Dupont, Tourpes (Hainaut)
The leading light of the new genre makes its beers in a modern plant sited within Wallonia's cutest-looking ancient farm complex. Wafts of herb and haystack augment a hop bitterness best appreciated when in 75cl bottles.
www.brasserie-dupont.com

SAISON VOISIN (5%)

Brasserie des Géants, Ath (Hainaut)
The best of the sweeter, lighter *saison* beers originated at the Voisin brewery in Flobecq and after its closure was re-created in 2002 with the former brewer's assent.
www.brasseriedesgeants.com

ULTRA-FRAÎCHE (3.5%)

Brasserie d'Ecaussinnes, Ecaussinnes (Hainaut)
One of few authentic light *saison* beers, from a successful export-orientated micro that uses dry hops to brighten this simple *blonde* ale.
www.brasserieecaussinnes.be

Spiced Wheat Beers

As early as the ninth century AD, records survive of brewing with wheat in much of the north of Charlemagne's Holy Roman Empire, suggesting at some level a shared history between Dutch-Flemish "white" (or *wit*) beers, *Berliner Weisse*, Bavarian *Weizen*, and lambics.

In 1966, dairy manager Pierre Celis decided to revive a brew he recalled from the Tomsin brewery, next to his childhood home. He added coriander, a little cumin, and the dried peel of Curaçao oranges to flavour a mash with 30 per cent unmalted wheat and a few oats. He named it Oud Hoegaards, after his town of Hoegaarden.

The tradition of lacing beers with spices may have originated from the age-old use of *gruut* mixes as preservatives and flavourings (*see* p.15), although whether Belgian wheat beer always used to be spiced is a moot point. Up the way in Leuven, the now-defunct *peeterman* style was definitely not spiced, but Celis's imitators, who came in droves, almost all included dried peel and coriander because this made an already cloudy beer, full of the taste of fresh bread, subtly perfumed and enjoyably drinkable.

Celis did not intend to become either a hero or a millionaire. He was a small businessman, a bit of a dreamer, and a likable old-fashioned grafter, who recognized a good opportunity. His beer looked and tasted completely different from those that dominated the market, at a time when conformity was going out of fashion.

White beers in Belgium have since diversified to include spelt, buckwheat, rye, and other grains. Some have gone spicier or plainer, weaker or stronger, clearer or murkier, and occasionally dark, redefining their place in a changing market.

Oud Hoegaards eventually mutated into Hoegaarden, the first beer of recent craft origin to become a worldwide hit, although by the time that happened it had left behind its creator and its panache.

Coriander   Cumin   Wheat   Oats   Orange peel

BEER SELECTION

AUGRENOISE (6.5%)
Brasserie d'Augrenoise, Casteau (Hainaut)
A sharp, slightly green variant on a heavier-end wheat beer made at a brewhouse providing employment for people with learning disabilities, overseen by Orval's head brewer (*see* p.54).
www.augrenoise.com

BLANCHE DES HONNELLES (6%)
Brasserie de l'Abbaye des Rocs, Montignies-sur-Roc (Hainaut)
Blanche Double in the USA, this fuller-bodied, slightly herbal, mandarin-laced golden *bière blanche* brewed with oats stands slightly to one side of the others.
www.abbaye-des-rocs.com

LIMBURGSE WITTE (5%)
Brouwerij Sint-Jozef, Opitter-Bree (Limburg)
Eschewing refermentation in the bottle does little harm to this undersung "standard" Belgian white beer from near the Dutch border.
www.brouwerijsintjozef.be

Above: Brewers' wheat, at a farm in Flanders.

SARA BRUNE (6%)

Brasserie de Silenrieux, Silenrieux (Namur)
This southern brewery was founded to promote the use of ancient grains in brewing, leading by example with this dark, spiced brew made using buckwheat.

SAISON D'ÉPEAUTRE (6%)

Brasserie de Blaugies, Blaugies (Hainaut)
One of the most distinctive beers in Belgium, made with spelt and a yeast–hop combination that brings a barn's worth of character to the glass. Best served cloudy.
www.brasseriedeblaugies.com

WAASE WOLF (6%)

Brouwerij Boelens, Belsele (East Flanders)
Kris Boelens' beers from Waasland have a history of being honeyed, spicy, and foggy, none more so than this chewy and opaque off-white example.
www.brouwerijboelens.be

The British Influence

Belgium is, according to France's former president Charles de Gaulle, a country invented by the British to annoy the French. Created at the 1830 London Conference, its first king was Queen Victoria's brother-in-law and before the end of the century the person holding most influence over its brewers was an Englishman.

George Maw Johnson brewed in Canterbury, but developed a great fondness for the town of Hal (now Halle), south of Brussels, after he was approached by local brewers to advise on how to make a beer that imitated one made haphazardly by local publicans adding sugar to open casks. His editorship of *Le Petit Journal du Brasseur* followed in 1899.

Johnson it was who persuaded Belgian brewers to greet the new century by creating a light style of pale ale called *spéciale*, some adding "1900" to its designation (*see* tasting note for Special De Ryck, opposite). Sweet black beers based on British milk stout followed, as did strong, dark, malt-packed Scotch ales and robust export stout.

Larger British brewery companies like Whitbread, Bass, and Watney exported beers in hogsheads for decanting into bottles after resting in Belgian warehouses, while importers such as John Martin of Antwerp struck deals to bring in ales from Guinness, McEwans, and Barclay Perkins, the brews often surviving in Belgium long after they had disappeared from Britain.

It was only a matter of time before the best ideas were absorbed into Belgian brewing culture and local talent took over.

Right: The brewery at Silly in northern Hainaut continued to produce a classic Scotch ale long after Scottish brewers had forgotten how.

Opposite left: Rich, malty, and warming, Scotch ales seem as much designed for the intemperate Belgian weather as they are for Scotland's colder climes.

Opposite top right: Wort is separated from the spent grain at Brouwerij De Ryck in Herzele.

Opposite bottom right: Increased interest in draught beer, especially in export markets, has led many Belgian breweries to invest heavily in kegs.

BEER SELECTION

BELLEVAUX BLACK (6.3%)
Brasserie de Bellevaux, Bellevaux (Liège)
The British influence on this winter brew comes directly from founder-brewer Will Schuwer's excellent recollection of the taste of Theakston's Old Peculier in 1980 (*see* p.121).
www.brasseriedebellevaux.be

HERCULE STOUT (9%)
Brasserie Ellezelloise, Ellezelles (Hainaut)
One of the boldest of Belgian-made stouts, full of caramel and cocoa, it follows the tradition of Guinness Export but is named in honour of Monsieur Poirot.
www.brasserie-ellezelloise.be

HOFBLUES (5.5%)
't Hofbrouwerijke, Beerzel (Antwerp)
One-man band Jef Goetelen brews whatever takes his fancy, but he keeps returning to this black, dry, roasted stout that could compete with Ireland's best.
www.thofbrouwerijke.be

SCOTCH SILLY (7.5%)
Brasserie de Silly, Silly (Hainaut)
This polished example of a strong, sweet, malty Scotch ale with modest hopping comes from a 160-year-old, family-run village brewery near Ath.
www.silly-beer.com

SPECIAL DE RYCK (5.5%)
Brouwerij De Ryck, Herzele (East Flanders)
The best of the beers that evolved from the "*spéciale* 1900" style of soft pale ales (*see above*), made by one of the most respected, small family breweries in Belgium.
www.brouwerijderyck.be

STOUT LEROY (5%)
Brouwerij Leroy, Boezinge (West Flanders)
Unlikely to win prizes but an interesting throwback to the days when sweet, caramelized Kentish milk stout looked good, tasted good, and by golly did you good.
www.brouwerijhetsas.be

Regional Beers

The great joy of drinking beer in Belgium is the fabulous diversity of styles and one-off creations found among the local brewers. These are known as *streekbieren* or *bières regionaux*.

In Limburg, they make light blond ales with summer grass hopping. Brewers in Brabant and elsewhere blend lambic into some of their ales. Southern brewers vaguely follow the *blonde*, *brune*, and *ambrée* principles found in France. Others put honey, mustard flour, a dab of coriander seed or aniseed into the mash.

Not all new Belgian beers are products of imagination. When a beer becomes successful, it will acquire imitators. For example, when Moortgat brewery's Duvel (dialect for "Devil") took off (*see* below), numerous other brewers began to make light blond ales of around 8.5 per cent alcohol with names like Lucifer and Judas.

Nor is everything of high quality. A recent vogue for making "fruit beers" to mimic the tradition of *oude kriek* has seen few brewers create beers with any a degree of authenticity. Most use syrups or juice concentrate to create drinks that are banal and insulting to a great cultural tradition.

The use of spices and other flavourings can be suspect, too. While the practice has strong historical roots and spices used with subtlety can enhance a beer, many producers follow their ancestors in using such tricks to hide fouling from poor technique or to add flavour to beers that derive little from thin recipes and cut-price methods.

The Proefbrouwerij in Lochristi, East Flanders, which has links to one of the country's brewing schools, was set up specifically to help professional, semi-professional, and amateur brewers experiment with creating new beers. Run

WHEN YOU ARE THERE

- 80 per cent of Belgian café owners know remarkably little about beer.
- When in doubt, drink local.
- Brussels is quieter at weekends and in summer; Bruges on weekday evenings.
- Buy knowledgeable one-upmanship from www.booksaboutbeer.com.
- Must see: the Cantillon lambic brewery and museum in Brussels (*see* p.63).
- Must drink: as much as you think wise.

Opposite: Dirk Naudts, brewmaster at Proef in Lochristi, East Flanders, has produced over 2,000 different beers for clients from Belgium and beyond.

BEER SELECTION

3 SCHTÉNG (6%)
Brasserie du Grain d'Orge,
Hombourg (Liège)
Soft, sweetish, portery, and spiced dark ale brewed for a local drinks wholesaler and named after the Three Stones landmark at the Belgian-Dutch-German border.
www.grain-dorge.com

ALPÄIDE (10%)
Brouwerij Nieuwhuys, Hoegaarden
(Flemish Brabant)
Surprisingly mature and balanced sweet, strong brown ale from a relatively new producer, unconnected to his town's other brewer but with solid plans.
www.hoegaardsbier.be

BELLA MÈRE (6.5%)
Brasserie Artisanale Millevertus,
Breuvanne (Luxembourg)
More complex than a typical modern *saison*, this pale amber ale is one of a dozen from this highly inventive village brewer with a forgiving mother-in-law.
www.millevertus.be

BINK BLOND (5.5%)
Brouwerij Kerkom,
Kerkom-Sint-Truiden (Limburg)
"Making bitter beer is easy — hoppy beer is more difficult," says brewer Marc Limet, defining the appeal of his elegant, delightfully drinkable, full-on Limburg blond ale.
www.brouwerijkerkom.be

BLACK ALBERT (13%)
Brouwerij 't Oude Schooltje, Oostvleteren
(West Flanders)
The Struise Brouwers collective produces easy beers for locals and challenging ones for foreigners, such as this massive "Royal Belgian" stout, brimming with roasted malts and firm hop bitterness.
www.struise.noordhoek.com/eng/

CARACOLE (7.5%)
Brasserie Caracole, Falmignoul (Namur)
This classic, middle-strength *ambrée* is made with five malts and some dried peel for good measure, in a reawoken 200-year-old brewhouse in the northern Ardennes.
www.brasserie-caracole.be

CUVÉE DE RANKE (7%)
Brouwerij De Ranke, Dottignies (Hainaut)
Every De Ranke beer is excellent and this blend of pale ale and lambic, retaining hop esters from one side and musty sourness from the other, is a must-try.
www.deranke.be

DUVEL (8.5%)
Brouwerij Duvel Moortgat, Breendonk (Antwerp)
This palest blond of bottle-conditioned strong ales is not so much a regional beer as a global success story, but it still manages to avoid going bland. Just.
www.duvel.be

EMBRASSE (9%)
Brouwerij De Dochter van de Korenaar, Baarle-Hertog (Antwerp)
The basic beer is somewhere between a strong stout and a dark *tripel* before any experiments to enhance it by oak ageing.
www.dedochtervandekorenaar.be

ESTIVALE (5.2%)
Brasserie Artisanale de Rulles, Rulles-Habay (Luxembourg)
The lightest of the world-class ales made at Grégory Verhelst's village brewery is this aromatic, pale amber brew, billowing hop esters like they were back in fashion.
www.larulles.be

FANTÔME (8%)
Brasserie Fantôme, Soy (Luxembourg)
Founder-brewer Dany Prignon has enjoyed a lifetime's success producing odd beers, of which the most regular is this apple-and-pear-edged, strong yet summery ale.
www.fantome.be

GOUDEN CAROLUS CLASSIC (8.5%)
Brouwerij Het Anker, Mechelen (Antwerp)
The longest-established beer from this revitalized brewery in Antwerp's second city is this heavy, red-brown ale said to be true to the old Mechelen tradition.
www.hetanker.be

GRUUT AMBER (6.6%)
Gentse Stadsbrouwerij Gruut, Ghent (East Flanders)
Annick De Splenter's family sold the brewery she hoped one day to run, so she built her own for making *gruut* beers without hops for a twenty-first-century audience.
www.gruut.be

GULDEN DRAAK (10.5%)
Van Steenberge, Ertvelde (East Flanders)
The tacky white bottle undermines the image of this half-brown, top-of-the-range, yeast-spiced barley wine from this hard-working, quintessentially Flemish brewery.
www.vansteenberge.com

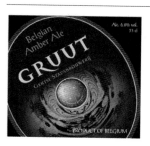

by a highly skilled team, it creates hundreds of new beers a year, saving many from ever seeing the light of day but creating others that go on to become modern classics.

Variety is reflected in the country's cafés and eating houses, some of which stock massive beer lists equivalent to, in some cases alongside, a lengthy wine list in a successful restaurant. These are supplied through a network of drinks warehouses, many of which also sell direct to the public. Those near the French and Dutch borders frequently see their car parks filled with foreign number plates, the drivers stocking their cellars for an entire season.

Left: Belgium is also blessed with more than its fair share of elegant cafés.

Opposite: Some Belgian ales have become big business, as seen at the high-tech brewhouse at Duvel Moortgat, near Puurs.

BEER SELECTION

HOPUS (8.3%)
Brasserie Lefebvre, Quenast
(Wallonian Brabant)
Having grown a reputation for efficiently made yet restrained, spicy-sweet beers, this family-run southern Belgian brewery put out this high-hopped strong *blonde* ale to applause.
www.brasserielefebvre.be

LA BINCHOISE SPÉCIALE NOËL (9%)
Brasserie La Binchoise, Binche (Hainaut)
If you are going to spice a beer, then do it at Christmas and ladle it in, as with this great bread pudding of a strong *ambrée*.
www.brasserielabinchoise.be

LA SAMBRESSE BLONDE (8%)
Brasserie Brootcoorens,
Erquelinnes (Hainaut)
Few beyond Erquelinnes have heard of Alain Brootcoorens, a typical Belgian craft brewer whose big ales include this earthy, strong *blonde*.
www.brasserie-brootcoorens-erquelinnes.be

MALHEUR DARK BRUT (12%)
Malheur Bieren, Buggenhout
(East Flanders)
Conditioning by the *méthode champenoise* gives this heavy, black coffee and chocolate-laden imperial stout a disconcertingly frisky edge.
www.malheur.be

ONDINEKE OILSJTERSEN TRIPEL (8.5%)
Brouwerij De Glazen Toren, Erpe-Mere
(East Flanders)
This lush, moreish, bittersweet strong blond ale is the official beer of Aalst, using hops from the local area in its recipe.
www.glazentoren.be

PALM DOBBEL (5.5%)
Palm Breweries, Steenhuffel (East Flanders)
Belgium's fourth-largest independent brewery produces this incongruous but appealing variant of a northern England, pre-war bitter as its winter brew.
www.palmbreweries.com

PATER LIEVEN BRUIN (6.5%)
Brouwerij Vanden Bossche,
Sint-Lievens-Esse (East Flanders)
Made in an old tower brewery in the
village square by a fourth-generation
family brewer, this plain but polished
brown ale is one of the best in Belgium.
www.paterlieven.be

STRUBBE PILS (5%)
Brouwerij Strubbe, Ichtegem
(West Flanders)
Most smaller Belgian breweries have
given up on pilsner, but this one from the
Strubbe family is unusually well hopped,
crisp, and light.
www.brouwerij-strubbe.be

'T SMISKE (7%)
Brouwerij Smisje, Oudenaarde
(East Flanders)
Former small-batch brewer Johan Brandt risked
all on a purpose-built brewhouse to make his
fresh-tasting pale ale with spring water and
100 per cent West Flanders hops.
www.smisje.be

TARAS BOULBA (4.5%)
Brasserie de la Senne, Brussels
While Belgium is famed for strong and
outlandish beers, some of its finest brewers
produce simpler brews magnificently, as
with this light, hoppy ale from the capital.
www.brasseriedelasenne.be

TONNEKE (5%)
Brouwerij Contreras, Gavere
(East Flanders)
Fruity, slightly sharp, light amber ale,
in a sub-style all of its own, is made
at a family brewery south of Ghent.
www.contreras.be

VICARIS GENERAAL (8.8%)
Brouwerij Dilewyns, Dendermonde
(East Flanders)
This strong brown ale smells heavily roasted
and tastes of bread crust, falling somewhere
between a Scotch and a dark *tripel*.
www.vicaris.be

VIVEN PORTER (7%)
Proefbrouwerij, Lochristi (East Flanders)
One of the ultimate service brewery's finest
products is this all-guns-blazing stronger
porter made with North American clarity
for a West Flanders wholesaler.
www.viven.be

GERMANY

Germany is the world's fifth-largest beer producer, brewing almost 100 million hectolitres annually, yet it is alone in the top 40 for the fact that less than half its output – 38 per cent – comes from large companies. By comparison, in the fourth- and seventh-largest producers, Brazil and Mexico, the brewing behemoths control 99 per cent of the market.

Not that Germany is immune to the fancies of global brewers. Four of the "Big Six" companies that show at Munich's Oktoberfest each year, plus many instantly recognizable German beer brands such as Beck's and St Pauli, are owned directly or in effect by Anheuser-Busch InBev or Heineken. However, their influence is subdued and most of the larger producers – such as the Radeberger and Oettinger groups Bitburger and Krombacher – are German-owned.

The remainder of the market is split among roughly 1,300 breweries, almost half based in Bavaria. While some are little more than commercialized hobbies and others are single-pub concerns, the majority are diminutive, local companies happily mired in approaches to brewing that are centuries old.

The natural conservatism of the market owes a great deal to the strictures of the legally defunct 500-year-old "Purity Order" (*see* panel, right), which ensured that German beer was always reliable, if not necessarily exceptional. Even brands like Krombacher Pils, which at 4.5 million hectolitres per annum is the country's bestseller, and the more travelled Bitburger (*see* p.82) retain reasonably authentic flavours.

Most German brewers seek to produce beers of high quality, with a tight ceiling on price. It is rarely their purpose to create something

Below: As the third-largest city in Bavaria and home to a major German university, it is perhaps not surprising that Augsburg boasts a half-dozen breweries.

THE REINHEITSGEBOT

In 1516, Duke Wilhelm IV of Bavaria agreed with his co-ruler Duke Ludwig X to sign off a masterpiece of legislation, accepted by historians as the world's longest-lasting consumer protection law.

A price war had developed between brewers and bakers over the purchase of wheat. Coming on top of growing concerns that brewers were putting all sorts into local beers, including herbs, root vegetables, fungi, and animal products, this latest annoyance brought a response known until the late nineteenth century as the "Surrogate Prohibition" and more recently the "Purity Order" (or *Reinheitsgebot*).

This diktat stipulated that beer must be made only with barley, hops, and water. Yeast escaped mention, as it had yet to be discovered. Within a decade, an exemption was made, ironically, for malted wheat.

As the German states came together under Bismarck, many adopted the standard, outlawing numerous historical and local beer styles in so doing. It only became universal in 1919, when Bavaria made it a condition for accepting its absorption into the new Germany.

The *Reinheitsgebot* was withdrawn in 1988 after the European Union declared it a restraint of free trade, although few German breweries to this day use the sugar, substitute grains, and additives allowed by the law that has replaced it.

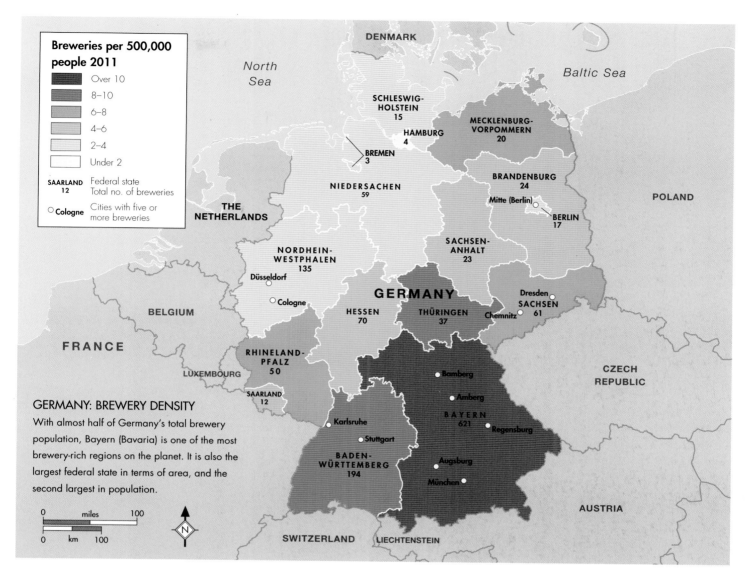

GERMANY: BREWERY DENSITY

With almost half of Germany's total brewery population, Bayern (Bavaria) is one of the most brewery-rich regions on the planet. It is also the largest federal state in terms of area, and the second largest in population.

spectacularly different or to ape other countries' brewing preferences.

Northern Germany has innumerable brewpubs, most created within the last 20 years and offering a predictable portfolio of a light lager, a dark one, and a wheat beer – plus, from time to time, a seasonal brew. In the south, older, small-town, and typically family-run breweries dominate, ranging from single beer producers to those that offer a broad array of brands, although many also stick with the light-dark-wheat triptych.

The contrasts across the country are compelling. A Munich *Biergarten* will offer beer in a litre-(1.76 pint-) sized *Maß* or stein, but venture north to Cologne and the glass shrinks to a 20cl (7fl oz) *Stange*. *Märzen* in Bamberg may arrive smelling like a smoked ham, whereas in Augsberg it will

be clean, malty, and warming. A wheat beer from Berlin should be light and tart, while one from Bavaria should yield a fruity, spicy brew.

More so perhaps in Germany than anywhere else, it is the nomadic drinker who will enjoy the greatest selection of beers and make the most enjoyable discoveries. Most of Germany's great brewers are local heroes, unknown beyond their parish.

German-style craft brewing is arriving, but in the bigger picture the question will be whether German-owned brewing groups will keep their nerve and not succumb to cutting costs and standards. As even the most undemanding of drinkers begin to tire of industrial beers, the prospects for those who have mastered quality large-scale brewing must be interesting.

BEST-SELLING LOCAL LABELS

Beck's	(Anheuser-Busch InBev)
DAB	(National)
Franziskaner	(Anheuser-Busch InBev)
Hacker-Pschorr	(Heineken)
Hasseröder	(Anheuser-Busch InBev)
Holsten	(Carlsberg)
Kulmbacher	(Heineken)
Löwenbräu	(Anheuser-Busch InBev)
Oettinger	(National)
Paulaner	(Heineken)
Radeberger	(National)
Spaten	(Anheuser-Busch InBev)
Warsteiner	(National)

Helles & Other Pale Lagered Beers

The word used in southern Germany to describe a pale-gold, lightly to moderately hopped, crisp and refreshing, bottom-fermented beer is *Helles*, meaning "light" or "bright", whereas "lager", derived from the German *lagern*, meaning "to store", is reserved for slightly aged beers. "Pils" may be used interchangeably, but more frequently refers to a hoppier, drier brew.

Helles is the everyday drinking beer of Munich – the one that fills the imposing steins featured in countless images of jubilant Bavarians. At its best, it is a refined and elegant thirst-quencher, a sublime expression of subtlety and finesse in the brewing arts, while even at its most awkward it should be a pleasing if mundane quaffer.

Possibly as early as the fourteenth century, brewers in the Munich area came to realize that whatever it was that ruined beer brewed in the summer could be prevented from doing so by refrigerating it in caves found under the foothills of the Alps. They began storing their late-spring brews there, lowering the temperature of fermentation and unwittingly encouraging the arrival of what we now know to be cool-activated lager yeasts (*see* p.20).

Pale malts arrived in southern Germany soon after light blond lagered beers appeared in Bohemia and it was not long before they had reached the northern states. These German pilsners have a drier, leaner, and paler malt profile than their Bohemian kin, leading to a greater degree of perceived, if not necessarily measurable, bitterness. Travel south from the Teutonic pilsner heartland

Above: The one-litre *Maß* is the preferred drinking vessel for *Helles* throughout Bavaria.

of Lower Saxony and the Upper Rhine and these beers grow by stages less aggressively hoppy, more elegant, and finally maltier, coming closer to the Pilsen original.

The firmly malty style associated by foreigners with the northern city of Dortmund is not formally recognized in Germany, where beer categorization is based more on format than character. For example, there are yeast-containing varieties, essentially bottle- or barrel-conditioned in the manner of British "real" ales, known variously as *Zwickel*, *Ungespundet*, *Kräusen*, and *Kellerbier*, some of which are at best amber and a few plainly dark. *Landbier* is similarly low in carbonation but is usually filtered.

Märzen was the name given to those beers sent for cold storage and consumed over the summer before brewing recommenced in September, the remainder being enjoyed at late summer festivals.

BEER SELECTION

ANDECHSER SPEZIAL HELL (5.8%)
Klosterbrauerei Andechs, Andechs (Bavaria)
The Andechs monastery near Munich produces a rich bounty of great beers and serves them all in a truly heavenly setting, including this generously hoppy *Spezial*.
www.andechs.de

AUGUSTINER EDELSTOFF (5.6%)
Augustiner-Bräu Wagner, Munich (Bavaria)
This Export beer from one of the two independent breweries in Munich's "Big Six" (see p.80) is brilliant gold with an elegant, hop-kissed sweetness, finishing dryly malty and only faintly bitter.
www.augustiner-braeu.de

AYINGER JAHRHUNDERT-BIER (5.5%)
Brauerei Aying, Aying (Bavaria)
Created in celebration of this well-marketed brewery's centennial year in 1978, this firmly malty Bavarian brew is in a stronger style reminiscent of what foreigners term *Dortmunder* beer.
www.ayinger.de

BITBURGER PREMIUM BEER (4.8%)
Bitburger Braugruppe, Bitburg (Rheinland-Pfalz)
The centrepiece of one of Germany's largest domestic brewing concerns, this light-hued and brilliantly crisp pilsner remains every bit the "sessionable" refresher it has always been.
www.bitburger.com

BRAUBERGER ZWICKELBIER (4.8%)
Brauberger zu Lübeck, Lübeck (Schleswig-Holstein)
Lübeck – another UNESCO World Heritage Site, along with the magnificent Bamberg (see p.84) – has one brewpub that makes one beer: an unfiltered, hazy light amber served from wooden barrels.
www.brauberger.com

HOFBRÄU OKTOBERFESTBIER (6.3%)
Hofbräu Munich, Munich (Bavaria)
Typical of a modern *Märzen*, this is only slightly richer and deeper gold in colour than this state-owned brewery's *Helles*, though stronger and more spicy-malty.
www.hofbraeu-muenchen.de

Classically of light amber hue, they tended to be stronger, maltier, and richer. The newer Export and *Spezial* varieties are not necessarily aged but lie on a spectrum of strength that eventually stretches out towards the paler forms of *Bock*.

Above: The interiors of many a Bavarian beer hall are dwarfed by the great expanses of the outdoor *Biergartens*, some of which can seat thousands.

JEVER PILSENER (4.8–5.2%)
Radeberger Gruppe, Jever (Lower Saxony)
A flagship for northern German pilsners of all stripes, Jever's success lies in the balance it strikes between assertive bitterness and a firmly malty base.
www.jever.de

KEESMANN BAMBERGER HERREN PILS (4.5%)
Brauerei Keesmann, Bamberg (Bavaria)
An exquisite, delicate, floral, grassy, crisp, light straw-coloured, and innocent-looking but delicious brew, arguably more *Helles*-like than pilsneresque.
www.bamberg.info/en/poi/keesmann_brewery-5205

KELLER BIER (4.9%)
St Georgen Bräu, Buttenheim (Bavaria)
The yeasty amber-pale calling card of this centuries-old Franconian brewery is spicy and faintly herbal on the nose, with a tangy body finishing just off-dry.
www.kellerbier.de

MÄRZEN (5.5%)
Staffelberg-Bräu, Loffeld (Bavaria)
A true old-style *Märzen*, deep amber and bready sweet, from an unusual butchery-cum-brewery on the outskirts of Bamberg (see p.84).
www.staffelberg-braeu.de

ROTHAUS PILS (5.1%)
Badische Staatsbrauerei Rothaus AG, Grafenhausen-Rothaus (Baden-Württemberg)
Known as Tannenzäpfle in 33cl (11.6fl oz) bottles, this well-made, hoppy beer has done remarkably well in export markets for being brewed at a large plant owned by the state government.
www.rothaus.de

WAGNER PILS (4.5%)
Wagner-Bräu, Kemmern (Bavaria)
Best enjoyed from a gravity-poured keg at the brewery tap, this rich and herbaceous take on the pilsner style reserves the bulk of its bitterness for the appetizing finish.
www.brauerei-wagner.de

The Beers of Franconia

The Germans consume a lot of beer – 105 litres (23 gallons) per head in 2009. This figure is said to double in Bavaria and some claim that, if the geographic constraints are narrowed further to include only its northern area, Franconia, it might treble.

As the most densely brewery-populated part of Europe, and possibly the world, Franconia is home to close on 300 breweries, reaching one per 50 square kilometres (19 square miles) in Oberfranken (Upper Franconia), the area around Bamberg.

Most are small, local operations producing no more than 10,000 hectolitres per year and, while best known for their smoke beers (*see* panel, right), Franconia's breweries produce a wide variety of local styles. Using subtly different terminology from other parts of Germany, visitors will encounter *Vollbier* (used here to identify the brewery's main beer), *Landbier* (denoting a "country-style beer" but little else), and occasionally the modestly carbonated, fresh-from-the-barrel *Ungespundet* or "unstoppered" beer.

With Bamberg alone supporting ten breweries, a gorgeous UNESCO-designated cityscape, and innumerable artfully preserved buildings, the area of Oberfranken belongs on the itinerary of any traveller visiting Germany.

Left: The brewing town of Bamberg is also an architectural paradise, recognized by UNESCO as a World Heritage Site.

BREWERIES OF FRANCONIA ▶

The world's most intensively breweried area is Upper Franconia, in the northernmost part of Bavaria. Here pure beer is the rule, most breweries offer a taphouse, and many a bed for the night. Our map shows communities that are home to at least one brewery, and more where indicated.

BAMBERG'S RAUCHBIERS

Before the development of coking allowed for a more controlled malting of barley, all malt had a degree of colour and smokiness to it, courtesy of the wood fire used to dry the germinated grains. While most of the world's breweries have moved away from this flavour profile, in Bamberg it persisted, eventually becoming an area speciality.

Known as *Rauchbier*, these smoky brews are made with varying percentages of malt that has been kilned over a beechwood fire. In the best-known example of the style, Aecht Schlenkerla, Heller-Bräu Trum brewery (*see* below) employs generous amounts of smoked malt to great effect, while cross-town Spezial (*see* opposite) produces more gently smoky beers from smaller quantities. Both have their own maltings. An estimated 70 other brewers in the region now brew this way on an occasional basis.

BEER SELECTION

AECHT SCHLENKERLA RAUCHBIER MÄRZEN (5.1%)
Heller-Bräu Trum, Bamberg
The brawny flagship of Bamberg's most famous brewer, boasting a gloriously rich smokiness some deride as "smoked ham in a glass" but others rightly hail as a regional classic.
www.schlenkerla.de

GOLDENER LÖWE ALTFRÄNKISCHES LAGER-BIER (4.9%)
Brauerei Först (Brauerei Goldener Löwe), Drügendorf
Golden Lion Old Franconian Stored Beer is orangey gold and malt-centric, best at the centuries-old, timbered *Gästhaus* in "Franconian Switzerland" next to where it is made.
www.brauerei-foerst.de

MERKENDORFER HUMMEL-BRÄU RÄUCHERLA (5.6%)
Brauerei Hummel, Memmelsdorf-Merkendorf
This 150-year-old, family-run village brewer makes half a dozen fine beers, of which the best is probably this five-times-yearly, lightly smoked *Märzen*.
www.brauerei-hummel.de

MÖNCHSAMBACHER LAGER (5.5%)
Brauerei Zehendner, Mönchsambach
From a family-owned brewery producing uniformly impressive beers comes this hoppy brew that speaks more of aroma than bitterness.
www.moenchsambacher.de

BREWERIES OF FRANCONIA

● Birkach — Brewery town/city
○ **Coburg** — Other town/city
(10) — Number of breweries if more than one

Ludwigstadt

Coburg
Mitwitz
Kronach (2)
Weißenbrunn
Maroldsweisach
Untersiemau
Stadtsteinach
Seßlach
Birkach am Forst
Burgkunstadt
Heilgersdorf
Großheirath-Rossach
Hofheim
Altenkunstadt
Itzgrund
Lichtenfels
Kulmbach (3)
Unterneuses
Bad Staffelstein (8)
Main
Mürsbach
Weismain
Trebgast
Ebensfeld (2)
Schweinfurt
Wattendorf (2)
Zeil am Main
Rattelsdorf (2)
Schederndorf
Neudrossenfeld
Main
Reckendorf (2)
Ebing
Stadelhofen
A70-E48
A70-E48
Stettfeld
Scheßlitz (3)
Warmensteinach
Eltmann-Eschenbach
Würgau
Breitengüßbach
Appendorf
Merkendorf
Schammelsdorf
Bayreuth (6)
Trunstadt (2)
Oberhaid (2)
Kemmern
Drosendorf
Königsfeld
Trossenfurt
Hallstadt
Lohndorf (2)
Rauhenebrach-
Priesendorf
Bischberg
Tiefenellern
Theinheim
Trabelsdorf
Bamberg (10)
Melkendorf
Memmelsdorf (2)
Zettmannsdorf
Geisfeld (2)
Aufseß (3)
Ahorntal (2)
Stegaurach
Heiligenstadt (2)
Ampferbach
Untergreuth
Roßdorf am Forst
Waischenfeld (3)
Creussen-Lindenhardt
Burgebrach (2)
Reundorf
Hirschaid
Gunzendorf
Mönchsambach
Frensdorf
Büchenbach
Röbersdorf
Buttenheim (3)
Schlüsselfeld (2)
Zentbechhofen
Weigelshofen
Pottenstein (3)
Pommersfelden
Eggolsheim (2)
A3-E45
Elsendorf
Hallerndorf (5)
Ebermannstadt (2)
Pegnitz (3)
Aisch
Pretzfeld (3)
Höchstadt an
Adelsdorf
Forchheim (4)
der Aisch (3)
Aisch
Neuhaus
Leutenbach (2)
Münchsteinach
Gräfenberg (4)
Neuhaus an
Pahres
der Pegnitz
Gutenstetten
Weißenohe
A9-E51
Neustadt an der Aisch
Oberreichenbach
Neunkirchen am Brand
Pegnitz
Herzogenaurach
Erlangen (2)
Schnaittach (3)
Lauf an der
Neunkirchen am Sand
Pegnitz (2)
Hersbruck
Fürth
Leinburg
A6-E50
Nuremberg

N

miles 0 — 20
km 0 — 10

GERMANY
Berlin
Munich

ROPPELT KELLERBIER (4.9%)
Brauerei Roppelt, Stiebarlimbach
The stone krug in which this is served at the village *Bierkeller* obscures its deep gold colour, but only heightens the experience of what is very much a rustic, traditional brew.
www.brauerei-roppelt.de

SPEZIAL RAUCHBIER (4.7%)
Brauerei Spezial, Bamberg
If a beer that smells and tastes of wood smoke can be finely nuanced, this is it. Less boisterous than others, it is well suited to sessions in the brewery's atmospheric beer hall.
www.brauerei-spezial.de

UNGESPUNDET-HEFETRÜB (5.2%)
Mahr's Bräu, Bamberg
To avoid tripping over your tongue, just order an "U" ("oooh") if you wish to enjoy this unfiltered, unpasteurized draught treat filled with earthy, bready malt and spicy accents.
www.mahrs.de

ZWERGLA (6%)
Brauerei Fässla, Bamberg
Across the street from Spezial in Bamberg, Fässla's Vollbier is an unsmoked dark alternative in the toasty style of a stronger *Dunkles* (see p.92), straying towards *Bock*.
www.faessla.de

The Altbiers of North Rhine Westphalia

There are basic beer styles that can be understood almost at first sip. Dry stout, American-style pale ale, and many types of wheat beer reveal themselves quickly and may be reasonably defined in a word or three. Then there are those that take their time in revealing themselves, beers that, ideally, should be tracked all the way to their source in order to be properly appreciated. *Altbier*, or *Alt*, from North Rhine Westphalia is such a beer.

Literally, *Altbier* means "old beer" and its heartland is Düsseldorf's Altstadt, or "old town", although there are variants throughout the region. The rest of its story is more involved.

As cool-temperature fermentation spread across Germany and other parts of Europe in the years following its discovery (*see* p.82), pockets of resistance were formed, particularly in Germany's northwest. In Düsseldorf, concession was made to lager's long and cool conditioning period (*see* p.22), but top-fermenting ale yeasts were retained (*see* p.20), creating a hybrid between the two families of beer.

Yet there is more to the enigma of *Alt* than this. Although often deep brown, it typically displays more earthy than roasty character and its significant hoppiness speaks more to dryness than bitterness. Additionally, its cool

BEER SELECTION

BOLTENS UR-ALT (4.7%)
Privatbrauerei Bolten, Korschenbroich
Dark hued and slightly roasty, the unfiltered version of Bolten's very traditional *Altbier* delivers an experience not unlike stepping through the centuries for a beer.
www.bolten-brauerei.de

FÜCHSCHEN ALT (4.5%)
Brauerei im Füchschen, Düsseldorf
In comparison with its near neighbours, the "Fox Cub" brewery's *Alt* is fruitier, less assertively hopped, more roundly malty, and even a bit creamy.
www.fuechschen.de

ORIGINAL PINKUS OBERGÄRIG (5.1%)
Brauerei Pinkus Müller, Münster
From Münster's Altstadt comes this often misunderstood local variant of *Alt* – not as sharp as the last but still lactic-edged by ageing in an otherwise classic *Alt* flavour.
www.pinkus-mueller.de

ORIGINAL SCHLÜSSEL (5%)
Hausbrauerei Zum Schlüssel, Düsseldorf
Its location within the old town makes the "Key" brewery's *Altbier* likely to be one of the first visitors taste. Dry and earthy, with a gentle background fruitiness, it is also one of the best.
www.zumschluessel.de

NORTH RHINE WESTPHALIA ▶

The tri-city region of Cologne-Düsseldorf-Dortmund
is not only a hotbed of brewing activity, and
home to two very specific beer styles, *Kölsch*
and *Altbier*, it is also a major convention and
trade-fair destination.

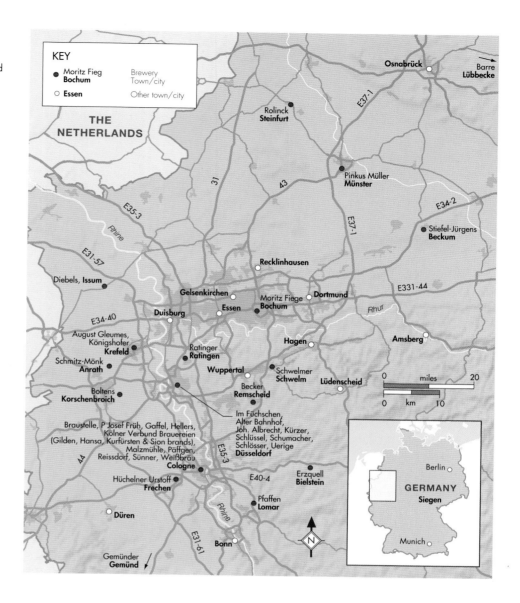

conditioning means that the round, ale-like
qualities, although apparent, are restrained.

Further, just when you think you might
have grasped the style, the Düsseldorf
breweries complicate matters with the
occasional production of special *Sticke* or
"secret" *Altbier*: stronger, often darker, but
no less beguiling.

Düsseldorf's convenient location and
the seductive appeal of its Altstadt make a
compelling case for pilgrimage. A few trips
out on a DB train bring you to towns where
they do things their own way.

Opposite: The brewery at Zum Schlüssel in
Düsseldorf often goes overlooked amid the
bustle of the beer hall.

SCHUMACHER ALT (4.6%)
Brauerei Schumacher, Düsseldorf
The lighter side of *Altbier* is presented
by this relatively pale and delicate
interpretation of the style, more floral
than earthy with an undercurrent of
lightly fruity maltiness. Available in the
Altstadt at "brewery tap" restaurant
Im Goldenen Kessel.
www.schumacher-alt.de

STIEFL-JÜRGENS UR-ALT DUNKEL (4.8%)
Brauhaus Stiefl-Jürgens, Beckum
From a ninth-generation, local evenings-
only *Hausbrauerei* comes this intentionally
acidic "wild" *Alt* that is an authentic
survivor from the styles of yesteryear.
www.stiefel-juergens.de

UERIGE ALT (4.7%)
Uerige Obergärige Hausbrauerei, Düsseldorf
The *Altbier* against which all others are
judged is made in an iconic *Hausbrauerei*
in the old town, supplemented in January
and October for one day by a much-
prized, dry-hopped, and aromatic 6%
ABV *Sticke*.
www.uerige.de

Kölsch

Any list of the most misunderstood beer styles would surely position *Kölsch* at or near the top. Pale of hue and delicately fragrant, with neither high strength nor aggressive hopping to trumpet its presence, it is often dismissed as trivial – fine for slaking a thirst but unsuitable for serious beer drinking.

Kölsch's claim to respectability is not helped by the traditional style of service, in cylindrical *Stange* glasses that accommodate just 20cl (7fl oz). Small wonder that Bavarians, with their exaggerated *Maß* steins, pour nothing but ridicule upon the drinking houses of Cologne.

Yet *Kölsch* is indeed serious stuff. Its two-dozen makers have achieved the tightest style protection afforded to any beer in the European Union and may yet attain a full *appellation contrôlée*. Within the EU, all claimants to the name must be brewed within an area of the city and its environs outlined in a 1985 Convention, plus a few specified older producers from nearby. The emphasizing effects of adjectives such as "premium" are banned from labels and advertising, and even the shape and size of a *Stange* is proscribed.

All of this might seem a lot of fuss for a pale beer that is, like *Altbier*, fermented at ale temperatures and conditioned like a lager

Above: The Päffgen beer hall is filled every evening with a mixture of locals and scattered tourists.

Below: Cologne's Cathedral is a good starting point for a tour of the city's Kölsch breweries.

(*see* p.82). To understand why *Kölsch* should not be dismissed as just another in the ranks of forgettable blond "lawnmower beers", you need to sample it at its best. This means visiting its city of origin and finding one of the many bars where it is served straight from an unpressurized barrel that has been tapped within the hour. In any other form its teasing complexity, quite at odds with its visual simplicity, is often missed.

Between an initial soft fruitiness and a dry, appetizing finish, *Kölsch* should segue through a range of subtle palate tweaks, some hoppier, others almost pillowy on the tongue, still others portraying a more assertive maltiness.

The city's *Ausschänke* ("brewery taps"), many of which sit on twisting laneways in the shadow of brooding Cologne cathedral, offer beers and environs that vary, though the rituals are the same: blue-clad waiters known as *Köbesse* wandering the aisles with trays of freshly poured beer, replacing glasses the moment they empty and marking the sale on a coaster beneath. The cycle stops when the customer places the coaster atop their glass, at which time the pencil marks are counted and the bill tallied.

Left: Trays of *Stangen* circulate regularly at busy Cologne beer halls, with *Köbesse* replacing empty glasses with great swiftness.

BEER SELECTION

FRÜH KÖLSCH (4.8%)
Cölner Hofbräu P Josef Früh, Cologne
Standing opposite the cathedral, Früh's rambling beer hall is the tourists' favourite, its subtly fruity and highly approachable *Kölsch* providing an additional reason to linger.
www.frueh.de

GAFFEL KÖLSCH (4.8%)
Privatbrauerei Gaffel Becker & Co, Cologne
The hoppiest *Kölsch*? Perhaps, and almost certainly the driest, with an enticingly floral aroma and quenchingly bitter finish.
www.gaffel.de

MÜHLEN KÖLSCH (4.8%)
Brauerei Zur Malzmühle, Cologne
The "Malt Mill" brewery presents a somewhat farmhouse-like atmosphere in its beer hall, suitable for a beer with an almost rustic maltiness and fresh hop aromatics.
www.muehlenkoelsch.de

PÄFFGEN KÖLSCH (4.8%)
Brauerei Päffgen, Cologne
Located near where the city walls once stood, the brewery draws a mix of locals and visitors with a well-hopped *Kölsch* that is more spicy than bitter in its hoppiness.
www.paeffgen-koelsch.de

German Wheat Beers

The story of those German beers known both as *Weiss* ("white") and *Weizen* ("wheat") is hidden among a pile of politically convenient myths of one persuasion or another, but it focuses on Bavaria.

Although the *Reinheitsgebot* or "Purity Order" (*see* p.80) at first banned the use of wheat in brewing, this was rapidly reinstated, volumes being held down by the application of heavy taxation over and above regular beer duty. In 1602, the elector of Bavaria, Maximilian I, removed the tax differential but licensed its production. With the fall in price, wheat beers enjoyed a massive increase in popularity, which played well for the elector's family, the Wittelsbachs, who had bought all the licences!

This monopoly ended in 1798, as the popularity of wheat beer faded, but it was not until a Munich brewer named Georg Schneider (*see* opposite) bought his licence in 1872 that efforts were made to revive types of beer that by then were badly on the wane.

Bavarian wheat beers, particularly when they appear with the prefix *Hefe* (roughly translated as "with yeast") are notable for

BEER SELECTION

GOEDECKE DÖLLNITZER RITTERGUTS GOSE (3.9%)
Brauhaus Hartmannsdorf, Hartmannsdorf (Saxony)
Gose beers are tangy, citrusy, and coriander-accented, shocking to the palate for their light saltiness but by the third sip a welcome refresher. Bayrischer Bahnhof's Leipziger Gose (4.5%) is most frequently encountered, but this one has the edge.
www.braha.de

GUTMANN WEIZENBOCK (7.2%)
Brauerei Friedrich Gutmann, Titting (Bavaria)
The Gutmann family are wheat beer specialists making excellent dark, blond, and even light (3.1%) wheat beers, but their strong, pale *Weizenbock* is a world-beater.
www.brauerei-gutmann.de

KARG WEIZEN-BOCK (7%)
Brauerei Karg, Murnau (Bavaria)
Intense and caramelly fruitiness characterizes this strong, ruddy amber beer from a century-old wheat specialist brewery in Bavaria's alpine foothills.
www.karg-weissbier.de

MAISEL'S WEISSE KRISTALL (5.1%)
Brauerei Gebr Maisel, Bayreuth (Bavaria)
Filtration often knocks the life out of wheat beers, but not in the case of this crystal clear, bright golden example, which is blessed with citrusy malt and a crisp, almost bracing finish.
www.maisel.com

Opposite: Gutmann Brauerei, Wasserschloss, Germany.

Right: Skimming yeast from a traditional open fermenter at a wheat-beer brewery.

more than just their grain content. Properly, such beers are fermented with one of a distinctive family of yeasts that imbue the beers with banana-like esters (*see* pp.20–1) and/or clove-accented spiciness. Citrus notes may also come from the wheat, along with some peppery character.

Filtered and clarified, they are often termed *Kristall*, while with darker malts they become *Dunkel Weiss* ("dark white") or occasionally even *Schwarzer Weiss* ("black white"). Stronger *Weizenbock* beers

have emerged in recent years, too, although whether these revive an old style or create a new one is unclear.

Other parts of Germany have wheat beer traditions that are quite different from those of the south. *Gose*, originally from the town of Goslar, near Hannover but adopted in the nineteenth century as a Leipzig speciality, is a sour style of top-fermented (*see* p.20) wheat beer that died out in the 1960s. It was revived after the fall of both the *Reinheitsgebot* and the Berlin Wall, to

be made by a handful of breweries using traditional recipes that include coriander and, of all things, salt.

The *Berliner Weisse* style was typically low strength and lactic, with a trademark tangy acidity. The best of these are now brewed in the USA, the lone German example with wide availability having been disarmed by simplification. The beer's engaging tartness is often muted, indeed vanquished, by the addition of sweetened syrup flavoured with raspberry or the herb woodruff.

MEHRINGER ALTBAYERISCHES WEISSBIER DUNKEL (4.8%)
Weißes Brauhaus Wolfgang Mehringer, Neunburg vorm Wald (Bavaria)
A mouthful in more ways than one, this small-town brewery in the Oberpfalz Forest packs its remarkably soft, chestnut brown beer with chocolate, fruit, and vanilla.
tel: +49 967 2871

SCHNEIDER WEISSE (5.4%)
G Schneider & Sohn, Kelheim (Bavaria)
Weissbier's longest-surviving champion, now brewed in Kelheim instead of Munich, is darker than now typical, low in banana and other fruity esters, and classically spicy on both the nose and palate.
www.schneider-weisse.de

UNERTL URSUD (5.8%)
Unertl Weißbier, Haag in Oberbayern (Bavaria)
This sumptuous, dark, top-fermented *Hefeweiss* is from a family-owned specialist brewery that puts 70 per cent wheat in the mash and uses open fermenters.
www.unertl.de

WEIHENSTEPHANER HEFE WEISSBIER (5.4%)
Bayerische Staatsbrauerei Weihenstephan, Freising (Bavaria)
A consummately refreshing beer, filled with banana and tropical-fruit notes yet finishing quite dry, from one of the world's oldest breweries, said to date from 1040.
www.brauerei-weihenstephan.de

Dark Beers & Bock

When new kilning techniques allowed the production of ultra-pale malt, German brewers and drinkers alike took to blond beers with gusto, consigning to the margins many darker local varieties. With the revival of interest in "anything but Pils" that jogged the German beer market in the 1980s, the southern varieties began to cluster together under the name *Dunkles*, or sometimes *Münchener*, in which case they should be made in the city of Munich from Munich malt (*see* p.17).

In the north, the same period saw the re-creation or emergence of yet darker beers known as *Schwarzbier* (literally "black beer").

However, unquestionably the most significant of the hold-outs is *Bock*, said to date from fourteenth-century Einbeck, a Lower Saxon city once also recorded as Eimbock. This being the case, it was probably first an ale, and records indicate it might also have been a wheat beer before it ultimately became an all-barley, cool-fermented beer. It was also strong, perhaps because Einbeck brewers, dependent as they were on exports, believed – rightly – that high potency would help protect the beer during its journey to Munich, France, England, and beyond.

Today's *Bock* is usually sweetly malty and dark, although a few light-hued ones exist, sometimes known as *Maibock* ("May *Bock*"). Typically they measure between six and

seven per cent alcohol, although there is a more formidable variant known as *Doppelbock* (or "double *Bock*").

Though modern sensitivities might suggest it would be otherwise, a deal of historical evidence suggests that these beers were developed as a form of "liquid bread" to sustain fasting monks, and that indeed Martin Luther was thus sustained throughout his most challenging debates at the Diet of Worms in 1521, supping from a donated barrel of Einbeck beer. This may explain why he lost.

Left: Because of their higher strength, *Bock* beers are sometimes served in smaller, more stylized glasses than are other German lagers.

BEER SELECTION

EINBECKER UR-BOCK DUNKEL (6.5%)
Einbecker Brauhaus, Einbeck
(Lower Saxony)
"Ur-" denotes "original", though unchanged since 1378 is unlikely. Dark amber and richly but also dryly malty, it finishes with a slightly bitter bite and soothing warmth.
www.einbecker.com

ETTALER CURATOR (9%)
Klosterbrauerei Ettal, Ettal (Bavaria)
Still overseen by Benedictine monks, this monastic brewery both brews and distils with acumen, producing among other brands this decadently spicy *Doppelbock* with roasted malt accents.
www.kloster-ettal.de

KNEITINGER BOCK (6.8%)
Brauerei Johann Kneitinger,
Regensburg (Bavaria)
Brewed for winter, this is surely among Germany's darkest *Bocks*, with an almost black hue, balanced sweetness, and hints of pumpernickel bread-like spiciness.
www.kneitinger.de

KÖNIG LUDWIG DUNKEL (5.1%)
König Ludwig Schloßbrauerei Kaltenberg, Fürstenfeldbruck (Bavaria)
The flagship brand of the brewery helmed by the descendant of the Bavarian prince whose marriage inspired Oktoberfest is a mocha-ish delight, unusually (for Germany) dry hopped for added aroma and character.
www.koenig-ludwig-brauerei.com

Above: Enjoying a beer and the last of the daylight at a café in Lower Saxony.

WHEN YOU ARE THERE

- Most breweries sell beer directly to the public during working hours.
- Sharing tables is normal, but always request permission first.
- The *Stammtisch*, however, is reserved for regulars and accessible by invitation only.
- For best updates, follow www.german-breweries.com or, for Franconia only, www.bierfranken.eu.
- Local beer festivals are common in Bavaria, usually as part of larger celebrations.
- Must visit: Bamberg, Munich, Düsseldorf, Cologne, and Berlin.

NEW GERMAN BEERS

The fact that even large German breweries produce uniformly "good enough" beers probably accounts for the country's lack of noisy groups protesting about the parlous state of beer. However, national detachment is being challenged from within by demands for beers that reflect best modern practice elsewhere, either via importation or local imitation, even if this turns away from purity.

The nascent German new wave revives a few older styles, produces a few "me too" brews from other traditions, and, more recently, seeks to grow new styles out of existing ones.

For example, the range at Camba Bavaria in southern Bavaria (www.cambabavaria.com) includes several ales, not least the excellent Eric's IPA (8%). Freigeist of Stolberg's sour AbraxXxas (6%) is made for the firm by Braustelle of Cologne (www.braustelle.com), who also has a *Tripelbock* called Helios (9.5%). Gänstaller-Bräu of Schnaid, north of Nürnberg, smoked the recipe to create Affumicator (9.6%), and even modern wheat beer originator Schneider (*see* p.91) gets in on the act with its Tap X Mein Nelson Sauvin (7.3%).

The "craft" component of the German beer market may be minuscule at present, but lest anyone doubt its serious intent, we recommend the house brewery at leading speciality malt producer Weyermann of Bamberg, which has brewed around 40 different styles to date to show the locals it can be done.

KÖSTRITZER SCHWARZBIER (4.8%)
Köstritzer Schwarzbierbrauerei,
Bad Köstritz (Thüringen)
Included for being typical rather than excellent, this modern black beer is lightly sweet, liquorice-accented, and, while not quite as black as stout, in that flavour zone.
www.koestritzer.de

KULMBACHER MÖNCHSHOF SCHWARZBIER (4.9%)
Kulmbacher Brauerei, Kulmbach (Bavaria)
One of Germany's largest beer factories produces one of its finest black beers, with hop bitterness, firm malting, and dabs of liquorice and chocolate on its tail.
www.kulmbacher.de

PAULANER SALVATOR (7.9%)
Paulaner Brauerei, Munich (Bavaria)
Allegedly the first *Doppelbock* and the origin of the "-ator" naming convention is made entirely with *Münchener* (Munich) malt, creating a molasses-accented aroma and treacly body.
www.paulaner.de

SCHÖNRAMER ALTBAYRISCH DUNKEL (5%)
Brauerei Schönram, Petting/Schönram (Bavaria)
A judicious mix of dark, roasted malts gives "Old Bavarian" a distinctive maltiness, more earthy than sweet, with fragrant hops adding floral notes to the nose and bitterness to the finish.
www.brauerei-schoenram.de

SCHWARZER SPECHT (6.1%)
Privatbrauerei Specht,
Ehrenfriedersdorf (Saxony)
Made by a small eastern German brewery, this fruity, sweetish black beer has a gentle and mild character that belies a strength revealed by its name, "Woodpecker".
www.privatbrauerei-specht.de

WELTENBURGER KLOSTER ASAM BOCK (6.9%)
Klosterbrauerei Weltenburg, Regensburg (Bavaria)
This Benedictine cloister has brewed for the greater part of the last millennium, most impressively in modern times with this faintly nutty, toffeeish beer, so densely malted that it seems thick on the palate.
www.weltenburger.de

AUSTRIA

It is never easy running a small shop next to a great department store, especially when a well-respected competitor is on the opposite corner. Austria's brewers may be forgiven for feeling ignored by those who tour Germany and the Czech Republic in search of fine beer.

Anton Dreher, one of the early greats of lager brewing, worked at Schwechat (*see* below, opposite), where he perfected Vienna malt, the basis of ruddy, amber-hued *Wiener*

Above: Austria's beer-drinking tradition includes a fondness for elaborate headgear.

(Viennese) lagers. Yet neither brewers nor bar owners in Austria today trumpet this style as a local speciality, preferring to mimic German styles such as *Helles* and *Märzen*, *Dunkles* and *Schwarzbier*.

The fact that Austria never had to accept the *Reinheitsgebot* or "Purity Order" (*see* p.80) gave Germans an excuse to be sniffy about beers made at the Alpine end of the German-speaking world. Had the story of the Austro-Hungarian Empire after 1918, and especially after 1948, been different, who knows what similarities Austrian beer would now share with those of Bohemia?

Austria has around 180 operating breweries, including many brewpubs like the highly inventive 1516 Brewing Company in Vienna. Roughly 55 per cent of Austrian beer comes from Brau Union AG, part of

Heineken, which runs nine breweries. There are also numerous family-owned companies that trace their origins back an implausible number of centuries.

The hop-growing area that stretches from Styria (now Steiermark) into Slovenia gave the world Styrian hops and some of the first to be grown organically. This has added fuel to the growing desire by the country's brewers to source local ingredients and produce fully organic beers.

Another national speciality emerging by dint of disappearing elsewhere is the tradition of *Steinbier*, in which the wort (*see* p.22) is brought to the boil by dropping red-hot stones into it, causing it to caramelize and go slightly smoky.

Next page: Haystacks in early autumn, Zillertal, in the northern Tyrol.

BEER SELECTION

DIE WEISSE HELL (5.2%)
Salzburger Weissbierbrauerei,
Salzburg (Salzburg)
Gorgeous-looking 1901 microbrewery that survived the twentieth century to brew wheat beers in classical Bavarian styles, mainly conditioned in flip-top bottles.
www.salzburgerweissbier.at

EGGENBERG URBOCK 23° (9.6%)
Stöhr GmbH & Co, Vorchdorf
(Upper Austria)
This amber *Doppelbock* is one of the most intense beers in the world, conditioned for nine months in cellars at a family-owned brewery where beer has been made since 1680.
www.schloss-eggenberg.at

FORSTNER STYRIAN ALE (6.6%)
Forstner Biere Handbrauerei, Kalsdorf bei Graz (Steiermark)
A pre-pilsner style of beer made at an excellent newish brewery using British pale ale yeast and American hops. The 5 vor Zwölf 13% barley wine is equally fine.
www.forstner-biere.at

GRANITBOCK (7.3%)
Brauerei Hofstetten, St Martin
(Lower Austria)
Occasional *Steinbock* made by a successful family brewery, where granite tuns hold wort boiled by stones heated over an open fire, creating a smoky, caramelized flavour (*see* above).
www.hofstetten.at

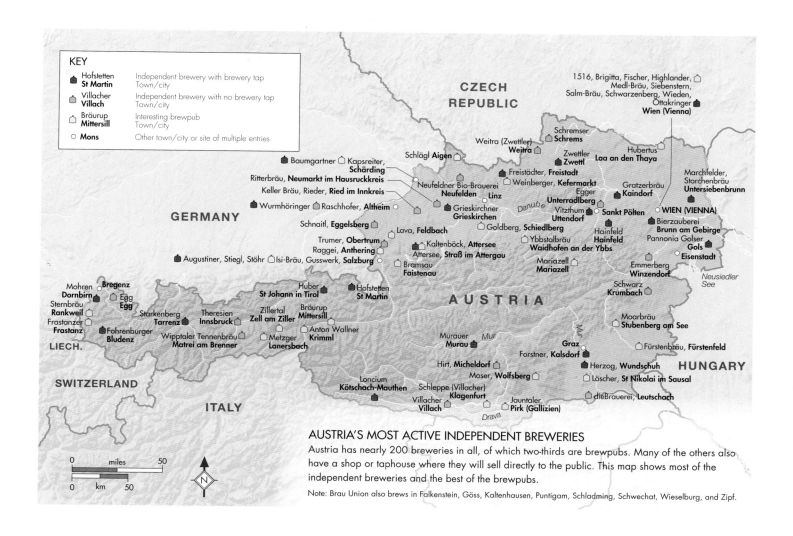

KEY

Hofstetten **St Martin**	Independent brewery with brewery tap Town/city	
Villacher **Villach**	Independent brewery with no brewery tap Town/city	
Bräurup **Mittersill**	Interesting brewpub Town/city	
○ **Mons**	Other town/city or site of multiple entries	

CZECH REPUBLIC

1516, Brigitta, Fischer, Highlander, Medl-Bräu, Siebenstern, Salm-Bräu, Schwarzenberg, Wieden, Ottakringer **Wien (Vienna)**

GERMANY

Baumgartner ○ Kapsreiter, **Schärding**
Ritterbräu, **Neumarkt im Hausruckkreis**
Keller Bräu, Rieder, **Ried im Innkreis**
Wurmhöringer ○ Raschhofer, **Altheim** ○
Schnaitl, **Eggelsberg**
Trumer, **Obertrum**
Raggei, **Anthering**
Augustiner, Stiegl, Stöhr ○ Isi-Bräu, Gusswerk, **Salzburg**

Schlägl **Aigen**
Neufeldner Bio-Brauerei **Neufelden**
Grieschirchner **Grieskirchen**
Lava, **Feldbach**
Kaltenböck, **Attersee**
Attersee, **Straß im Attergau**
Bramsau **Faistenau**

Weitra (Zwettler) **Weitra**
Schremser **Schrems**
Zwettler **Zwettl**
Freistädter, **Freistadt**
Weinberger, **Kefermarkt**
Linz
Goldberg, **Schiedlberg**
Ybbstalbräu **Waidhofen an der Ybbs**

Hubertus **Laa an den Thaya**
Gratzerbräu **Kaindorf**
Egger **Unterradlberg**
Vitzthum **Sankt Pölten**
Uttendorf
Hainfeld **Hainfeld**
Mariazell **Mariazell**

Marchfelder, Storchenbräu **Untersiebenbrunn**
○ **WIEN (VIENNA)**
Bierzauberei **Brunn am Gebirge**
Pannonia Golser **Gols**
Eisenstadt
Emmerberg **Winzendorf**
Neusiedler See

AUSTRIA

Danube

Mohren **Bregenz**
Egg **Egg**
Sternbräu **Rankweil**
Frastanzer **Frastanz**
Fohrenburger **Bludenz**
LIECH.
Starkenberg **Tarrenz**
Theresien **Innsbruck**
Zillertal **Zell am Ziller**
Huber **St Johann in Tirol**
Bräurup **Mittersill**
Hofstetten **St Martin**
Wipptaler Tennenbräu **Matrei am Brenner**
Metzger **Lanersbach**
Anton Wallner **Krimml**

SWITZERLAND
ITALY

Loncium **Kötschach-Mauthen**
Murauer **Murau**
Hirt, **Micheldorf**
Moser, **Wolfsberg**
Forstner, **Kalsdorf**
Graz
Villacher **Villach**
Schleppe (Villacher) **Klagenfurt**
Jauntaler **Pirk (Gallizien)**
Drava

Schwarz **Krumbach**
Moarbräu **Stubenberg am See**
Fürstenbräu, **Fürstenfeld**
Herzog, **Wundschuh**
Löscher, **St Nikolai im Sausal**
dieBrauerei, **Leutschach**

HUNGARY

Mur
Mur

0 — miles — 50
0 — km — 50

N

AUSTRIA'S MOST ACTIVE INDEPENDENT BREWERIES

Austria has nearly 200 breweries in all, of which two-thirds are brewpubs. Many of the others also have a shop or taphouse where they will sell directly to the public. This map shows most of the independent breweries and the best of the brewpubs.

Note: Brau Union also brews in Falkenstein, Göss, Kaltenhausen, Puntigam, Schladming, Schwechat, Wieselburg, and Zipf.

HIRTER MORCHL (5%)
Brauerei Hirt, Micheldorf (Upper Austria)
Fulsome black beer, full of caramel and cocoa, and better than most German varieties, from an independent brewery dating from 1270. The *Märzen* turns heads, too.
www.hirterbier.at

SCHWECHATER ZWICKL (5.4%)
Brauerei Schwechat, Schwechat (Lower Austria)
Leaving a blond lager unfiltered often improves it significantly, as with this cleverly hopped one made by Brau Union in Anton Dreher's home town (*see above*).
www.schwechater.at

TRUMER PILS (4.9%)
Trumer Privatbrauerei, Salzburg (Salzburg)
Few countries have genuine affection for a pilsner, but this award-winning beer with a floral aroma and flavour has been popular enough to fund a sister brewery in California, USA.
www.trumer.at

URBAN-KELLER'S STEINBIER (5.6%)
Brauhaus Gusswerk, Salzburg (Salzburg)
Brewed by the hot-stone method (*see opposite*) at an ecologically sound, arty brewpub-cum-microbrewery, to create a prize-winning *Märzenbier*.
www.brauhaus-gusswerk.at

WÄLDER SENN (2.5%)
Brauerei Egg, Egg (Vorarlberg)
Numerous normal beers come from this friendly, family-run brewery, but none beats this extraordinarily tasty light beer made with whey.
www.brauerei-egg.at

WEITRA BRÄU HADMAR (5.2%)
Bierwerkstatt Weitra, Weitra (Lower Austria)
The best of Austria's real Viennese lagers, amber and malt-laden, from a small brewery in an historic brewing town, to a 100-per-cent organic recipe.
www.bierwerkstatt.at

CZECH REPUBLIC

Czechs are among the world's most dedicated beer drinkers, consuming around 140 litres (30 gallons) per head each year. Their preferred style appears on menus as *světlý ležák* or pale lager. So it comes as no surprise that in the land of Pilsen (now Plzeň) and Budweis (České Budějovice), where Pilsner Urquell and Budweiser Budvar are respectively produced, 90 per cent of the beer (*pivo*) consumed is blond lager, although the history of Czech brewing is less conservative.

In Bohemia, the western half of the Czech Republic, hops were being farmed in the seventh century and by 1089 were subject to taxation. By the thirteenth century, numerous towns had their own brewery (*pivovar*), beginning a tradition of public ownership that survives in some form to the present day.

Beer quality here is defined by the Balling scale, on which an expression of malt density is measured in degrees Plato. There are four categories, although the lightest, *lehké* (less than 8°) has virtually disappeared. *Výčepni* (8–10.99°) means "draught", even when it is bottled, while *ležák* (11–12.99°) means "lager", even when referring to ale. Stronger beers are *speciál*.

Classic Czech beers are generally brewed with soft water, use decoction mashing (*see* p.22 and p.102), feature Saaz hops (*see* p.18), and are cool-fermented and then lagered for up to three months (*see* p.22 and p.103).

When the Velvet Revolution saw off Soviet influence (1948–89), there were around 100 breweries left. All were in public ownership,

Above: A worker loading Saaz hop bines onto a trailer at Lhota, near Žatec in western Bohemia.

Above: The Czech capital of Prague was, like its brewing industry, preserved by inaction during the Soviet era.

THE CZECH REPUBLIC'S LOCAL BREWERIES ▼

The Czech Republic's 150 or so breweries are dispersed throughout its 13 provinces (*kraje*) and the capital, Prague. Around 40 pre-date the Velvet Revolution though, in many of these, traditional methods of production have been superseded.

Newer enterprises tend to be brewpubs or small local breweries that seek to provide higher standards of beer-making by ancient and modern methods. The best way to discover the finest of local Czech brewing is to visit those breweries,

shown here, which have remained outside the grip of foreign ownership and large-scale production and welcome visitors to their taphouse.

KEY	
● Hubertus Kácov	Brewery Town/city
○ Opava	Other town/city

most nursing elderly equipment used to make delicate beers on a shoestring. The Russians had made little investment.

The return of market economics brought many foreign companies keen to enter a market of habitual beer drinkers and gain a foothold in Eastern Europe. They bought breweries by the cluster, closed many, and fitted others with new equipment to make lagers the international way, which is to say cheaper and faster.

At its low point around 1997, fewer than 50 breweries remained. The new beers were often poor and the normally uncomplaining

Czech drinkers turned against them, state-owned Budvar taking the role of national hero and adamantly refusing to cut corners or sell out to a global buyer.

There has followed a slow revival, led by some adventurous brewpubs, followed by a few new entrepreneurial microbreweries. More recently, the fortunes of the longer-established regional companies have improved and there are even signs of re-evaluation in the largest, though much will depend on whether the world's better-informed beer lovers ever trust lager again.

BEST-SELLING LOCAL LABELS

Budweiser Budvar	(National)
Gambrinus	(SABMiller)
Kozel	(SABMiller)
Master	(SABMiller)
Pilsner Urquell	(SABMiller)
Staropramen	(MolsonCoors)

Pale Lagers

Despite their massive scale of production, two of the best-known Czech pale lagers, Pilsner Urquell and Budweiser Budvar (*see* below), remain close to the authentic pilsner style – the latter appearing as Czechvar in North America, to distinguish it from the US Budweiser, which is totally unrelated.

Below: A worker at a Czech maltings takes samples of germinated Moravian barley for examination.

Authentic pilsner is a beer of elaborate simplicity, reaching perfection through the use of top-end ingredients, carefully managed brewing, and slow maturation.

Budvar 12°, for example, uses only Saaz aromatic whole hops from northern Bohemia (*see* pp.18–9), three malted varieties of South Moravian barley, 12 days' fermentation at 12°C (54°F), then 90 days lagering in horizontal cellar tanks at 0–3°C (32–37°F) (*see* p.22).

A shorter lagering period will show itself in subtly rougher edges, although beers rated 10° or 11° can usually soften in six to eight weeks.

Wariness of blond lagers among informed drinkers has led to some brewers bringing in subtle enhancements. For example, krausening – the addition of wort in the early stages of fermentation to a conditioning tank of nearly finished beer – brings a fuller, breadier flavour with a yeasty edge.

Such beers are described variously as *kroužkovaný*, *kvasnicové*, or *kvasničak*, often translated as "yeast beer".

Simply leaving a draught lager unpasteurized can add noticeable character.

Leaving it unfiltered (*nefiltrované*) injects more but at the cost of losing its "polished" appearance, blond lager's biggest selling point.

Such techniques are a boon to brewpubs, their mechanics being simple to manoeuvre

BEER SELECTION

BERNARD SVÁTEČNÍ LEŽÁK 12° (5%)
Bernard, Humpolec (Vysočina)
The brewery is 50 per cent owned by Duvel Moortgat (*see* p.77) but left free to make old-style lagers, sometimes with new twists, including this dryish yeast beer with a hint of bitterness.
www.bernard.cz

BUDVAR KROUŽKOVANÝ LEŽÁK (5%)
Budějovický Budvar, České Budějovice (South Bohemia)
Budweiser Budvar 12° (Czechvar in North America) in its lightly krausened (*see* p.102) version is found on draught and in the Czech Republic only. Combines the easy charm of its delicate and reliable international version, with a bit extra.
www.budvar.cz

ČERNÁ HORA MORAVSKÉ SKLEPNÍ 10° (4%)
Černa Hora, Černa Hora (South Moravia)
An easy-drinking, slightly bitter and unfiltered lighter lager from Moravia. Typical of newer, light *výčepni*-style beers (*see* p.98).
www.pivovarcernahora.cz

CHOTĚBOŘ PRÉMIUM 12° (5.1%)
Chotěboř, Chotěboř (Vysočina)
A prize-winning pale lager from a multiple prize-winning new brewery, bringing back the bittersweet tastes associated with the days of properly coaxed pilsners.
www.pivovarchotebor.cz

Above: In the Czech Republic only beers brewed in the town of Plzeň are referred to as Pilsner. The standard term for a pale lager is *světly ležák* (pronounced 'luj-ack').

KLÁŠTER LEŽÁK 11° (4.6%)
Klášter, Klášter Hradiště nad Jizerou (Central Bohemia)
A lighter lager that packs a lot of beery flavours into its small frame, its makers crediting a monastic recipe while we suspect absence of pasteurization.
www.pivovarklaster.cz

KRAKONOŠ SVĚTLY LEŽÁK KVASNICOVÉ 12° (5.1%)
Krakonoš, Trutnov (Hradec Králové)
More golden than blond, with an orange tinge and, coincidentally, leaving a dab of bitter peel on the palate.
www.pivovar-krakonos.cz

LITOVEL SVÁTEČNÍ SPECIÁL 13° (6%)
Litovel, Litovel (Olomouc)
A fulsome favourite that stands out from the crowd of blond Czech lagers for its big grain flavour and rounded presence. One of the best.
www.litovel.cz

OPAT MEDOVÝ KVASNIČÁK 12° (5%)
Broumov, Broumov (Hradec Králové)
Delightfully malt-led lager with a distinctly fruity edge, from a Silesian brewery with its own maltings. The 13° is said to be even better.
www.pivovarbroumov.cz

and sometimes even resulting in cutting costs. Their enhanced character is beginning to build respectability for a modern view – sacrilegious to older drinkers – that tastier, handcrafted beers will be cloudier.

Because most Czech bars will in practice sell only beers from one brewery and few smaller producers export their beers yet, discovering the full scope of blond lager in the country that invented it requires dedicated research and enjoyment of the road less travelled.

In addition to the beers featured here, other brews worth tracking down include Strakonický Nektar from Strakonice, Bohemia Regent of Třeboň, Herold Bohemian of Březnice, Samson Budweiser of České Budějovice, Zlatopramen of Ústí nad Labem, and Březňák of Velké Březno.

Opposite: At the Budějovický Budvar brewery in České Budějovice, an unlikely combination of state ownership, large scale production and a site filled with much steel and concrete assist in creating world-class beers of elaborate simplicity.

OF PILSEN, BUDWEIS & THE LAW

In the Czech Republic, only beers made in the town of Plzeň (Pilsen) are termed "Pilsner" (or "from Pilsen"). By the same token, only those made in České Budějovice (Czech Budweis) are known as Budweiser.

The world's first blond lager was created in 1842 at Pilsen. Its early success came from the marriage of technique and glamour. The technical innovations were decoction mashing to make perfect wort, cold fermentation to minimize spoiling, and lengthy lagering to achieve stabilization (see pp. 22–3).

But just as moving pictures turned good-looking actors into stars, so it was affordable, crystal-clear glassware that helped the world's first transparent blond beer achieve world renown. In the late nineteenth century, it spread

across central Europe, a landmark ruling in a Munich court in 1899 formally stripping its original brewers of any exclusive use of its name.

From then on, pilsner took on the world, shedding excellence as it advanced. Making blond beer was easy. Creating the beer made in Bohemia took time, know-how, and expensive storage.

High on looks but delicate in structure, by the time "pils" had become the world's favourite beer style, it was not just its name that had been abbreviated. Maize, rice, and syrups replaced malted barley. Fermentation quickened and filtration replaced lagering. Appearance had triumphed over content.

BEER SELECTION

PILSNER URQUELL UNPASTEURIZED TANK BEER (4.4%)
Pilsner Urquell (SAB-Miller), Plzeň (Plzeň)
Available on draught only, mainly in the Czech Republic. The beer goes from boil to bottle in five weeks, losing subtlety obviously in the pasteurized bottled version.
www.pilsnerurquell.com

RYCHTÁŘ NATUR 12° (4.9%)
Rychtář, Hlinsko v Čechách (Pardubice)
Light-tasting lager with a fresh hop taste that dovetails with an indefinable yeast tang in its body to make a most agreeable drink.
www.rychtar.cz

SVIJANSKÝ RYTÍŘ 12° (5%)
Svijany, Příšovice (Liberec)
A deceptive lighter lager that starts soft but fills up as higher hopping creeps in down the glass.
www.pivovarsvijany.cz

ŽATECKÝ BARONKA PREMIUM 13° (5.4%)
Žatecký, Žatec (Ústí nad Labem)
Sweeter than average, almost honeyed, with remarkably little hop presence for the last brewery left in the home of Saaz hops.
www.zateckypivovar.cz

Darker Lagers & Other Czech Beers

The Czech beers that are enjoying the greatest renaissance since local interest in brewing began to regrow in the late 1990s are those beers that had become defunct or neglected.

Dark beer has been part of the Czech brewing landscape for over 1,000 years. Most are now lagers, coming – as with paler beers – in the lighter *výčepní* and regular *ležák* formats, although there are numerous *speciál* versions at 14° and upwards (*see* p.98).

Dark lagers vary hugely in sweetness, colour, clarity, and quality. The designations black (*černé*) and dark (*tmavé*) are largely interchangeable, but stronger examples (15° plus) are more often branded "Tmavé" or "Tmavý", with the occasional "Porter".

Amber lagers have enjoyed a revival, appearing as *polotmavé* (medium-dark), *granát* (garnet), and *jantar* (amber). *Řezané* (meaning "cut") implies a beer made by "cutting" or mixing together two separately brewed blond and dark beers.

In a nod to modernity, the first Czech-style IPAs have appeared, though ale brewing is rare, so these are mostly bottom-fermented (*see* p.20) – a dubious claim to originality that might yet grow.

Above: Dark (*tmavý*) beers have likely been produced at U Fleků (The Flask) in Prague for over 500 years.

BEER SELECTION

FERDINAND SEDM KULÍ POLOTMAVÝ LEŽÁK 13° (5.5%)
Ferdinand, Benešov (Central Bohemia)
Ruddy amber lager, with more caramel than expected and hints of liquorice and dry plum.
www.pivovarferdinand.cz

FLEKOVSKÝ TMAVÝ LEŽÁK 13° (4.9%)
U Fleků, Prague
This lightly flavoured dark beer – caramel with a touch of car tyre – is fit for all seasons and served only at the Prague brewpub that has made beer since 1499.
www.ufleku.cz

HAVRAN TMAVÝ LEŽÁK 12° (4.5%)
Vyškov, Vyškov (South Moravia)
This unique dark beer is made by the Republic's "other" state-owned brewery, and is a classic of its kind, finishing full of dried fruit.
www.pivovyskov.cz

KOCOUR TMAVÝ LEŽÁK (5%)
Kocour, Varnsdorf (Ústí nad Labem)
A soft brown lager with prominent vanilla and mixed fruit, representative of the brewery's gently shocking intentions.
www.pivovar-kocour.cz

Above: Adam Matuska, pictured in 2010 when aged just 20, already a master brewer with his own brewery and the up-coming radical voice of new Czech brewing.

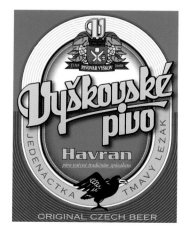

KOUT NA ŠUMAVĚ TMAVÝ SPECIÁL 14° (6%)
Kout na Šumavě, Kout na Šumavě (Plzeň)
This classic dark lager, which is brewed by a small company in an old town brewhouse, epitomizes the steady, sweetish style well enough to appear in top Prague restaurants.
www.pivovarkout.eu

MATUŠKA RAPTOR IPA 15° (6.3%)
Matuška, Broumy (Central Bohemia)
A clever Czech take on American IPA, malt-packed and hoppy enough but bottom-fermented (see p.20). Different enough to lead a worthy new fad.
www.pivovarmatuska.cz

MERLIN ČERNÝ TMAVÉ LEŽÁK (4.7%)
Platan, Protivin (South Bohemia)
Commissioned dark lager with the character of an upbeat, candied milk stout made bitter by roasted malts.
www.pivo-merlin.cz

NÁCHOD PRIMÁTOR WEIZENBIER (5%)
Primátor, Náchod (Hradec Králové)
Hazy wheat beer with prominent toffee flavour from the boil, and banana nose from its yeast.
www.primator.cz

Wheat beer (*pšeničné* or *bílé*) has reappeared after many decades, mostly in the Bavarian *Hefeweizenbier* style. There are also beers flavoured with cherry, coffee, hemp, and so on, although these build on no local tradition and offer little beyond novelty.

For the most historic Czech dark lager, visit U Fleků (*see* p.104), Prague's 500-year-old brewpub. To taste the future, follow the Matuška brewery (*see* p.105) from west of Prague and Kocour, on the German border at Varnsdorf in northern Bohemia, each intent on introducing Czechs to foreign beer styles with a Bohemian twist.

For a journey of discovery that will introduce you to a different and changing world of Czech beer, and to a historic and beautiful country at the heart of Central Europe that is not yet awash with visitors, plot your way round the nation's brewpubs, which are often sited in towns that have other reasons to be visited.

WHEN YOU ARE THERE

- The cosmopolitan beer scene is mainly a Prague phenomenon.
- Most bars serve only draught pale lagers from a single brewery.
- Etiquette dictates that men enter bars ahead of women – to check for brawling.
- Find brewpubs and brewery news by taking a translation tool to www.pivni.info.
- Must see: the Budvar museum and brewery in České Budějovice.
- Must drink: black lager at the 500-year-old U Fleků brewpub in Prague (11 Křemencova – *see* p.104).

Left: There has been a functioning brewhouse at U Fleků in Prague for over 500 years, making it probably the world's oldest brewpub.

BEER SELECTION

PERNŠTEJN PARDUBICKÝ PORTER 19° (8%)
Pernštejn, Pardubice (Pardubice)
This national treasure is related to the Baltic-style porters of Poland and northeastern Europe. Its burned-grain aroma heralds a hefty body with a medium-dry finish.
www.pernstejn.cz

REBEL ČERNÝ 11° (4.7%)
Rebel, Havlíčkův Brod (Vysočina)
Prize-winning, innocent, ruby-brown lager with a memorable build-up of raisins at its end.
www.hbrebel.cz

TAMBOR TMAVÝ SPECIÁL 13° (5%)
Dvůr Králové nad Labem (Hradec Králové)
Off-centre dark lager from a rising-star brewery, with elements of tobacco, lashings of caramel, and a fruity edge.
www.pivo-tambor.cz

U MEDVÍDKŮ X BEER 33 (12.6%)
U Medvídků, Prague
The world's most intense lager, brewed at 33° Plato (*see* p.100), the brewer squeezing wort from a porridge mash like a cider maker pressing a cheese. Intensely sweet and alcoholic.
www.umedvidku.cz

Above: Even the most modest of Bohemian villages once boasted its own brewery, but Communism and attrition brought the national number down to fewer than 50 by 1997. Today, however, brewing is back on the rise.

GREAT BRITAIN & IRELAND

Many of the types of beer that feature in craft brewing globally owe their origins to the oddly shaped islands off the northwest coast of continental Europe known collectively as the British Isles. Pale ale (Indian or otherwise), stout – oatmeal, imperial, or oyster – Scotch ale, and porter all began life here.

Yet the daily beers of choice in the UK and the Irish Republic are altogether less robust. Industrial lagers dominate markets shared, in Britain, with low-carbonation light ales and, in Ireland, nitrogenated ordinary stouts.

In 1971, reacting to a further downturn in beer quality, four young English journalists decided to form a protest group to make beer better. An industry intent on making high-volume convenience brews was about to collide with a crusade promoting inconvenient ones – the Campaign for Real Ale (CAMRA).

Top-fermented beers (*see* p.20) that condition in the cask were dubbed "real ale" and in turn became synonymous in Britain with "good beer". CAMRA's early successes made beer lovers in other countries take heart, sparking what eventually developed into a worldwide revival of craft brewing, with even Ireland's dutiful adoption of global brands starting to be challenged.

The unintended downside of this in Britain has been to freeze-frame an idea of what constitutes "proper beer" around 1960, when it was already in a bad way. Only recently have the two nations begun to re-create the older styles which, despite having made their brewers famous, had been allowed virtually to disappear from their lands of origin.

ESTABLISHED INDEPENDENT BREWERIES IN SCOTLAND ▶

The Scottish beer scene is currently undergoing a strong revival, its greater willingness to experiment perhaps being attributable to the relative dearth of longer-established breweries in comparison with the rest of mainland Britain.

Note: Greene King plc also brews at Belhaven Brewing in Dunbar (East Lothian). Heineken owns Caledonian in Edinburgh.

BEST-SELLING LOCAL LABELS

Bass	(various*)
Boddingtons	(Anheuser-Busch InBev)
Carling	(MolsonCoors)
Foster's	(Heineken)
Greene King	(National)
John Smith's	(Heineken)
McEwan's	(National)
Newcastle Brown	(Heineken)
Tennent's	(C&C Group)
Tetley's	(Carlsberg)
Worthington	(MolsonCoors)

*In the UK, most but not all Bass brands are produced by Anheuser-Busch InBev

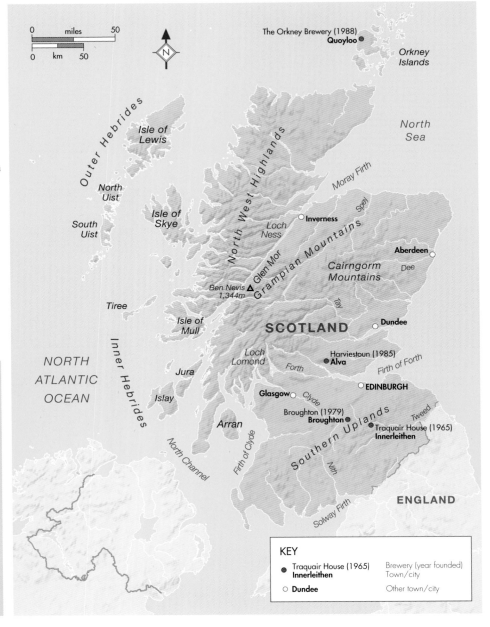

KEY

● Traquair House (1965) Innerleithen — Brewery (year founded) Town/city

○ Dundee — Other town/city

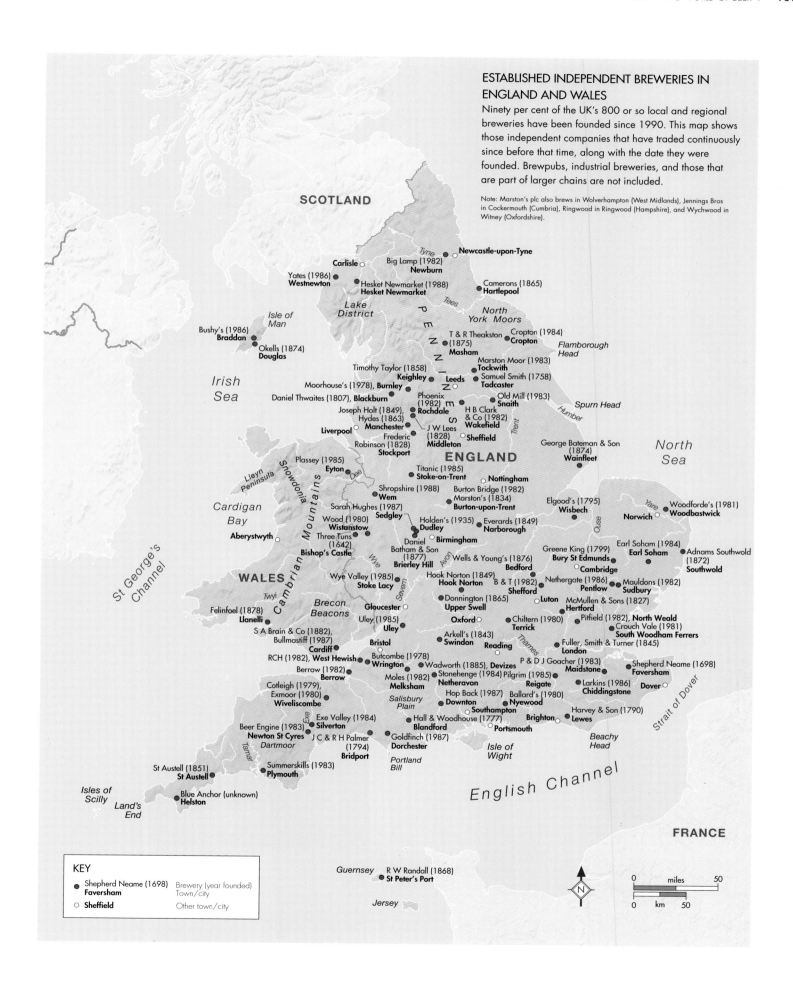

ESTABLISHED INDEPENDENT BREWERIES IN ENGLAND AND WALES

Ninety per cent of the UK's 800 or so local and regional breweries have been founded since 1990. This map shows those independent companies that have traded continuously since before that time, along with the date they were founded. Brewpubs, industrial breweries, and those that are part of larger chains are not included.

Note: Marston's plc also brews in Wolverhampton (West Midlands), Jennings Bros in Cockermouth (Cumbria), Ringwood in Ringwood (Hampshire), and Wychwood in Witney (Oxfordshire).

SCOTLAND

Newcastle-upon-Tyne
Big Lamp (1982)
Newburn
Carlisle
Yates (1986)
Westnewton
Hesket Newmarket (1988)
Hesket Newmarket
Camerons (1865)
Hartlepool

Lake District

North York Moors

T & R Theakston (1875)
Masham
Cropton (1984)
Cropton
Flamborough Head

Isle of Man
Bushy's (1986)
Braddan
Okells (1874)
Douglas

Marston Moor (1983)
Tockwith
Timothy Taylor (1858)
Keighley
Leeds
Samuel Smith (1758)
Tadcaster
Moorhouse's (1978), Burnley
Daniel Thwaites (1807), Blackburn
Phoenix (1982)
Rochdale
Old Mill (1983)
Snaith
Spurn Head
Joseph Holt (1849),
Hydes (1863)
Manchester
H B Clark & Co (1982)
Wakefield
Liverpool
J W Lees (1828)
Middleton
Sheffield
Frederic Robinson (1828)
Stockport
George Bateman & Son (1874)
Wainfleet

Irish Sea

ENGLAND

North Sea

Plassey (1985)
Eyton
Titanic (1985)
Stoke-on-Trent
Nottingham
Shropshire (1988)
Wem
Burton Bridge (1982)
Marston's (1834)
Burton-upon-Trent
Elgood's (1795)
Wisbech
Woodforde's (1981)
Woodbastwick
Norwich

Cardigan Bay

Sarah Hughes (1987)
Wood (1980)
Wistanstow
Sedgley
Holden's (1935)
Dudley
Everards (1849)
Narborough

Three Tuns (1642)
Bishop's Castle
Daniel Batham & Son (1877)
Brierley Hill
Birmingham
Wells & Young's (1876)
Bedford
Greene King (1799)
Bury St Edmunds
Cambridge
Earl Soham (1984)
Earl Soham
Adnams Southwold (1872)
Southwold

Aberystwyth

WALES

Wye Valley (1985)
Stoke Lacy
Hook Norton (1849)
Hook Norton
B & T (1982)
Shefford
Nethergate (1986)
Pentlow
Mauldons (1982)
Sudbury

Felinfoel (1878)
Llanelli
Donnington (1865)
Upper Swell
Luton
McMullen & Sons (1827)
Hertford

Brecon Beacons
Gloucester
Oxford
Chiltern (1980)
Terrick
Pitfield (1982), North Weald
Crouch Vale (1981)
South Woodham Ferrers

S A Brain & Co (1882),
Bullmastiff (1987)
Cardiff
Uley (1985)
Uley
Arkell's (1843)
Swindon
Reading
P & D J Goacher (1983)
Fuller, Smith & Turner (1845)
London

RCH (1982), West Hewish
Berrow (1982)
Berrow
Bristol
Butcombe (1978)
Wrington
Wadworth (1885), Devizes
Stonehenge (1984)
Pilgrim (1985)
Maidstone
Shepherd Neame (1698)
Faversham

Cotleigh (1979)
Exmoor (1980)
Wiveliscombe
Moles (1982)
Melksham
Netheravon
Hop Back (1987)
Downton
Ballard's (1980)
Nyewood
Reigate
Larkins (1986)
Chiddingstone
Dover

Salisbury Plain
Southampton
Harvey & Son (1790)
Lewes
Brighton
Beachy Head

Beer Engine (1983)
Silverton
Newton St Cyres
Exe Valley (1984)
Dartmoor
J C & R H Palmer (1794)
Bridport
Hall & Woodhouse (1777)
Blandford
Goldfinch (1987)
Dorchester
Portsmouth
Isle of Wight

St Austell (1851)
St Austell
Summerskills (1983)
Plymouth
Portland Bill

Isles of Scilly
Land's End
Blue Anchor (unknown)
Helston

English Channel

FRANCE

KEY
- Shepherd Neame (1698) Faversham — Brewery (year founded) Town/city
- ○ Sheffield — Other town/city

Guernsey
R W Randall (1868)
St Peter's Port

Jersey

N

0 miles 50
0 km 50

Pale Ale & Bitter Beers

When it comes to packing flavour, variety, and subtlety (or lack of it) into remarkably dilute beer, pale British ales drawn naturally carbonated from the cask deserve all the adulation poured upon them.

PUNCH'S FANCY PORTRAITS.—No. 89.

SIR ARTHUR M. BASS, M.P.

Above: In the 19th century, British brewers became so prominent in both the Houses of Parliament that they were known collectively as "the Beerage".

Pale-ale brewing became possible in the seventeenth century when newly invented coke ovens allowed maltsters to avoid burning their malt for the first time. A high-hopped variety bound for India had appeared in London by 1780, but its acrid, unfettered bitterness, which dissipated on the long sea journey to Bombay, made it unpopular at home.

In 1820, Samuel Allsopp's newish brewery at Burton-upon-Trent in the English Midlands decided to ape the style using their local hard water, which is alkaline and packed with gypsum. This they found absorbed the hops' bitterness without harming their floweriness, creating graceful beers that contrasted sharply with the malty sweetness of brown ales and wall-of-flavour onslaught of porters and stouts.

Burton brewers were well used to exporting beer by this time but had recently lost a lucrative market in strong brown ale and stout to Russia. The opportunity to ship large quantities of paler brews to the outposts of a growing empire – coupled with the fact that these Burton-brewed beers, bearing the exotic mark of India Pale Ale (IPA), were much better suited to immediate consumption in the English market – made the fortunes of the Allsopp family and of other Burton brewers like Worthington and Bass.

Brewers elsewhere soon learned how to "Burtonize" water by adding sulphates, and throughout Britain took to brewing highly hopped pale ales and "bitter beer", which attracted a premium price when it first appeared in the mid-nineteenth century.

Growers in Kent, Sussex, Herefordshire, and Worcestershire used rail and sea to supply hops by the ton, though some brewers preferred to play with pale malt combinations to distinguish their lighter coloured ales. Scotland honed brews to different tax bands, "70 shilling" and "80 shilling", while Irish brewers made ruddy-hued ales akin to Vienna lagers.

BEER SELECTION

BATEMANS XXXB (4.5%)
George Bateman & Son, Wainfleet (Lincolnshire)
The strongest of three regular paler ales from this much-loved, nineteenth-century family-owned brewery. Drier and more bitter than many, with a strong hop aroma and clever mixed-grain backdrop.
www.bateman.co.uk

BATHAMS BEST BITTER (4.3%)
Daniel Batham & Son, Brierley Hill (West Midlands)
In the Black Country, northwest of Birmingham, the tradition of sweet mild ales extends to pale bitters with a light malt character, of which the uncrowned champion is from this fifth-generation family brewer.
www.bathams.com

BISHOPS FAREWELL (4.6%)
Oakham Ales, Peterborough (Cambridgeshire)
This successful, forward-thinking brewery first challenged drinkers with a near-albino bitter called JHB, then followed up with this even more robustly hopped light golden ale.
www.oakhamales.com

BLUEBIRD BITTER (3.6%)
Coniston Brewing Co, Coniston (Cumbria)
Challenger hops and a distinct hint of orange help shape this Cumbrian take on light bitter beer, from a part of the country awash with brewers and beautiful scenery.
www.conistonbrewery.com

Above: As well as exploiting Burton's hard water, the town's brewers used a re-fermentation method known as the Union System, which is shown here at its National Breweing Centre.

Hoppy pale ale became popular with gentlemen and southerners, coming to enjoy a status somewhere between England's riposte to blond lager and a gauche alternative to regular brown ale and porter. The rise of modern "bitter" was a 1950s phenomenon.

In August 1914, at the outbreak of World War One, the Liberal government passed the Defence of the Realm Act. Temperance campaigners had been active in the party for

Above: A hop farm in Kent, where layers of hops are dried in hot air rising from a "kell", or kiln, in traditional oast houses.

COPPER COAST RED ALE (4.3%)
Dungarvan Brewing Co, Dungarvan (Waterford)
Although by far the best of Ireland's Vienna malt-influenced "red" ales, this is the least-lovely beer from an impressive new brewer whose Black Rock stout and sharp, hoppy Helvick Gold are chart-toppers.
www.dungarvanbrewingcompany.com

EXMOOR GOLD (4.5%)
Exmoor Ales, Wiveliscombe (Somerset)
The first of Britain's golden ales, designed in 1986 to have the visual appeal of blond lager but a fuller, grainier flavour, drawing more than a few canned beer drinkers into real ale.
www.exmoorales.co.uk

GALWAY HOOKER IRISH PALE ALE (4.4%)
Hooker Brewery, Roscommon (Galway)
The best so far of Southern Ireland's attempts at floral, citrus, light pale ale, setting a trend with younger Irish drinkers and deserving a crack at Britain.
www.galwayhooker.ie

HARDCORE IPA (9.2%)
BrewDog, Fraserburgh (Aberdeenshire)
British brewing's horribly bright adolescent has an awkward streak, leading it to spearhead extreme beers such as this 150 IBU (International Bitterness Units)-strong IPA, which does better in a sealed container than an open cask, to the annoyance of the grown-ups.
www.brewdog.com

decades and with a single blow increased beer duty and imposed compulsory pub closing times and the abolition of stronger beers.

Until 1914, British and Irish beer was generally 5–6.5% ABV, as elsewhere. This now fell to an eccentric 3–3.5% ABV. The Great Depression that followed the war led to stronger beers returning only slowly. By the time they had, a second cycle of cataclysm and economic recession was imminent.

During World War II, British cities suffered heavy bombing, which destroyed many of the pubs that provided smaller urban brewers with their income. Food rationing subsequently remained in place until 1954, reducing consumer expectations. Surviving brewery companies adopted newer business methods and courted new technology. For example, pasteurization allowed flat beer to be transported in sealed kegs, provided its fizz was replaced shortly before dispensing. All of this ushered in global trends that continue to this day, higher profits being made by creating economies of scale through takeovers, mergers, and closures, rather than by crafting better beers.

By 1970, bottled beers were disappearing, and fashionable drinkers preferred national brands of draught,

Left: Food pairing, UK-style: a light English bitter with pork scratchings – pieces of cold, salt-roasted rind.

BEER SELECTION

HOPPIT CLASSIC BITTER (3.5%)
Loddon Brewery, Dunsden Green (Oxfordshire)
The Oxford-based television detective Inspector Morse would have enjoyed this perfect post-war English "session" bitter made from a pale ale malt mash flavoured with Kentish Goldings.
www.loddonbrewery.com

JAIPUR IPA (5.9%)
Thornbridge Brewery, Bakewell (Derbyshire)
Expect great beers from this strident and successful newish brewer of more authentic ale styles, including this credibly old-fashioned IPA made with assertive, newer-strain citrus hops.
www.thornbridgebrewery.co.uk

LANDLORD (4.3%)
Timothy Taylor & Co, Keighley (West Yorkshire)
A classic Yorkshire ale in which Styrian Goldings hops dominate a lush-bodied pale brew that has been festooned with more awards than any other UK beer.
www.timothy-taylor.co.uk

MOORHOUSE PENDLE WITCHES BREW (5.1%)
Moorhouse's Brewery, Burnley (Lancashire)
This typically Northern England pale ale, darker, sweeter, and less overtly hopped, has remained little changed from when the brewery first emerged in the early days of CAMRA's success (see p.108).
www.moorhouses.co.uk

PALE RIDER (5.2%)
Kelham Island Brewery, Sheffield (South Yorkshire)
Sheffield's largest brewery celebrated its 20th birthday by winning the Supreme Champion Beer of Britain award for this American-hopped but essentially English light-coloured pale ale.
www.kelhambrewery.co.uk

THREE TUNS XXX (4.3%)
Three Tuns Brewery, Bishop's Castle (Shropshire)
An exquisitely simple, floral straw-coloured pale ale from this expensively renovated, authentic tower brewery, which has had a continuous brewing tradition since 1642.
www.threetunsbrewery.co.uk

Above: Beer in modern Britain means a combination of centuries-old operations, such as Palmers, established in 1794...

Above: ...and Thornbridge, founded in 2005, but already considered a vanguard of the new breed of British brewers.

Above: Before the days of statutory paid holidays, working-class families from East London would take a week of paid leave in Kent to help with the hop harvest, pictured here ca. 1900.

recarbonated light ales drunk mainly by men from pint glasses, the shape of which mattered more than their contents. Brand catchphrases were nurtured using the new medium of television advertising.

Such mundane brews were no match for "real" ales, which seemed to have infinite variety: colour ranging from light blond to deep ruddy amber, malt character from wispy to improbably heavy, and hop presence from nuanced to moderately assertive. Some whistled past the palate quietly, while others brought impressions of new-mown hay, home-baked bread, and intense nostalgia, although in truth most were just better-made light ales.

In 1880, pale ale was typically 6% ABV and could contain a prodigious quantity of hops; by 1980, it was 3.5–4% ABV and had relatively few hops, but provided it was "real", it was deemed good. It was 2005 before a few brave souls dared to suggest that there might be more to making a great beer than that.

TRIBUTE (4.2%)
St Austell Brewery Co, St Austell (Cornwall)
Head brewer Roger Ryman created his own Cornish Gold malt as the base for this Willamette-hopped, distinctive light bronze ale, available nationally but brewed in the far South West.
www.staustellbrewery.co.uk

WORKIE TICKET (4.5%)
Mordue Brewery, North Shields (Tyne & Wear)
At the other end of the spectrum is this mellow, near-brown bitter from North East England, with a strong local following, defining another edge of the UK pale-ale footprint.
www.morduebrewery.com

WOODFORDE'S WHERRY (3.8%)
Woodforde's Broadland Brewery, Woodbastwick (Norfolk)
Instantly recognizable to local cognoscenti, this floral, sweetish bitter with slight grapefruit backtaste is a permanent fixture in many pubs in the East of England.
www.woodfordes.co.uk

WILLIAM WORTHINGTON'S WHITE SHIELD (5.6%)
William Worthington's Brewery (Molson Coors), Burton-upon-Trent (Staffordshire)
A bottle-conditioned, ester-laden Burton-brewed pale ale that survived the twentieth-century's travails to become as great a British icon as thick-cut marmalade and Marmite.
www.worthingtonswhiteshield.com

Porters & Stouts

Previous page: The causeway to the holy island of Lindisfarne, for which an Elizabethan beer has been recreated brewed with hyssop, a herb from the eponymous castle garden.

Although the image of stout is closely associated with Ireland, this family of beers actually originated in early eighteenth-century London. Local maltsters had created a dark malt suited to making a multipurpose beer, dubbed Entire. When young it was dry and refreshing, gaining such popularity with stevedores and porters at the docks and in the city that, by 1721, it had become known as porter. However, it was its ability to age beautifully in the barrel, or butt, that secured its fame.

Porter was as revolutionary in its time as lager would be a century later. It could be made in huge quantities – massive oak tuns being constructed for fermentation – and its flavour development over time made it suitable for export to the British colonies in North America, Australasia and India. In Ireland, by 1790, it accounted for one-third of the beer drunk.

Stronger versions became known as "stout porter", later abbreviated to "stout". These were sold successfully to Scandinavia and the countries around the Baltic Sea, including the Russian empire, leaving a legacy to this day of Baltic porters and Imperial Russian stouts.

Stout in Ireland was to follow a different path. The London government assisted English brewers to ship vast quantities of

Above: Wooden tuns have given over to stainless steel at London's Meantime Brewing Company, where a broad stable of beers includes the exemplary London Porter.

BEER SELECTION

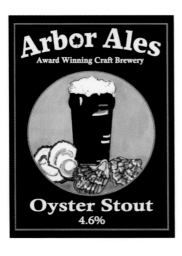

ARBOR OYSTER STOUT (4.6%)
Arbor Ales, Kingswood (Bristol)
A highly drinkable, smooth, chocolaty light stout from one of Bristol's numerous, interesting new breweries. Whole oysters are added at the end of mashing.
www.arborales.co.uk

DARK ARTS PORTER (4.4%)
Trouble Brewing, Allenwood (Kildare)
One of few Irish porters, thus designated for the absence of roasted barley. Found on draught and locally only thus far, although this careful new brewery should blossom.
www.troublebrewing.ie

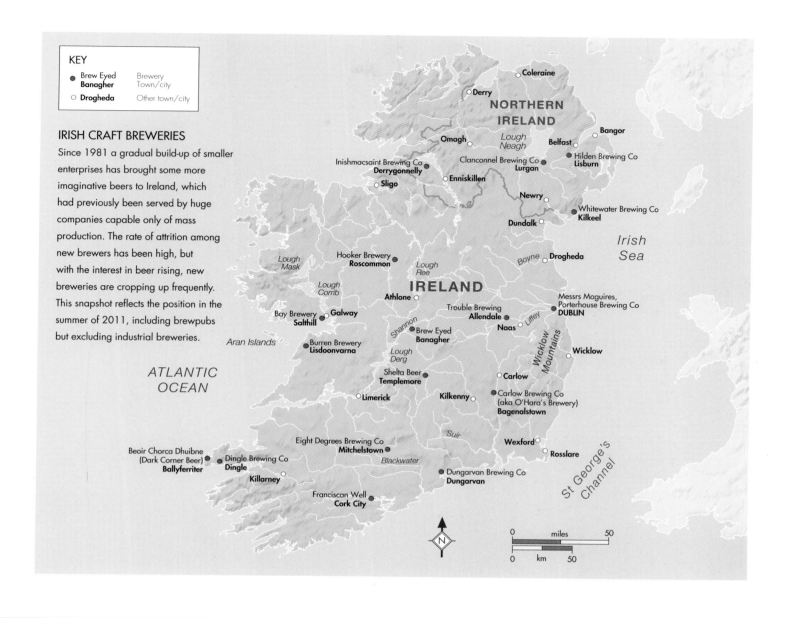

IRISH CRAFT BREWERIES

Since 1981 a gradual build-up of smaller enterprises has brought some more imaginative beers to Ireland, which had previously been served by huge companies capable only of mass production. The rate of attrition among new brewers has been high, but with the interest in beer rising, new breweries are cropping up frequently. This snapshot reflects the position in the summer of 2011, including brewpubs but excluding industrial breweries.

DOROTHY GOODBODY'S WHOLESOME STOUT (4.6%)

Wye Valley Brewery, Stoke Lacy (Herefordshire)
Burned enough yet smooth and satisfying stout, from a family-run brewery in hop country, which has now passed to the second generation.
www.wyevalleybrewery.co.uk

IMPERIAL EXTRA DOUBLE STOUT (9%)

Harvey and Son, Lewes (Sussex)
Imperial stouts are returning piecemeal to the UK, but this mighty beast, from one of the most gorgeous breweries in Britain, has kept going after the demise of Courage Barclay's original and now awaits reinforcements.
www.harveys.org.uk

MCGRATH'S IRISH BLACK (4.3%)

Clanconnel Brewing Co, Lurgan (Armagh)
An exceptional modern take on a light-bodied stout from Northern Ireland, plain chocolate nestling alongside something reminiscent of moss, slate, and rainwater.
www.clanconnelbrewing.com

MEANTIME LONDON PORTER (6.5%)

Meantime Brewing Co, Greenwich (London)
Straightforward, clean, dark medium-strength porter, with liquorice and caramel to the fore and a whisky-like lacing not far behind.
www.meantimebrewing.com

porter across the Irish Sea by imposing a heavy duty on local brewers – so much so that a young Arthur Guinness almost moved production to North Wales, from there to reimport his beers to Dublin.

When this tax was withdrawn in 1795, Ireland was freed to develop its own preferences, leading typical nineteenth-century Irish brewers to make three grades of porter and stout, often called "plain", "extra", and "export". These tended to be drier, made so by the addition of a little salt to the mash. A much-misunderstood variant on this was oyster stout, made by using a layer of crushed oyster shells to filter the beer before fermentation, thus infusing it with sea salt.

Back in Britain, a more overtly political beer was being born. Around 1870, sensing that the previously beer-friendly Temperance Society was about to flay English brewers, they invented "invalid stout". These sweetened black beers of 3–4.5% ABV were so rich in malty goodness as to be claimed suitable for the frail and infirm, the elderly, and even nursing mothers. The style lived on in forms like milk (or cream) stout, made with the unfermentable milk sugar lactose, and more wholesome-sounding oatmeal stout, which derives its sweetness from oats added to the mash.

THE LONG ROAD TO IRISH INDEPENDENTS

The story of black beers in twentieth-century Ireland mirrors that of pale ales in Britain. By 1970, porter was a distant memory and the three domestic brewing companies – Guinness, Murphy's, and Beamish & Crawford – marketed only basic stout in their home markets.

While a Campaign for Real Irish Stout & Porter (CRISP, maybe?) might have appealed to some, it never existed. Industrial lager was to be the future, single-brand-name stouts would cover for heritage, and light "red" ales of doubtful provenance would do for the cusses who liked neither.

The craft beer movement that began to engulf the rest of the world in the 1990s failed to penetrate an island on which, by then, 99 per cent of the brewing capacity was in the hands of multinationals.

The most assertive proponent of Irish craft brewing has been Dublin-based Porterhouse (see opposite), which even owns a pub in London's Covent Garden. Carlow Brewing's O'Hara beers (see below) are growing steadily in their second decade, while

north of the border pioneer real ale brewer Hilden of Lisburn has entered its fourth.

Among more recent arrivals, Dungarvan of Waterford (see p.111) and, in the north, Clanconnel of Lurgan (see p.117) have earned plaudits for recapturing old-style flavours, while the auspiciously named Trouble Brewing of Kildare (see p.116) skilfully seduces mainstream drinkers with brews that are drinkable but different.

Watch out, too, for Shelta of Tipperary, whose White Gypsy beers increasingly use their own locally planted hops, while maturing some stronger stouts in purpose-bought winemakers' oak casks.

With Ireland's larger brewers still unwilling to entertain producing craft-quality stout or porter – the obvious way to go for anyone seeking to rebuild the reputation of Irish brewing – and a new consumer group, Beoir, actively engaging younger drinkers in discovering the world of beer from the backyard outwards, the future for new Irish brewers is looking brighter than for many decades.

BEER SELECTION

NIGHTMARE (5%)
Nick Stafford's Hambleton Ales, Melmerby (North Yorkshire)
A perfectly balanced, surprisingly rich, fulsome yet not acrid prize-winning stout from a brewery company possessed of confidence and apparently limitless common sense.
www.hambletonales.co.uk

O'HARA'S LEANN FOLLÁIN (6%)
Carlow Brewing Co, Bagenalstown (Carlow)
A fuller-bodied, darker-headed, coffee-laced, and smoky stout that points the way for future Irish craft brewers intent on being less afraid of assertive flavours.
www.carlowbrewing.com

PITFIELD'S 1850 LONDON PORTER (5%)
Pitfield Brewery, North Weald (Essex)
Dry, black, and earthy, with burned caramel in the aroma. At the end of the swallow, this beer re-creates the "plain porter" style from an organic 1850 recipe.
www.pitfieldbeershop.co.uk

ST PETER'S OLD-STYLE PORTER (5.1%)
St Peter's Brewery, St Peter South Elmham (Suffolk)
Clever bottle design has shaped the fortunes of this modern brewery, set in a fifteenth-century manor, whose stronger porter is, unconventionally, a blend of older and younger beers.
www.stpetersbrewery.co.uk

Above: It has taken 30 years for pioneering small brewers to find a receptive market in Ireland, but now younger drinkers are discovering the sort of beers their great-grandparents once enjoyed.

St Peter's Brewery
OLD STYLE PORTER
ALC. 5.1% VOL.
St Peter's Brewery, St. Peter's Hall, Nr. Bungay, Suffolk, U.K.

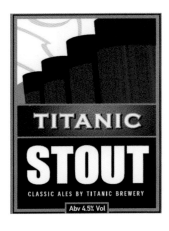

TITANIC STOUT (4.5%)
Titanic Brewery, Stoke-on-Trent (Staffordshire)
Straightforward, reliable, velvety English-tasting lighter stout from a popular brewery that makes a sound range of reliable beers.
www.titanicbrewery.co.uk

WRASSLERS XXXX (5%)
Porterhouse Brewing Co, Dublin
Brewed with malted wheat and some unmalted barley in the mash to re-create an authentic, fuller-bodied early twentieth-century stout from County Cork.
www.porterhousebrewco.com

Brown Ale & Dark Mild

While the twentieth century was bad for pale ale in Britain, its effect on those ales – called variously mild, dark, or brown – that reflected a sweeter, softer, and longer tradition was far greater.

Such beers had, historically, come in three strengths. Regular beer, or "common", was around 5–6% ABV. "Small beer", made from thinner wort often run off after sparging (see p.22), would more typically be around

Above: Bitter, mild, red ale or brown? The designation given to a British beer often affects its popularity more than the taste.

3% ABV and provided routine daytime hydration for farm workers and industrial labourers. There were also stronger ales, as high as 9% ABV, made for religious festivals, the harvest supper, or, in the case of college breweries at the universities of Oxford and Cambridge, the annual audit.

Regular and stronger ales would often be conditioned in oak casks. The term "mild ale" originally indicated a beer that was decanted before it had started to turn vinous or acidic and become "old ale". Such mild ales could be pale, too.

As with their paler counterparts, 1914's Defence of the Realm Act (see pp.111–12) and the cycle of war and economic hardship that characterized the 50 years that followed inflicted considerable damage on all dark beers, so that by 1970, Britain's dwindling stock consisted mostly of brews in the 3–3.5% ABV small-beer range.

Despite the efforts of CAMRA (see p.108) and others, these weaker beers have failed to

appeal to baby boomers. Although interest in darker British ales has started to grow in recent years, it seems still to be the case that they do better if the word "mild" is omitted from their name.

Above: Heavily bearded temperance advocate Sir Wilfred Lawson (1829–1906), pictured in 1890.

BEER SELECTION

DARK RUBY (6%)
Sarah Hughes Brewery, Sedgley (West Midlands)
Dark mild ales are synonymous with the industrial West Midlands, but few retain the rich fruitiness or authenticity of this excellent dark brew that has become the definitive old-style mild.
www.sarahhughesbrewery.co.uk

DOUBLE MAXIM (6%)
Maxim Brewery, Houghton-le-Spring (Co Durham)
Originally from Vaux Breweries, which closed in 1999, this (usually) bottled ale is possibly the last of the well-attenuated, uncluttered, dry light brown ales from North East England.
www.maximbrewery.co.uk

HOBSON'S MILD (3.2%)
Hobsons Brewery, Cleobury Mortimer (Worcestershire)
This delicious Midlands, postwar, cask-conditioned dark-mild ale packs an implausible amount of flavour into a beer so light that other countries would serve it to patients.
www.hobsons-brewery.co.uk

MIDNIGHT BELL (4.8%)
Leeds Brewery, Leeds (West Yorkshire)
Founded in 2007 by a young crew to make "very Yorkshire" beers using high-tech kit and top-quality ingredients, this proper old-fashioned mild is the top of their regular range.
www.leedsbrewery.co.uk

Above: An 1836 caricature from *McCleans Monthly*, entitled "Meeting of the Temperance Society, with Chairman Mr Drainmedry and his deputy J. Ditch-Water Esq."

OSCAR WILDE (3.7%)
Mighty Oak Brewing, Maldon (Essex)
At the light, mellow but nutty end of the dark-mild spectrum, from a part of South East England where such beers are reviving against the trend.
www.mightyoakbrewery.co.uk

OTT OLD TONGHAM TASTY (6%)
Hog's Back Brewery, Tongham (Surrey)
A stronger brown beer from a Home Counties brewer with a reputation for making solid English ales, this one in the manner of a twentieth-century old ale.
www.hogsback.co.uk

OTTER MILD (3.8%)
The Otter Brewery, Luppitt (Devon)
In the region traditionally least associated with mild ale, this well-established newer brewer has created a fine example: soft, with a gentle fruity underlay and a dab of hop.
www.otterbrewery.com

RUDGATE RUBY MILD (4.4%)
Rudgate Brewery, Tockwith (North Yorkshire)
Prize-winning, black-cherry-tinted gentle ale that would pass for a lighter mild of a bygone era but for the lacing of American hops.
www.rudgatebrewery.co.uk

THEAKSTON'S OLD PECULIER (5.6%)
T & R Theakston, Masham (North Yorkshire)
A ruby-brown, slightly fruity, Fuggle-hopped iconic ale that counts for strong in Britain, taking its name from an ancient local court and its fame from being misread.
www.theakstons.co.uk

Stronger British Ales

Britain and Ireland have always enjoyed an ambivalent relationship with stronger beers, including those that can lay claim to a more authentic heritage than most "traditional ales".

Perhaps the most poignant illustration of Britain's ambivalent attitude to craft brewing is that the three strong bottle-conditioned ales to survive the twentieth century – the original Russian Imperial Stout, Thomas Hardy's Ale, and George Gale's Prize Old Ale – have either faded from view or dimmed, as did the massively hopped style of barley wine called Burton Ale before them.

Scotch ales, too, disappeared from the UK or else were redefined as lighter beers. The principle of these beers in their original form was to extract the maximum amount of sugar from the grain, using the caramelized residues to add flavour and some preservative power. Hops, which tasted a bit English anyway, were muted.

The historical spread of English stock ale is less clear. These high-strength beers, often pale ales, were matured in oak and used mainly for blending into regular beers to add strength and character, a practice that survives in only one mainstream British brewery today but which may yet revive.

Above: Greene King plc of Bury St Edmunds, home to Old 5X, Britain's last stock ale.

Right: The new owner of Gale's Prize Old Ale ages it in steel tanks rather than oak tuns.

BEER SELECTION

ADNAMS TALLY HO! (7.2%)
Adnams, Southwold (Suffolk)
This heavy, dark brew, all malt loaf, burned crust, and sultana, was once a Christmas bonus for friends and loyal publicans but is now available year-round in the bottle.
www.adnams.co.uk

BODGERS BARLEY WINE (8.5%)
Chiltern Brewery, Terrick (Buckinghamshire)
This elegant brewery has passed to a second generation, along with a fine collection of ales that includes this delicious golden chestnut soup of a beer, tasting of Goldings and Fuggles hops and nudging towards old-style Burton Ale.
www.chilternbrewery.co.uk

GOLDEN PRIDE (8.5%)
Fuller Smith & Turner, Chiswick (London)
This 100 per cent malt, amber strong ale from London's longest-established independent brewery is sweet, overtly alcoholic, and warming, with a touch of orange liqueur in its afterburn.
www.fullers.co.uk

ROBINSON'S OLD TOM (8.5%)
Frederic Robinson, Stockport (Cheshire)
From a fifth-generation family brewery comes this dark barley wine that retains a port-like vinous finish after a taste onslaught that includes hop, dried fruit, and a faint smokiness.
www.frederic-robinson.co.uk

Above: Adnams Brewery of Southwold – masterful movers from age-old tradition to modern ideas.

STRONG SUFFOLK VINTAGE ALE (6%)

Greene King, Bury St Edmunds (Suffolk) The brewery's oak-aged stock ale, 5X, is blended into a brown ale to create an earthy, dark, dry British version of an oak-aged Flemish brown ale. www.greeneking.co.uk

TRAQUAIR HOUSE ALE (7%)

Traquair House, Innerleithen (Peeblesshire) In 1965, an early pioneer of the Scottish beer reopened the brewhouse at this historic house to brew authentic, dark, sweet, and heavy Scotch ales, bound mostly for export. www.traquair.co.uk

Local Heroes & New Beginnings

The story of Britain's beer revival is a tale with two strands. The main storyline shows the little guy winning, illustrated by the successful expansion of every established regional British brewer of "real" ales that chose not to sell out to a rich buyer, and the parallel creation of over 700 new craft breweries to make broadly similar products.

The uneasy subplot focuses on the narrow vision imposed on smaller UK breweries by a conservative beer-drinking audience that mistrusts modern production methods, is wary of new tastes, and approaches any beer stronger than 5% ABV with trepidation. Yet, as with everything else in an era when superhighways are transporting people, goods, and information around the world in previously unthinkable volumes, those beer fans thirsting for experiences that lie beyond the horizon can explore far more easily than their forebears.

A new generation of brewers and drinkers are learning to make and enjoy beers from a grander heritage than those championed by British beer campaigners of the 1970s. They are beginning to play with new forms of production and flavours to the extent of provoking what may become a second phase of the UK beer revolution, adopting different rules.

The beers that we have chosen here and earlier in this chapter to represent the best of modern British brewing will, in some cases, prove to be works in progress. Yet we hope that we have at least been able to pick beers made in styles that represent the way the industry will head in the next 20 years, and

Right: The Blue Anchor in Helston, Cornwall; quietly brewing its own thing since the 1400s.

BEER SELECTION

CHIMERA DARK DELIGHT (6%)
Downton Brewery Co, Downton (Wiltshire)
The roasted coffee and chocolate flavours in this strong-for-England dark beer are not matched by heavy hopping, thus avoiding a porter label – just deep and interesting.
www.downtonbrewery.com

CHOCOLATE MARBLE (5.5%)
Marble Brewery, Chorlton (Manchester)
Marble is one of the ones to watch among the new elite, making interesting and technically sound beers like this organic black porter-cum-strong mild out of an extended brewpub.
tel: +44 161 819 2694

Above: Silly hats and evolving ales at the Great British Beer Festival.

also highlighted some of the brewers who will lead that future.

The emerging beers are unquestionably of mixed pedigree. Some attempt to rekindle old-fashioned styles that may not have been seen inside beer glasses for many decades, while using ingredients and technology that would likely be the envy of British brewers of the eighteenth and nineteenth centuries.

But in a fast-developing worldwide beer culture where any brewer can imitate IPAs, porters, and imperial stouts, should not brewers in the lands that invented them have something useful to say? The real question is

Right: British drinkers are so used to associating hand-pulled, cask-conditioned ales with the notion of "Good Beer" that higher quality ales and lagers derived from other brewing traditions have been slow to develop in the UK.

DARK STAR ORIGINAL (5%)
Dark Star Brewing Co, Partridge Green (West Sussex)
Nobody would be surprised if this well-established offbeat micro's next brew was a cocoa bean porter, although its longest-standing beer is an amber mild with porterish leanings.
www.darkstarbrewing.co.uk

FRAOCH HEATHER ALE (5%)
Williams Bros Brewing Co, Alloa (Clackmannanshire)
From a recipe claiming Pictish connections from four millennia past, heather flowers are infused into a brew of malted barley and sweet gale to make a unique light amber ale that is an acquired taste.
www.williamsbrosbrew.com

IMPERIAL BROWN STOUT (10.1%)
The Kernel, Southwark (London)
This tiny new brewery in the capital has big ideas, currently bottled as an evolving range of IPAs, plus this massive not-quite stout based on an old Barclay Perkins brew.
www.thekernelbrewery.com

ISLAND BERE (4.2%)
Valhalla Brewery, Baltasound (Shetland Isles)
Brewed in the most northerly community in the UK from island-grown bere (primeval barley planted by the Vikings) to create a unique, sweet, scented yet highly drinkable orange-amber ale.
www.valhallabrewery.co.uk

whether or not a new generation of brewers will feel it should impose some sort of proprietary authenticity on these old British inventions, or simply imitate the sometimes avant-garde interpretations placed on them by North American or Scandinavian producers.

The British talent for squeezing more flavours from fewer ingredients is already showing itself in some of the pioneering efforts. A few brewers are even starting to extend their efforts to creating a British take on some distinctly unBritish styles, such as wheat beers, spiced ales, and even the odd authentic blond lager, although none has yet reached a standard we felt justified illustration here.

Hopefully, whichever way things go, some room will remain for local specialities – eccentric brews created because the owner-brewer wanted to see what would happen if they made a beer this way or that, or beers that continue to be made simply because they always have been.

There is a fear that too many breweries are now seeking to trade in a UK market that, although growing and exciting, is distinctly volatile and under further challenge from the foreseeable and inevitable rise in the volume of craft beers that will be imported. However

Left: After settling, freshly made beer is racked into a cask of real ale at the Dark Star brewery in Horsham, Sussex.

BEER SELECTION

MARCUS AURELIUS (7.5%)
Milton Brewery, Milton (Cambridgeshire)
This Imperial Roman stout is one of 40 beers from this brewery of the imagination near Cambridge. It is dark and deep, with a dried-fruit character and a mocha edge.
www.miltonbrewery.co.uk

O8 (8%)
Otley Brewing Company, Pontypridd (Mid-Glamorgan)
The simple vision of this adventurous new Welsh brewery is epitomized in its bold logo and its entertaining, aromatic, prize-winning blond bitter strong ale that tops off a fine range.
www.otleybrewing.co.uk

OLA DUBH (8–8.5%)
Harviestoun, Alva (Clackmannanshire)
When Old Engine Oil 6% dark ale is decanted into Highland Park whisky casks, the amalgam Gaelicizes its name and gains something godly.
www.harviestoun.com

ORKNEY DARK ISLAND RESERVE (10%)
Orkney Brewery, Quoyloo (Orkney)
An extraordinary strong black ale fermented in whisky casks and presented starkly in tall black bottles. A burned syrup, coal-fired drinking experience somehow appropriate to the far north.
www.orkneybrewery.co.uk

DARK ISLAND
RESERVE
THE EXTRAORDINARY ORCADIAN ALE

Dark Island Reserve is a rich, robust ORCADIAN ALE. After a gentle fermentation at our brewery in Quoyloo, the beer is finished in old oak casks formerly used to MATURE FINE MALT WHISKIES. This unhurried process creates a timeless classic tasting of fruit, spice, oak & roast malt aromas. An Extraordinary ale.

Andrew Fulton
Head Brewer, The Orkney Brewery
LIMITED EDITION
BREWED IN SCOTLAND
HAND CRAFTED IN SMALL BATCHES
Alc. 10%/vol   Alc. 10%/vol

things pan out, a reversal of the trend away from beers of industrial convenience seems highly unlikely, and a continuing healthy growth in the range and volume of British-made craft beers seems virtually predestined.

Indeed, beer in Great Britain generally seems set to become more diverse and interesting than it has been for over a hundred years. Although the island of Ireland has further to catch up, signs there, too, are encouraging.

Right: The cask is sealed with a round "shive", in the centre of which is a small "spile" hole that, once in the pub cellar, is broached to let the cask breathe.

WHEN YOU ARE THERE

- In most British and Irish pubs, drinks are bought for cash at the bar.
- Plan your tour, then pick pubs to fit from the *Good Beer Guide* and *Good Pub Guide*.
- Find the best Irish beer information on www.beoir.org.
- Do not expect to find good beer in many hotels or restaurants yet.
- Must see: The National Brewery Centre in Burton-on-Trent.
- Must drink: at the meticulously preserved Sun Inn at Leintwardine (Herefordshire) and Bridge Inn at Topsham (Devon).

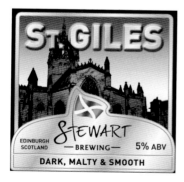

SPINGO MIDDLE (5.1%)
Blue Anchor Inn, Helston (Cornwall)
A distinctly tangy dollop of living history, made in the tiny granite brewhouse at the back of this thatched, 500-year-old former travellers' rest house, once run by monks.
www.spingoales.com

ST GILES (5%)
Stewart Brewing, Loanhead (Midlothian)
Edge-of-Edinburgh micro that is forging a Scottish dimension to craft brewing UK style with ales such as this dark, tangy, stewed, caramel-laced, and indefinably north-of-the-border example.
www.stewartbrewing.co.uk

TWIN RAM (4.6%)
Penlon Cottage Brewery, Pencae (Ceredigion)
This 100 per cent malt, bottle-conditioned amber ale is beautifully flavoured with whole hops at a cottage industry brewery on a smallholding deep in rural west Wales.
www.penlon.biz

WANDLE (3.8%)
Sambrook's Brewery, Battersea (London)
Founded by a former accountant with a dream of resurrecting commercial brewing in the centre of London. Duncan Sambrook launched his brewery in 2008 with this copper-hued bitter with a leafy aroma and refreshingly spicy, biscuity malt body.
www.sambrooksbrewery.co.uk

FRANCE

When Charles de Gaulle became President of France in 1959, it was home to an economically battered but recognizable network of small regional breweries. By the time his successor, Georges Pompidou, died in office 15 years later, all but a handful had been absorbed into six corporations, none of which proved solid enough to remain French owned.

BEST-SELLING LOCAL LABELS

33	(Heineken)
Desperados	(Heineken)
Fischer	(Heineken)
Kanterbräu	(Carlsberg)
Kronenbourg	(Carlsberg)
Pelforth	(Heineken)

By the turn of the millennium, there were a few signs of a revival in French brewing culture, particularly in regions where wine production is absent or low key, such as in the far north along the Belgian border, or Brittany in the northwest.

Little more than a decade later, France is seeing a massive increase in the number of small breweries, from the Alps to the Pyrenees and La Manche to Le Med. By 2012, only five of the country's 95 mainland *départements* was without a brewery. The fear is no longer of loss of interest but rather of lack of prowess.

Many French people remain delightfully chauvinistic about food and drink but become rapidly scornful of poor quality. Few of the beers from these new ventures have to date made the brew masters of Belgium or Bavaria begin quaking in their boots. Many producers brew less beer in a week than some people keep in their cellar, while others are no more than brewpub franchises making rather dull beers not far off the mainstream.

However, when it comes to spirit and sheer numbers – nearly 400 at the last count – they may prove eventually to have something to send brewers at larger companies searching for their old textbooks. In a country famed not just for its wines but also for its brandies, pastis, and *eaux de vie*, it would be naive to assume other than that among these pioneers are the cult brewers of tomorrow.

France enjoys some of the lowest rates of tax on beer – not that you would know this from the top-end prices charged by Parisian beer cafés and restaurants for any beer with a good reputation or foil top. What remains to be seen is whether France's new brewers will in time earn the right to charge high prices through merit alone.

Below: Northern France's bars, like the Java in St Malo, shown here, have more in common with the pub traditions of northern Europe than the café culture of Paris and the south of the country.

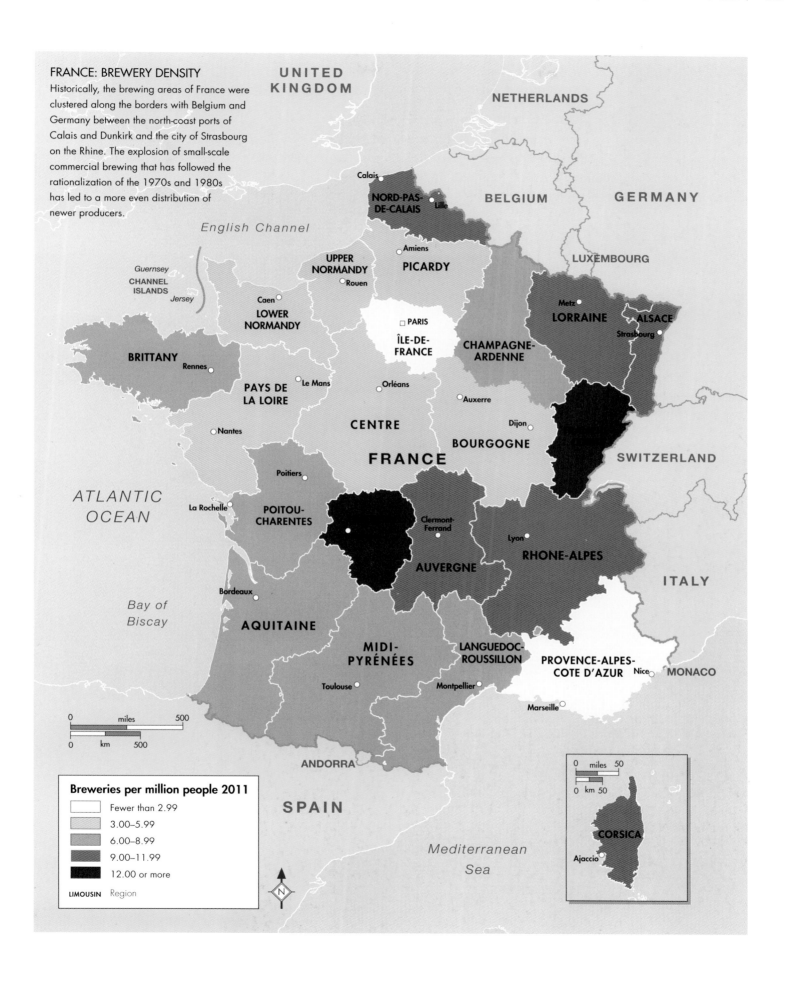

FRANCE: BREWERY DENSITY

Historically, the brewing areas of France were clustered along the borders with Belgium and Germany between the north-coast ports of Calais and Dunkirk and the city of Strasbourg on the Rhine. The explosion of small-scale commercial brewing that has followed the rationalization of the 1970s and 1980s has led to a more even distribution of newer producers.

Breweries per million people 2011

- Fewer than 2.99
- 3.00–5.99
- 6.00–8.99
- 9.00–11.99
- 12.00 or more

LIMOUSIN Region

Bière de Garde

The term *bière de garde* means "stored beer". Although its origins pre-date the development of ice-cold lagering by some centuries (*see* p.22), its principles are similar, referring to the practice of letting a beer mature on its lees at the brewery for a time before dispatch, either lying in oak tuns like a fine wine or developing in its bottle.

Opposite: In the northeastern *départements* of France, beer-making is as much a part of the fabric of life as is wine-growing in the valleys of the country's south and west.

These French beers share a common heritage with *saison* (*see* pp.68–9), made in the former French *départements* that are now the southern provinces of Belgium.

Their home territory runs from that part of northeast France between Calais and Lille sometimes referred to as French Flanders, down through Picardy, the Ardennes, and on into Lorraine and Alsace, a wide strip of country that borders Belgium and the German Rhineland.

Traditionally, brewers produced beers on the one-*blonde*, one-*ambrée*, one-*brune* principle, found across much of the Francophone beer world and beyond, particularly in the Americas.

A few breweries can still trace their roots back to the nineteenth century. The most entrepreneurial of these has been Duyck

Above: The landscape of French Flanders is, like its beers, in many ways similar to its Belgian neighbour's.

BEER SELECTION

3 MONTS (8.5%)
Brasserie de St Sylvestre, St Sylvestre Cappel (Nord – Pas-de-Calais)
The first strong golden ale to persuade their Belgian neighbours that the French can brew. A fulsome, honeyed ale with herbal notes that needs to mature in its bottle for a few months.
www.brasserie-st-sylvestre.com

ANOSTEKÉ (8%)
Brasserie du Pays Flamand, Blaringhem (Nord – Pas-de-Calais)
A newish strong *blonde* ale that is attracting much attention for its ability to pack a large hop presence into a French-style, yellow-*blonde* ale that is not an IPA clone.
www.bracine.com

JENLAIN AMBRÉE (7.5%)
Brasserie Duyck, Jenlain (Nord – Pas-de-Calais)
The most widely available northern French *bière de garde* is a clean but multifaceted, unpasteurized brew from this small, commercially focused brewery near Valenciennes, run by the fourth generation.
www.jenlain.fr

LA CHOULETTE BRUNE (7.5%)
Brasserie La Choulette, Hordain (Nord – Pas-de-Calais)
A regular example of the northern French *bière de garde* take on a stronger brown ale, with dabs of chocolate and liquorice in among the caramel and old books.
www.lachoulette.com

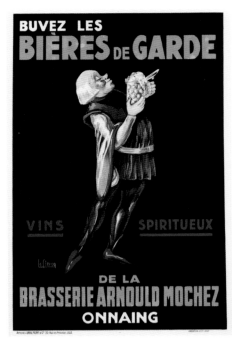

(*see* opposite), whose Jenlain beers are widely exported, even to Paris! St Sylvestre's 3 Monts (*see* opposite) has earned space on many lists, although its other beers have failed to penetrate thus far, and La Choulette (*see* opposite) gets about enough to give the impression that it brews more than it does.

Of the new breed, Thiriez of Esquelbecq (*see* p.132) has grown a following while others remain just local heroes in the north. Here, mistrust of anything that goes on in the capital and annoyance at being excluded historically from the national tourism map has manifested itself in the growth of a distinct local culture, with its own dialect, ales, and some fabulously authentic pubs.

Above: The bottling line at the Duyck family's Jenlain brewery is geared mostly to filling corked 75cl bottles.

LA CUVÉE DES JONQUILLES (7%)
Brasserie Bailleux Café-Restaurant, Au Baron, Gussignies (Nord – Pas-de-Calais)
Tiny French brewpubs show up more on the radar when they are 200 metres (240 yards) from the Belgian border, especially when they produce a more than passable impression of fragrant *saison* such as this one.

LA BAVAISIENNE AMBRÉE (7%)
Brasserie Theillier, Bavay
(Nord – Pas-de-Calais)
Possibly the finest French *bière de garde* of all – a simple, straightforward, full-of-grain *ambrée*, made at a tiny nineteenth-century family-run brewery using 100 per cent single-strain malt and only one hop variety.

LA P'TITE SYLVIE (7%)
Micro Brasserie "Le Paradis",
Blainville-sur-l'Eau (Lorraine)
The flagship high-hopped pale ale from a tiny idiosyncratic producer, southeast of Nancy. The brewery's range also includes perfumed wheat beers and others, sometimes featuring local oil of bergamot.
www.brasserieleparadis.com

Bière de Blé Noir & Other Local Specialities

If the British were to dub France's northwesternmost region "Little Cornwall", would it be taken as a sign of affection, returning the compliment for having been condemned to live a thousand years in "Big Brittany" or *Grande Bretagne?*

As with the Cornish, remoteness from the capital and familiarity with the skills of surviving winter on a gale-blown granite peninsula stuck in the North Atlantic as a shipping hazard has bred a strong regional spirit among the Bretons. This is seen in their music, plain cooking, and, in recent decades, the creation of a unique beer culture.

Bière de blé noir ("black wheat beer") is as Breton as the pipes and pancakes, although whether local brewers of old used to mash with blackened buckwheat is anyone's guess. Regardless, their modern counterparts adopted it as their own and in so doing have created a classic modern style that lies somewhere between Bavarian *Weizenbier* and Irish plain porter.

The re-emergence of Brittany as a centre of craft brewing was also aided by that most British icon, the counter-mounted handpump,

used as a method of dispensing locally made, reddish cask-conditioned pale ales.

In the vanguard were brewers like Lancelot, near Morlaix (below opposite), and Coreff of Carhaix (*see* below). At the latest count, 20 producers had joined in, though fears of recession have brought unwise corner-cutting and none has yet plotted an export drive to the "English Peninsula", or Southern Ireland.

In a nation of chefs serving a people who delight in discovering and celebrating flavours sometimes cultivated over centuries, French craft brewing is in its infancy and its styles are derivative for the present. Spices, syrups, and additives are used to imitate the worst of Belgian brewing, while some brewers choose originality over developing sound technique.

However, if asked 20 years ago about the survival prospects of a brewery on the

Mediterranean island of Corsica that intended to master the inclusion of sweet chestnut in its mash, who would have predicted two decades of steady growth for Brasserie Pietra?

We have no idea whose efforts we will be lauding in our next edition of this book, but the sheer weight of numbers guarantees there will be many.

WHEN YOU ARE THERE

- Always nod, make eye contact, and wish customers *"Bonjour!"* on entering a café.
- Most French craft breweries are tiny and only sell their beers locally.
- Expect to pay eye-watering prices for craft beers in Paris.
- Must see: the hilltop town of Cassel – a great base for touring the far north.
- Must drink: hand-drawn Breton ale at the Ty Korn on the island of Ushant (Ouessant), off the coast of Le Conquet.
- To keep abreast of developments, try www.brasseries-france.info.

BEER SELECTION

COREFF AMBRÉE (4.7%)
Brasserie Coreff, Carhaix (Brittany)
Included for the sheer nerve of it, this hand-drawn, cask-conditioned "real *ambrée*" amuses the French and bemuses the British, whenever it appears. *Une bière Franglaise.*
www.coreff.com

L'AGRIVOISE LA COMMUN'ALE (5%)
Micro Brasserie L'Agrivoise, St-Agrève (Rhône-Alpes)
This light, hoppy *blonde* ale is the most frequently encountered rather than the best of the beers from this consistently high-performing brewer in the Ardèche hills.
www.lagrivoise.fr

LA BLONDE D'ESQUELBECQ (6.5%)
Brasserie Thiriez, Esquelbecq (Nord – Pas-de-Calais)
Daniel Thiriez began producing beer commercially in 1996 with this slightly spicy but unspiced *blonde* ale made with locally grown hops. Since then, his charming farmhouse brewery has sprung seven other ales, a cute café, and small lodgings.
www.brasseriethiriez.com

MATTEN LA SCHWORTZ (5.8%)
Brasserie Artisanale de Matzenheim, Matzenheim (Alsace)
Although it is Red Fox IPA, the brewery's high-hopped *bière rousse*, that may make its name, this confident, full-flavoured lightish stout speaks volumes about its competence as a brewer of the future.
www.matten.fr

Above: The continuity of the Celtic fringe drinking culture is seen in bars like Ty Elise in Plouye, Britanny, where five French real ales are served in a public bar littered with bric-a-brac.

Next page: While other regions in France are fast developing their own craft-beer cultures, it is in brewpubs, like this one in Lille and others in Alsace, that French brewing history lives on.

METEOR PILS (5%)
Brasserie Meteor, Hochfelden (Alsace)
A rare example of a commercial pilsner with enough strength of character to cut through to the taste-buds at the end of the evening.
www.brasserie-meteor.fr

NUIT DE GOGUETTE (6%)
Brasserie des Garrigues, Sommières (Languedoc-Roussillon)
Accomplished and steady dark-brown ale from a new brewery in the southwest that shows signs of wishing to make beers to push French tastes.
www.brasseriedesgarrigues.fr

ODO (6.6%)
Le-Brewery, Joue du Bois (Lower Normandy)
Set up by expats in 2001 to bring English-style beers to the Orne, this tiny brewery's offbeat "milk stout" – black, sweet, and all-enveloping – is its most unusual brew.
www.le-brewery.com

TELENN DU (4.5%)
Brasserie Lancelot, Le Roc St André (Brittany)
One of the first of these extraordinary *blé noir* darkened buckwheat beers found in Brittany, packing roasted stout flavours into a rounded wheat beer to unique effect, when not flirting with mainstream.
www.brasserie-lancelot.com

25ᵈ **Cocktails de Bière** 3,90€

Le Habanna : Bière blanche, Rhum blanc
Sirop de banane.

Le Boucanier : Bière ambrée, Rhum brun
Sirop de Canne.

Tonnelet 5l

- Blonde 14,00€
- Ambrée 15,00€
- Blanche 15,00€

Bière Bouteille 75cl

- Blonde 3,20€
- Ambrée 3,90€
- Blanche 3,90€

Tripack (3 Bouteilles) 10,80€
Bipack (2 Bouteilles) 8,60€

3
Flammekueches
Emportées
1
Bouteille de Bière
OFFERTE

TIRAGE
AUJOURD'HUI:
N'... ASSIN:

L'AMBREE
LA BRUNE
LA BLANCHE

NETHERLANDS

The Netherlands is a nation of traders. Its wealth, like much of its land mass, comes from the Dutch ability to conquer the seas. In the staunchly Protestant north, drink was eschewed as a sign of human weakness, while in the Catholic south, it was celebrated as God's way of helping mankind survive a trying world. The western provinces of North and South Holland, and their respective port cities of Amsterdam and Rotterdam, took the sailor's view.

Meticulous excise records mean we know more about beer sales here in past centuries than in most other countries. For example, we know that beers made in Louvain and Bremen were shifted in vast quantities through the ports of Holland in the fifteenth century.

Less is known about actual brewing and drinking habits, although it is likely that the emphasis was on regular brown ales, with traditions of special brews made for the autumn, New Year, and possibly the coming of spring.

The Netherlands' better-known contribution to world brewing was its role in forming a global vision of simple, shiny beer for all. The

Below: Amsterdam's riverside Brouwerij 't IJ, one of four breweries in the city, is instantly identifiable by the windmill that looms behind it. Its tasting room is a popular after-work spot for locals.

BEST-SELLING LOCAL LABELS

Amstel	(Heineken)
Bavaria	(National)
Dommelsch	(Anheuser-Busch InBev)
Grolsch	(SABMiller)
Oranjeboom	(Anheuser-Busch InBev)
Wieckse	(Heineken)

THE HEINEKEN LEGACY

More than in any other country, the rise and fall of brewing in the Netherlands owes its fate to one person, Alfred "Freddie" Heineken (1923–2002), the man who said, "In the end, life is all about advertising."

The small Heineken family brewery had been good enough to win international awards in the late nineteenth century, but it hit bad times in the interwar period and fell out of family control – a fact that irked Freddie badly.

After spending time in the USA in the late 1940s, he became passionately interested in the power of product imaging and determined he would use this to promote what we now term the Heineken "brand".

Even after the company's empire had grown beyond his wildest expectations, he continued to take a keen interest in the minutiae of its advertising campaigns and logo design, although he also found time to be the architect of its financial success, too.

A huge character, he survived three weeks as a kidnap victim in 1983, but eventually succumbed, as he had predicted, to the consequences of "too much smoking".

ill-fated "Skol project", which sought to create a new, pan-European beer brand, was born here, as was the world of beer's first and arguably greatest marketing man, Freddie Heineken (*see* panel, opposite).

By 1970, most small-scale commercial brewing had disappeared from the Netherlands and those independent brewers that remained simply aped the beers of larger producers. Even the brewery at the Trappist abbey of Koningshoeven near Tilburg (*see* p.139) produced mainly a blond lager called Abdij Pilsener.

The Dutch beer revival began around 1975, when a string of independent cafés started to sell unusual bottled beers, mainly imported from Belgium and elsewhere. The consumer group PINT (rhymes with "mint") followed in 1980.

Interest built in a traditional seasonal beer style, the dark autumn lager called *bok*, which to this day is the only type of beer sold at the country's national beer festival, held each October.

To most Dutch people, beer is a ritually poured, blond, foam-topped drink made by one of two global corporations with a national connection. Curious beer drinkers still tend to drink Belgian.

INDEPENDENT DUTCH BREWERIES ▲

All but seven of the 84 smaller breweries operating in the Netherlands in 2011 were founded since 1980. Only two are run by multinationals. Omitted from the map are the 20 or so firms that hire breweries (sometimes along with their brewers) to make own-brand beers.

The older regional brewers that survived the era of standardization – Budel, Gulpener (*see* pp.138–9), Alfa, and Lindeboom – dotted along the Belgian border in north Brabant and Limburg have taken a while to start trading on their independence.

In the 1980s, new microbreweries emerged that rejected the mainstream styles of the larger corporations but also, sadly, ignored their technical standards. Yeast infections and

other forms of spoiling became a routine hazard, as naive owners tried to save money by skimping on key production safeguards.

In recent years, a new wave of entrepreneurial craft brewers has emerged, as good at mastering technique as they are at shocking the old order. One of these, De Molen of Bodegraven (*see* p.138), near Gouda, south of Amsterdam, has also mastered the art of world-class presentation of its bottles.

Dutch craft brewing has a long way to go to catch up with the rest of northern Europe, but at least its ship has now left the harbour.

Left: The shadow of brewing giant Heineken looms large over the Netherlands, but smaller Dutch breweries are making progress.

Bok & Meibok

The Dutch *bokbier* tradition is in one way an extension of German *Bockbier* (*see* pp.92–3), learned by Dutch brewers from German colleagues in the late nineteenth century, and in another way the custom of using up the previous year's residual malt shortly after harvest time (*herfst*) to brew an extra-strong beer for consumption in the autumn.

The first week of October sees virtually every Dutch brewer launch a seasonal dark brew that is typically available from the brewery only for a couple of weeks. There was a time when every one of these was a dark lager of exactly 6.5% ABV, within a narrow range of caramel sweetness, backed by low to medium hopping.

The last two decades have seen style creep. Most are now ales, colour runs from dark amber to jet black, and the alcohol content has been nudged upwards. A couple contain wheat or are smoked.

Mei- ("May") or *lente-* ("spring") *bok* is a more recent development, the honeyed sweetness of these generally light amber ales

Right: Jong & Onbedorven (or Young & Unspoilt), the *meibok* from De Molen; the first Dutch brewers to enjoy rock-star status among their fans.

and lagers being more obviously related to German *Maibock* (*see* p.92). These appear in the first week of April, exactly six months out of synch with their autumnal equivalents, but have been receding recently.

The tradition of broaching a *nieuwjaarsbier* ("New Year beer") on 1st January has been succeeded by "winter beers", typically first appearing in late November, thus ending the opportunity to launch a summer style in the first week of July to complete an agreeably neat marketing cycle.

Opposite: The Dutch beer consumers group PINT presents several beer fests, including the Meibokfestival (pictured) in spring and Bokbierfestival in autumn.

BEER SELECTION

BUDELS HERFSTBOK (6.5%)
Budelse Brouwerij BV, Budel
(North Brabant)
This old family brewery's autumn *bok* is in the classic bottom-fermented style (*see* p.20), made dark and caramel by the use of *Münchener* (Munich) malt; a beery equivalent of lightly roasted chestnuts.
www.budels.nl

CHRISTOFFEL BIER (6%)
Sint Christoffel Bier BV, Roermond (Limburg)
Unfiltered, unpasteurized, rugged blond lager fermented in open vessels before lagering (*see* p.22), ending bitter with a well-formed body. The best Dutch lager.
www.christoffelbier.nl

DE HEMEL GODELIEF (5%)
Stadsbrouwerij De Hemel, Nijmegen
(Gelderland)
A good example of the plain style of slightly sweet, not quite spicy, and smooth pale ale preferred by Dutch beer drinkers, available mainly at the superb brewpub-hotel-restaurant where it is made.
www.brouwerijdehemel.nl

DE MOLEN HEL & VERDOEMENIS (11.9%)
Brouwerij de Molen, Bodegraven
(North Holland)
This imperial Russian stout is brewed with authentic specialist ingredients to make it one of the biggest and finest beers in this book, created by a master chef of brewing.
www.brouwerijdemolen.nl

DE PRAEL JOHNNY (5.7%)
Stichting Brouwerij de Prael, Amsterdam
(North Holland)
This social enterprise firm employs people with mental health problems to create a range of pretty good craft beers in premises on the edge of Amsterdam's Red Light District, including this typically Dutch pilsner-coloured ale.
www.deprael.nl

EMELISSE RAUCHBIER (6.2%)
Bierbrouwerij Emelisse,
Kamperland (Zeeland)
Smoked dark-amber ale, with the smokiness found more in the body than the nose, made by emerging heroes who understand consistency and technical quality.
www.emelisse.nl

GULPENER LENTE BOCK (6.5%)

Gulpener Bierbrouwerij, Gulpen (Limburg)
The most experimental of the longer-
established independent Dutch breweries
makes this typical unpasteurized, golden
amber, clear, honeyed, herbal-edged
spring bok.
www.gulpener.nl

JOPEN EXTRA STOUT (5.5%)

Jopen BV, Haarlem (North Holland)
Bitter, dryish stout brewed in a former
church. Like an Irish stout but with dark
chocolate on the palate and café espresso
in the finish.
www.jopen.nl

KLEIN DUIMPJE HILLEGOMS TARWE BIER (5.5%)

Huisbrouwerij Klein Duimpje, Hillegom
(South Holland)
The "Little Thumb" is one of the most
consistent Dutch picobreweries, producing
up to 30 beers each year, of which this
light, spicy wheat beer is as good as any.
www.kleinduimpje.nl

LA TRAPPE QUADRUPEL (10%)

Brouwerij De Koningshoeven,
Berkel-Enschot (North Brabant)
The only Trappist brewery outside Belgium,
which invented the term quadrupel in
1991 to describe a new, strong, sweet
winter brew. The beer has gained greater
respect in recent years, since ageing in a
mix of old port barrels and on new oak
has brought greater complexity.
www.latrappe.nl

Other Dutch Beers

In contrast to the conformity and orderliness of the large-scale Dutch brewers, patterns of production among the newer, smaller ones, now numbering nearly 80, are virtually impossible to spot.

The country's lone Trappist brewery (*see* p.139) is now operated by Bavaria, an independent family brewer that otherwise concentrates on making canned beers for supermarket contracts. In the abbey brewery, however, it makes some increasingly experimental fine strong ales for the order.

Microbreweries like Sint Christoffel of Roermond (*see* p.138) took a couple of decades to expand their range beyond one or two beers, but others find making less than a dozen varieties in their first year an unacceptable constraint.

While only a handful brew solely for one café, few have any substantial presence in the beer trade or in local bars and eateries. Sense of pride in one's local brewery is not yet a prominent feature of the Dutch beer scene. The sticking point might be quality.

At the top of the tree, some craft brewers, including those from which we have chosen our selection, usually deliver reliable production quality. However, standards elsewhere can be embarrassingly poor, as owners and brewers try to hide the use of cut-price ingredients or poor technique behind the "folksy" and "alternative" nature of their products.

For the best of what is to come, we recommend following the gradual development of Menno Olivier's brewery De Molen (*see* p.138) and its associated restaurant, where international beer styles old and new are re-created and sometimes even invented, with great aplomb.

Above: Koningshoeven Abbey, near Tilburg.

WHEN YOU ARE THERE

- Dutch craft beers are found mainly in specialist beer shops and a few cafés.
- For up-to-date information, try the Dutch beer portal www.cambrinus.nl.
- Bars with peanuts expect the shells to be thrown on the floor to keep it oiled.
- Must see: a traditional smoke-stained brown café (*kroeg*) while stocks last.
- Must drink: beers from every Dutch brewery at the 't Arendsnest in Amsterdam (90 Herengracht).

Opposite: La Trappe, at present the only Trappist beers brewed outside Belgium, being savoured by an admirer.

BEER SELECTION

MOMMERIETE BLOND (6%)
Mommeriete, Gramsbergen (Overijssel)
Husband-and-wife team brewing world-class beers on a small scale in the Protestant north. This full-on rustic blond ale mixes great yeast-shaped, grassy-hoppy character into a sound malt base.
www.mommeriete.nl

VAN VOLLENHOVEN'S EXTRA STOUT (7%)
De Schans, Uithoorn (North Holland)
This tiny brewery near Schiphol Airport produces a wide range of beer, of which the steadiest is this re-creation of *kopstout*, or "heady stout", once made by Heineken.
www.schansbier.nl

SCANDINAVIA & THE BALTIC

If any part of the world embodies the unexpected nature of the revival of top-quality brewing, it is Scandinavia. The nations that lie between the Baltic Sea and Europe's icy north have taken on "craft beer" as a cultural obsession.

Unlike other parts of the beer-drinking world, the destruction inflicted on Scandinavian brewing in the twentieth century did not come from Europe's 1914–8 war, which did cause problems sourcing raw materials but brought little of the economic devastation seen farther south. Rather, it came from self-inflicted wounds.

Born out of an odd mix of religious conviction and concern for public health, a fetishistic belief in the evil of alcohol has pervaded the politics of Scandinavia and the Baltic for a century and remains an issue. People here, it seems, prefer to elect politicians who take the potential lethality of alcohol far more seriously than its life-enhancing properties.

While only Norway and Iceland ever voted to criminalize the trade in alcohol, all bar the Danes introduced tight controls on its production, importation, and sale. As well as giving governments a sense of control over alcoholism, this generated, through the imposition of impressive levels of "sin tax", considerable cash for their treasuries.

Alcohol in beer was often taxed more punitively than that in wine, as beer drinkers were considered in greater need of protection from their own proclivities. Additionally, while Europe's winemakers have for centuries been a powerful political lobby, its beer makers have preferred jovial internecine combat, ensuring that such liberties went unquestioned for decades.

Ironically, it was this high taxation that eventually fuelled the return to making bigger, stronger beers. Emerging craft brewers reasoned that, if beer drinkers were condemned to pay an exorbitant price for the ordinary, they may as well pay a little more for something excellent.

The earliest stirrings of the Scandinavian beer revival were in the last years of the old millennium. Denmark has enjoyed the most success, although Sweden, Norway, Finland, and Iceland (*see* panel, p.144) have all made remarkable progress against steeper odds.

Above: The remote Faroe Islands, between Iceland and the Shetlands, are home to one long-established family brewery and a more recent craft producer.

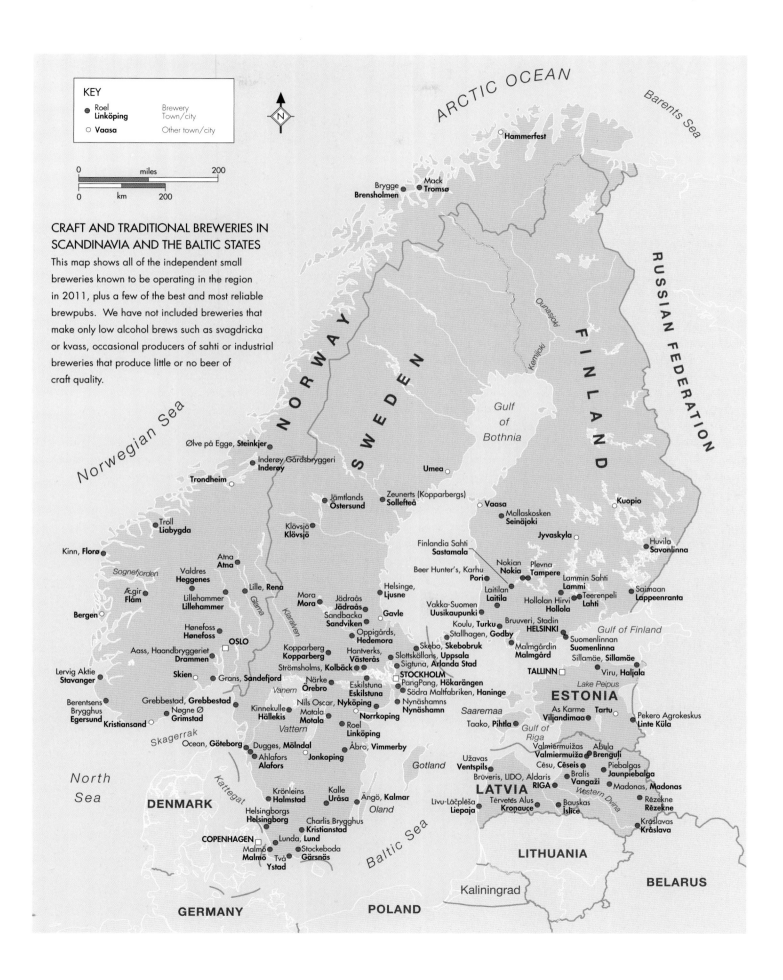

KEY

● Roel **Linköping** — Brewery Town/city

○ **Vaasa** — Other town/city

miles 0 — 200

km 0 — 200

CRAFT AND TRADITIONAL BREWERIES IN SCANDINAVIA AND THE BALTIC STATES

This map shows all of the independent small breweries known to be operating in the region in 2011, plus a few of the best and most reliable brewpubs. We have not included breweries that make only low alcohol brews such as svagdricka or kvass, occasional producers of sahti or industrial breweries that produce little or no beer of craft quality.

ARCTIC OCEAN

Barents Sea

Hammerfest

Brygge **Brensholmen** Mack **Tromsø**

RUSSIAN FEDERATION

Ounasjoki

Kemijoki

N O R W A Y

S W E D E N

F I N L A N D

Gulf of Bothnia

Norwegian Sea

Ølve på Egge, **Steinkjer**

Inderøy Gårdsbryggeri **Inderøy**

Trondheim

Umea

Jämtlands **Östersund** Zeunerts (Kopparbergs) **Sollefteå** **Vaasa** **Kuopio**

Mallaskosken **Seinäjoki**

Jyvaskyla

Huvila **Savonlinna**

Troll **Liabygda**

Klövsjö **Klövsjö**

Finlandia Sahti **Sastamala**

Kinn, **Florø**

Nokian **Nokia** Plevna **Tampere**

Sognefjorden

Atna **Atna**

Beer Hunter's, Karhu **Pori**

Lammin Sahti **Lammi**

Valdres **Heggenes**

Helsinge, **Ljusne**

Laitilan **Laitila** Teerenpeli **Lahti**

Ægir **Flåm**

Lille, **Rena**

Lillehammer **Lillehammer**

Mora **Mora** Jädraås **Jädraås**

Vakka-Suomen **Uusikaupunki** Hollolan Hirvi **Hollola**

Saimaan **Lappeenranta**

Bergen

Sandbacka **Sandviken** **Gavle**

Koulu, **Turku**

Bruuveri, Stadin

Gläma

Klaralven

Oppigårds **Hedemora**

Stallhagen, **Godby** **HELSINKI**

Gulf of Finland

Hønefoss **Hønefoss**

Kopparberg **Kopparberg**

Hantverks **Västerås**

Skebo, **Skebobruk**

Malmgården **Malmgård**

Suomenlinnan **Suomenlinna**

Aass, Haandbryggeriet **Drammen**

OSLO

Strömsholms, **Kolbäck**

Slottskällans, **Uppsala**

Sillamäe **Sillamäe**

Lervig Aktie **Stavanger**

Skien

Närke **Örebro**

Sigtuna, **Arlanda Stad**

STOCKHOLM

TALLINN

Viru, **Haljala**

Grans, **Sandefjord**

Eskilstuna **Eskilstuna**

PangPang, **Hökarängen**

Berentsens Brygghus **Egersund**

Grebbestad, **Grebbestad**

Nøgne Ø **Grimstad**

Vanern

Nils Oscar, **Nyköping**

Södra Maltfabriken, **Haninge**

ESTONIA

Lake Peipus

Kristiansand

Kinnekulle **Hällekis**

Motala **Motala**

Nynäshamns **Nynäshamn**

Saaremaa

As Karme **Viljandimaa**

Tartu

Pekero Agrokeskus **Linte Küla**

Vattern

Roel **Linköping**

Norrkoping

Taako, **Pihtla**

Gulf of Riga

Ocean, **Göteborg**

Dugges, **Mölndal**

Åbro, **Vimmerby**

Gotland

Uzavas **Ventspils**

Valmiermuižas **Valmiermuiža**

Abula **Brenguļi**

Ahlafors **Alafors**

Jonkoping

Cēsu, **Cēseis**

Piebalgas **Jaunpiebalga**

North Sea

Kattegat

Krönleins **Halmstad**

Kalle **Uråsa**

Ängö, **Kalmar** Oland

Bruveris, LIDO, Aldaris **RIGA**

Bralis **Vangaži**

Madonas, **Madonas**

Livu-Lāčplēša **Liepaja**

Tērvetēs Alus **Kronauce**

Bauskas **Īslīce**

Rēzekne **Rēzekne**

DENMARK

Helsingborgs **Helsingborg**

Charlis Brygghus **Kristianstad**

LATVIA

Western Dvina

Kråslavas **Kråslava**

COPENHAGEN

Lunda, **Lund**

Malmö **Malmö**

Tvá **Ystad**

Stockeboda **Gärsnäs**

Baltic Sea

LITHUANIA

BELARUS

Kaliningrad

GERMANY

POLAND

At times, the speed of development has been so great that even assiduous locals have found it hard to stay abreast, progress being made possible in part by the dog that did not bark in the night.

While it would be wrong to credit the Copenhagen-based Carlsberg group of companies with instigating the craft-beer revolution in the region, it was highly significant that the group put up less-than-total resistance to its emergence. Indeed, in some cases they even provided training, practical assistance, and moral support to aspiring newcomers.

Their reasons were not entirely based on altruism or comradeship. Carlsberg knew that other global brewers were lined up to take chunks out of their home market, backed by massive resources. While the products from these incomers had little to recommend them, they would have the advantage of being new, so some in Carlsberg reasoned that allowing a rash of genuinely innovative small-scale producers might usefully queer their rivals' pitch.

They have even followed through with some interesting beers of their own, commercializing a microbrewery (Jacobsen – *see* p.146) on their Copenhagen site and ensuring the continued production of various strong porters at breweries they own in each of the countries around the Baltic rim.

Porters and stouts have been around this part of the world for 250 years, but this is just a bat of the eye in comparison with the folk origins of *sahti*, a home brew flavoured with juniper, which clings on in Finland and parts of Estonia (*see* p.152).

The Baltic States – Estonia, Latvia, and Lithuania – emerged from 70 years of communist control with their own challenges. Each had a long tradition of brewing that had been lost or else gone underground during Soviet times, only re-emerging at the end of the occupation.

In total, there are now roughly 300 breweries in Scandinavia and the Baltic. The vast majority are new, but many already produce well-made beers of great integrity, including some of the finest on the planet.

Small brewers in the region are well set to capitalize not only on the rising interest in fine beer in growing markets throughout the Western world, but also, when the time comes, to rerun history by responding to the eventual import demands of their waking neighbour – mother Russia.

ICELAND'S ANNUAL BEER DAY

When Ronald Reagan met Mikhail Gorbachev to discuss nuclear disarmament in Reykjavik in 1986, they could not share a beer, as to do so would have been illegal. Their talks ended without agreement.

All alcohol was banned in Iceland by a referendum that took effect in 1915. Wine reappeared in 1921, after a Spanish boycott of Icelandic fish, and in 1935 a further referendum reinstated spirits.

Beer of over 2.25% ABV remained illegal until March 1, 1989. While drinking beer in Iceland remains an expensive hobby, several new breweries have sprung up since then. Beer liberation is still celebrated each year on the anniversary of its legalization, with pubs staying open until 4am.

NEW ICELANDIC BEERS

ISLENSKUR ÚRVALS STOUT (5.8%)
Viking Ölgerd, Akureyri
This unlikely black beer is made at a brewery five hours' drive from its nearest neighbour, in Iceland's second city, a north-coast port with an ice-free harbour.
www.vifilfell.is

KALDI DÖKKUR (5%)
Bruggsmidjan ehf, Dalvík Árskógssandur
Icelanders being out of practice, this 2005 start-up called on a Czech brew master to shape its two lagers, the darker ending more assertive than the lighter.
www.bruggsmidjan.is

LAVA (9.4%)
Ölvisholt Brugghús, Selfoss
The finest achievement of modern Icelandic brewing is this amazing, top-class smoked imperial stout, which hit the beer world, as it will your palate, like a volcanic eruption.
www.brugghus.is

Denmark

In 1995, a well-researched trip to Copenhagen yielded two basic ales from a newly established brewpub in the city centre, plus a couple of half-interesting porters from larger producers. Nothing else crossed the radar. Venturing outside of the capital would have added little more.

THE CRAFT BREWERIES OF DENMARK ▼
Denmark is one of the crucibles of the craft beer movement in Europe, its smaller breweries setting the standards that others in Scandinavia aim to beat. Industrial breweries are not shown.

Less than two decades on, Denmark has well over 100 breweries. Almost all of these have pulled on the finest habits of the American new wave, classical German, older British brewing styles, and the ingenious end of the Belgian brewing spectrum to create countless beers that range from local takes on simpler styles to experimental ones designed to shock even the most world-weary beer hunter.

There is no such thing as a typical Danish craft brewery. Some originated as brewpubs, others were created by enthusiastic home brewers, and a few arrived with business plans written by graduate brewers with a second business degree. A handful result from little more than artistry and imagination.

The country's most acclaimed new-wave brewery company, Mikkeller (see p.147), does not even own a commercial-sized brewery, its principal product being owner-brewer Mikkel Borg Bjergsø himself. His reputation is such that various brewers, both domestic and international, number among his apostles, acolytes, and heroes, many of whom let him turn up at their doors and brew in their kit.

As everywhere, the most successful of these new businesses combine rigorous technical quality with an eye for a winning style, a desire to add recognizably homespun originality, and a sound understanding of business. Many find their sales split between their localities and some far-off export market such as North America.

Ironically, the many fine specialist beer cafés that have sprung up in the capital, Copenhagen (København), more often serve Belgian and American beers than these home-grown creations, despite the fact that the small brewery sector has taken four per cent of the Danish beer market

in roughly a decade. The reputation of new-wave producers is for audaciously challenging convention in a conservative beer market.

Some old hands fear that too great a gap is growing between "the regular beer drinker" and those seeking ever more extreme brews. However, in practice, newer brewers appear to be taking different paths to immortality, some specializing in so-called extreme beers, others moving to brighten

up the mainstream. Most seem to produce at least one imaginatively hopped pale ale, plus a few porters or stouts. It may well be that, in time, "typically Danish" beers will emerge from within these, through the application of a high-tech approach to old brewing traditions.

Today, the craft-brewing scene in Denmark seems both disparate and confident. If you know where to go, you will find dark beers that stretch from soft and toffee-sweet to hard, acrid, and desert-dry, in strengths as low as two per cent and as high as 13 per cent, and encompassing flavours that are recognizably light Irish, lagered Baltic, or imperial Russian, some with additional coffee grounds, cocoa powder, coconut or vanilla extract, and even chilli.

The new brewers seem to have no idea where they are heading, but we have enough confidence to suspect that they will know when they get there. With the madness of adolescence behind it, the best days of craft brewing in Denmark are surely yet to come.

BEST-SELLING LOCAL LABELS

Albani	(National)
Ceres	(National)
Faxe	(National)
Tuborg	(Carlsberg)
Wiibroe	(Carlsberg)

Above: Once a city awash with golden lager, Copenhagen is now one of northern Europe's great beer destinations, with breweries, brewpubs, beer bars and an enthusiastic public to partake of it all.

BEER SELECTION

BLACK MAGIC WOMAN (9.9%)
Hornbeer, Kirke Hyllinge (Sjælland)
A huge stout made with both wood- and peat-smoked malts tops an extraordinary range of beers from an inventive brewery that always rises to a challenge, often successfully.
www.hornbeer.dk

BØGEDAL (5.5–7.3%)
Bøgedal Bryghus, Vejle (Syddanmark)
This unique, wood-loving, gravity-powered folk producer of godtøl – or ancient Scandinavian oak-aged ales – creates one-off beers distinguished only by their batch number, in a range of apparently authentic styles.
www.boegedal.com

DET LILLE BRYGGERI INDIAN PALE ALE (7.5%)
Det Lille Bryggeri, Ringsted (Sjælland)
Typical of the reverential type of American-style IPA found commonly among newer Danish breweries, including this accomplished, if rather shy, one.
www.detlillebryggeri.dk

FYNSK FORÅR (4.8%)
Ørbæk Bryggeri, Ørbæk (Nyborg)
This organic wheat beer with spelt and oats in its mash gets to taste of permanent springtime through the additional tang of elderflowers, with a yeast-hop underlay that unmistakably says rustic.
www.oerbaek-bryggeri.nu

INFANTØL (2.8%)
Beer Here, Køge (Sjælland)
The room for error in light beers is relatively small, the full flavour in this modern take on Malzbier (caramel beer), speaking volumes about its creators' skills with the rest of their excellent range.
www.beerhere.dk

ISTEDGADE HIPSTER ALE (5.5%)
Evil Twin Brewing, Copenhagen
Mikkel Bjergsø's (see p.145) twin brother Jeppe has taken to brewing his own range of beers, with this American pale ale pointing to a less-acrobatic direction of travel that is worth watching.
www.facebook.com/EvilTwinBrewing

JACOBSEN EXTRA (5.5%)
Huisbryggeriet Jacobsen, Copenhagen
Carlsberg's play brewery has produced a few great beers since opening in 2005, although this is a well-made ordinary pilsner from 100 per cent organic malt and German noble hop varieties.
www.jacobsenbryg.dk

LIMFJORDS PORTER (7.9%)
Thisted Bryghus, Thisted (Nordjylland)
From one of Denmark's longer-established regional breweries comes this re-creation of a legendary "double brown stout" from Aalborg, made with malted rye and English liquorice.
www.thisted-bryghus.dk

MIDTFYNS ALE (6.5%)
Midtfyns Bryghus, Broby (Syddanmark)
This middle-market craft brewery, founded in 2004, makes reliable stouts and wheat beers, plus two English "special bitters" – this one and the strong Gunners.
www.midtfyns-bryghus.dk

MIKKELLER BEER GEEK BREAKFAST (7.5% AND UP)

Mikkeller, Copenhagen
Among the 200 beers created by Mikkeller since 2007, this "breakfast accompaniment" (ho, ho) is the nearest to a hardy perennial – a jet-black, lightly smoked, chocolate-oatmeal stout brewed with gourmet coffee beans.
www.mikkeller.dk

NØRREBRO PACIFIC SUMMER ALE (5.6%)

Nørrebro Bryghus, Copenhagen
Perhaps the foremost of Denmark's many brewpubs, assisted by being in the capital, was making this appealingly citrus, New Zealand-hopped pale ale long before they became fashionable.
www.noerrebrobryghus.dk

OKKARA PORTARI (5.8%)

Okkara, Velbastaður (Faroe Islands)
The North Atlantic's Faroe Islands are a self-governing province of Denmark, and home to two independent breweries making a dozen pleasant beers, of which this liquorice porter is the best.
www.okkara.fo

RAASTED TRIPPEL NELSON (10.8%)

Raasted Bryghus, Randers (Midtjylland)
Great chefs recognize flavour combinations that work, as with this perhaps overly strong *tripel* flavoured with New Zealand Nelson Sauvin. The get-up-and-dance beer from a great range.
www.raasted-bryghus.dk

SORT HVEDE (6.5%)

Indslev Bryggeri, Åby (Syddanmark)
This revival of an old brewhouse specializes in non-barley beers, adding malted rye to this black wheat beer-cum-oatmeal stout, with a smoked-fish nuance. They do a spelt *Bock*, too.
www.indslevbryggeri.dk

SUNDBY STOUT (6.2%)

Amager Bryghus, Kastrup (Hovedstaden)
These magnificent producers of all kinds of beer excel with this clever, medium-strength, coffee, chocolate, and liquorice-wearing stout, with delicate floral hopping that lasts throughout.
www.amagerbryghus.dk

SVANEKE MØRK GULD (5.7%)

Svaneke Bryghus, Svaneke, Bornholm (Hovedstaden)
One of the first (established in 2000) and smartest micros, from the eastern island of Bornholm, now makes single-hop pilsners and numerous oddities like this well-made amber lager.
www.svanekebryghus.dk

Norway

The ancient Gulating code stipulated that any Norwegian farmer who did not brew ale (*øl*) would be fined. Beer lovers in Norway might yet demand its reinstatement.

BEST-SELLING LOCAL LABELS

Borg	(Heineken)
Hansa	(Heineken)
Lysholmer	(Carlsberg)
Munkholm	(Carlsberg)
Ringnes	(Carlsberg)

In the nineteenth century, concerns about alcoholism and domestic violence found their voice in Norway's Lutheran Church. Independence from Sweden in 1905 was soon followed by universal suffrage, a critical precursor to the 1921 decision to prohibit trade in alcohol.

This ruling was short-lived, as the French reacted to the loss of this wine market by excluding Norwegian fish from France. The political compromise that followed created a state-controlled network of alcohol producers, importers, and retailers called the *Vinmonopolet* (or "wine monopoly").

Ninety years on, the monopoly is confined to take-home sales of wines, spirits, and "stronger beers" – *i.e.* those over 4.5% ABV – and is a modern chain of well-stocked retailers selling super-taxed goods.

The market is dominated by Ringnes (part of Carlsberg) and Hansa Borg (Heineken), with only two established independent breweries, Aass and Mack (*see* below and opposite),

having survived the twentieth century. Production is mostly blond lager and lower-tax light beers (*lettøl*), with some darker lagers. Deep amber *bayer* is based on *Münchener*, *bock* is dark, autumnal, and more Dutch than German, while Christmas sees *juleøl*.

Above: Nøgne Ø's Grimstad brewery is located within a converted hydro-electric plant.

Then, in 2002, came Nøgne Ø ("Naked Island") and its strapline, *Det Kompromissløse Bryggeri* (The Uncompromising Brewery) (*see* opposite). Its name refers to Norwegian playwright Henrik Ibsen's description of a weather-beaten outcrop off Norway's southern coast. The brewery's bold experiments immediately impressed, its massively framed beers selling successfully at equally large prices in enough Oslo bars to prove that there is always a market for excellence.

They soon attracted importers from abroad and a trade formed into which others have followed, causing Norwegian craft brewers to gain a reputation for daring journeys that their Viking forebears would appreciate, although their contributions to the nation's wealth might be improved if the wind were less icy.

Opposite: Fermenters at Nøgne Ø. The southern Norwegian brewery is the vanguard in the country's youthful but growing craft-brewing movement.

BEER SELECTION

AASS BOCK (6.5%)
Aass, Drammen (Buskerud)
Considered one of the best Norwegian *bocks*, its full-grain, caramel-laced, deep, dark styling has more in common with the Netherlands than Germany.
www.aass.no

ÆGIR INDIA PALE ALE (6.5%)
Ægir Bryggeri, Flåm (Sogn og Fjordane)
By the famous Flåm railhead, at the upper reach of Aurlandsfjord, comes this IPA, its firm, not-too-bitter hopping balanced just the right side of extremity.
www.flamsbrygga.no

ATNA STABBURØL (4.7 %)
Atna Øl, Atna (Hedmark)
A lightish lager made with 100 per cent malt and hops by a new small brewery that has yet to produce classic ales but does simpler beers well.
www.atnaol.no

HAAND BRYGGERIET NORWEGIAN WOOD (6.5%)
Haand Bryggeriet, Drammen (Buskerud)
This memorable dark ale re-creates old-style Norwegian farmhouse brewing, using wood-smoked malt and fresh juniper (twigs and all), to create something near to *sahti* (see p.152).
www.haandbryggeriet.net

KINN SJELEFRED (4.7%)
Kinn Bryggeri, Florø (Sogn og Fjordane)
The big beers from this micro all get rave reviews, but the simple confidence of this plainer, roasty brown ale shows raw talent.
www.kinnbryggeri.no

LUCKY JACK (4.7%)
Lervig Aktiebryggeri, Stavanger (Rogaland)
Although the product range darts about a bit, this local take on an American pale ale is becoming a mainstay and stands its ground with the best.
www.lervig.no

MACK JULEØL (6.5%)
Macks Ølbryggeri, Tromsø (Troms)
Famed as the world's northernmost brewery, Mack's high-tech standards are shown off well in this, the stronger of two lightly spiced Christmas beers.
www.mack.no

NØGNE Ø IMPERIAL STOUT (9%)
Nøgne Ø, Grimstad (Aust-Agder)
Norway's original and best craft brewery makes beers that, like this one, ping every taste-bud on the palate.
www.nogne-o.com

Sweden

With the sole exceptions of Norway and Singapore, Sweden is the most expensive brewing nation anywhere on Earth in which to buy a beer.

The system of alcohol control is tough but both logical and generally even-handed. The only exception is that direct advertising of beers above 3.5% ABV is not allowed, while the European Union has insisted that wines and spirits may be advertised – those lobbyists again. The drinking age is 20, photo-ID is checked for any customer who looks under 25, and those caught handing alcoholic drinks to children in public can be prosecuted.

The state-owned Systembolaget chain of drinks stores holds the retail monopoly for all beers above 3.5% ABV, although none would fault its range of nearly 1,200 different brands, including those from local microbreweries and many of the world's finest producers. While it clearly sees its primary social role as the control of alcohol provision, it also claims to make its full product range available across the whole country via its 420 stores and over 500 order points serving smaller communities.

Above: Sweden's Systembolaget drinks stores sometimes carry a phenomenal range of craft beers from around the world – but at a price.

BEER SELECTION

BARONEN BARLEY WINE (12.7%)
Hantverksbryggeriet, Västerås (Västmanland)
This creative new brewery, founded in 2003 and led by its heart as much as its head, makes much-loved ales like this wilfully strong barley wine, full of dried-fruit flavours and designed to be kept forever.
www.hantverksbryggeriet.se

DUGGES BOLLOX! (7.8%)
Dugges Ale- & Porterbryggeri, Mölndal (Västra Götaland)
Forgive the name – the owners are still young – yet their beers are born of live minds capable of creating this sweet, fruity, flower-powered strongish IPA, flavoured with Centennial hops.
www.dugges.se

HELL (5.1%)
Jämtlands Bryggeri, Östersund (Jämtland)
One of Sweden's longest-established micros, producing a dozen beers, including this blond lager packed with flavour from Yorkshire malt and Slovenian hops. The dark version is called Heaven.
www.jamtlandsbryggeri.se

KAGGEN! STORMAKTS PORTER (9.5%)
Närke Kulturbryggeri, Örebro (Örebro)
Sweden's most challenging brewery, founded in 2003, creates several versions of this imperial stout, this example creating one of the most impressive taste sensations of any beer in this book or elsewhere.
www.kulturbryggeri.se

Exporting beer to Sweden can, however, carry risks, as one monastic brewery discovered to its embarrassment a few years back. The Swedish authorities not only regularly check that the alcohol content declared on the label is correct but they also inform their counterparts in the country of origin if they discover any anomalies.

The number of breweries in the country peaked around the end of the nineteenth century and hit an all-time low of 13 in 1990, although since then around 50 breweries and brewpubs have opened. The market is dominated by Carlsberg's Pripps and Falcon brands, followed by those from local yet unimaginative Spendrups and the brewing arm of cider maker Kopparbergs.

The average Swedish beer drinker still takes light lager to be the norm, but this is slowly changing as newer breweries adopt an uncoordinated two-pronged approach of creating a few memorably fabulous beers at the top end of the spectrum and an increasingly impressive array of well-made beers in simpler styles at the other.

Right: In a country with fewer than 10 million people, nearly 600 inhabited islands and high tax on alcohol, Swedish craft brewers like to think small and stay top quality.

NILS OSCAR RÖKPORTER (5.9%)
Nils Oscar Company AB, Nyköping (Södermanland)
One of Sweden's earliest microbreweries sets the standards others must beat, this smoked porter standing out from a steady range that runs from blond lager to imperial stout.
www.nilsoscar.se

OCEAN BRYGGERIET JULÖL (5.8%)
Ocean Bryggeriet, Göteborg (Västra Götaland)
Gothenburg brewery that is producing a changeable range of well-made light and medium beers in numerous popular and craft styles, this one a typical old-style Christmas beer.
www.oceanbryggeriet.se

OPPIGÅRDS AMARILLO (5.9%)
Oppigårds Bryggeri, Hedemora (Dalarna)
Successful small brewery based on an old family farm, making a range that includes some single-hop pale ales that began with this beautifully restrained beer, softened by some wheat.
www.oppigards.com

SIGTUNA EXTRA BITTER (5.6%)
Sigtuna Brygghus, Arlandastad (Stockholm)
This Challenger-hopped British-style bitter would be seen as strong in its home country, but here it fits the portfolio of a specialist in lighter styles.
www.sigtunabrygghus.se

SLOTTSKÄLLANS RED ALE (5%)
Slottskällans Bryggeri, Uppsala (Uppsala)
This well-established but safety-conscious microbrewery makes mainly elegant versions of simpler beer styles, such as this Munich-malted, Swedish-tilted "Irish" red ale.
www.slottskallan.se

SMÖRPUNDET PORTER (5%)
Nynäshamns Ångbryggeri, Nynäshamn (Stockholm)
Successful micro concentrating on perfecting brews such as this straightforward, lightish porter, which must be one of the tastiest regular-strength beers in the world.
www.nyab.se

Finland

A quarter of the Finnish population lives in or around its capital, Helsinki, and most of the rest live in the country's southern third, which is why its 30 or so craft breweries appear to huddle here, with Tampere having become a new brewing centre.

BEST-SELLING LOCAL LABELS

Hartwall	(Heineken)
Lapin Kulta	(Heineken)
Olvi	(National)
Sinebrychoff	(Carlsberg)

It is remarkable that any new breweries emerge in this nation, given the Finnish politicians' obsession with taxing and otherwise restricting locally made beers beyond people-friendly limits. Microbreweries and brewpubs contribute only 1.5 per cent of beer production but most of the originality in Finland, a market that sees 90 per cent made by Sinebrychoff (owned by Carlsberg), Hartwall (Heineken), or Olvi, which also imports many of the beers that account for the rest.

The country's nationwide chain of state-owned liquor stores, Alko, stocks hundreds of imported beers, yet it is reluctant to sell brews from small native producers. Meanwhile, other shops and supermarkets are barred from selling beer above 4.7% ABV and pub sales have halved in a decade as the population takes to drinking at home to minimize the cost.

The political belief that high taxation affords protection against alcohol problems is undermined by the massive importation by ordinary Finns of beer via the Estonian ferry, equivalent each year to double the total amount sold by Alko.

It is hard to imagine worse conditions in which to be a craft brewer, let alone to try to preserve one of the world's longest-surviving traditions of folk brewing – the heavy, dark beers known as *sahti* (*see* panel, left).

A UNESCO WORLD HERITAGE BEER?

Always largely the domain of the home brewer, *sahti* (a word of two distinct syllables) may be as old as Nordic civilization itself.

Traditionally, it was brewed in a hollowed-out tree trunk, heat and caramel coming from the addition of red-hot stones to a mash of malted barley, sweetened perhaps by rye or wheat. The wort is then filtered through juniper before being top-fermented by baker's yeast to add banana to the mélange of flavours (*see* p.20).

High on spice but low on hops, its short shelf life renders it virtually unexportable, although you will still find it in some Helsinki beer cafés.

Opposite top left: Helsinki's Spårakoff pub tram runs tours of the city from May to August, the conductor being replaced by a drinks waiter.

Opposite bottom left: Probably the ultimate folk beer, Finnish sahti does not travel well. The curious are advised to visit Finland and drink it *in situ*.

Opposite right: Finland's two dozen craft breweries are huddled mainly in the south, where lakes and forests give way to centres of population.

BEER SELECTION

KEISARI ELOWEHNÄ (5.3%)
Nokian Panimo Oy, Nokia
This distinct remodelling of a Bavarian-style *Hefeweizen*, with lots of grain and prominent banana, comes from a micro with national distribution.
www.nokianpanimo.fi

LAITILAN KUKKO TUMMA (4.5%)
Laitilan Wirvoitusjuomatehdas Oy, Laitila
This simple, light amber lager, termed "dark", is typical of Finnish brewing in that it packs hop aroma and taste into a beer of little bitterness.
www.laitilan.com

LAMMIN SAHTI (7.5%)
Lammin Sahti Oy, Lammi
Flat as old lambic and spicy as aftershave, this hazy brown liquid cake of a beer is a rare surviving commercial example of the farm-crafted folk brew.
www.sahti.fi

MALMGÅRD X-PORTER (7.3%)
Malmgårdin Panimo Oy, Malmgård
Baltic porter from a manor-house brewery east of Helsinki that also makes light ales from ancient grains and a Finnish take on "Belgian ale" called Ceci n'est pas un Belge.
www.malmgard.fi

PRYKMESTAR SAVU KATAJA (9%)
Vakka-Suomen Panimo Oy, Uusikaupunki
Highly professional German-style set-up on
the west coast making eye-catching offbeat
lagers that include this heavy, deep-brown,
smoked-juniper-laced ruby.
www.vasp.fi

SEVERIN EXTRA IPA (5.9 %)
Koskipanimo Plevna, Tampere
The best of the Tampere brewpubs also
supplies this exquisitely hopped pale ale,
plus Sam's Stout and Siperia strong porter,
to specialist beer cafés in Helsinki.
www.plevna.fi

The Baltic States

The English word "ale" comes via the Scandinavian *øl*, which in turn is predated by the Estonian *ölu*, and *alus* from the Latvian and Lithuanian languages.

Estonia may see itself as the most advanced of the Baltic States, but in brewing it is stagnant, with global groups controlling its two largest breweries – Saku (Carlsberg) and A. Le Coq (Heineken). These dominate a market in which third-place Viru, owned by Harboe of Denmark, holds just five per cent of the share.

Sillamae (*see* below, opposite) produces good *Müncheners*, and we might have included Oü Taako's Pihtla Ölu (7% ABV) had we found any. The expansion of brewpubs beyond the Austrian-styled Beerhouse in Tallinn, which opened in 2002, is mired in red tape and risk-avoidance. Rumours of *sahti* producers on the island of Saaramaa will interest intrepid readers.

Further south, Latvia once had hundreds of breweries, most exporting beer to Imperial Russia. However, between 1915 and 1950, two wars, the Russian Revolution, anti-alcohol laws, and Soviet-style nationalization conspired to close all but two. Find the full and fascinating story at http://labsalus.lv/beer-guide/.

Nowadays, three large modern breweries, Aldaris (*see* below), Cēsu, and Lāčplēša-Līvu, each of them funded by foreign investment, produce mainly industrial beers, but a dozen or so smaller brewers supply a healthy 13 per cent of the market, taking advantage of tax breaks for those whose production stays below 50,000 hectolitres a year. The best draught beers are those that are marked *nefiltrētais* ("unfiltered"). For a more folksy style, try brews from the Krāslava and Madonas breweries.

For those with time to explore, we recommend heading for Lithuania. The country has its usual share of new brewpubs, particularly in its capital, Vilnius. But it is in the more rural north that an old culture of farmhouse and small-town brewing is starting slowly to re-emerge from the shadows. For tips, try www.alutis.lt/aludariai/.

Left: Carlsberg has invested significantly in the future of Baltic brewing, here at the Aldaris brewery in Riga, Latvia.

BEER SELECTION

ALDARIS PORTERIS (6.8%)
AS Aldaris, Riga (Latvia)
Carlsberg Latvia's quietly impressive Baltic Porter is a brown beer laced with muscatel and vanilla, putting it among that country's finest.
www.aldaris.lv .

KAUNO BIRŽIEČIŲ (8%)
Kauno Alus, Kaunas (Lithuania)
This heavy, sweet black porter may not be the finest, but it is the most noticeable of the many beers from this long-established brewer in the country's second city.
www.kaunoalus.lt

KEPTINIS (5.7%)
Kupiškio Alus, Kupiškis (Lithuania)
Track down this scruffy, sourish, cloudy brown, "naturally fermented" old-style ale and you will start to understand why we think northern Lithuania needs exploring.
www.visalietuva.lt/imones/info/
kupiskio-alus-uab

PONORAS KAIMIŠKAS NEFILTRUOTAS ŠVIESUSIS BIRŽIETIŠKAS (5.5%)
Alaus Darykla Ponoras, Biržai (Lithuania)
This organized northern brewer still makes a few delightfully disorganized brews, like this cloudy, wild blond lager, made by cold-conditioning beer from open fermenters (*see* p.22).
www.ponoras.com

Above: Vilnius, capital of Lithuania – one of the last unexplored frontiers of traditional brewing.

Next page: Snow-covered rooftops of the Old Town, Tallinn, Estonia.

SILLAMÄE MÜNCHEN VASKNE (6.3%)
Sillamäe Õlletehas, Sillamäe (Estonia)
An accomplished draught *Münchener*,
full of malt with a hint of maple, that is
made at a tiny brewery not far from the
Russian border.
www.beerguide.ee/sillamae.html

TĒRVETES ORIĢINĀLAIS (5.4%)
Agrofirma Tērvete, Kroņauce (Latvia)
Latvia's best blond lager is made on a
large farm, changing recipe from time
to time but flying a flag for higher-quality
pilsners that do not cut (many) corners.
www.tervete.lv

UŽAVAS TUMŠAIS NEFILTRĒTAIS (4.9%)
SIA Zaksi, Užavas, Ventspils (Latvia)
Unfiltered, unpasteurized amber lager with
a toffee underlay, from a well-respected
new brewery near the port city of Ventspils.
www.uzavas-alus.lv

ITALY

Italians have always drunk beer, and from 2000 – when craft brewing really began to take off – to 2009, per capita beer consumption in Italy has remained virtually unchanged. What *has* changed, however, is the way Italians drink beer.

UNIONBIRRAI IN NORTHERN ITALY ▶
The Italian craft-beer scene has undergone vigorous fermentation in recent years. Although this map shows only the member breweries of the craft-beer association Unionbirrai, representing around a quarter of the breweries currently in existence, it includes the most influential and some of the most consistent.

In the twentieth century, most of the beer consumed in Italy filled the role of refresher or restorative, pale lagers enjoyed cold and in small measures, either out of the refrigerator at home or standing at a bar. Seldom was beer thought of as a celebratory drink or a beverage for mealtimes.

With the arrival of craft breweries, all that has changed. A 2010 study by the Makno research group for the beer and malt organization Assobirra found that the number of Italians enjoying beer while eating out had more than doubled since just the previous year, and beer had actually overtaken wine as the beverage of preference for consumption outside of the home. Even where celebrations were concerned – holidays and weekends in particular – beer was found to stand head to head in popularity with wine.

What instigated this change in attitude is not only the number of craft breweries – exceeding 300 as of 2011 – but the character and quality of their beers. Few nations in the world can lay claim to such steep increases in brewery count and reliability over such a short time.

Uniquely, Italy's craft breweries have successfully focused much of their marketing efforts at the restaurant goer and fine dining enthusiast rather than the casual beer drinker, seeking to complement and sometimes replace wine in its traditional roles. They have accomplished this through a high-profile combination of aesthetics and beer style, crafting remarkably complex and food-friendly brews, and packaging and serving them in elegant bottles and glassware.

On this level, at least, Italian brewers have created one of the most innovative and intriguing craft beer markets in the world.

Below: Even in Tuscany, where wine has long ruled, craft beer is beginning to make an impact.

THE WORLD'S CRAFT BEER ECCENTRICS

In their constant quest for beer flavours that rival the nation's great wines in complexity and character, Italy's craft brewers have embraced some of the most unorthodox and inventive brewing methods and ingredients in the world. Indeed, it is becoming almost commonplace to find Italian craft beers containing spices, fruits, herbs, or other ingredients outside of the norm, from garlic powder and cardamom to gentian root and pink peppercorns.

And if the beers are not flavoured in some fashion, do not be surprised to find that they have been prepared in an odd or unusual way. Barrel ageing is, of course, far from unusual in the modern age of craft brewing, but the Italians embrace it with an enthusiasm seldom seen elsewhere, employing all manner of barrels – wine, whisky, and Cognac – and maturing their beers in them for up to several years.

If all this was not enough, one of the latest trends in ultra high-end Italian beer is sherry-style oxidation, which sees high-strength ale intentionally exposed to oxygen and carefully monitored until it reaches the desired almost sherry-like character. It is then bottled without carbonation, intended to be sipped and enjoyed over the course of days or even weeks.

Cardamom

Chestnut

Lemon

Peach

Garlic powder

Basil

Peppercorn

Sage

Watermelon

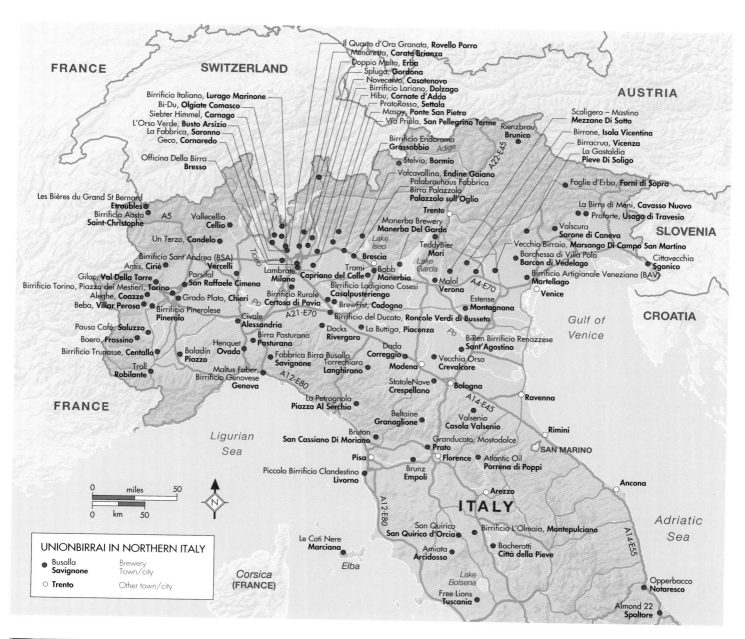

FRANCE

SWITZERLAND

AUSTRIA

SLOVENIA

CROATIA

Il Quarto d'Ora Granata, **Rovello Porro**
Menaresta, **Carate Brianza**
Doppio Malto, **Erba**
Spluga, **Gordona**
Novecento, **Casatenovo**
Birrificio Lariano, **Dolzago**
Hibu, **Cornate d'Adda**
PratoRosso, **Settala**
Maspy, **Ponte San Pietro**
Via Priula, **San Pellegrino Terme**

Birrificio Italiano, **Lurago Marinone**
Bi-Du, **Olgiate Comasco**
Siebter Himmel, **Carnago**
L'Orso Verde, **Busto Arsizio**
La Fabbrica, **Saronno**
Geco, **Cornaredo**

Officina Della Birra
Bresso

Rienzbrau
Brunico

Scaligero – Mastino
Mezzane Di Sotto

Birrone, **Isola Vicentina**
Birracrua, **Vicenza**
La Gastaldia
Pieve Di Soligo

Foglie d'Erba, **Forni di Sopra**

La Birra di Meni, **Cavasso Nuovo**
Praforte, **Usago di Travesio**

Birrificio Endorama
Grassobbio *Adige*

Stelvio, **Bormio**

Valcavallina, **Endine Gaiano**
Palabrauhaus Fabbrica
Birra Palazzolo
Palazzolo sull'Oglio

Les Bières du Grand St Bernard
Etroubles

Birrificio Aosta
Saint-Christophe

A5

Vallecellio
Cellio

Un Terzo, **Candelo**

Birrificio Sant'Andrea (BSA)
Vercelli

Gilac, **Val Della Torre**

Amis, **Cirlè**

Birrificio Torino, Piazza dei Mestieri, **Torino**

Aleghe, **Coazze**

Beba, **Villar Perosa**

Birrificio Pinerolese
Pinerolo

Pausa Café, **Saluzzo**

Boero, **Frassino**

Birrificio Trunasse, **Centallo**

Troll
Robilante

Parsifal
San Raffaele Cimena

Grado Plato, **Chieri**

Civale
Alessandria

Henquet
Baladin **Ovada**
Piozzo

Maltus Faber,
Birrificio Genovese
Genova

Manerba Brewery
Manerba Del Garda

Lake Iseo

Trento

TeddyBier
Mori

Lake Garda

Brescia

Lambrate
Milano

Trami
Capriano del Colle
Babb
Manerbio

Birrificio Lodigiano Cosesi
Casalpusteriengo

BrewFist, **Codogno**

Birrificio Rurale
Certosa di Pavia

Birrificio del Ducato, **Roncole Verdi di Busseto**

Docks
Rivergaro

La Buttiga, **Piacenza**

Birra Pasturana
Pasturana

Fabbrica Birra Busalla
Torrechiara
Savignone **Langhirano**

Dada
Correggio

Modena

StataleNove
Crespellano

La Petrognola
Piazza Al Serchio

Beltaine
Granaglione

San Cassiano Di Moriano

Bruton

Vecchio Birraio, **Marsango Di Campo San Martino**
Barchessa di Villa Pola
Barcon di Vedelago

Malol
Verona

Estense
Montagnana

Birrificio Artigianale Veneziano (BAV)
Martellago

Venice

Gulf of Venice

Valscura
Sarone di Caneva

Cittavecchia
Sgonico

BiRen Birrificio Renazzese
Sant'Agostino

Vecchia Orsa
Crevalcore

Bologna

Ravenna

Valsenio
Casola Valsenio

Rimini

Granducato, Mostodolce
Prato

Pisa

Florence
Atlantic Oil
Porrena di Poppi

SAN MARINO

Ancona

Piccolo Birrificio Clandestino
Livorno

Brunz
Empoli

Arezzo

Birrificio L'Olmaia, **Montepulciano**

Le Coti Nere
Marciana

San Quirico
San Quirico d'Orcia

Bacherotti
Città della Pieve

Amiata
Arcidosso

Elba

Lake Bolsena

Free Lions
Tuscania

Opperbacco
Notaresco

Almond 22
Spoltore

Ligurian Sea

Corsica (FRANCE)

ITALY

Adriatic Sea

0 miles 50
0 km 50

N

UNIONBIRRAI IN NORTHERN ITALY

● Busalla
Savignone
Brewery
Town/city

○ **Trento**
Other town/city

BEST-SELLING LOCAL LABELS

Castello	(National)
Dreher	(Heineken)
McFarland	(Heineken)
Moretti	(Heineken)
Peroni	(SABMiller)
Poretti	(Carlsberg)
Splügen	(Carlsberg)

Left: Changes to the way Italians drink beer are fuelling the craft-beer movement, with bottles of beer even appearing at the dinner table.

Italian Breweries

Prior to the 1990s, if you were in search of beer beyond pale lager brewed in Italy, you needed to rely principally on two words: *doppio malto*. These beers, basically malty, higher-alcohol lagers not dissimilar to *Doppelbocks* (*see* p.92), were one end of the spectrum, with mass-market lagers light of both hue and palate at the other. In between lay very little.

Small wonder, then, that Italians were in general unenthusiastic beer consumers, accounting for fewer than 17 litres (3.7 gallons) per person in 1980.

The first changes to this state of affairs began as the 1980s morphed into the 1990s and the first brave craft brewers began to redefine how Italians viewed beer. Anchored primarily in the country's highly gastronomically oriented north, breweries such as the now-iconic and grandfatherly Birrificio Baladin (*see* p.163), led by Teo Musso, sought inspiration not in Germany but in Belgium and, increasingly thereafter, the USA.

The Belgian connection, although seemingly remote, made and continues to make sense on multiple levels. The Low Countries are popular holiday destinations for Italians and, owing at least in part to this fact, Belgian speciality beers have long sold well in Italy. Further, Belgium's are among

Above: Enjoying beer in Chianti country. The annual beer festival at the TNT Pub near Buonconvento – the Villaggio della Birra, or "Village of Beer".

Opposite: Agostino Arioli, head brewer at Birrificio Italiano, cleans out the spent grains after the mash and lauter. Local farmers use them to feed livestock.

BEER SELECTION

BRÙTON STONER (7.5%)
Birrificio Brùton, Lucca (Tuscany)
Brewed from three grains, this ale is loaded with tropical fruit notes balanced by spice from both the hop and the rye grain. Full-bodied yet light on the palate.
www.bruton.it

CONFINE (6%)
Birrificio BI-DU, Olgiate Comasco (Lombardy)
A remarkably smooth and rounded – and unflavoured! – seasonal porter with mocha and molasses notes in the body and gentle coffee flavours in the finish. A northern Italian restorative.
www.bi-du.it

DOMM (5%)
Birrificio Lambrate, Milan (Lombardy)
One of the older craft breweries in Italy (c. 1996) and one that retains some German influence in its beers, as this spicy, faintly peppery *Weissbier* with a dry, citrusy finish illustrates so well.
www.birrificiolambrate.com

IMPER ALE CHIARA (6%)
Collesi, Apecchio (The Marches)
From a brewery that epitomizes the gastronomic approach of many Italian craft breweries comes this light and yeasty blond ale with a refreshing, zesty character and slightly bitter finish.
www.collesi.com

PANIL BARRIQUÉE (8%)

Birrificio Torrechiara, Torrechiara (Emilia-Romagna)
Although there is some batch-to-batch variation in this beer, at its best it is a true delight, with cherry and other berry notes backing earthy, woody ones. The export version is more aggressive than the domestic edition.
www.panilbeer.com

PINK IPA (6%)

Almond '22, Spoltore (Abruzzo)
Not a pink beer but an ale brewed with pink peppercorns for a spicy, citrusy hop nose and bitter, faintly "hot" body. A delicious IPA with an attractive twist.
www.birraalmond.com

REALE (6.4%)

Birra del Borgo, Borgorose (Lazio)
Inspired by British best bitter but constructed with an eye to the USA, this bottle-fermented pale ale, the brewery's flagship, balances round malt and citrusy-spicy hop to emerge robust and food-friendly.
www.birradelborgo.it

SHANGRILA (8.5%)

Birrificio Troll, Vernante (Piedmont)
A beer that should be a disaster, spiced with a kitchen full of seasonings, but it somehow survives to deliver a unified and complex spiciness that ends dry and warming.
www.birratroll.it

Opposite: Checking the wort at the Almond '22 brewery, named for the building in which it is housed, which in 1922 was an almond-processing plant.

Above: Beer has always been part of Italian life, as illustrated by this 1906 poster.

Europe's most food-friendly beers, and the benefits of adding culinary utility to their beers were not lost on the nation's craft brewers.

Perhaps most significantly, however, Belgians have long placed a great deal of emphasis on the aesthetics of beer drinking, everything from proper pouring rituals to glassware and bottle design, and this appealed to the always fashionable Italians.

So, as craft brewing began to take hold in Italy through the 1990s and into the twenty-first century, its expansion was strongly dependent on style as well as substance, featuring often extravagantly stylized and cork-finished bottle design, emulating wine bottles in size and substance, and elegant glassware. A strong embrace of Belgian and American "anything goes" brewing attitude did not hurt, either, although it deserves noting that, as in the USA, while the more unusual beers are the ones that achieve notoriety, the great majority of Italian craft brews are more conventional ales and lagers.

But as where craft brewing has taken off elsewhere, the early days were not without their

A CHESTNUT OBSESSION

Of all the myriad ingredients Italian brewers add to their beers, the one most ubiquitous is the humble chestnut. Although to our knowledge the first-ever modern chestnut beer emerged from Corsica, it is in Italy that the "style" has been pursued with fervent enthusiasm.

Most common is the addition of chestnut flour to flavour a beer, but by no means does the use of this unusual brewing ingredient stop there. We have seen Italian beers brewed with crushed raw chestnut pieces, chestnut honey, roasted chestnuts, and even chestnut jam. So great is their popularity that in their annual beer competition, the Italian craft brewers' association Unionbirrai includes a category devoted exclusively to chestnut beers.

WHEN YOU ARE THERE

- Speciality beers are just as likely to be found in restaurants as cafés or bars.
- Expect to pay as much for fine beer as you would for a wine of good quality.
- Plan for September's Tuscan festival of Belgian and Italian craft beers (www.villaggiodellabirra.com).
- Research breweries at www.unionbirrai.it.
- To find out what craft beers are on the menu, ask about *la birra artigianale*.

BEER SELECTION

STRADA SAN FELICE (8%)
Birrificio Grado Plato, Chieri (Piedmont)
A chestnut beer that showcases flavours of roasted chestnut within a fruity, warming character. Entirely approachable and miles ahead of most Italian chestnut beers.
www.gradoplato.it

TOSTA (12.5%)
Pausa Cafe, Turin (Piedmont)
Brewed with Costa Rican chocolate and not at all shy about it, with robust chocolate and port wine notes throughout. From a cooperative that supports sustainable trade with indigenous peoples.
www.pausacafe.org

TIPOPILS (5.2%)
Birrificio Italiano, Lurago Marinone (Lombardy)
A golden lager given an unusually short conditioning, this refreshing brew combines a sweet, slightly appley front with a dry, faintly yeasty body and lingering bitter finish.
www.birrificio.it

VECCHIA BASTARDA (9.6%)
Birra Amiata Artisanale, Arcidosso (Tuscany)
Intensely spicy and vanilla-accented on the nose, this beer is brewed from malt and 40 per cent crushed chestnuts, then aged in Tuscan wine barrels. The result is a fruity ale with ample vanilla notes throughout and great complexity.
www.birra-amiata.it

problems. As recently as 2006, judging beer at a national contest in Italy was a task filled with at least equal parts disappointment and joy, as a youthful craft-brewing industry suffered through teething pains of uninspired flavours, technical flaws, and misguided recipes.

That all changed in a hurry during the second half of the first decade of the new millennium. Almost as one, Italy's craft brewers seemed to find their footing and suddenly the beers flowing both north and south were of roundly impressive quality, with even the most seemingly bizarre of recipes featuring multiple spice cabinets' worth of ingredients coming together in exciting and delicious ways. Led by the always experimental Musso, alongside other pioneering and/ or innovative breweries like Panil (officially Birrificio Torrechiara), Birrificio Grado Plato, and Birrificio Lambrate (*see* p.162 and p.164), Italian craft brewers have taken an "us against them" approach and with gleeful irreverence transformed the country into one of the continent's most exciting beer markets.

Next page: A Tuscan afternoon, a little cheese and a bottle of *birra artigianale*. What could be better?

VERDI IMPERIAL STOUT (8.2%)
Birrificio Del Ducato, Roncole Verdi di Busseto (Emilia-Romagna)
An homage to Verdi's birthplace, this spicy, roasty stout mixes hot pepper with roasted malt and espresso flavours with an elegance worthy of the great composer.
www.birrificiodelducato.it

VIENNA (5.3%)
Antica Birreria Theresianer, Trieste (Friuli-Venezia Giulia)
A proper Vienna-style lager is a great companion to pizza, which makes this malty, faintly roasty, and dry-finishing lager a natural for the Italian table. Lightly nutty hop notes add to the complexity.
www.theresianer.com

XYAUYÙ ETICHETTA ARGENTO (SILVER LABEL) (13.5%)
Birrificio Baladin, Piozzo (Piedmont)
Intentionally oxidized to a carbonationless complexity that rivals the finest Pedro Ximénez sherry, this is a compelling, fascinating brew, as are its Gold and Bronze Label mates.
www.birreria.com

REST OF EUROPE

Going back a century or so, the parts of Europe that had substantial beer cultures could be fairly reliably defined as those lying north of a line that ran from Picardy on the French coast, through northeastern France to Strasbourg, then south of the Alps to bisect Austro-Hungary before heading northeast through Poland to hit the Baltic near St Petersburg, the area also including the British Isles and Scandinavia.

Nowadays it is not so simple. The international trade in wine expanded massively during the twentieth century and now beer is following suit, although the latter is conferred interesting advantages by the fact that any importing nation can also make its own beer, commissioning brewers' skills to add distinctive local interpretations.

If asked which country's craft beer industry will advance furthest in the five years after this edition is published, one intuitive answer would be Spain. The home of Rioja and Penedès, Jerez and Málaga has acquired its new passion for brewing not by trying to reconnect with a beery past or via the colonization of its Mediterranean coastline by herds of British expats. Rather, it has been learned from the acquisition of new tastes by Spaniards travelling in the new world of beer.

In the more traditional beer-drinking part of Europe, the nation that might feel most aggrieved at not being granted its own chapter in this book is Switzerland, where, depending on who you ask, between 130

NEW AND OLD EUROPE ▶
The regions of Europe where beer has for centuries been the cultural drink of choice do not always represent the areas where traditional and craft beers are enjoying their strongest renaissance. This map contrasts the current strength of the revival in different areas with those that represent the historic homelands of beer brewing.

Right: The beer revival in Greece is still in its early days.

Above: Increasingly, glasses of beer are replacing wine and Sherry when the Spanish enjoy their early evening tapas.

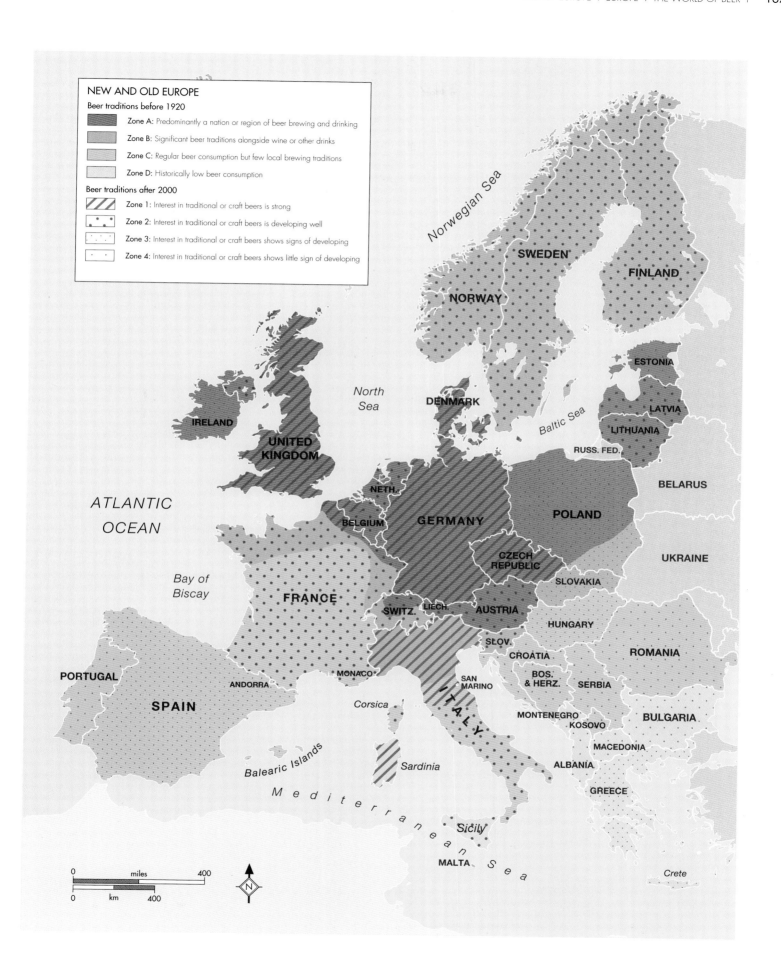

NEW AND OLD EUROPE

Beer traditions before 1920

Zone A: Predominantly a nation or region of beer brewing and drinking

Zone B: Significant beer traditions alongside wine or other drinks

Zone C: Regular beer consumption but few local brewing traditions

Zone D: Historically low beer consumption

Beer traditions after 2000

Zone 1: Interest in traditional or craft beers is strong

Zone 2: Interest in traditional or craft beers is developing well

Zone 3: Interest in traditional or craft beers shows signs of developing

Zone 4: Interest in traditional or craft beers shows little sign of developing

and 190 breweries are active. Swiss brewers in the three different language areas (French-German-Italian) seem to reflect the brewing habits of their linguistic homelands, but sadly, many produce either technically pristine yet rather dull beers or else a massive range of which not one has been perfected.

Poland, too, might be considered worthy of more space for its variations on Baltic porter and various Germanic styles. However, the rapid assimilation of its larger brewers by global companies, coupled with a lack of distinctive products from its 50 or so independent companies and virtual absence of brewpubs, has failed as yet to spark the sort of entrepreneurial craft brewing seen elsewhere. Indeed, the only native Polish beer style, a type of smoked wheat beer called *Grodziskie* (or *Grätzer Bier*), appears to have died out completely.

In those countries where local beers are being reseeded into the culture or seen for the first time, the early settlers are often brewpubs. These arrive in degrees of sophistication that vary from full-on North American restaurants with beer to small saloons that are little more than offshoots from the owner's kitchen.

For example, when Slovenia peeled away from the old Yugoslavia in 1991, its route to full European Union membership in 2004 included encouraging the development of new small businesses. Inevitably, some involved brewing, and by 2002 a country that had historically been home to few breweries boasted a dozen or more brewpubs. Nowadays, it has twice that number, plus some commercial microbreweries.

The rest of the Balkans has seen considerably more conflict in the past two decades, but nonetheless Croatia is showing early signs of a rising interest in beer, as is an unlikely aspiring beer country – Greece.

Left: Banská Bystrika, home of Urpina beers, perhaps the best in the Slovak Republic.

Opposite: Having seen their historic breweries gobbled up by the major multinationals, Poles are gradually turning towards a nascent craft-brewing culture.

BEER SELECTION

ADAM RAVBAR KVASNO SVETLO PIVO (4.5%)
Pivovarna Adam Ravbar, Domžale (Slovenia)
Based in a brewpub northeast of Ljubljana, this modern Slovenian brewery makes interesting unfiltered beers like this cloudy blond, well enough to get commissions from others.
www.pivnica-adamravbar.si

AGULLONS PURA PALE (5%)
Cervesa Artesana Masia Agullons, Mediona, Alt Penedès (Spain)
One of Spain's most interesting new brewers, not averse to blending ale with lambic, makes this spot-on English pale ale from imported British malt and mostly English hop varieties.
www.masia-agullons.com

BLACK BOSS PORTER (8.5%)
Browar Witnica, Witnica (Poland)
This 160-year-old brewery not far from the German border supplements its range of local brews with several export porters, of which this ruddy brown heavyweight is the most frequently encountered.
www.browar-witnica.pl

BLACK ROSE (9%)
Békésszentandrási Sörfőzde, Békésszentandrás (Hungary)
This unplaceable strong black lager comes from a Hungarian brewery set up in 1993, which makes some of the country's best beers, many featuring fruit.
http://serfozde.uw.hu/

BRAUHAUS MALBU-BOCK (6.8%)
Liechtensteiner Brauhaus AG, Schaan (Liechtenstein)
The principality of Liechtenstein has 36,000 citizens, 24 Alpine peaks, and, since 2007, a brewery making four year-round beers and this, the strongest, a fruity, autumnal amber *bock*.
www.brauhaus.li

CORFU BEER REAL ALE SPECIAL (5%)
Corfiot Microbrewery, Arillas, Corfu (Greece)
We could not resist including this incongruously English pale ale, one of two bottled with its yeast at a purpose-built brewery on the holiday island of Corfu.
www.corfubeer.com

ESTRELLA DAMM INEDIT (4.8%)
Grupo Damm, Barcelona (Spain)
This long-established Spanish brewery has always made better-than-industrial beers and is now nudging gingerly towards a wider world of styles, such as this competent Belgian-style wheat beer.
www.damm.es

GRAND IMPERIAL PORTER (8%)
Browar Amber, Bielkówko (Poland)
This state-of-the-art brewery, located not far from the Baltic coastal port of Gdansk, impresses most with its pasteurized bottled black porter, which seems to have an imperial air.
www.browar-amber.pl

GUINEU MONTSERRAT (6%)
Ca L'Arenys, Valls de Torroella (Spain)
Early signs that Spain intends to do craft brewing its own way include this Catalan creation, an overtly sweet but full-flavoured, chocolaty, and substantial clean stout.
www.calarenys.cat

HUMAN FISH PALE ALE (4.4%)
Pivovarna Človeška Ribica, Slovenj Gradec (Slovenia)
Named after the eel-like olm, or "humanfish", that lives in the rivers of northern Slovenia, this punchy young bunch of brewers make international beer styles, including this confident pale ale, packed with local hops.

Much of the rest of Eastern Europe lies firmly within grape-growing territory. Even the Slovak Republic, which made up the eastern half of former Czechoslovakia, had few breweries historically, although enough for one or two independents to flourish.

The largest breweries in the southern countries of the former Soviet bloc have frequently been subject to takeover by global brewers, who often closed the worst plants and renovated the best, usually improving beer quality, but then fell shy of producing anything memorable.

In the old Union of Soviet Socialist Republics (USSR), it was virtually impossible for foreign beer writers to gauge how many breweries were in production, let alone what range of beers they made. Those that reached the export trade were as untypical as they were often undrinkable.

The quality and quantity of information in the new Russia has risen somewhat – how could it not? – but insufficiently as yet to bring clarity. The most likely place for craft

Above: In many parts of southern Europe, including the Iberian Peninsula, beer was seen traditionally as something designed strictly to quench a thirst.

Above: European brewers are increasingly aware of new markets for better-quality beers.

BEER SELECTION

INDIA PALE ALE (6.3%)
Brasserie Trois Dames, Sainte-Croix (Switzerland)
Precision and passion combine to make this perhaps the finest of the newer Swiss brewers. Its American-hopped, Burton-bodied pale ale (La Victorienne in the USA) brings it the most praise.
www.brasserietroisdames.ch

L'ABBAYE DE SAINT BON-CHIEN (10–11%)
Brasserie des Franches-Montagnes, Saignelégier (Switzerland)
Named after the brewer's late cat and created in different incarnations, this hefty amber sipping ale, aged in spirits casks, sits close to the boundary of beer and wine, frightening the connoisseurs of both.
www.brasseriebfm.ch

LEŽIAK TATRAN 12° EXPORT LAGER (5%)
Pivovar Pilsberg, Poprad (Slovak Republic)
Top-quality pilsner is still made in the less-beery half of the former Czechoslovakia, at this brewery that can trace its tortuous history back 200 years. Its 1715 Münchener is also worth trying.
www.pilsberg.sk

OBOLON PSHENICHNE (5%)
Obolon, Kiev (Ukraine)
The largest Ukrainian-owned brewery is concentrating on brand rather than flavour to create a wider reputation, but it does produce this well-constructed German-style Hefeweizen.
www.obolon.ua

SAN MARTINO GOLD (7.6%)
Birrificio Ticinese, Stabio (Switzerland)
The most interesting of the new breweries emerging from the Italian Swiss cantons mirrors the inventiveness of its neighbour in this sweet, honey-laced doppio malto golden Bock.
www.birrasanmartino.ch

SCHWARZER KRISTALL (6.3%)
Brauerei Locher AG, Appenzell (Switzerland)
The best of the longer-established Swiss family brewers produces German styles of beer, including this chocolate-driven, slightly smoky, coffee-tinged confident black lager.
www.appenzellerbier.ch

brewing to take root is St Petersburg, where rival beer festivals feature aspiring local microbrewers alongside a few craft imports.

Of the new republics, enough is known to suggest that Ukraine is "one to watch". As well as having four large brewery companies, a couple under local ownership, its national tourist board promotes visits to five microbreweries in its second city, the brewing town of Lviv.

Perhaps the most endearing indication that craft brewing is making real progress in Europe is that even the smallest nations feel they must have a decent brewery. Monaco has seen the return of the Brasserie de Monaco as a smart brewpub restaurant serving nicely crafted beers to beautiful people, while Liechtenstein has its first commercial brewery in nearly a century (*see* p.168).

Expansion may also be on the cards in Luxembourg, where craft brewing had consolidated under a single privately owned company, and in Malta, where the large local producer Cisk-Farsons has to date failed to recognize the potential of its old-fashioned brewing habits but might be about to get some competition.

Above: The shape of things to come? The early success of two rival beer festivals in St Petersburg bodes well for the future development of craft brewing and, more importantly, an enthusiastic audience.

STOLICHNO TEMNO (6.5%)
Pivovarna Zagorka, Stara Zagora (Bulgaria)
Perhaps the best beer from around the Black Sea, is this clean, dark *Bock* – or *bok* maybe, as it comes from a Heineken subsidiary.
www.zagorka.bg

TAMNO VELEBITSKO PIVO (6%)
Pivovara Ličanka, Donje Pazarište (Croatia)
This central Croatian brewery was founded in 1997 to produce a couple of sound all-malt lagers to the standards of the *Reinheitsgebot* or "Purity Order" (*see* p.80). This is the darker, stronger one.
www.pivovara-licanka.hr

VERGINA WEISS (5%)
Macedonian Thrace Brewery, Komotini (Greece)
A new northern Greek brewery, founded by an American-trained local brewer and expanding nicely to make four beers, including this clove-and-banana-nuanced Bavarian-style wheat beer.
www.verginabeer.com

URPINER LEŽIAK VÝČAPNÝ TMAVÝ 11% (4.5%)
Banskobystrický Pivovar, Banská Bystrika (Slovak Republic)
In the ancient brewing town of Banská Bystrika, this recently overhauled regional company make six Urpiner beers, of which this sweet, mellow black lager is the standout.
www.urpiner.eu

WËLLEN OURDALLER (6.5%)
Ourdaller Brauerei, Heinerscheid (Luxembourg)
The small, independent Simon family brewery now owns two of the Grand Duchy's tiny craft producers, including the makers of this tasty, strongish, brown, hazy buckwheat beer.
www.beo.lu

Collaboration Beers

From the early days of what used to be known as microbrewing, craft beer has oft-times seemed more like a chummy club than a competitive marketplace. Brewers were regularly photographed sporting shirts bearing the logos of other breweries, tasting events would see reps from competing companies hobnobbing over glasses of ale or lager – their own or that of yet another brewery – and if a brewery ran into a problem, be it with fermentation or keg delivery, another local beer operation could usually be counted upon to help overcome it.

Given this state of heightened camaraderie, it seemed only a matter of time before breweries eventually joined forces to create special, one-off beers. Which is, of course, precisely what happened.

The first collaboration brews we recall seeing were in the USA, the result of head brewers spending increasing amounts of time on the road promoting their wares. One brewer would talk to another in advance of visiting the latter's district for a festival, tasting, or beer dinner and ideas would be hatched, schedules adjusted, and brew times arranged. The resulting beer would sometimes be released only by the brewery being visited, other times replicated later on at the travelling brewer's facility.

From such humble beginnings, it did not take long for the collaboration concept to assume a life of its own, and an international one at that.

Thanks to the near-instantaneous connectivity we enjoy today via smart phones, email, Facebook, and other modern methods of communication, brewers were soon planning promotional tours around their collaboration efforts, rather than vice versa. And the emergence of the so-called "gipsy brewer", or brewer without a brewery, furthered the cause by leading these peripatetic brewers by necessity into collaborations.

Even with all the above, however, the collaboration beer would probably never have taken off but for the "us versus them" nature of the global craft-brewing industry.

As the massive, international brewing companies grew ever larger through mergers and acquisitions, so, too, grew the sense among craft brewers that they were less individual concerns and more a collective movement against the worldwide status quo of light lagers.

From that premise, collaboration was but a short, logical step. Underlying the now international nature of brewing collaborations is the diversity of prominent collaborators, including Stone (USA), Mikkeller (Denmark), BrewDog (Scotland), Nøgne Ø (Norway), Epic (New Zealand), and even the monastic brewers of La Trappe (Netherlands), all of whom have crossed numerous borders in the pursuit of new ideas and ever more inventive brews.

At the time of writing, there have been far too many collaboration efforts to list them all, but among the more notable have been: Infinium (Weihenstephan of Germany with Boston Beer of the USA); Collaboration Not Litigation (the product of the realization by two American breweries, Russian River and Avery, that they had beers with the same name); Portamarillo (Epic of New Zealand with Dogfish Head of the USA for the Discovery Channel series *Brew Masters*); and VCBW Cascadian Dark Ale (a 2011 Vancouver Beer Week collaboration worked on by 28 brewers from different breweries in British Columbia, Canada).

Left: Collaboration beers, such as the three seen here, are usually bottled in such a manner as to emphasize their special, limited-edition nature.

Above: Danish "gypsy brewer" Mikkel Borg Bjergsø relies on the breweries of colleagues to make his many distinctive beers.

Above: An early start for the team from New Zealand's Renaissance Brewing Company.

Above: Friendly beer-making rivals, the Yeastie Boys, check their levels.

Above: Collaboration brewing is not just about crafting great beer, but also having fun in the brewhouse.

THE AMERICAS

As a catalyst for the global craft beer renaissance, North America in the 1970s must have seemed a most unlikely candidate. Famous as little more than the butt of the world's beer-soaked humour, the USA and Canada were at the time awash in a sea of similarly styled lagers, each seemingly vying with the other in a race towards the ultimate in bland predictability.

Opposite: Beers enjoyed straight from the tank – a scene that could be a US brewpub circa 1995, captured at a beer restaurant in the fashionable Palermo Viejo district of Buenos Aires.

There were pockets of character to be found, such as the still-extant Anchor Brewing in California (see p.180) and Yuengling in Pennsylvania (see p.196), and Nova Scotia's Oland Brewing prior to its absorption by Labatt. But by and large, for the 45 or so years following Prohibition's repeal, the North American beer market was bleak and industrial. As the 1980s approached, the USA boasted scarcely more than 50 brewing companies, Canada a mere seven.

Thirty years on, although lager brands like Budweiser and Coors Light still dominate in Canada as well as in the USA, the reality of beer drinking in North America is far, far different. The numbers alone tell a large part of the tale: in 2011, the USA claimed more breweries than the nation has seen in well over a century, possibly ever, at over 1,800. With a much smaller population base, Canada is, on a per capita basis, even more brewery-rich.

This growth in the number of breweries has been accompanied by massive expansion in market share and influence, as in 2010 craft beer approached five per cent market share by volume in the USA. (Statistics on craft beer sales in Canada are not compiled on a national basis, but it could be assumed that they roughly parallel those of the USA.) In terms of volume growth, the craft beer market saw gains in excess of ten per cent in 2010.

As impressive as these numbers may be, they are dwarfed by the influence that North American breweries, particularly those in the USA, have exerted on the global craft brewing community since the dawn

Above: And they would have their beer, too, once Prohibition was repealed one year following this 1932 New York protest.

Previous page: It has been a long road for American craft beer, but the reward is wildfire-like growth in the new century.

of the new millennium. After years spent following the lead of Belgian, English, and German brewers, many North American brewers have turned the tables on their European counterparts and now inspire creativity in beer markets both well established, such as Belgium and Great Britain, and new, like Italy, Japan, and Denmark.

Above: Craft beer weeks have taken off in cities and regions across the United States, and even spawned a national celebration supported by Congress.

South America, meanwhile, stands poised to emulate the North American craft beer renaissance, with a small but enthusiastic and optimistic base of breweries centred mainly in Brazil, Argentina, and Chile. Standing up to major breweries that are both larger and more powerful than those faced by North American brewers in the 1980s, however, may yet prove to be a serious test of their mettle.

In between the dominant nations of North and South America, Central America, Mexico, and the Caribbean all remain very much under the thumb of the large, international brewing concerns. This is not to say that no craft brewing initiatives have been undertaken – there are more than two dozen such operations in Mexico, for example – but their size and scope is so small as to be almost invisible. It remains to be seen whether that will change in the years to come.

Above: D G Yeungling & Son in Pottsville, Pennsylvania, is the oldest operating brewery in the United States.

THE USA

When Jack McAuliffe first opened the doors of California's New Albion Brewing Company in Sonoma in May 1976 he could not have possibly imagined the movement he was about to ignite. For even though the first American craft brewery of the modern age failed to survive beyond a mere half-dozen years, like the biblical Adam, its offspring grew to populate the whole of the USA, from Sarasota, Florida, to Anchorage, Alaska.

In 2011, with now hundreds of breweries and brewpubs scattered across all 50 states, the story of craft brewing in the USA was not even one of growth already realized but potential growth yet to come. As brewery after brewery scrambling to meet rising demand is the norm, some are refraining from entering new cities and states for fear of running out of the beer required to meet the needs of their existing markets, while others are actually exiting smaller market states so as to meet the wants of larger ones.

Taken together, and augmented by the estimated 700 or more breweries in the planning stages as of mid-2011, these volumes of unrealized craft beer sales are likely to represent many tens of thousands of barrels, on top of the close to ten million barrels the segment sold in 2010.

So great has been the craft beer success story in the USA that aficionados even talk of so-called "rock star" brewers, individuals like Sam Calagione of Delaware's Dogfish Head Craft Brewery (*see* p.198), Tomme Arthur of San Diego's The Lost Abbey (*see* p.183), and Adam Avery of Boulder, Colorado's Avery Brewing (*see* p.188), who literally tour the country to promote their wares, often "playing" to truly impressive crowds.

Beyond more beer, US craft brewers are also producing different beer, sometimes radically so. To the delight of some and the bemusement of others, America's craft brewers have proved time and again true to the culture of excess that often appears to define their society. If a beer style is strong and well hopped, as in a traditional India pale ale or even a paler and hoppier American-style IPA, then it

BEST-SELLING LOCAL LABELS

Blue Moon	(MillerCoors*)
Bud Lite	(Anheuser-Busch InBev)
Busch	(Anheuser-Busch InBev)
George Killian's	(MillerCoors*)
Leinenkugel's	(MillerCoors*)
Michelob	(Anheuser-Busch InBev)
Pabst	(National)
Samuel Adams	(National)
Shock Top	(Anheuser-Busch InBev)
Yuengling	(National)

*In the USA, SABMiller and MolsonCoors operate jointly as MillerCoors

Left: Jack McAuliffe pioneered craft brewing in the USA with his New Albion Brewing Company in northern California.

is worth making it yet hoppier and more potent, as witnessed by the development and popularity of the so-called "double" IPA. Similarly, a malty and warming barley wine or imperial stout can easily be made intensely so by ageing it six months in a former bourbon barrel or dramatically increasing its malt content so that it ferments at close to 20 per cent alcohol.

Some of these style-twisting experiments – indeed, one is tempted to say most of them – have resulted in a body of brews that has greatly increased the range of flavours and aromas available to beer connoisseurs worldwide. At their best, they have even served to inspire brewers in distant lands, from Belgium to northern England and Italy to Japan.

Thirty years is not a long time in the greater scheme of things, but it has proved time enough for American craft brewers to make an indelible and expanding mark on their own culture and that of many others, and change the way their fellow citizens drink, probably forever.

WHEN YOU ARE THERE

- Beer bars and brewpubs in the USA vary widely, from screen-festooned sports bars to casual but upmarket venues with white tablecloths.
- Unless you are seated or standing at the bar, ordering is normally directed through the waiter.
- While most establishments will place the emphasis on their draught taps, don't overlook the bottled beer menus, which may list much-sought-after rarities.
- As most serious beer destinations hire people who are enthusiastic about beer, discovering a great beer you have never heard of can be as simple as asking the bartender for advice.

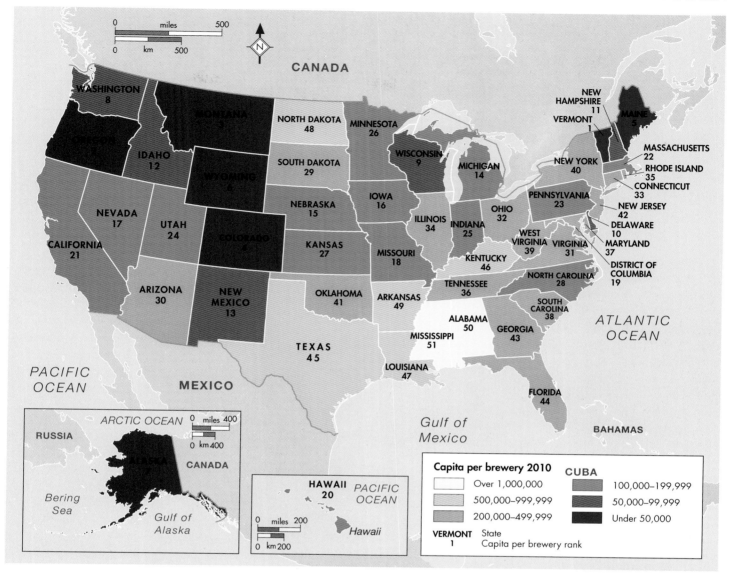

STATE	BREWERIES	CAPITA/BREWERY
Vermont	21	29,797
Oregon	121	31,662
Montana	27	36,645
Colorado	118	42,620
Maine	31	42,850
Wyoming	12	46,969
Alaska	15	47,349
Washington	123	54,671
Wisconsin	72	78,986
Delaware	11	81,630
New Hampshire	19	82,279
Idaho	21	82,504
New Mexico	85	98,056
Michigan	15	116,278
Nebraska	24	121,756
Iowa	19	126,931
Nevada	40	142,134
Missouri	40	149,723

STATE	BREWERIES	CAPITA/BREWERY
District of Columbia	4	150,431
Hawaii	9	151,145
California	245	152,057
Massachusetts	42	155,896
Pennsylvania	77	164,966
Utah	16	172,743
Indiana	35	185,251
Minnesota	28	189,426
Kansas	15	190,208
North Carolina	47	199,010
South Dakota	4	203,545
Arizona	30	213,067
Virginia	37	216,244
Ohio	47	245,458
Connecticut	14	255,293
Illinois	49	261,850
Rhode Island	4	263,142
Tennessee	23	275,918

STATE	BREWERIES	CAPITA/BREWERY
Maryland	19	303,871
South Carolina	15	308,358
West Virginia	6	308,832
New York	59	328,442
Oklahoma	9	416,817
New Jersey	20	439,595
Georgia	21	461,300
Florida	39	482,085
Texas	48	523,866
Kentucky	8	542,421
Louisiana	8	566,672
North Dakota	1	672,591
Arkansas	4	728,980
Alabama	4	1,194,934
Mississippi	2	1,483,649

California

From almost the moment it joined the union in 1850, California has been enshrined in the collective American consciousness as the land of milk and honey, where opportunity awaits and possibilities abound. So it is particularly appropriate that consensus places the roots of modern American craft brewing firmly in the north of the state.

The story begins with a young man named Fritz Maytag, part of the famous appliance manufacturing family, pursuing his graduate studies while living in San Francisco during the 1960s. Partial to a beer called Anchor Steam, enjoyed with friends at a local institution known as the Spaghetti Factory, Maytag was dismayed to hear from a bartender there that the Anchor brewery was nearing closure (see below). A visit was quickly organized.

Touring the decaying regional brewer, Maytag was struck by the opportunity it afforded and speedily secured a deal to assume partial ownership. As he fought to resuscitate the ageing plant, the fledgling

Right: Many visitors are drawn to San Francisco as much for the beer as they are for the iconic sights.

entrepreneur became increasingly enamoured with his purchase and, as the 1960s gave way to the next decade, obtained full ownership.

By the mid-1970s, Maytag had not only turned around the fortunes of Anchor but he had also begun to introduce new brands into the brewery's line-up, including a porter in 1974 and, in 1975, Liberty Ale and Old Foghorn Barley Wine, the latter labelled a "barleywine-style ale" as a sop to perplexed authorities who could not understand how a wine could be made from barley.

Maytag's commitment to crafting intensely flavourful beer during a time when American breweries seemed caught in a race to produce the blandest and most inoffensive lager possible served as inspiration to other would-be brewing entrepreneurs, including Sonoma's

BEER SELECTION

ANNIVERSARY ALE (+/-12%)
Firestone Walker Brewing Company, Paso Robles
Every year since the brewery's tenth anniversary, brewer Matt Brynildson has crafted a special ale blended from up to seven barrel-aged beers and named for the anniversary it celebrates (2012's ale is Sixteen). Always intense, warming, and profoundly flavourful, they never disappoint.
www.firestonebeer.com

ANCHOR STEAM BEER (4.9%)
Anchor Brewing Company, San Francisco
A hybrid, fermented with what would normally be deemed a lager yeast at temperatures more in keeping with an ale, this post-Prohibition brew is caramelly on the nose but dry of body, with roundly malty notes and a crisp, gently bitter finish.
www.anchorbrewing.com

ARROGANT BASTARD ALE (7.2%)
Stone Brewing Co., Escondido
Incredibly, Stone Brewing has built a large degree of the brewery's success on the back of this strong, dark, and aggressively hopped ale, bracing in its bitterness with fruity, caramelly malt to match.
www.stonebrew.com

AUTUMN MAPLE (10%)
The Bruery, Placentia
This seasonal ale brewed with yams, molasses, maple syrup, and spices actually offers a taste that is, well, yammy, alongside notes of allspice, caramelized root vegetables, maple, and nutty-spicy hop. A unique experience.
www.thebruery.com

SAN FRANCISCO BAY ▶

The spiritual home of American craft brewing, the San Francisco Bay area is a top beer destination not only for its large number of breweries, but also for the many beer bars and beer-oriented restaurants it boasts.

Jack McAuliffe, Chico's Ken Grossman and Paul Camusi, and Ted DeBakker of Novato, each of whom had opened a new brewery prior to 1980, respectively New Albion Brewing, Sierra Nevada Brewing (*see* p.182), and the DeBakker Brewery.

The 1980s saw craft brewing – then known as microbrewing – spread across California and the rest of the USA, stronger in some regions than in others, but always with the Golden State at the forefront. In 1982, the brewpub, defined as a brewery with the ability to sell directly to the public through a restaurant setting, was formally recognized in the state, and thereafter opened two in rapid succession, beaten to the title of America's first modern brewpub only by Bert Grant's Yakima Brewing in Washington State.

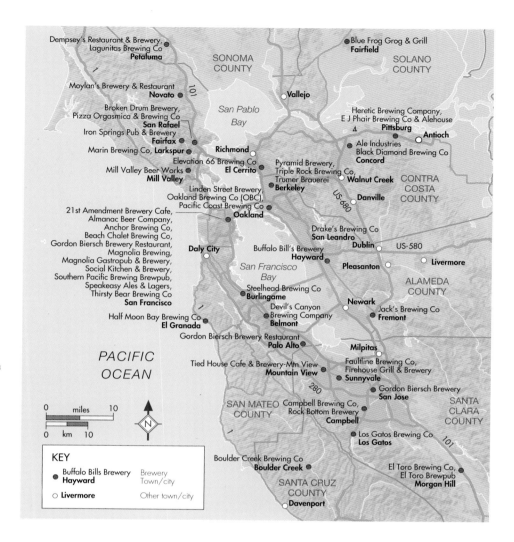

BARNEY FLATS OATMEAL STOUT (5.7%)
Anderson Valley Brewing Company, Boonville
The oats used in its creation add both their textbook silkiness and a slight porridge-like sweetness to this stout, both of which blend beautifully with roasted malt flavours that never stray to bitter and slightly nutty hoppiness that keeps it all just off-dry.
www.avbc.com

LAGUNITAS PILS (6.2%)
Lagunitas Brewing Company, Petaluma
What happens when northern California meets the Czech Republic. The bitterness of this flowery, herbaceous lager builds slowly over an almost sweet, nectar-like malt base, eventually leading to a boldly hoppy and quenching finish.
www.lagunitas.com

ORGANIC CHOCOLATE STOUT (5%)
Bison Brewing Company, Ukiah
Boasting a nose of raw cocoa and coffee, this black ale begins lightly sweet with soft liquorice notes before developing a creamy, mocha-led body with a bitter and chocolaty finish. A happy marriage of chocolate and stout.
www.bisonbrew.com

POPPY JASPER AMBER ALE (5.3%)
El Toro Brewing Company, Morgan Hill
Evidence that amber need not equal boring is this quaffable ale with a tame fruitiness, gentle bitterness, and just enough roasted malt character to keep it all interesting. A great Californian pub ale.
www.eltorobrewing.com

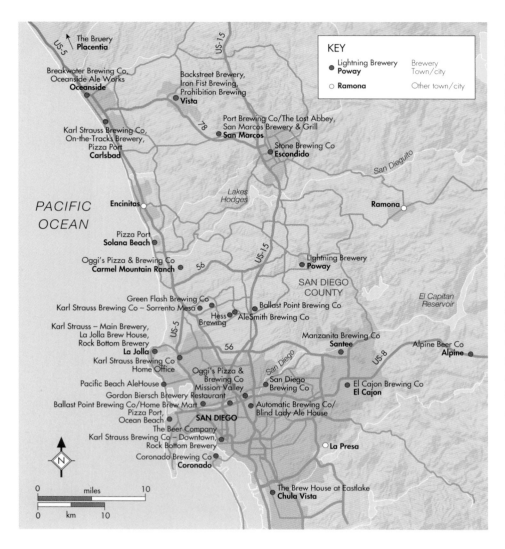

Craft beer continued to grow in popularity throughout California during the 1990s, but it was with the dawn of the new millennium that the state really hit its stride, most notably through the dramatic transformation of the southern region from craft beer wasteland into brewery-rich nirvana. Led by such attention-grabbing operations as the defiantly local AleSmith (*see* below, opposite), attitudinal Stone Brewing, and the more recent arrival The Bruery (*see* p.180), San Diego has in short order established itself as one of the west's major craft-brewing capitals.

Along the way, California's brewers have proved themselves to be, if not necessarily the instigators of certain creative brewing movements, then certainly some of their most successful early adopters. Among these recent innovative trends are the use of bacteria and wild yeasts in the creation of so-called sour ales, practised extensively by Vinnie Cilurzo of Russian River (*see* below), and the barrel ageing of beer, championed by The Lost Abbey's Tomme Arthur (*see* below).

◄ SAN DIEGO AREA

Although initially slow to develop a craft-beer culture, the San Diego area has blossomed in the 21st century into one of America's top centres of brewing innovation and experimentation.

BEER SELECTION

MY BLOODY VALENTINE (6.66%)
AleSmith Brewing Company, San Diego
Almost crimson in colour, this seasonal – released around Valentine's Day, of course – presents a gloriously fragrant and hoppy aroma, all pine and alfalfa, before a lightly caramelly, red apple body, ending in a final tannic and hoppy assault.
www.alesmith.com

PRANQSTER (7.6%)
North Coast Brewing Company, Fort Bragg
Proof that this veteran craft brewery was conscious of Belgium before Belgium was cool, this fruity golden ale offers an effusively floral nose and moderately sweet, peachy body that dries as it crosses the palate, ending spicy and off-dry.
www.northcoastbrewing.com

RACER 5 IPA (7%)
Bear Republic Brewing Company, Healdsburg
The use of four "c-hops" – the kind that produce citrus-like bitterness – gives this ale an abundance of lemon zest and grapefruit notes, along with resinous herbals laid over the top of balancing, biscuity malt.
www.bearrepublic.com

SIERRA NEVADA PALE ALE (5.6%)
Sierra Nevada Brewing Company, Chico
This classic American-style pale ale showcases the aromatic, spicy character of the Cascade hop, more orange than grapefruit in its citrus appeal, to produce a faintly fruity, moderately bitter beer that has quite deservedly become an icon of craft brewing.
www.sierranevada.com

Left: Sit at the Anderson Valley Brewing Company bar and you might just hear some "Boontling", an esoteric dialect spoken only in Boonville.

THE BIRTH OF THE "BREWSPAPER"

It was a young Canadian by the name of Bret Nickels, then living in the San Francisco Bay area, who first realized that there might lie opportunity in the craft beer business beyond the making and selling of ales and lagers. And so, on Valentine's Day, 1988, Nickels and his then-wife Julie launched the first issue of the *California Celebrator* – today just the *Celebrator* – and the "brewspaper" was born.

Since that first issue, brewspapers have blossomed across the USA, with one covering almost every major market from coast to coast. They all emulate the modern *Celebrator* in style, featuring reports on brewery developments in specific regions, columns by established regulars, and, perhaps most importantly for the consumer, addresses of breweries, brewpubs, and beer bars scattered across the covered area.

Other than the *Celebrator*, titles to look for include *Ale Street News* and the *Brewing News* chain, the latter of which covers numerous markets from the south to the northwest.

TEMPTATION (7.25%)
Russian River Brewing Company, Santa Rosa
A year spent with a *Brettanomyces* culture in French oak barrels that previously held Chardonnay wine gives this blond ale a depth that belies its appearance, with a tropical-fruit entry that yields quickly to a miasma of oaky vanilla, grape, and tart, earthy flavours.
www.russianriverbrewing.com

THE ANGEL'S SHARE (12.5%)
The Lost Abbey, San Marcos
Aged one year in the brewery's barrel room, this bold ale assumes flavours from what the wood had previously held – mostly bourbon, but sometimes brandy – and emerges with a complex, vanilla-accented malt body laden with notes of molasses and dark dried fruits.
www.lostabbey.com

TRIPPEL BELGIAN STYLE ALE (9.7%)
Green Flash Brewing Company, San Diego
Although known for its highly hopped ales, Green Flash also boasts a Belgian-inspired side, which includes this dryly fruity and floral golden ale with a hoppy aroma that belies its complicated, malt-fuelled flavour.
www.greenflashbrew.com

Pacific Northwest, Alaska & Hawaii

While California can rightly lay claim to both the inspiration and first commercial application of the American craft-brewing ethos in, respectively, Anchor Brewing (*see* p.180) and New Albion (*see* page 178), it is in the Pacific Northwest that it has thrived as nowhere else. Throughout Washington and Oregon, and even into Alaska and the Hawaiian islands, one is challenged to find a city, town, or village unserved by a nearby brewery or brewpub, and in the odd location where those are lacking, one can normally find a beer bar nearby.

It should come as no surprise, really. Residents of Oregon and Washington state are notoriously antagonistic where conventions are concerned, preferring to bicycle or take public transit where others would drive, and embracing the culture of the "locavore" long before it was fashionable to do so. Additionally, America's most fertile hop fields sit on their doorstep, in Washington's Yakima Valley, providing a ready source of seasoning for the hoppy ales they so adore.

Indeed, even prior to Bert Grant's founding of America's first modern brewpub in Washington (*see also* p.202) and the 1982 opening of Seattle's Red Hook Brewery, Cascadians, as the locals sometimes like to call themselves, were a contrary bunch where beer was concerned. In the late 1970s, as mainstream beer brands grew increasingly bland, Portland's Blitz-Weinhard brewery called attention to itself by producing what

Above: Remote though it is (or maybe for that very reason), Alaska is home to many fine craft breweries.

BEER SELECTION

ADAM (10%)
Hair of the Dog Brewing Company, Portland (Oregon)
The first beer ever brewed at this iconoclastic brewery, this rich and warming ale imbued with flavours of brandy-soaked raisins and other concentrated fruits is fashioned after a long-dead style once native to Dortmund, Germany.
www.hairofthedog.com

ARCTIC DEVIL BARLEY WINE (13.2%)
Midnight Sun Brewing Company, Anchorage (Alaska)
Aged in oak barrels and then blended before bottling, this malt-forward barley wine offers the predictable vanilla on the nose, backed with a contemplative mix of stewed fruit, toffee, and other malty goodness, dried rather than bittered by soft hoppiness.
www.midnightsunbrewing.com

AVATAR JASMINE IPA (6.3%)
Elysian Brewing Company, Seattle (Washington)
The use of jasmine flowers in the creation of this ale gives it an abundantly floral character that complements well the unabashedly spicy-citric bite of the Amarillo hops also used.
www.elysianbrewing.com

BLACK BUTTE PORTER (5.2%)
Deschutes Brewery, Bend (Oregon)
Well on its way to becoming a craft beer legend, this is American porter's proper evolution, creamy and a bit sweet, with chocolate malts balancing on the edge of hop bitterness.
www.deschutesbrewery.com

SEATTLE AREA ▶

Washington state was home to the first modern brewpub in the United States (Grant's in Yakima), and today maintains a great fondness for pub breweries. The state's largest city, Seattle, is the epicentre of this brewpub culture.

Opposite: For more than a century, Washington's Yakima Valley has been the heartland of US hop cultivation.

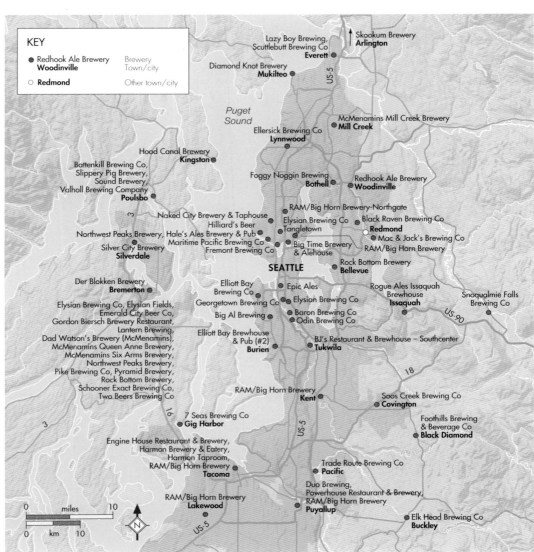

KEY

● Redhook Ale Brewery   Brewery
  Woodinville   Town/city

○ **Redmond**   Other town/city

Lazy Boy Brewing, Scuttlebutt Brewing Co
Everett

↑ Skookum Brewery
Arlington

Diamond Knot Brewery
Mukilteo

Puget Sound

McMenamins Mill Creek Brewery
● **Mill Creek**

Ellersick Brewing Co
Lynnwood

Hood Canal Brewery
Kingston

Battenkill Brewing Co, Slippery Pig Brewery, Sound Brewery, Valholl Brewing Company
Poulsbo

Foggy Noggin Brewing
Bothell

Redhook Ale Brewery
● **Woodinville**

RAM/Big Horn Brewery-Northgate

Naked City Brewery & Taphouse
Hilliard's Beer

Northwest Peaks Brewery, Hale's Ales Brewery & Pub
Maritime Pacific Brewing Co
Fremont Brewing Co

Elysian Brewing Co
Tangletown

Black Raven Brewing Co
○ **Redmond**
● Mac & Jack's Brewing Co

Big Time Brewery & Alehouse

RAM/Big Horn Brewery

Silver City Brewery
Silverdale

SEATTLE

Rock Bottom Brewery
Bellevue

Der Blokken Brewery
Bremerton

Elliott Bay Brewing Co
Georgetown Brewing Co
Big Al Brewing

Epic Ales
Elysian Brewing Co
Baron Brewing Co
Odin Brewing Co

Rogue Ales Issaquah Brewhouse
Issaquah

Snoqualmie Falls Brewing Co

Elysian Brewing Co, Elysian Fields, Emerald City Beer Co, Gordon Biersch Brewery Restaurant, Lantern Brewing, Dad Watson's Brewery (McMenamins), McMenamins Queen Anne Brewery, McMenamins Six Arms Brewery, Northwest Peaks Brewery, Pike Brewing Co, Pyramid Brewery, Rock Bottom Brewery, Schooner Exact Brewing Co, Two Beers Brewing Co

Elliott Bay Brewhouse & Pub (#2)
Burien

BJ's Restaurant & Brewhouse – Southcenter
Tukwila

RAM/Big Horn Brewery
Kent

Soos Creek Brewing Co
Covington

Foothills Brewing & Beverage Co
Black Diamond

7 Seas Brewing Co
Gig Harbor

Engine House Restaurant & Brewery, Harmon Brewery & Eatery, Harmon Taproom, RAM/Big Horn Brewery
Tacoma

Trade Route Brewing Co
Pacific

Duo Brewing, Powerhouse Restaurant & Brewery, RAM/Big Horn Brewery
Puyallup

RAM/Big Horn Brewery
Lakewood

Elk Head Brewing Co
Buckley

miles 0 — 10
km 0 — 10
N

BRIDGEPORT INDIA PALE ALE (5.5%)
Bridgeport Brewing Company,
Portland (Oregon)
The brewery's history of honouring British brewing traditions gives this quaffable ale, Bridgeport's flagship, a soft maltiness and less assaultive hop character than most northwestern IPAs.
www.bridgeportbrew.com

CASCADE KRIEK ALE (7.3%)
Cascade Brewing Barrel House,
Portland (Oregon)
As its name suggests, Cascade ages many of its beers in oak barrels, including this sweet and tart ale that spends eight months in the company of cherries to develop a deeply fruity, cherry-stone-accented flavour.
www.cascadebrewing.com

the late beer writer Michael Jackson deemed "perhaps the most distinctive lager in the United States" – Henry Weinhard's Private Reserve. It was, it almost goes without saying, especially notable for its hop character.

As was the case for most of America's fabled regional breweries, however, the final decades of the century were not kind to Blitz-Weinhard, and the old brewery eventually shut its doors for good in 1999. In its place arose a wealth of craft breweries, located in not just Portland or even Oregon but all across the Pacific Northwest and as far afield as Hawaii and Anchorage, Alaska.

Prime catalysts in the expansion of craft brewing throughout Washington and Oregon were the McMenamin brothers, Mike and Brian, who began with a single Portland pub eventually to build a sprawling network of pubs, brewpubs, hotels, and even licensed movie theatres. Now counting in excess of 50 fully owned and operated outlets, the McMenamins personify the community-mindedness of the region by limiting sales of

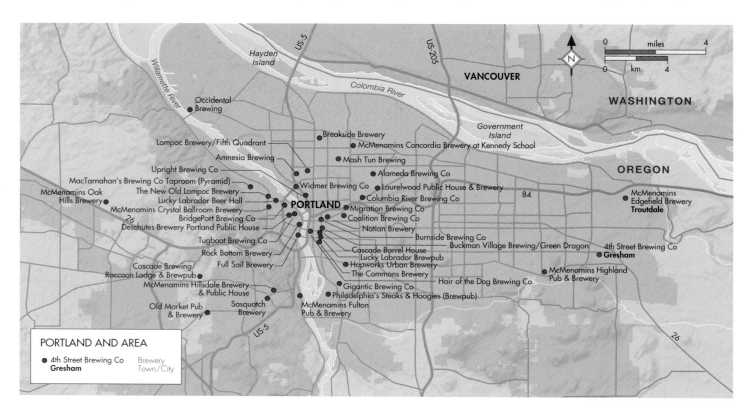

BEER SELECTION

FIVE (5.5%)
Upright Brewing Company, Portland, (Oregon)
Eschewing style classifications, Upright identifies its main beers solely by number, hence the unusual name of this fruity, pear-accented, and copper-hued ale with spicy, herbal hop notes and a dryly appetizing finish.
www.uprightbrewing.com

HAZELNUT BROWN NECTAR (6.2%)
Rogue Brewery, Newport (Oregon)
Hazelnut extract is added to this malty brown ale, not only softening the bitter hop edges so common to other Rogue ales but also providing nutty aromatics and contributing to its round and full-bodied character.
www.rogue.com

KOKO BROWN (5.5%)
Kona Brewing Company, Kona (Hawaii)
A mix of toasted coconut and "natural flavour" contributes obvious coconut aromas and taste to this ale, supported by notes of chocolate and plum, hints of freshly brewed coffee appearing towards the off-dry finish.
www.konabrewingco.com

SESSION LAGER (5.1%)
Full Sail Brewing Company, Hood River (Oregon)
Arguably stronger than one would normally expect of a "session" beer, this is nevertheless a welcome break from the big and hoppy ales that so populate the Northwest. Crisp, balanced, and refreshing, with just a hint of caramelly malt.
www.fullsailbrewing.com

SMOKED PORTER (6.5%)
Alaskan Brewing Company, Juneau (Alaska)
The beer that first garnered Alaskan Brewing copious attention in the lower 48 states, this black ale blends a rich mix of woodsmoke with dark fruits and a whiff of burned caramel.
www.alaskanbeer.com

SOMNAMBULATOR DOPPELBOCK (10%)
Walking Man Brewing Company, Stevenson (Washington)
Bourbon-barrel ageing is not often bestowed upon Doppelbocks, but here it works well. Clean but sweet malt flavours blend with vanilla and oak to form a rich and supple sipper that could easily be likened to dessert in a glass.
email: info@walkingman.com

their ales to their own establishments, resisting all temptation to package for off-site retailing.

From the urban centres of Portland and Seattle, craft brewing quickly spread to all parts of the two states, and even north to such unlikely milieus as the Alaskan capital of Juneau, accessible only by sea or air, where the Alaskan Brewing Company put far-north beer on the map with its much-awarded Smoked Porter (see opposite). It extended still further north to Anchorage, where brewers mined the decidedly bohemian bent of the citizenry to develop a vivacious beer culture. Eventually, the movement also came ashore at Maui, where the short-lived Pacific Brewing Company heralded the return of brewing to the islands seven years after Schlitz transferred production of Hawaii's beloved Primo Beer to Los Angeles.

◄ PORTLAND AND AREA

Sometimes referred to as "Beervana" or "Munich on the Willamette", Portland is the most brewery-rich city in the United States and is home to one of the country's top beer events, the Oregon Brewers Festival, held annually on the last full weekend in July.

Right: The mash tun at the Grand Teton Brewing Company has suffered a few dents through the years, but still it keeps ticking along nicely.

TAMERLANE BROWN PORTER (5.8%)
Black Raven Brewing Company, Redmond (Washington)
Treading the line between brown ale and porter, this chocolaty ale mixes spicy hops with ample amounts of roasted malt to form a most quaffable treat. Dedicated to the early works of Edgar Allan Poe.
www.blackravenbrewing.com

VIENNA LAGER (7.1%)
Chuckanut Brewery & Kitchen, Bellingham (Washington)
Will Kemper of the long-gone – and much-mourned – Thomas Kemper Brewery now brews mostly lagers up near the Canadian border, including this caramelly and unusually strong Vienna-style lager that blends lightly biscuity malt with grassy hop.
www.chuckanutbreweryandkitchen.com

XXXXX EXTRA STOUT (7%)
Pike Brewing Company, Seattle (Washington)
There were some uncomfortable years for Pike, but now back under the stewardship of founders Charles and Rose Ann Finkel, beers like this full-bodied, well-roasted, and coffee-accented warmer are returning to their original, delicious form.
www.pikebrewing.com

Rocky Mountains

Opposite: The Brewers Association is the voice of craft brewing in the USA.

The Rocky Mountain states, more specifically Colorado, achieved brewing infamy long in advance of craft beer. Well before Coors became a national brand, it had cult status in the east as a result of both its general unavailability outside of a jumble of western states – easterners were known to "bootleg" home cases of the stuff at a time – and a clever ad campaign that touted the purity of the mountain-stream water with which the beer was brewed.

Below: Coors once launched an effective advertising campaign based on the water from the Rocky Mountains, but dozens of Colorado craft brewers are putting it to better use.

More substantial fame arrived in 1979, when two former Colorado University professors founded the Boulder Brewing Company, now Boulder Beer (*see* below), in a goat shed outside of Denver. Around that same time and in that same town, an association of home brewers was set up by Charlie Papazian, who probably did not realize that what he was really doing was sowing the seeds for a national organization of small-scale breweries.

The American Homebrewers Association eventually spun off several wings, including

BEER SELECTION

5 BARREL PALE ALE (5.2%)
Odell Brewing Company,
Fort Collins (Colorado)
A showcase for the difference between hop flavour and hop bitterness, this flagship brew has a spicy aroma and caramelly, earthy drying body.
www.odellbrewing.com

DALE'S PALE ALE (6.5%)
Oskar Blues Brewery, Longmont (Colorado)
The leader of the canned craft beer movement – or "apocalypse", to use the brewery's term – is this piney, almost chewy pale ale with a quenching, off-dry finish.
www.oskarblues.com

HOG HEAVEN BARLEY WINE (9.2%)
Avery Brewing Company,
Boulder (Colorado)
Bitter both coming and going, with classic American hop notes, a wealth of fruity, toffee-like malt breaks up the citric bite.
www.averybrewing.com

INDIA PALE ALE (6.2%)
Marble Brewery, Albuquerque
(New Mexico)
Where some breweries use American hops to attack the palate with citrus and pine, Marble cannily mixes flavours of over-ripe fruit with juicy and tangy hop notes. The result is a tantalizingly restrained ale that proves that, sometimes, less really can be more.
www.marblebrewery.com

OAK AGED YETI IMPERIAL STOUT (9.5%)
Great Divide Brewing Company,
Denver (Colorado)
Part of a range of Yeti imperial stouts, this bourbon-barrel-matured beauty blends vanilla and oak with coffee and roast, and keeps it all in perfect harmony.
www.greatdivide.com

MOJO INDIA PALE ALE (6.8%)
Boulder Beer Company,
Boulder (Colorado)
Massively fragrant with tropical-fruit notes, the taste of this showpiece of balance segues deftly from a fruity, toffee-accented front to a sparkling, resinous finish.
www.boulderbeer.com

the Brewers Association, a now-vital trade group representing the interests of craft brewers, a publishing house, and the largest beer event in the Americas: Denver's annual Great American Beer Festival (GABF). Along the way, of course, craft brewing spread from Boulder all the way up and down the Rockies, from Montana to Arizona and New Mexico.

The heart of mountain brewing today remains Denver, Colorado, perhaps because the GABF places it at the epicentre of American craft beer. Or maybe it is thanks to the way locals have embraced the movement, or owing to the efforts of the talented brewers who both populate and surround the city. Most likely, though, it is because of a combination of the three.

Above: The Great American Beer Festival draws thousands to Denver every year, usually selling out months in advance.

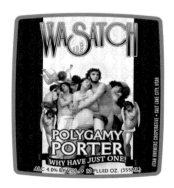

POLYGAMY PORTER (4%)
Wasatch Brew Pub & Brewery,
Park City (Utah)
Utah's upper alcohol limit of 4% produces some interesting results, like this mocha-ish ale. Its controversial tagline: "Why have just one?"
www.wasatchbeers.com

PROVO GIRL PILSNER (4%)
Squatters Pubs & Beers, Salt Lake City (Utah)
Another of Utah's unusual low-alcohol brews, this "session" lager has an unusually sweet and fragrant aroma but a flavour that is crisp, dry, and wonderfully palate-cleansing.
www.squatters.com

RAIL YARD ALE (5.2%)
Wynkoop Brewing Company,
Denver (Colorado)
As befits one of America's largest brewpubs, Wynkoop's flagship is a consummate pub ale, with a light fruitiness, caramelly malt, and quaffably off-dry character.
www.wynkoop.com

RANGER INDIA PALE PALE (6.5%)
New Belgium Brewing Company,
Fort Collins (Colorado)
A citrus-accented nose plentiful in sweet floral notes precedes a flavour that might lean a tad heavily on the bitter side but balances things with sweet, honey-like malt.
www.newbelgium.com

SNOW GHOST (5.9%)
Great Northern Brewing Company,
Whitefish (Montana)
A satisfyingly strong lager that is neither *Bock* nor *Märzen* but still big, malty, and delicious, this winter treat offers notes of chocolate, roasted malt, and sweetened espresso.
www.greatnorthernbrewing.com

TROUT HOP BLACK IPA (8.5%)
Grand Teton Brewing Company,
Victor (Idaho)
Molasses and earthy caramel mix with citrus-accented bitterness and liquorice notes in this jet-black and nutty fixture, one of the brewery's "Cellar Reserve" series.
www.grandtetonbrewing.com

Midwest & Great Lakes

The Midwest was once America's brewing heartland. Immortalized in song and story, Milwaukee was its capital, home at one time or another to such celebrated breweries as Schlitz and Blatz, Pabst and Heileman, and – still standing today – Miller.

LAKE MICHIGAN SHORELINE ▶
America's "third coast", the Lake Michigan area has been popular with breweries since the industrialization of brewing in the 19th century. Today, craft breweries dot almost the entire shoreline, from northern Michigan to the top of Wisconsin.

Further south, the brewing anchor was provided by St Louis, Missouri, where were rooted Falstaff, Anheuser-Busch, and the latter's fierce rivals, the Griesedieck Brothers. Cincinnati laid claim to Hudepohl-Schoenling, while St Paul, Minnesota, had Hamm's, and Detroit, Michigan, boasted the "fire-brewed" flavour of Stroh.

The 1970s and 1980s, however, were unkind to the breweries of the Midwest, as one by one they fell from favour to be devoured by the competitors, which were in turn consumed by their even larger competitors. Nowhere was this beer Darwinism more apparent than in the case of Schlitz, which took little more than a decade to tumble from its position as America's number-one brewery to a state of general irrelevance.

Phase one of the craft-brewing renaissance returned a small degree

Above: America's "Motor City", Detroit, appears to be on the cusp of a comeback following years of hard times – and craft beer is there to toast its recovery.

BEER SELECTION

ALPHA KING (6.5%)
Three Floyds Brewing Company, Munster (Indiana)
A mash-up of massive American hop character and juicy malt brings to life this aggressively grapefruity powerhouse of a pale ale, one of the Midwest's original ultra-hoppy craft beers.
www.3floyds.com

BAM BIÈRE (4.5%)
Jolly Pumpkin Artisan Ales, Dexter (Michigan)
Barrel aged, like all of Jolly Pumpkin's wares, this "session" ale has a light and very dry character, with muted fruitiness and a tart, appealingly woody character.
www.jollypumpkin.com

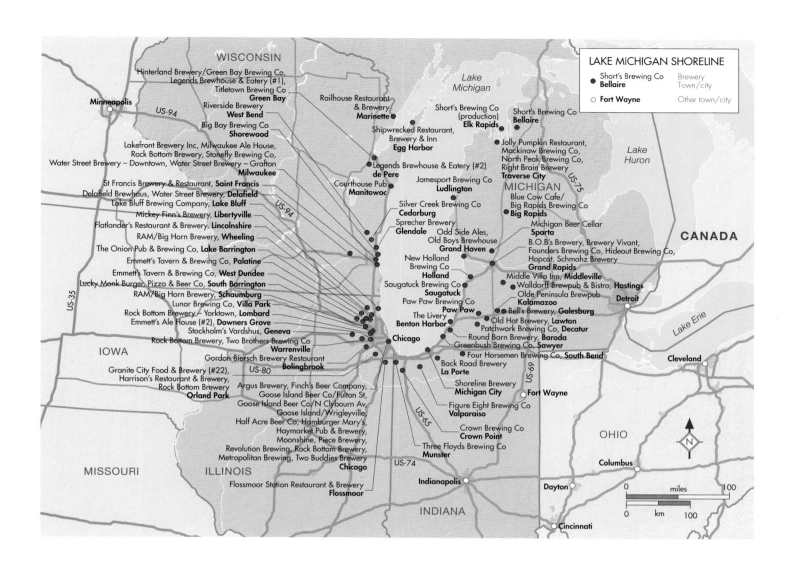

WISCONSIN

Hinterland Brewery/Green Bay Brewing Co,
Legends Brewhouse & Eatery (#1),
Titletown Brewing Co
Green Bay
Riverside Brewery
West Bend
Big Bay Brewing Co
Shorewood
Lakefront Brewery Inc, Milwaukee Ale House,
Rock Bottom Brewery, Stonefly Brewing Co,
Water Street Brewery – Downtown, Water Street Brewery – Grafton
Milwaukee
St Francis Brewery & Restaurant, **Saint Francis**
Delafield Brewhaus, Water Street Brewery, **Delafield**
Lake Bluff Brewing Company, **Lake Bluff**
Mickey Finn's Brewery, **Libertyville**
Flatlander's Restaurant & Brewery, **Lincolnshire**
RAM/Big Horn Brewery, **Wheeling**
The Onion Pub & Brewing Co, **Lake Barrington**
Emmett's Tavern & Brewing Co, **Palatine**
Emmett's Tavern & Brewing Co, **West Dundee**
Lucky Monk Burger, Pizza & Beer Co, **South Barrington**
RAM/Big Horn Brewery, **Schaumburg**
Lunar Brewing Co, **Villa Park**
Rock Bottom Brewery – Yorktown, **Lombard**
Emmett's Ale House (#2), **Downers Grove**
Stockholm's Vardshus, **Geneva**
Rock Bottom Brewery, Two Brothers Brewing Co
Warrenville
Gordon Biersch Brewery Restaurant
Bolingbrook
Granite City Food & Brewery (#22),
Harrison's Restaurant & Brewery,
Rock Bottom Brewery
Orland Park
Argus Brewery, Finch's Beer Company,
Goose Island Beer Co/Fulton St,
Goose Island Beer Co/N Clybourn Av,
Goose Island/Wrigleyville,
Half Acre Beer Co, Hamburger Mary's,
Haymarket Pub & Brewery,
Moonshine, Piece Brewery,
Revolution Brewing, Rock Bottom Brewery,
Metropolitan Brewing, Two Buddies Brewery
Chicago
Flossmoor Station Restaurant & Brewery
Flossmoor

Minneapolis
US-94

IOWA

US-35

MISSOURI

ILLINOIS

US-80

US-65

US-74

Railhouse Restaurant
& Brewery
Marinette
Shipwrecked Restaurant,
Brewery & Inn
Egg Harbor
Legends Brewhouse & Eatery (#2)
de Pere
Courthouse Pub
Manitowoc
Silver Creek Brewing Co
Cedarburg
Sprecher Brewery
Glendale

Lake
Michigan

Short's Brewing Co
(production)
Elk Rapids
Jolly Pumpkin Restaurant,
Mackinaw Brewing Co,
North Peak Brewing Co,
Right Brain Brewery
Traverse City
Jamesport Brewing Co
Ludlington

Short's Brewing Co
Bellaire

MICHIGAN

Lake
Huron

US-75

Short's Brewing Co
Traverse City

Blue Cow Cafe/
Big Rapids Brewing Co
Big Rapids
Michigan Beer Cellar
Sparta
B.O.B's Brewery, Brewery Vivant,
Founders Brewing Co, Hideout Brewing Co,
Hopcat, Schmohz Brewery
Grand Rapids
Middle Villa Inn, **Middleville**
Walldorff Brewpub & Bistro, **Hastings**
Olde Peninsula Brewpub
Kalamazoo
Bell's Brewery, **Galesburg**
Old Hat Brewery, **Lawton**
Patchwork Brewing Co, **Decatur**
Round Barn Brewery, **Baroda**
Greenbush Brewing Co, **Sawyer**
Four Horsemen Brewing Co, **South Bend**

CANADA

Lake Erie

Odd Side Ales,
Old Boys Brewhouse
Grand Haven
New Holland
Brewing Co
Holland
Saugatuck Brewing Co
Saugatuck
Paw Paw Brewing Co
Paw Paw
The Livery
Benton Harbor

Chicago

Back Road Brewery
La Porte
Shoreline Brewery
Michigan City
Figure Eight Brewing Co
Valparaiso
Crown Brewing Co
Crown Point
Three Floyds Brewing Co
Munster

Detroit

US-69

Cleveland

OHIO

Columbus

Dayton

N

Indianapolis

INDIANA

Cincinnati

0   miles   100

0   km   100

LAKE MICHIGAN SHORELINE

●	Short's Brewing Co	Brewery
	Bellaire	Town/city
○	**Fort Wayne**	Other town/city

BLACK BAVARIAN (5.86%)
Sprecher Brewing Company,
Glendale (Wisconsin)
Think of this as a midpoint between
Dunkel and *Doppelbock*, with fistfuls of
roasted malt thrown in for good measure.
Sweet and chocolaty turning borderline
smoky by the finish.
www.sprecherbrewery.com

BREAKFAST STOUT (AKA KBS, CBS)
(8.3–11.2%)
Founders Brewing Company,
Grand Rapids (Michigan)
A beer that changes name and character
with barrel ageing – bourbon barrels for
K(entucky)BS, maple syrup barrels for
C(anadian)BS – this oatmeal stout starts life
rich, mocha-ish, and incredibly full-bodied,
and only gets better from there.
www.foundersbrewing.com

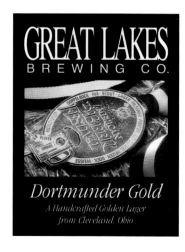

DORTMUNDER GOLD LAGER (5.8%)
Great Lakes Brewing Company,
Cleveland (Ohio)
Evidence that "malty" need not correspond
directly with "sweet", this dry beauty
has an almost chewy malt appeal, hints
of minerality, and a satisfying, mildly
bitter finish.
www.greatlakesbrewing.com

EXPEDITION STOUT (10.5%)
Bell's Brewery, Kalamazoo (Michigan)
With a brewery this stout-obsessed –
13 in the present line-up – you would
expect something special of its imperial,
like this roasty behemoth, rough when
young but mellowing nicely in the cellar.
www.bellsbeer.com

Above: Filling growlers and drinking pints at Thr3e Wise Men Brewing in Indianapolis, Indiana.

BEER SELECTION

HOPFEN (6.2%)
Urban Chestnut Brewing Company,
St Louis (Missouri)
IPA-style hopping with German Hallertau hops gives this unique brew a seductively floral aroma and a flavour evocative of a lightly fruity pale ale crossed with aromatic Riesling.
www.urbanchestnut.com

MAD HATTER INDIA PALE ALE (5.25%)
New Holland Brewing Company,
Holland (Michigan)
A spicy, floral, and alfalfa-tinged aroma precedes a dry, herbaceous, and citric body that follows quenchingly through to a generously bitter finish – sessionable IPA at its best.
www.newhollandbrew.com

MATILDA (7%)
Goose Island Beer Company,
Chicago (Illinois)
Inspired by the Trappist ale Orval (see p.54), this is a noble homage, with slightly tart and spicy accents layered appetizingly over tangy fruitiness and earthy malt.
www.gooseisland.com

TANK 7 FARMHOUSE ALE (8%)
Boulevard Brewing Company,
Kansas City (Missouri)
After an aromatic nose suffused with tropical fruit and spice, this flagship of Boulevard's "Smokestack Series" of speciality ales offers peppery spice and even a hint of tamarind in a lively, refreshing body.
www.boulevard.com

of brewing glory to the Midwest, with breweries such as Lakefront and Sprecher (*see* p.191) in Milwaukee, Bell's in western Michigan (*see* p.191), Summit in St Paul, and Goose Island in Chicago (*see* below, opposite) speeding out of the starting gate in the mid- to late 1980s. Then things really got interesting.

Through the 1990s and into the new millennium, breweries opened at a voracious rate all across the Midwest, from Schlafly Beer's "David" act in the shadows of Anheuser-Busch's "Goliath" to a host of operations on America's "Third Coast" in Michigan and throughout Indiana and Ohio. Certain areas fared better than others, of course – Chicago was a notoriously difficult market, and the Dakotas struggle still – but, by and large, the heartland is once more spoiled for choice in fine ales and lagers.

Right: At the Schlafly Brewing Company, in St Louis, they joke that neighbour Anheuser-Busch spills more beer in a day than their brewery produces in a year.

Next page: It took a while for craft beer to take off in the Windy City, but Chicago is now home to dozens of breweries, brewpubs, and beer bars.

WEE MAC SCOTTISH ALE (5.3%)
Sun King Brewing Company,
Indianapolis (Indiana)
The Scots would love such a beer. Copper-coloured, it has a nutty, toffeeish nose and a body boasting sweet raisin and caramel notes throughout, without ever growing sticky or cloying, finishing off-dry and slightly minerally.
www.sunkingbrewing.com

WISCONSIN BELGIAN RED (4%)
New Glarus Brewing Company,
New Glarus (Wisconsin)
With more than a pound of cherries per 75cl (26.4fl oz) bottle, this is an unapologetic fruit beer that remains nonetheless a beer first and fruit-flavoured second.
www.newglarusbrewing.com

Northeast

Being the birthplace of the USA, it stands to reason that the northeast would hold a considerable amount of brewing history within its borders. George Washington brewed here, or at least we think he did, as did Thomas Jefferson, or at least his wife, Martha. And the oldest operating brewery in the country, Yuengling, still stands proudly in Pottsville, Pennsylvania.

MAJOR BREWERIES OF THE METROPOLITAN NEW YORK CITY AND PHILADELPHIA AREAS ▶
While New York City was slow to take to craft beer, Philadelphia rapidly developed into one of the best beer cities in the United States. Today, both areas are replete with craft breweries.

Below: Portland, Maine, just minutes from picturesque Cape Elizabeth (pictured), has evolved into one of the northeast's most interesting cities for craft beer.

Somewhere along the line, however, New England and the mid-Atlantic states were marginalized where beer and brewing were concerned. Sure, Ballantine had some outstanding years in New York and New Jersey, as did Narragansett in Rhode Island and Rheingold in New York. But as the brewing industry became more of a national concern, it also grew increasingly centralized, not in the northeast but in the industrial and increasingly Germanic Midwest. Until, that is, the Boston Beer Company came along (*see* pp.198–9).

While Jim Koch's company was not the first craft brewery to bloom in the northeast – it was beaten to the punch by the since-closed Newman Brewing Company in Albany, New York, and a small handful

BEER SELECTION

BROOKLYN LAGER (5.2%)
Brooklyn Brewery, Brooklyn (New York)
German and American hops combined with toasted grain notes give this brew a most distinctive character, neither fish nor fowl in the style-categorization game but impressively balanced with spicy, citric, biscuity notes and an off-dry finish.
www.brooklynbrewery.com

CERISE CASSÉE (9%)
Cambridge Brewing Company, Cambridge (Massachusetts)
Sour mashing, wild yeasts, sour cherries, and barrel aging all contribute to this beer's unusual character, both sweet and tart, fresh on the palate, and aged and oak-accented on the finish. The brewery uses a *solera*-style system (*see* p.28), which means that this brew literally never ends.
www.cambrew.com

CURIEUX (11%)
Allagash Brewing Company, Portland (Maine)
A Belgian-inspired *tripel* aged in bourbon barrels should not work, and in the early years of this beer it did not. Now, however, Allagash has nailed the wood-to-beer proportions and created a stunningly approachable, vanilla-tinted strong ale.
www.allagash.com

CUVÉE DES FLEURS (8.2%)
Southampton Publick House, Southampton (New York)
Multiple varieties of edible flowers contribute to the intensely floral aroma of this mischievously potent ale. Floral notes also dominate in the taste, but in such a way that they might be welcomed by even the most macho of palates.
www.publick.com

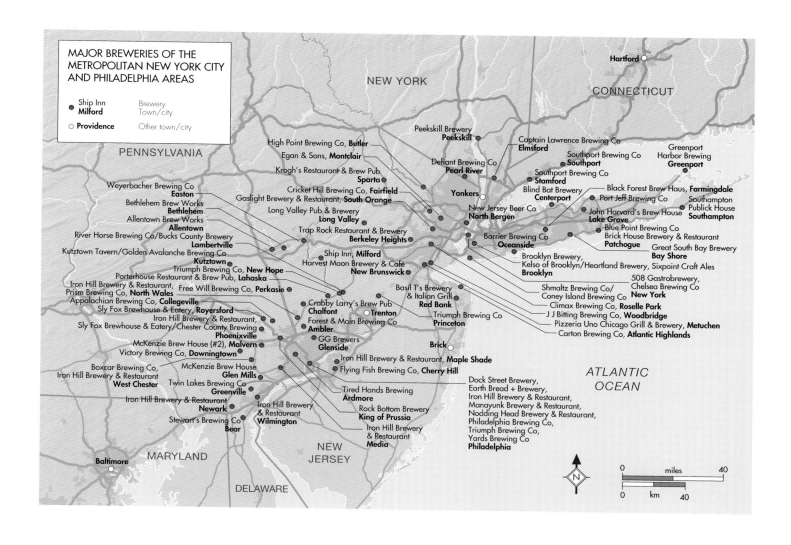

MAJOR BREWERIES OF THE
METROPOLITAN NEW YORK CITY
AND PHILADELPHIA AREAS

● Ship Inn / **Milford** — Brewery / Town/city
○ Providence — Other town/city

SOUTHAMPTON
750 Series
Cuvée
des Fleurs
Ale brewed with Flowers
750 mL (1 PINT, 9.4 FL. OZ.)

EXIT 4 AMERICAN TRIPPEL (9.5%)
Flying Fish Brewing Company, Cherry Hill
(New Jersey)
"American" indeed, as one sniff of this
hop-laden paean to Belgian monastic
brewing will tell. Take the soft malt and
vaguely brandyish appeal of a Belgian
tripel and layer on top a bunch of spicy
American hops for a sense of this beauty.
www.flyingfish.com

GEARY'S HAMPSHIRE SPECIAL ALE (7%)
D L Geary Brewing Company,
Portland (Maine)
Born a winter ale, "available while the
weather sucks", this astute blend of big
malt and drying, Christmas-cake spiciness
culled from a mix of British and American
hops is now brewed year-round. Still at its
best as the snow blows.
www.gearybrewing.com

**HE'BREW ORIGIN POMEGRANATE
ALE (8%)**
Shmaltz Brewing Company, Saratoga
Springs (New York)
Gimmicky names and graphics aside,
Shmaltz produces some serious ales,
including this unlikely blend of rich,
moderately bitter hoppiness and luscious,
berryish malt, leading to a dry, almost
tannic finish.
www.shmaltzbrewing.com

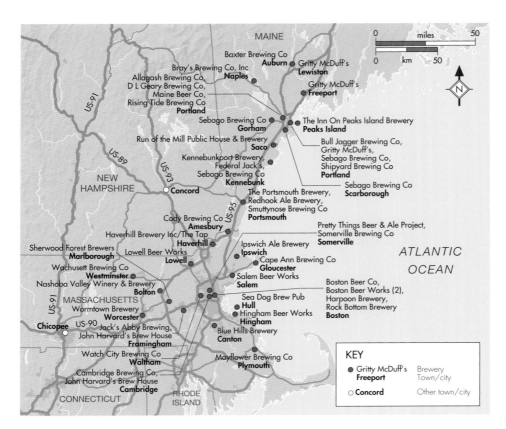

Map legend:

MAINE

Baxter Brewing Co
Auburn
Gritty McDuff's
Lewiston

Bray's Brewing Co, Inc
Naples
Gritty McDuff's
Freeport

Allagash Brewing Co,
D L Geary Brewing Co,
Maine Beer Co,
Rising Tide Brewing Co
Portland

Sebago Brewing Co
Gorham
The Inn On Peaks Island Brewery
Peaks Island

Run of the Mill Public House & Brewery
Saco
Bull Jagger Brewing Co,
Gritty McDuff's,
Sebago Brewing Co,
Shipyard Brewing Co
Portland

Kennebunkport Brewery
Federal Jack's,
Sebago Brewing Co
Kennebunk
Sebago Brewing Co
Scarborough

NEW HAMPSHIRE
Concord

The Portsmouth Brewery,
Redhook Ale Brewery,
Smuttynose Brewing Co
Portsmouth

Cody Brewing Co
Amesbury

Pretty Things Beer & Ale Project,
Somerville Brewing Co
Somerville

Haverhill Brewery Inc/The Tap
Haverhill

Ipswich Ale Brewery
Ipswich

ATLANTIC
OCEAN

Sherwood Forest Brewers
Marlborough
Lowell Beer Works
Lowell
Cape Ann Brewing Co
Gloucester

Wachusett Brewing Co
Westminster
Salem Beer Works
Salem

Nashoba Valley Winery & Brewery
Bolton

MASSACHUSETTS
Wormtown Brewery
Worcester
Sea Dog Brew Pub
Hull
Hingham Beer Works
Hingham

Boston Beer Co,
Boston Beer Works (2),
Harpoon Brewery,
Rock Bottom Brewery
Boston

Chicopee
Jack's Abby Brewing,
John Harvard's Brew House
Framingham

Blue Hills Brewery
Canton

Watch City Brewing Co
Waltham

Cambridge Brewing Co,
John Harvard's Brew House
Cambridge

Mayflower Brewing Co
Plymouth

RHODE ISLAND

CONNECTICUT

0 miles 50
0 km 50

KEY

● Gritty McDuff's
Freeport — Brewery Town/city

○ **Concord** — Other town/city

▲ MAJOR BREWERIES OF COASTAL NEW ENGLAND, BOSTON TO PORTLAND

Since the founding of the Boston Beer Company in 1985 and Portland's D L Geary in 1986, the coastal stretch between these two New England cities has proved fertile ground for craft-beer development.

Dogging Boston Beer throughout its first two decades of existence were criticisms that because it hired other breweries to produce the majority of its beer, a practice known as contract brewing, it was somehow not a "real" brewery. So great were these concerns, in fact, that they persist in some quarters even today, despite the fact that Boston Beer has long since become responsible for the creation of all its beer.

Regardless of its occasionally impugned credentials, what Koch's company did accomplish was the bringing of craft beer into the mainstream for millions of Americans. As the label image of colonial founding father Samuel Adams became a sight increasingly familiar to beer buyers, first throughout the east and eventually across the country, it helped transform beer other than that of the major brewers – Anheuser-Busch, Miller, and Coors – from an oddity into a commodity.

of others – it certainly became the most significant over time. Buoyed by the success of its flagship Samuel Adams Boston Lager, Boston Beer evolved into the largest craft brewing concern in the country, today accountable for roughly one-fifth of all craft beer brewed in the USA. It is also a company not without its share of controversy.

BEER SELECTION

ICH BIN EIN BERLINER WEISSE (3.5%)
Nodding Head Brewery & Restaurant,
Philadelphia (Pennsylvania)
An unassuming brewpub in central Philly is hardly a likely source of a *Berliner Weisse* revival, but so it was with this lactic, appetizingly tart wheat beer, which started a movement in the USA, even as the style was dying in Germany.
www.noddinghead.com

OLD BROWN DOG ALE (6.5%)
Smuttynose Brewing Company, Portsmouth (New Hampshire)
A brown ale with an American accent of higher strength and more apparent hoppiness, this dog has no shortage of new tricks. American hops give it a spicy, nutty appeal on top of quaffable chocolate malt.
www.smuttynose.com

OMMEGANG ALE (8.5%)
Brewery Ommegang, Cooperstown (New York)
Unabashedly Belgian influenced – the brewery is owned by Duvel (*see p.77*) – this spiced and spicy brown ale offers dried dark fruit notes along with a moderate caramelly sweetness, all leading to a clove-accented and food-friendly finish.
www.ommegang.com

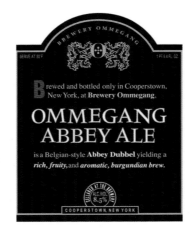

PALO SANTO MARRON (12%)
Dogfish Head Craft Brewery, Milton (Delaware)
Deep mahogany in colour, ageing in vats made of Paraguayan wood gives this ale aromas of perfumy vanilla, cinnamon, and other spices, and a Madeira-esque body of rum-soaked raisins, chocolate fudge, stewed tropical fruits, and fireplace embers.
www.dogfish.com

PIKELAND PILS (4.9%)
Sly Fox Brewing Company, Royersford (Pennsylvania)
Styled after the pilsners of northern Germany, this is the equal of the best of its Teutonic kin. Brilliant gold with a dryly malty nose, the body speaks of fragrant malt in the first half and grassy, appetizing bitterness the rest of the way.
www.slyfoxbeer.com

As elsewhere in the USA, the 1990s saw an explosion of craft breweries across the northeast, although with some surprising and notable exceptions. New York City, for example, although long noted as a fertile ground for sales of imported beer, was ponderously slow to embrace craft beer, despite the heroic efforts of the Manhattan Brewing Company, Zip City, and others. It was not until the twentieth-first century that craft beer actually began to thrive in the Big Apple.

Plucky Vermont, on the other hand, with its relatively small but progressively minded population, was quick to embrace the rebellious ethos behind the craft beer movement and took to breweries from the Vermont Pub & Brewery in the north to McNeill's Brewery in the state's southernmost reaches. Similarly, New Hampshire, Maine, and Pennsylvania all proved to be highly supportive of local brewing efforts.

Transformed from brewing also-ran into craft beer dynamo, the northeast today is considered one of the top beer markets in the country. Whether imbibing at a time-worn Boston tavern or dining at a white-tablecloth restaurant inside the Beltway in Washington DC, a quality ale or lager would seem to be never too far from reach.

Above: Boston Beer Company CEO Jim Koch samples oak-aged beer that will be blended to make the brewery's super-strong Utopias, which, in 2011, measured 27 per cent alcohol.

ST BOISTEROUS HELLERBOCK (7.3%)

Victory Brewing Company, Downingtown (Pennsylvania)

Although arguably better known for hoppy and intense ales, this suburban Philadelphia brewery is also adept at crafting lagers, including this pale gold and perfumy jewel that segues beautifully from a honey-malt front to a bitter and warming finish.

www.victorybeer.com

THE MAD ELF ALE (11%)

Tröegs Brewing Company, Harrisburg (Pennsylvania)

The brothers Trogner have created an East Coast holiday classic with this cherry-infused mix of yeasty spice, chocolaty malt, and, of course, tart cherry flavour. A warming end to a Christmas feast.

www.troegs.com

UTOPIAS (27%)

Boston Beer Company, Boston (Massachusetts)

A behemoth of a brew that changes with each release, the latest edition of this cellar-worthy sipper is a blend of multiple ales, some barrel-aged for years, resulting in complex flavour of spicy toffee and praline, chocolate and allspice, vanilla and muddled fruit, and so much more.

www.samueladams.com

South

For any number of varied and occasionally unusual reasons – economic, cultural, historic, and legislative – the South for years lagged badly in the development of its craft-brewing industry. With few exceptions, notably the Spoetzl Brewery in Texas (*see* p.202), there was no great tradition of brewing in the region, and the hot weather often experienced in the southern states tends to have people reaching for ice-cold and light-bodied lagers: precisely the sort of beer the major breweries specialize in.

Below: Not all breweries make it. Some, like Nashville, Tennessee's Market Street Brewery, succumb to commercial pressures, but leave their trademark behind.

Furthermore, the South has long been plagued by disproportionately higher rates of poverty than the rest of the country, which hardly provided fertile ground for the development of premium-priced artisanal ales and lagers.

What might have played the biggest role in the suppression of southern craft brewing, however, was the web of odd and arcane laws that governed states from North Carolina to Texas. Regulations capping the percentage of alcohol allowed in beer were relatively commonplace, for example, and one of the USA's most bizarre alcohol laws must have been that which once required all bottles of beer sold in Florida to have the letters "FL" inscribed on the side of their caps.

BEER SELECTION

BOSCOS FAMOUS FLAMING STONE BEER (4.8%)
Boscos Restaurant & Brewing Company, Memphis (Tennessee)
The stones in question are heated in the restaurant's pizza oven before being added to the beer during the boil, an act that contributes a caramelly quality to this otherwise light-bodied brew.
www.boscosbeer.com

COMMERCIAL SUICIDE (3.3%)
Jester King Craft Brewery, Austin (Texas)
From a brewery known for its edgy styles and irreverent approach to labelling comes this suitably malty, British-style mild ale, a portion of which is aged in American oak barrels. A newer version is fermented with a Belgian yeast and known as Farmhouse Commercial Suicide.
www.jesterkingbrewery.com

DUCK-RABBIT MILK STOUT (5.7%)
Duck-Rabbit Craft Brewery, Farmville (North Carolina)
The use of lactose, or milk sugar, in this beer gives it a rounded sweetness that mellows any rough edges on the bitter chocolate, coffee, and roasty flavours resulting from the dark malts involved.
www.duckrabbitbrewery.com

FANCY LAWNMOWER (4.9%)
Saint Arnold Brewing Company, Houston (Texas)
A different take on the hot weather "lawnmower beer" is this offering from the oldest craft brewery in Texas. Styled after the *Kölsch* beers of Cologne (Köln), Germany, it has a crisply quenching character buoyed by a mildly full and fruity body. A dark-hued version is also made, called Santo.
www.saintarnold.com

GREEN MAN IPA (6.2%)
Green Man Brewing Company, Asheville (North Carolina)
Although unarguably well hopped, this IPA boasts dry toffee maltiness and hints of toasted nuts more reminiscent of the British style.
www.greenmanbrewery.com

Above: Notorious for the sale of "Big Ass" cups of cold and largely flavourless beer, even New Orleans' famed Bourbon Street is welcoming the arrival of beers from Abita, NOLA Brewing, and other craft breweries.

HEAVY SEAS SMALL CRAFT WARNING ÜBER PILS (7%)
Clipper City Brewing Company,
Baltimore (Maryland)
Part of the brewery's high-strength division, this floral-spicy delight could be likened to a ramped-up Bohemian pilsner with attitude.
www.hsbeer.com

HOPITOULAS IPA (6%)
NOLA Brewing Company,
New Orleans (Louisiana)
Seasoned with a half-dozen varieties of hops and dry hopped to boot, this draught-only offering provides a citric, spicy, and fruity alternative to the typically more mild-mannered brews available in the Big Easy. The brewery also crafts seasonal and occasional special edition brews.
www.nolabrewing.com

HORNY TOAD CERVEZA (5.3%)
Coop Ale Works,
Oklahoma City (Oklahoma)
Bright gold and pilsnerish on the palate, the apricot notes in the aroma suggest that this is fermented with ale yeast rather than lager, although to its benefit rather than detriment. A satisfying quaff for the Southern heat.
www.coopaleworks.com

LIVE OAK PILZ (4.7%)
Live Oak Brewing Company, Austin (Texas)
Old World brewing methods imbue this draught-only lager with an almost bready maltiness, over which is laid ample amounts of floral, lightly spicy, and quenching hop bitterness.
www.liveoakbrewing.com

MADURO BROWN ALE (5.5%)
Cigar City Brewing Company,
Tampa Bay (Florida)
Where oatmeal stout meets brown ale lies this milk chocolaty beer with berry-fruit notes, some caramel in the start, coffee in the finish, and an overall rich and silken character.
www.cigarcitybrewing.com

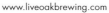

As those laws fell by the wayside and prosperity arrived in the South, craft beer boomed. Led by North Carolina, location of the headquarters of the pioneering beer magazine *All About Beer*, breweries began springing up in numbers through the late 1990s and into the twenty-first century. This resulted not just in pioneering

Southern breweries like Abita in Louisiana (*see* below) and Saint Arnold of Texas (*see* p.200) being able to expand their existing ranges to include more characterful styles, but also a foothold being put in place for such eclectic and innovative operations as Cigar City in Florida (*see* below) and Jester King in Texas (*see* p.200).

Today, while states such as Alabama and Arkansas continue to trail by some distance the craft beer *Zeitgeist*, urban areas like Atlanta, Austin, and even Tampa Bay have turned into hotbeds of creative brewing and warm-weather paradises for beer aficionados.

AMERICAN BREWPUB

The modern American brewpub was born a simple beast, producing beer intended to be served at the bar or restaurant adjoining the brewery only, thus eliminating the sometimes lengthy supply lines that have become pillars of our modern lives. What it evolved into, however, is the incubator of the US craft-brewing movement.

Beginning with the first brewpub in the USA, Bert Grant's Yakima Brewing & Malting Company, brewpubs took the lead in charting a course of innovation in brewing, with Grant's effusive use of hops helping pave the way for the far hoppier beers that were to follow. Further, like literally hundreds of the

brewpubs that were to follow his lead, Grant quickly grew tired of selling his beers only on premises and was not long in turning to bottling and distribution.

As the years progressed and craft beer grew increasingly popular, brewpubs flourished in number, size, and creativity, to the point that many of the biggest names in craft brewing today got their start as brewpubs, or began life as combined brewpub-production brewery operations. Delaware's Dogfish Head Craft Brewery (*see* p.198) began with a minuscule 12-US-gallon (45-litre) brewing system operating full-tilt to serve its resort town brewpub; San Diego's The Lost Abbey

(*see* p.183) first found its soul in a small chain of pizza restaurants; and the beers of Bell's Brewery (*see* p.191) are still found at their best in the aptly named Eccentric Cafe in downtown Kalamazoo, Michigan.

In their wake stand brewpubs like Cambridge in Massachusetts (*see* p.196) and Nodding Head in Philadelphia (*see* p.197), and Florida's Tampa Bay Brewing (*see* p.201), collectively pushing the envelope of creative brewing and awaiting their moment in the bottled- beer spotlight.

BEER SELECTION

RESTORATION PALE ALE (5%)
Abita Brewing Company, Abita Springs (Louisiana)
Launched as a charitable effort to help those affected by Hurricane Katrina, this is a highly fragrant, floral, and mildly hoppy pale ale with ample body and a peppery finish.
www.abita.com

RYE SQUARED (8.5%)
Terrapin Beer Company, Athens (Georgia)
As much as the spicy, caraway-ish rye grain defines Terrapin's Rye Pale Ale, it screams its presence in this intensified version, sharing the stage with citric bitterness and caramel malt.
www.terrapinbeer.com

SHINER DORTMUNDER (5.5%)
Spoetzl Brewery, Shiner (Texas)
Deep gold in colour, this firmly malty, even slightly flinty lager with a dry, engaging finish is mislabelled an ale in order to comply with Texas labelling law that restricts beers of such strength.
www.shiner.com

THE CARIBBEAN

Sun-seekers visiting the resorts of Negril, Jamaica, or the beaches of Barbados will end their trips with the impression that, in beer terms, at least, little has changed in the Caribbean over the last 40 or so years. Stores and bars, particularly those a tourist might frequent, remain dominated absolutely by the same, soon-familiar brands, mostly owned by all-too-familiar multinational brewing corporations.

BEST-SELLING LOCAL LABELS

Banks	(National)
Carib	(National)
Red Stripe	(Diageo)

And sadly, that impression is very close to the truth. While there has been over the past years some small growth in craft brewing, notably in the Cayman Islands and U.S. Virgin Islands, the beer giants still largely control to near-exclusivity the Caribbean beer markets. Defiant breweries like Jamaica's Big City Brewing, Trinidad's Samba Brewery and St. John Brewers (*see* below) in the U.S. Virgin Islands have their work cut out for them.

Yet even within the portfolios of the beer giants there lurks respite from the pallid lagers ubiquitous throughout the tropics. A legacy of the so-called export-strength (7% or higher) black beers once shipped to the Caribbean from the British Isles, the sweet, lager-fermented stout is considered almost *de rigueur* for any island brewery. Strong and malty golden lagers, once almost as common, have all but disappeared in recent years.

Left: Light lager brands like Carib, Banks, and Red Stripe still dominate the Caribbean, but there are signs things might slowly be beginning to change.

BEER SELECTION

DRAGON STOUT (7.5%)
Desnoes & Geddes, Inc.,
Kingston, Jamaica
There is not a great deal of complexity in this sweet, lightly roasty and thinnish stout with notes of toasted brown sugar and anise, but that's also part of its charm. Suited to sipping on a sultry evening.
www.redstripebeer.com

ISLAND HOPPIN' IPA (6.2%)
St. John Brewers, St. John,
U.S. Virgin Islands
Assertive hoppiness is a rarity in Caribbean beer, but it is abundantly evident in this deep copper, fruity-nutty IPA. Brewed in small batches on the island and, for bottled product, under contract in Maine.
www.stjohnbrewers.com

ROYAL EXTRA STOUT (6.6%)
Carib Brewery Trinidad Limited
Champs Fleur, Trinidad
An oddball beer of sorts, fortified with lactose, as one would use for a milk stout, but fermented with a lager yeast, this sweet black beer is light yet silky on the palate, with notes of sugary espresso and dark chocolate. Surprisingly refreshing when served chilled.
www.caribbrewery.com

Extreme Beers

You would need to have been in hiding for most of the first decade of the twenty-first century not to recognize that "extreme" has become a buzzword for our time. Extreme sports, extreme travel, extreme eating and, yes, even extreme drinking have become commonplace, if rather absurd, concepts.

It's no surprise, then, that we also have extreme beer.

It is uncertain precisely when the phrase came into popular use, but the "where" was most certainly the USA. Among craft brewers seeking to stretch the envelope on beer style, extreme became the watchword for more alcohol, higher hopping rates, intense flavours, barrel ageing, and almost any other outside-the-norm practice a brewer could employ.

Adherents soon followed. Fascinated by the newest, greatest notion, hardcore beer aficionados began chasing the latest and greatest exercise in the unconventional, never mind that such pursuits frequently necessitated early-morning concert ticket-style line-ups outside a brewery's door, battling crowds at hyper-exclusive launch parties, or shelling out ten or 20 times the price of an ordinary craft ale or lager. The collectors would not be denied their due.

Although they varied greatly in character – some were blended from multiple batches of different ales, others employed rare and unusual barrels for conditioning, while still others were crafted from exotic ingredients – extreme beers generally met on two levels: elevated strength and intensity of character.

Their appeal among both brewers and aficionados spread quickly to Europe and elsewhere, until the unusual began approximating the usual and the inevitable backlash finally took hold. It even developed in 2010 that there was a supposed, largely media-fabricated battle between the extremists and proponents of more moderate "session"-style beers, dubbed the "sessionistas".

It would have all made a very good story except for one thing: even at their most outrageous, extreme beers were nothing new.

As modern beer historians have shown, unusually high rates of hopping, the use of curious or unexpected ingredients, and the reuse of spirits barrels or blending of batches (*see* pp.28–9) are brewing practices that have been in play for centuries. Even the modern craft beer conceit of using various bacteria to sour ale has a long and fabled history, albeit without the modern understanding of the specific factors at work. And as for the high-strength beer battle between Scotland's BrewDog (*see* p.111) and Germany's Schorschbräu that so dominated the headlines in 2010, it was always more a question of who could freeze-distil their beer to greater strength than who could be more "extreme".

The fact is that, throughout its short modern history, craft beer has always been to some degree extreme – at least relative to the vast majority of the global beer market. The return to the fore of cask-conditioned ale in Britain was to a certain extent extreme (*see* p.108), as was Anchor Brewing's 1975 release of a barley wine into California's sea of steadily blander brews (*see* p.180), and the stubborn insistence of Italy's early craft breweries on producing beers other than pale or *doppio malto* lagers (*see* pp.158–9).

And the opening of a small business in a market utterly and vastly dominated by major corporations? That may be the ultimate in extremism.

Above: Led by breweries such as northern California's Russian River, American craft brewers are embracing the wood-aging of their beers like never before.

Above: In 2010, Germany's Schorschbräu battled it out with Scotland's Brew Dog for the title of the world's strongest brew, but because each used freeze-distillation, it was questionable whether either could be sold as beer under EU law.

Opposite: One of the highlights of the "extreme" beer calendar is the annual release of Russian River's strong and super hoppy Pliny the Younger, seen here in 2010.

CANADA

Canada's iconic twentieth-century prime minister, Pierre Trudeau, famously promoted the "cultural mosaic" to define his model of Canada, providing contrast to the "melting pot" approach of the USA. He could equally have been describing his nation's history of brewing.

CANADA ▶

The primary influences on brewing in Canada were first British and then, with westward expansion, German, augmented by 20th-century Belgian success in Québec. With increased influences from the US and elsewhere, plus the mingling of cultures and rise of an indigenous approach to brewing in French Canada, the map is becoming much more complicated.

Above: There are strong genealogical and emotional ties between Scotland and Nova Scotia, and ample Celtic influence in many of the province's craft ales.

Beer drinkers born near the middle of the last century will recall when the great national beer divide was Toronto's central Yonge Street, to the east of which, it was said, citizens drank predominantly ales, while lagers held sway to the west. It was a theory with some validity, since the ale-centric British and French immigrant cultures could be found largely in eastern Ontario, Québec, and the Atlantic Provinces, while the Germans and Eastern Europeans, who favoured lagers, led the county's westward expansion.

Since the dawn of craft brewing in the 1980s, a similar though more complex divide has continued to define beer in Canada, albeit based less on immigration patterns than on regional cultures.

In the Atlantic Provinces of Nova Scotia, New Brunswick, Prince Edward Island, and Newfoundland, where hospitality is held in high esteem and beer drinking is arguably more of a purely social act than anywhere else in Canada, "sessionable" English and Irish beer styles – those with a lower-alcohol content – have long held sway. From Halifax to St John's, pale ales and best bitters, porters and stouts dominate, the arrival of higher-alcohol contents, elevated hopping rates, and unconventional styles being but a recent development.

Travel westwards to Québec and the French embrace of gastronomy and *joie de vivre*, coupled with a small brewery-friendly taxation policy, have resulted in what is indisputably the country's most innovative brewing culture. Beer aficionados in search of oddball ingredients, mixed fermentations, and barrel ageing, frequently employed to delectable results, are advised to begin in Montréal and circle outwards from there.

Canada's most populous province, Ontario, is also that with the most firmly conservative traditions, save perhaps for much smaller Alberta. This has resulted in a craft-brewing market that embraces reliable and well-executed versions of traditional European beer styles from Bavarian *Weissbier* to Bohemian pilsner and northern English brown ale. More unusual efforts, such as ales flavoured with orange peel or fermented with *Brettanomyces* (*see* p.65), are generally newer brews of more unpredictable quality.

Although Saskatchewan boasts the country's greatest per capita number of brewpubs, this is due to legislation allowing packaged beer sales on site and has resulted in a slew of generally mediocre beers. Elsewhere on the Prairies, a methodical, practical approach to brewing has resulted, with a few notable exceptions, in generally

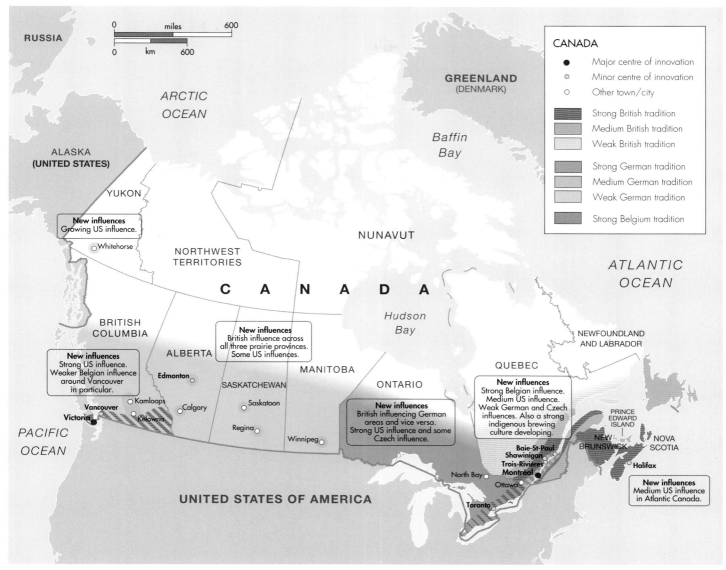

solid though unexciting beers from Manitoba to the Rockies.

Finally, in British Columbia, a long-lasting loyalty to British brewing traditions is finally giving way to influence from the province's "Cascadian" neighbours to the south, manifesting in a new generation of boundary-stretching beers, from highly hopped and potent IPAs to a miasma of seasonal specialities. Although brewing continues to be concentrated in the population centres of greater Vancouver and the capital region, a surprising number of breweries are now appearing in areas far more remote, such as upper Vancouver Island and the Kootenays.

BEST-SELLING LOCAL LABELS

Alexander Keith's	(Anheuser-Busch InBev)
Labatt	(Anheuser-Busch InBev)
Lakeport	(Anheuser-Busch InBev)
Molson	(MolsonCoors)
Moosehead	(National)
Pacific Western	(National)
Rickard's	(MolsonCoors)
Sleeman	(Sapporo)

Right: The O'Keefe name now belongs to MolsonCoors, although the Pilsner Lager and Special Extra Mild Ale are but distant memories.

Québec & the East

Best known for the family-owned Moosehead Brewing Company and a faux IPA called Alexander Keith's, brewed by Labatt (Anheuser-Busch InBev), Canada's easternmost Maritime Provinces were slow to embrace craft brewing, and can still today claim only a smattering of breweries located outside of Nova Scotia, the bulk of the east's best brewpubs and breweries residing in its attractive provincial capital, Halifax.

Similarly, Québec, once famous for a Molson-brewed malt liquor called Brador, came to craft brewing long after Ontario and British Columbia. However, in contrast to the Maritimes, Canada's largest province subsequently embraced it with such enthusiasm that it has become the most brewery-rich in the whole land.

Craft beer in Québec owes much of its success to government tax breaks for small breweries, which have caused the number of such operations to explode since the dawn of the new millennium. Its renown, on the other hand, is due largely to the efforts of the Belgian-inspired brewery Unibroue (*see* opposite).

Above: Québec's most famous ski resort, Mount Tremblant, is now home to two craft breweries.

Born in 1991 from the ashes of a failed brewery called Massawippi, Unibroue might not have pioneered Belgian styles in the province – Belgian brewer Brasserie d'Achouffe once sold a full third of its production in Québec – but it certainly popularized them with brands like Blanche de Chambly, a Belgian-style wheat, and Maudite, a strong, spiced ale. Although now owned by the Japanese brewery Sapporo (*see* pp.234–6), Unibroue's direct and indirect influence continues to help shape the works of such third-generation craft breweries as the much-lauded Dieu du Ciel! (*see* below, opposite) and newer Le Trou du Diable (*see* below).

BEER SELECTION

DOMINUS VOBISCUM BRUT (11%)
MicroBrasserie Charlevoix, Baie-Saint-Paul (Québec)
The brewery invested in special equipment to make this *méthode champenoise* beer with a dry, toasty aroma and rich body that begins perfumy and sweet before drying to a biscuity maltiness.
www.microbrasserie.com

DULCIS SUCCUBUS (7%)
Le Trou du Diable, Shawinigan (Québec)
Ageing in Californian oak that formerly held botrytis-affected wine adds extra dimensions to this tart, apricot-and-candied-citrus-accented ale, with a snappy appeal that belies its strength.
www.troududiable.com

GARRISON IMPERIAL IPA (7%)
Garrison Brewing Company, Halifax (Nova Scotia)
With a new emphasis on more experimental styles, such as this strong IPA with a chewy malt backbone supporting woody hop bitterness, this brewery appears finally to have found its niche.
www.garrisonbrewing.com

ISLAND RED (5.3%)
The Gahan House, Charlottetown (Prince Edward Island)
Like the Irish red ales of old, this quaffable brew boasts toffee and a whiff of butterscotch on the nose, red-apple fruitiness growing to a more bitter but still balanced body, and a drying finish.
www.gahan.ca

Above: Montréal is known throughout Canada as a city that comes alive at night, as illustrated by its boulevards lined with bars, cafés, and, more recently, brewpubs.

KRYPTONITE (8.5%)

Hart & Thistle Gastropub & Brewery, Halifax (Nova Scotia)
Another potent Haligonian IPA, this brewpub ale boasts a classic American-style citric bitterness but with a fruity, juicy malt character more typical of a British ale.
www.hartandthistle.com

MAUDITE (8%)

Unibroue, Chambly (Québec)
Arguably one of the most influential beers in Québec craft-brewing history, this dark, Belgian-inspired ale offers an off-dry mix of earthy chocolate, dried fruitiness, and coriander-led spice.
www.unibroue.com

PORTER BALTIQUE (10%)

Les Trois Mousquetaires, Brossard (Québec)
A textbook interpretation of the Baltic porter style, with a sweet espresso-scented nose and dark chocolate-accented body leading to a roasted, warming, and faintly cinnamony finish.
www.lestroismousquetaires.ca

POSTCOLONIAL IPA (6.5%)

Hopfenstark, L'Assomption (Québec)
Led by a remarkably floral and fragrant aroma, this American-style IPA bursts with bright hoppy notes of grapefruit and lemon, balanced by caramel malt and a restrained fruitiness.
www.hopfenstark.com

ROUTE DES ÉPICES (5%)

Dieu du Ciel!, Montréal & St Jérôme (Québec)
Dieu du Ciel! partner and lead brewer Jean-Francois Gravel has a deft hand with unusual ingredients, like the peppercorns flavouring this rye ale with a spiciness that never overwhelms the appeal of the bready, vaguely cocoa-like malt.
www.dieuduciel.com

ST-AMBROISE OATMEAL STOUT (5%)

Brasserie McAuslan Brewing, Montréal (Québec)
An early critical success, a healthy proportion of oats give this ale a silky mouthfeel, while dark and roasted malt contribute complex coffee, raisin, and roasted flavours.
www.mcauslan.com

ST JOHN'S STOUT (4.7%)

YellowBelly Brewery & Public House, St John's (Newfoundland)
Suitably for a beer crafted by a brewer who worked for years in Dublin, this quaffable stout evokes memories of Ireland with its dry, roasty character and coffeeish, mildly bitter finish.
www.yellowbellybrewery.com

Ontario & the Prairies

With a new generation of breweries having opened since the start of the new millennium, the craft breweries of central Canada are finally beginning to shed their conservative, Eurocentric approach to beer-making. But oh, what a long road it has been!

Below: Like many North American brewpubs, Toronto's Granite Brewery offers tasting flights of all its beers.

Without exception, every one of Ontario's first-generation craft breweries began with beers firmly founded on the traditions of the British Isles, Czech Republic, or Germany. These habits persisted with little variation for close to two decades, and when they finally began to give way to innovation and experimentation, most of the initial results left a considerable amount to be desired.

In Manitoba and Saskatchewan, meanwhile, with few exceptions, early craft breweries operated in a climate of disinterest and general apathy, resulting in a number of failures, and even more lamentable brewpubs operated mainly for the lucrative beer store licence that accompanied their brewing permit.

On a cheerier note, Ontario, Manitoba, and Saskatchewan today offer a patchwork of brewing styles that combines the practical traditionalism of breweries such as King Brewery, Beau's (*see* below), Denison's and Bushwakker (*see* below and opposite) with the iconoclastic adventurism of the likes of Half Pints (*see* opposite), Flying Monkeys in Barrie (Ontario), and Toronto's Great Lakes. Others such as Black Oak (*see* below), Grand River in Cambridge (Ontario), and Paddock Wood of Saskatoon (Saskatchewan) split the difference, with beers that are both style-specific and slightly eccentric.

Opposite: Grain elevators like this one in Saskatchewan are familiar sights on the Canadian Prairies, processing up to 2 million metric tonnes of malting barley per year.

BEER SELECTION

BEAU'S LUG•TREAD LAGERED ALE (5.2%)
Beau's All Natural Brewing Company, Vankleek Hill (Ontario)
Styled after the famed *Kölsch* beers of Germany, this golden ale has a restrained peach-and-apricot fruitiness on the nose and a crisp, more Helles-like body and flavour.
www.beaus.ca

BLACK CREEK PORTER (5%)
Black Creek Historic Brewery, Oakville (Ontario)
A vanilla-accented, faintly tangy porter born of a project designed to replicate the brewing methods of the pioneer. Look for nutty notes of tobacco, dried dark fruit, and burned toast.
www.blackcreekbrewery.ca

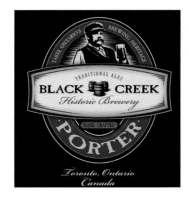

BLACK OAK NUT BROWN ALE (5%)
Black Oak Brewing Company, Toronto (Ontario)
As nutty as its name suggests, this deep-brown delight approaches the palate with a chocolate sweetness but finishes quite dry, suiting it well to dishes that feature red meat.
www.blackoakbeer.com

DENISON'S WEISSBIER (5.4%)
Denison's Brewing Company, Toronto (Ontario)
Contract brewed and canned, this Bavarian-style wheat offers a full and banana-accented nose and spicy (clove, black pepper), softly sweet flavour.
www.denisons.ca

GRANITE BEST BITTER (4.5%)
Granite Brewery, Toronto (Ontario)
Very much a bitter that would be at home in any London pub, this cask-conditioned ale begins with gentle, fruity malt before drying to a leafy, almost tobacco-accented finish.
www.granitebrewery.ca

HUMULUS LUDICROUS (8%)
Half Pints Brewing Company, Winnipeg (Manitoba)
Ex-Bushwakker (see below) brewer David Rudge crafts this massive ale with an amount of hops that is indeed ludicrous, but he balances it all with ample, toffeeish malt and a surprisingly subtle complexity.
www.halfpintsbrewing.com

KING PILSNER (4.8%)
King Brewery, Nobleton (Ontario)
Fresh and floral in aroma, like the Czech offerings that inspired it, this lager from north of Toronto has a light butterscotch maltiness, moderate bitterness, and a dry, quenching finish.
www.beerbanons.com

PALLISER PORTER (5.8%)
Bushwakker Brewpub, Regina (Saskatchewan)
An aroma of roasted malt and coffee introduces this off-dry ale. Laced with flavours of mocha and light and dark chocolate, its sweetness is held in check through the judicious use of hops.
www.bushwakker.com

Alberta, British Columbia & the North

Craft brewing got its Canadian start in and around Vancouver, with the first North American brewpub being the now-defunct Horseshoe Bay Brewing, which opened in 1982, and Granville Island Brewing, nowadays owned by Molson, commencing operations in 1984 as Canada's first craft brewery.

Alberta quickly followed, with the Big Rock Brewery (*see* below, opposite) opening its doors a few months later, followed by a period of intense excitement, then one of rather tedious copycat brewing.

First, hemp beer became fashionable in British Columbia, then blond ale, then pale ale. Imports might have moved the market forward, but these were scarce in both provinces. By the late 1990s, the west coast beer scene had grown so moribund that the region's only newspaper beer columnist quit.

The new century has been kind to brewing in western Canada, with inspired brewers like Matt Phillips of Phillips Brewing (*see* below), Gary Lohin of Central City Brewing (*see* below, opposite), and, to a lesser degree, Neil Herbst of the re-engineered Alley Kat Brewing (*see* below, opposite) pushing the boundaries.

In northern Canada, meanwhile, Arctic Brewing, the Northwest Territories' pioneering craft beer operation in Yellowknife, shut down after a short run, to be succeeded far more successfully, one territory over, by Yukon Brewing in Whitehorse (*see* below).

Left: Now a part of MolsonCoors, the showpiece Granville Island Brewery in Vancouver is more tourist attraction than working brewery.

BEER SELECTION

AMNESIAC DOUBLE IPA (8.5%)
Phillips Brewing Company, Victoria (British Columbia)
An iconoclastic brewer producing a style-busting ale, with chocolaty, cinnamon-accented maltiness significantly mellowing both the intense hoppiness and significant potency of this fine ale.
www.phillipsbeer.com

BACK HAND OF GOD STOUT (5.2%)
Crannóg Ales, Sorrento (British Columbia)
All organic and even growing its own hops, this farmhouse brewery in the British Columbia interior offers a number of draught-only ales, including this dry, tobaccoey, and roasty Irish-style stout.
www.crannogales.com

LEAD DOG ALE (7%)
Yukon Brewing Company, Whitehorse (Yukon)
Designed for long, cold nights, the country's northernmost brewery offers this raisiny, plummy malt bomb of a winter ale, sharpened by spicy, bittering hop.
www.yukonbeer.com

KING HEFFY IMPERIAL HEFEWEIZEN (7.7%)
Howe Sound Brewing Company, Squamish (British Columbia)
As ridiculous as an "imperial *Hefeweizen*" sounds, Howe Sound makes it work. A big banana and brown spice nose leads to a fruit cup and clove flavour, with a peppery finish.
www.howesound.com

WHEN YOU ARE THERE

- Brewing in Canada is concentrated in the urban areas, especially Montréal, Toronto, Vancouver, and, to a slightly lesser degree, Halifax and Victoria.
- Whether in a bar, tavern, or pub, table service is the norm, although you will find places where you will be expected to place your order British-style with the bartender.
- Especially where stronger beers are served, glass sizes will vary from place to place, although the standard is the US 16fl oz pint (473ml) in British Columbia and the imperial 20fl oz pint (568ml) in the rest of Canada.
- In Québec, expect to order your beer by colour: *blanche* for a wheat beer, *brune* for a brown ale, *rousse* for an amber ale or lager, and *noire* for a stout.

Next page: The Canadian Prairies are notoriously fertile, producing as much as 10 per cent of the world's barley, as well as wheat, mustard seed, rye, and canola, among other seeds and grains.

Above: Alberta's "Little Brewery That Could" is Alley Kat Brewing, based in the provincial capital of Edmonton.

MCNALLY'S EXTRA (7%)
Big Rock Brewery, Calgary (Alberta)
An early Canadian classic, this ale offers a caramel apple nose and plenty of toffeeish malt up front, backed by moderate hop bitterness and a dry, nutty finish.
www.bigrockbeer.com

MITCHELL'S EXTRA SPECIAL BITTER (5.2%)
Spinnakers Gastro Brewpub & Guest Houses, Victoria (British Columbia)
Canada's longest-surviving brewpub continues to excel with a floral-fruity bitter holding just a touch of smokiness in its dry finish. Named after craft-brewing pioneer John Mitchell.
www.spinnakers.com

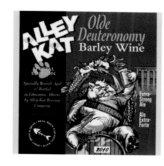

OLD DEUTERONOMY BARLEY WINE (11.4%)
Alley Kat Brewing, Edmonton (Alberta)
Perhaps Canada's best and certainly longest-serving barley wine, this seasonal gem offers ample raisin and date notes in the aroma and flavour, with malty accents of Christmas cake and a lengthy, warming finish.
www.alleykatbeer.com

RED RACER IPA (6.5%)
Central City Brewing Company, Surrey (British Columbia)
Loaded with citrus and pineapple hop notes, this ale from Canada's 2010 Brewery of the Year offers a floral, lemon-balm aroma and brilliant hoppiness balanced by dry, biscuity malt.
www.centralcitybrewing.com

LATIN AMERICA

As the first decade of the twenty-first century gives way to the second, beer in South America generally meets three basic criteria: it is pale and pallid, it is served ice-cold, and it is the product of a major multinational brewing conglomerate. By which measures, we could easily end this section here and move swiftly to the next.

However, there is a ray of light in the southern Americas. Much as North America overcame the tyranny of "fizzy yellow beer" in the 1980s and 1990s, the new millennium has witnessed the birth of craft brewing in South America, with legitimate movements appearing in Brazil, Argentina, and Chile, and rumblings being felt elsewhere.

The road ahead is steep and fraught with peril – the big breweries still enjoy almost 100 per cent market share throughout South America and, as it remains a growth market for them, are loathe to cede sales to other newcomers. But the continent's craft brewers can hardly be faulted for lack of enthusiasm, dedication, and, in some instances, sheer nerve.

This is not to say that all is rosy in South American craft brewing. Beer defects such as oxidation, diacetyl, and dimethyl sulphide (DMS) appear with sometimes surprising regularity in smaller-scale beers from São Paulo to Santiago de Chile, arguably hindering the popularization of the entire segment, much as it did in North America during the early 1980s.

Left: Tequila is the traditional drink of Mexico, but sometimes it must take second place to the refreshing nature of a cold beer.

WHEN YOU ARE THERE

- If you don't speak the native languages – Portuguese in Brazil, Spanish elsewhere – be sure to pack a phrase book, since English is less than commonplace.
- Be prepared for lengthy taxi rides through insanely congested traffic in big cities such as São Paulo and Buenos Aires.
- Do not judge every beer on first sip – some will vary significantly or even dramatically from bottle to bottle.

BEER SELECTION

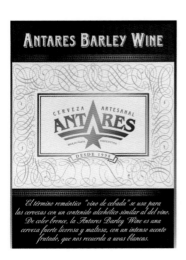

ANTARES BARLEY WINE (10%)
Cerveza Artesanal Antares, Mar del Plata, Buenos Aires (Argentina)
Much of this eminent Argentine craft brewery's beer is tanked to its own pubs, including this tropically fruity ale with a roundly malty body and slightly boozy finish, also found bottle-conditioned.
www.cervezaantares.com

COLORADO INDICA (7%)
Cervejaria Colorado, Ribeirão Preto, São Paulo (Brazil)
Better on tap than in the bottle, this pioneering Brazilian craft IPA presents appley fruitiness and fine flavour progression, from lightly sweet to firmly bitter and, finally, dry and nutty.
www.cervejariacolorado.com.br

KROSS 5 (7.2%)
Cerveceria Kross, Vitacura (Chile)
Created for the brewery's fifth anniversary and continued since, this oak-aged ale offers soft nuances of vanilla on the aroma and berry fruit, sweet malt, tobacco, and raisins in the robust body and finish.
www.kross.cl

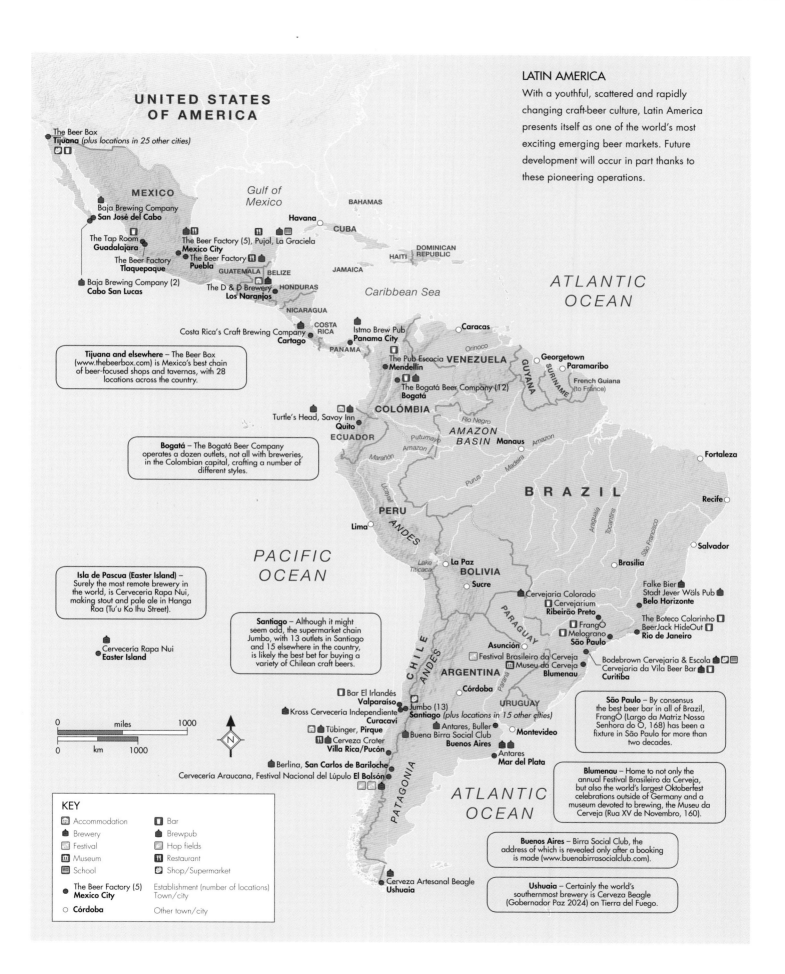

LATIN AMERICA

With a youthful, scattered and rapidly changing craft-beer culture, Latin America presents itself as one of the world's most exciting emerging beer markets. Future development will occur in part thanks to these pioneering operations.

Tijuana and elsewhere – The Beer Box (www.thebeerbox.com) is Mexico's best chain of beer-focused shops and tavernas, with 28 locations across the country.

Bogatá – The Bogatá Beer Company operates a dozen outlets, not all with breweries, in the Colombian capital, crafting a number of different styles.

Isla de Pascua (Easter Island) – Surely the most remote brewery in the world, is Cervecería Rapa Nui, making stout and pale ale in Hanga Roa (Tu'u Ko Ihu Street).

Santiago – Although it might seem odd, the supermarket chain Jumbo, with 13 outlets in Santiago and 15 elsewhere in the country, is likely the best bet for buying a variety of Chilean craft beers.

São Paulo – By consensus the best beer bar in all of Brazil, FrangÓ (Largo da Matriz Nossa Senhora do Ó, 168) has been a fixture in São Paulo for more than two decades.

Blumenau – Home to not only the annual Festival Brasileiro da Cerveja, but also the world's largest Oktoberfest celebrations outside of Germany and a museum devoted to brewing, the Museu da Cerveja (Rua XV de Novembro, 160).

Buenos Aires – Birra Social Club, the address of which is revealed only after a booking is made (www.buenabirrasocialclub.com).

Ushuaia – Certainly the world's southernmost brewery is Cerveza Beagle (Gobernador Paz 2024) on Tierra del Fuego.

KEY

Accommodation
Brewery
Festival
Museum
School
The Beer Factory (5)
Mexico City
○ **Córdoba**

Bar
Brewpub
Hop fields
Restaurant
Shop/Supermarket
Establishment (number of locations)
Town/city
Other town/city

Mexico & Central America

To millions of drinkers the world over, Mexican beer is synonymous with but a small handful of brands, almost all packaged in familiar clear-glass bottles and uniformly produced by one of the two companies that dominate brewing in Mexico to the point of near-exclusivity. And for most beer drinkers in Mexico, the *negro*, or amber to brown lager loosely fashioned in the Vienna style which remains popular with the two big brewers, is about as flavourful as their beer is going to get.

BEST-SELLING LOCAL LABELS

MEXICO	
Corona	(Grupo Modelo)
Modelo Especial	(Grupo Modelo)
Negro Modelo	(Grupo Modelo)
Sol	(Heineken)
Tecate	(Heineken)

CENTRAL AMERICA	
Gallo	(National)
Imperial	(National)
Pilsener	(National)

Scratch below the surface, however, and a youthful, sometimes cheeky craft beer movement will appear. Based largely in the Mexico City and Baja California regions, the two dozen or so brewers of *cerveza artesanal* produce everything from porters and pale ales to Belgian-inspired ales and even beers aged in used tequila barrels.

The barriers they face are hardly insignificant, since they receive no tax breaks as small breweries do elsewhere and must import the bulk of their ingredients, but still, breweries like Minerva, Cucapa and Cosaco persist, nurturing the slow development of a market for their wares. Some breweries have even opened their own stores so that they might address their customers directly.

In Central America, on the other hand, precious little craft-brewing activity has thus far been sited. Likely the most promising market is Costa Rica, with its burgeoning tourism industry and lone craft brewery, but elsewhere market development has been scarce to non-existent.

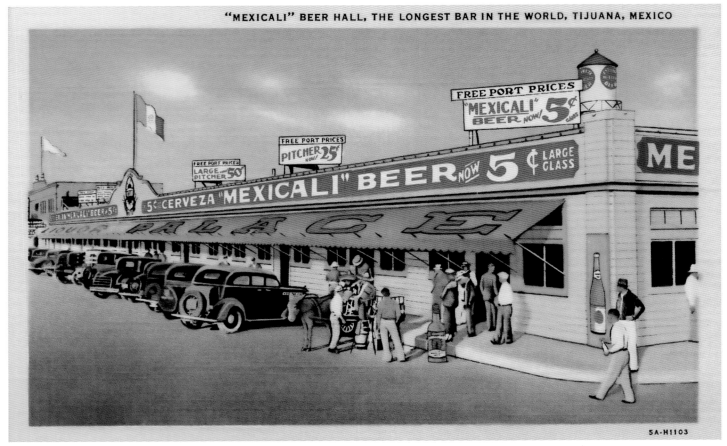

Above: The border town of Tijuana has always attracted visitors from the United States, and now it acts as home to another American import: craft beer.

Above: Beer today finds favour in all strata of Mexican society, from the urban, white-tableclothed restaurant to the rural *cantina*.

BEER SELECTION

SEGUA RED ALE (5%)
Costa Rica's Craft Brewing Company,
Cartago, Costa Rica
Evidence that hoppy beers exist in Central
America, this copper-hued gem exudes
equal parts nutty hop and fruity malt,
finishing just off-dry and refreshing. At
time of writing, the brewery is said to be
experimenting with tropical-fruit *saisons*,
making it one to watch.
www.beer.cr

TEMPUS DOBLE MALTA (7%)
Cervecería Primus, Mexico City, Mexico
One of the highest profile of Mexico's
struggling craft breweries produces a
trio of beers including this, styled as an
"Imperial altbier." Its dry maltiness gives
some credibility to the claim.
www.primus.com.mx

Brazil

Brazil is one of the largest beer-producing countries in the world and, along with its BRIC kin – Russia, India, and China – also one of the rare places where both production and consumption have increased in recent decades. Further, with a per capita consumption of only 51 litres (11.2 gallons) in 2009 and a booming middle class, there would appear to be nowhere to go but up for the nation's brewers.

BEST-SELLING LOCAL LABELS

Antarctica Original	(Anheuser-Busch InBev)
Bavaria Clássica	(Heineken)
Brahma Chopp	(Anheuser-Busch InBev)
Devassa	(Kirin)
Nova Schin	(Kirin)
Skol	(Anheuser-Busch InBev)
Xingu	(Kirin)

This might particularly apply to the growing ranks of Brazilian craft brewers, providing that they can overcome a few not insignificant obstacles. Prominent among these is the general preference of the populace at large for ultra-cold beer, a situation that obviously mutes the very flavour characteristics these brewers seek to highlight in order to differentiate their beers from those of the big, convenience breweries.

Of greater concern, however, is a stumbling block of the brewers' own creation, namely their borderline obsession with pasteurization. In and of itself, this is not necessarily a bad thing – it is not unheard of for craft breweries to pasteurize their wares – but the equipment widely used for this purpose is, by modern standards, antiquated, which results all too often in flat-tasting, "cooked" beer.

On the positive side, artisanal brewing does appear to be gaining in popularity in

Above: These beer-drinking Brazilian farmers trace their ancestry to Germany's Baltic coast.

BEER SELECTION

ABADESSA EXPORT (5%)
Cervejaria Abadessa, Porto Alegre
(Rio Grande do Sul)
Crafted in the fast-disappearing
Dortmunder export style of lager, this
boasts the dryly malty appeal of the
style with a touch of minerality. A lager
for pale-ale drinkers.
www.abade.com.br

ALBA WEIZEN (5.5%)
Cervejaria Coruja, Porto Alegre
(Rio Grande do Sul)
Introduced by a spicy, phenolic nose,
this faintly smoky wheat boasts a crisp,
green apple-citric body loaded with
clove-accented spice and a dry,
quenching finish.
www.cervejacoruja.com.br

BAMBERG RAUCHBIER (5.2%)
Cervejaria Bamberg, Votorantim
(São Paulo)
Sweetly smoky in the nose, this is a beer
with mild to modest smokiness, and some
sweet caramel apple notes to support the
flavours. Bamberg (the German city –
see p.84) would be proud of Bamberg
(the Brazilian brewery).
www.cervejariabamberg.com.br

Left: The familiar coastline of Rio de Janeiro. Spurred by a growing middle class, craft beer is poised to take off in the cities and towns of Brazil.

Next page: Chilean gauchos ride up a thirst, with the Cuernos del Paine mountains in the backdrop.

Brazil, albeit on a very small scale. With an estimated craft brewery count of well over 100 in 2010, perhaps as many as twice that number, a very firm foundation would certainly seem to have been laid.

Most common among Brazilian craft brews is the pilsner, which may denote anything from a mild-mannered *Helles*-style lager intended to wean drinkers off Brahma and Antarctica to a strongly hopped, Czech-, or German-influenced refresher. Also popular are pale ales and IPAs, the latter commonly referred to throughout South America as "eepahs", the hoppiness of which seems to suffer from the expense and scarcity of quality hops.

Without doubt, the trend most encouraging in Brazil, and to a lesser degree elsewhere on the continent, is the use of indigenous ingredients in the creation of beers loosely based on traditional styles. Included in this mix are breweries such as Cervejaria Colorado, which makes use of everything from local coffee to the hard sugar known as *rapadura*, and beers like Cervejaria Way's Amburana Lager (*see* below), aged in exotic Amazonian wood, and Falke Bier's highly limited edition Vivre pour Vivre (*see* below), which incorporates juice from the native *jabuticaba* fruit.

If Brazil is to continue to grow as a brewing nation and make its impact on the world stage, one suspects it will be largely on the back of initiatives such as these.

BODEBROWN WEE HEAVY (8%)
Bodebrown Cervejaria & Escola, Hauer Curitiba (Paraná)
A brewery and brewing school combination, Bodebrown favours style-bending brews such as this whisky-barrel-aged ale with notes of chocolate fudge, vanilla pod, date, and raisin – all leading to a spicy, warming finish.
www.bodebrown.com.br

FALKE TRIPEL MONASTERIUM (9%)
Falke Bier, Ribeirão das Neves (Minas Gerais)
Billed a *tripel*, this is more a thinnish and strong *dubbel* in character, with dried-apricot and pear notes layered over flavours of brown spice and vanilla. The base beer for Vivre Pour Vivre (*see* above).
www.falkebier.com.br

WAY AMBURANA LAGER (8.4%)
Cervejaria Way, Pinhais (Paraná)
When this high-strength lager spends time on chips of amburana wood, it develops a rich and vanilla spice-accented character that offers both a seductive appeal and a smoothness, belying its potency.
www.waybeer.com.br

Argentina & the Rest of South America

After the Argentine economy went into meltdown in 1989 and the peso had to be replaced for trading purposes by the US dollar, a new government determined to give entrepreneurs their head. There followed an explosion of microbreweries, which have come and gone with dizzying frequency ever since, although some are now well down their second decade.

Above: The garden patio at the Berlina pub brewery provides breathtaking views of the Andes to accompany its India Pale Ale, authentically hopped with imported East Kent Goldings.

BEST-SELLING LOCAL LABELS

Cristal	(Heineken – Chile)
Cristal	(SAB – Peru)
Paceña	(A-B InBev – Bolivia)
Polar	(National – Venezuela)
Quilmes	(A-B InBev – Argentina)
Schneider	(Heineken – Argentina)

Since 2002, at any one time there have been between 75 and 150 craft breweries extant in Argentina, with a couple of dozen consistently found around Bariloche and the hop-growing region of El Bolsón, in the spectacularly beautiful Lake District of northern Patagonia.

The further development of hop cultivation could bode well for the future of craft brewing, although Argentina's hop farms were originally created to supply those large South American breweries that eventually agglomerated to become the AmBev brewing group, the leading lights of which provide a driving force within the world's largest brewing group, Anheuser-Busch InBev.

The varieties historically grown are regarded by many northern hemisphere brewers as of

BEER SELECTION

BEAGLE FUEGIAN ALE (5.8%)
Cervecería Beagle, Ushuaia (Argentina)
The most southerly brewery in the world makes three beers of which the regular rubia, a copper-blond sweetish ale with fruity overtones on a bittersweet base is the lightest and best.
www.cervezabeagle.com.ar

DRY STOUT (5.8%)
Buller Brewing Company, Buenos Aires (Argentina)
In the fashionable and touristy Recoleta district stands this two-level brewpub with a most respectable selection of ales, including this dryish stout with a sweetened coffee nose and creamy, roasty body.
www.bullerpub.com

GROSA (9.5%)
Cerveza Jerome, Mendoza (Argentina)
From a brewery dedicated to barrel ageing comes a beer two-and-a-half years in Malbec wine barrels, yielding an oaky-fruity aroma and bittersweet body with notes of vanilla, peppery spice, and dried fruit.
www.cervezajerome.com

PALE ALE (6%)
Cerveza Zeppelin, Buenos Aires (Argentina)
Brewed entirely from Argentine ingredients, including a local hop called Mapuche, this brown-aleish pale is more spicy than bitter, with dried fruit maltiness and an enticing character.
www.cervezazeppelin.com.ar

inferior quality and woefully lacking in aromatics. Argentine Cascade, for example, rather than being fresh and citrus-spicy, is herbaceous and subtle, unsuited to creating American-style pale ales and IPAs. However, new hybrids, suited to the soil and climate, are being cultivated that should assist in the growth of those styles and others like them.

A typical Argentine microbrewery produces one light beer, one dark, and one in between. Most are brewed in foreign styles, but there the pattern ends. For example, the dark beer could be a milk stout, a super-strong porter, a soft German *Dunkles*, or a *Doppelbock*; the light one a Czech-style pilsner, a *Kölsch*, or even a blond *tripel*; and the middle one a British bitter, an attempt at American pale ale, or an amber *bière de garde*. And there is no set rule about which is weakest or strongest.

The craft beer destinations that do exist can be large and boisterous, such as the 12 brewpub-style bars owned and operated across the country's central belt by Antares. Others can be small and secretive, like the popular and successful speakeasy-style Buena Birra Social Club in Buenos Aires. Most encouraging, though, is that once outside the capital it is not unusual to find a couple of craft beers on the drinks list of ordinary bars and eating houses, even as far south as Ushuaia in Tierra del Fuego, home to the world's southernmost brewery, Cerveza Beagle.

Above: The brew-pub Cerveza Artesanal Blest at Bariloche is at the heart of the Patagonian Lake District.

After Argentina, the next advanced is Chile, followed at a fair distance by Uruguay and then, well, pretty much nowhere else. The building blocks of the future are in place, though. Home brewers, always vital to the development of new craft-beer cultures, are active throughout the continent, particularly in the capital city regions.

Hurdles remain to be overcome. The absence of a so-called "cold chain", for instance, in which beer is kept refrigerated during the entirety of its journey from brewery to consumer – essential in hot weather – results in the overuse of pasteurization. Equally, the lack of

experience in many breweries leads to far too many technically flawed examples of the brewing arts.

Competition should also speed the beer education of producers and consumers alike. Both The Great South Beer Cup in Buenos Aires and the Concurso Internacional de Cervezas en Chile marked their debuts in 2011.

If consumers increasingly demand characterful beer, as they appear to be doing with growing regularity, it will be up to the brewers to supply it. And if the south follows the lead of the north, that should result in a healthy craft beer market in South America for years to come.

STRONG ALE (7.5%)
Szot Microbrewery, Santiago de Chile (Chile)
A native Californian transplanted to Chile brews beers designed to appeal to what he says is a Chilean desire for stronger ales, such as this brew loaded with fruity malt not quite held in check by hoppy backnotes.
www.szot.cl

TRIGO (4.9%)
Cabesas Bier, Tacuarembó (Uruguay)
The use of peel from local navel oranges, rather than traditional bitter ones, lends this faintly acidic, Belgian-style wheat a seductive sweetness. Local, home-farmed wheat is also used.
www.cabesasbier.blogspot.com

TÜBINGER BROWN ALE (5%)
Tübinger Microbrews, Vitacura, Santiago de Chile (Chile)
A Brazilian-born brewer of German descent crafting ales in Chile is perhaps not the most obvious source for a slightly chocolaty-sweet ale but, as the beer's balance and nuttiness shows, it is a good one.
www.tubinger.cl

AUSTRALIA, NEW ZEALAND & THE FAR EAST

AUSTRALIA

South Australia is home to one of the brewing world's great survivors, but the rest of the country came relatively late to the global expansion in craft brewing. It is said that nothing provokes Australians to action more effectively than the suggestion that perhaps the New Zealanders are doing it better, which may explain why there is now no shortage of scurrying growth.

Lion Nathan (*see* p.229), which has connections with the Japanese brewers Kirin, plus Carlton & United Breweries, now part of SAB Miller, supply between them 95 per cent of the beer drunk in a nation that by tradition prefers its beer ice-cold, its brand names familiar,

and its advertising campaigns on the wry side. The oddity is the fourth-placed but relatively tiny Coopers Brewery of Adelaide (*see* below), a family-owned firm that for decades produced Australia's only unconventional beers – easily clouded ales that tasted of their yeast and drew scorn from mainstream drinkers, while nurturing the generation that has spearheaded a new brewing scene, one with similarities to that found in Japan.

A majority of the modern ventures are run by optimistic evangelists risking their savings and a few years of their lives on a plan they just know will work. A few are part- or wholly owned by larger brewers, or more often other businesses with serious money behind them, including several wineries – craft brewing being seen as a branch of the same tree.

Recent estimates suggest that there are now well over a hundred new breweries operating in Australia, though the exact number is hard to calculate meaningfully, as many of them operate more like marketing companies. These companies commission beers from contract brewers, which are designed solely for the production of beer for others and make no brands of their own.

Production breweries outnumber brewpubs roughly two to one, with the best crops currently found in Victoria, New South Wales and Western Australia.

BEST-SELLING LOCAL LABELS

Boag's	(San Miguel)
Carlton	(SABMiller)
Castlemaine	(Kirin)
Foster's	(SABMiller)
Tooheys	(Kirin)
Victoria Bitter (VB)	(SABMiller)

WHEN YOU ARE THERE

- Learn more about Australian craft beer from Matt Kirkegaard's *Beer Lover's Guide to Australia* or Willie Simpson's *Australian Beer Companion*.
- Australians are fanatical about ice-cold beer; if you prefer yours at a better-tasting temperature buy one round ahead to let it warm a bit.
- When drinking with friends, it is usual to buy rounds of draft beer in 1.15-litre (2-pint) jugs that serve five pot glasses (called 'midis' in New South Wales).
- The further north you go, the hotter it gets, so beer glasses get correspondingly smaller to prevent the beer from getting warm before you finish it.

Previous page: Eucalyptus trees in the rainy season, Australia.

BEER SELECTION

COOPERS EXTRA STRONG VINTAGE ALE (7.5%)
Coopers Brewery, Regency Park (South Australia)
Do not underestimate this toffee-sweet, initially simple dark amber ale. It comes from a fifth-generation family brewery and is made for lengthy cellaring, when character replaces innocence.
www.coopers.com.au

GRAND RIDGE BREWERY MOONSHINE (8.5%)
Grand Ridge Brewery, Mirboo North (Victoria)
In its third decade of brewing and offering an Australian take on world beers, this pioneering dark Scotch ale explains why locals call this brewery "The Monastery".
www.grand-ridge.com.au

MURRAY'S PILSNER (4.8%)
Murray's Craft Brewing Co, Port Stephens (New South Wales)
This archetypal beachside restaurant with a brewery and winery crafts massive ales as well as this thirst-quenching, crisp, floral north German-style pilsner with New Zealand Motueka hops.
www.murraysbrewingco.com.au

HOLGATE BREWHOUSE MT MACEDON ALE (4.5%)
Holgate Brewhouse, Woodend (Victoria)
This English pale ale brewed with German hops, orange-amber in colour, full of fruit flavours, and scented with grapefruit, is clean and clear with firm bitterness throughout.
www.holgatebrewhouse.com

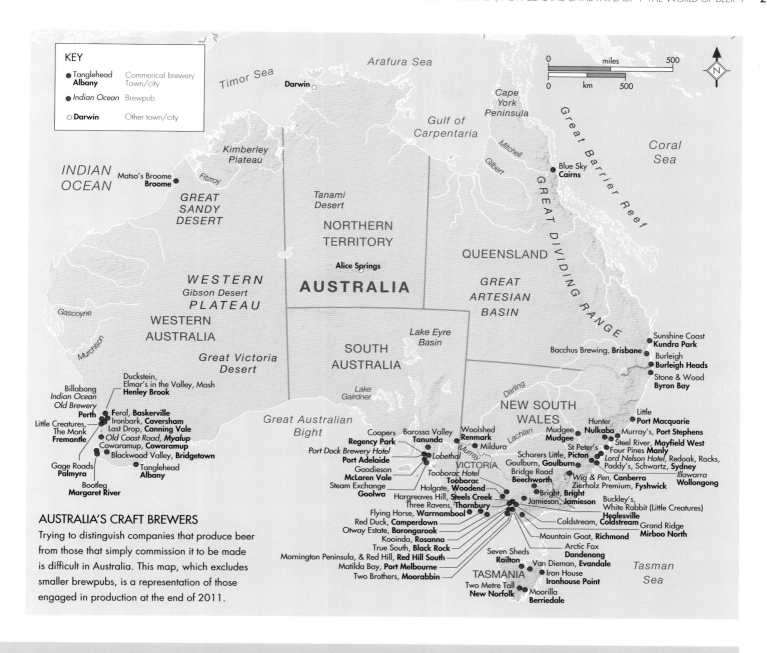

KEY

● Tanglehead **Albany**	Commerical brewery Town/city
● *Indian Ocean*	Brewpub
○ **Darwin**	Other town/city

Timor Sea

Arafura Sea

Darwin

Cape York Peninsula

Gulf of Carpentaria

Kimberley Plateau

INDIAN OCEAN

Matso's Broome **Broome**

GREAT SANDY DESERT

Tanami Desert

NORTHERN TERRITORY

Alice Springs

AUSTRALIA

QUEENSLAND

Coral Sea

Gascoyne

WESTERN Gibson Desert PLATEAU

WESTERN AUSTRALIA

Great Victoria Desert

SOUTH AUSTRALIA

GREAT ARTESIAN BASIN

Lake Eyre Basin

Blue Sky **Cairns**

Sunshine Coast **Kundra Park**

Bacchus Brewing, **Brisbane**

Burleigh **Burleigh Heads**

Stone & Wood **Byron Bay**

Lake Gairdner

Darling

NEW SOUTH WALES

Duckstein, Elmar's in the Valley, Mash **Henley Brook**

Billabong *Indian Ocean* Old Brewery **Perth**

Feral, **Baskerville**
Ironbark, **Caversham**
Last Drop, **Canning Vale**
Old Coast Road, **Myalup**
Cowaramup, **Cowaramup**
Blackwood Valley, **Bridgetown**

Little Creatures **The Monk Fremantle**

Gage Roads **Palmyra**

Tanglehead **Albany**

Bootleg **Margaret River**

Great Australian Bight

Coopers Barossa Valley **Regency Park** **Tanunda**
Port Dock Brewery Hotel **Port Adelaide**
Goodieson **McLaren Vale**
Steam Exchange **Goolwa**

Woolshed **Renmark**
Mildura
Lobethal

Murray

Tooborac Hotel

Hargreaves Hill, **Steels Creek**
Three Ravens, **Thornbury**
Flying Horse, **Warrnambool**
Red Duck, **Camperdown**
Otway Estate, **Barongarook**
Kooinda, **Rosanna**
True South, **Black Rock**
Mornington Peninsula, & Red Hill **Red Hill South**
Matilda Bay, **Port Melbourne**
Two Brothers, **Moorabbin**

Holgate, **Woodend**
Tooborac

VICTORIA

Lachlan

Mudgee Hunter **Nulkaba**
Mudgee
St Peter's
Scharers Little, **Picton**
Goulburn, **Goulburn**
Bridge Road **Beechworth**
Bright, **Bright**
Jamieson, **Jamieson**

Little **Port Macquarie**
Murray's, **Port Stephens**
Steel River, **Mayfield West**
Four Pines **Manly**
Lord Nelson Hotel, Redoak, Rocks, Paddy's, Schwartz, **Sydney**

Wig & Pen, **Canberra**
Zierholz Premium, **Fyshwick**

Illawarra **Wollongong**

Buckley's, White Rabbit (Little Creatures) **Healesville**
Coldstream, **Coldstream**
Mountain Goat, **Richmond**
Arctic Fox **Dandenong**
Van Dieman, **Evandale**

Grand Ridge **Mirboo North**

Seven Sheds **Railton**
Iron House **Ironhouse Point**

Tasman Sea

TASMANIA

Two Metre Tall **New Norfolk**
Moorilla **Berriedale**

0 ——— miles ——— 500
0 ——— km ——— 500

AUSTRALIA'S CRAFT BREWERS

Trying to distinguish companies that produce beer from those that simply commission it to be made is difficult in Australia. This map, which excludes smaller brewpubs, is a representation of those engaged in production at the end of 2011.

HOP HOG INDIA PALE ALE (5.8%)

Feral Brewing Co, Baskerville (Western Australia)
American-styled, sharply bitter pale ale with touches of citrus and pine essence – one of a strong range of mid-strength beers from this craft brewery-cum-winery north of Perth.
www.feralbrewing.com.au

LITTLE CREATURES PALE ALE (5.2%)

Little Creatures Brewery, Fremantle (Western Australia)
Annoyingly enjoyable, easily accessible, much exported, and deliciously hopped, this soft light ale tastes tropical while at the same time being 100 per cent beery.
www.littlecreatures.com.au

MOO BREW DARK ALE (5%)

Moorilla Estate, Barriedale (Tasmania)
This design-conscious Tasmanian winery and craft brewery uses beautiful bottles to show off its classy beers, which include this clearly stated, subtly hopped Anglo-American brown ale.
www.moobrew.com.au

SOUTHWARK OLD STOUT (7.4%)

South Australian Brewing Company (Lion Nathan), Thebarton (South Australia)
Virtually forgotten, strong bottled stout from Australasia's largest brewer, coffee-tinged with a fortified edge, hanging on from the days of empire – British or Russian.
www.lion-nathan.com.au

SUNSHINE COAST SUMMER ALE (3.5%)

Sunshine Coast Brewery, Kunda Park (Queensland)
This questing craft brewery, north of Brisbane, makes a range of international beers plus this unique, prize-winning lower-strength golden ale, with a distinctly tropical flavour.
www.sunshinecoastbrewery.com

NEW ZEALAND

From beery also-ran to rising star to flagging market to poster child for New World craft brewing, New Zealand's recent brewing history has certainly been one of peaks and valleys. With a cadre of earnest and gifted young brewers now in full creative flight, however, the island nation is poised to become the tail that wags the Australasian dog.

Craft breweries in New Zealand have not had an easy time of it. Of the over 60 breweries listed in the 1999 book, *Kerry Tyack's Guide to Breweries and Beer in New Zealand*, roughly half had shut down operations a mere decade later. This high rate of attrition, Kiwi brewing insiders suggest, was due in

SOME OF NEW ZEALAND'S PIONEERING SMALL BREWERIES ▾

Brewpubs and independent small breweries can be found all over New Zealand, with a greater concentration in the hop-growing region at the northern end of South Island. A high proportion have taphouses (bars) or cellar doors (shops) where their beers can be bought or sampled.

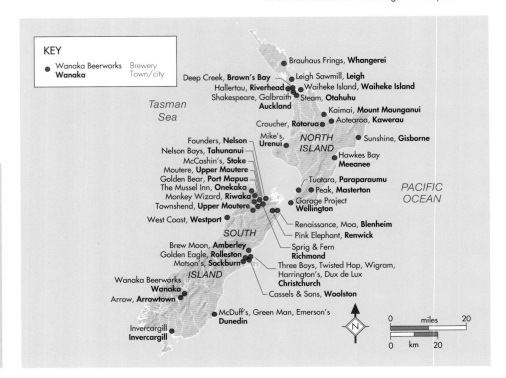

WHEN YOU ARE THERE

- For the best New Zealand brewery and beer bar information, go to www.beertourist.co.nz.
- You can mail order beer within New Zealand from www.beerstore.co.nz.
- Getting served at the bar ahead of someone who arrived before you is a sure-fire way to see easy-going attitudes freeze.

BEER SELECTION

APA (5.8%)

Tuatara Brewing Company, Paraparaumu (Wellington)
Originally conceived as an American Pale Ale, this beer has now been transformed by the reduced availability of US hops into an *Aotearoa* Pale Ale, with local hops giving its significant hop character more a tropical than a citrus fruitiness.
www.tuatarabrewing.co.nz

CAPTAIN COOKER MANUKA BEER (4%)

Mussel Inn, Onekaka (Tasman)
An industry survivor dating from 1995, the Mussel Inn's flagship is this unusual and intensely aromatic beer flavoured with freshly harvested tips from the local manuka tree.
www.musselinn.co.nz

EMERSON'S PILSNER (4.9%)

Emerson Brewing Company, Dunedin (Otago)
An organic offering that is seen by most as the vanguard of the New Zealand pilsner movement, this highly aromatic lager showcases Riwaka hops in its assertive tropical fruitiness.
www.emersons.co.nz

EPIC MAYHEM (6.2%)

Epic Brewing Company, Auckland (Auckland)
Epic was one of the earlier contract breweries – like 8 Wired and Yeastie Boys (*see below and p.231*) – and their fame has come largely thanks to big beers like this, seasoned to powerful fruitiness with American Cascade and New Zealand Riwaka hops.
www.epicbeer.com

HOPWIRED IPA (7.3%)

8 Wired Brewing Company, Blenheim (Marlborough)
An expat Dane who fell in love first with a Kiwi lass and then brewing, pushing the envelope whenever he can, as with this grapey, orangey IPA brewed entirely from New Zealand ingredients.
www.8wired.co.nz

MOA FIVE HOP (6.2%)

Moa Brewing Company, Blenheim (Marlborough)
Conceived as a tribute to the British brewer Young's, this tropically fruity ale features five varieties of New Zealand hop and a biscuity maltiness to underscore it all. Frequently seen served on handpump, but not necessarily cask-conditioned.
www.moabeer.com

BEST-SELLING LOCAL LABELS

Canterbury	(Kirin)
DB	(Heineken)
Lion	(Kirin)
Monteith's	(Heineken)
Speight's	(Kirin)
Steinlager	(Kirin)

part to the rather mundane offerings of some of the earliest small breweries but also to the country's modest population coupled with its celebrated remoteness and isolation.

With a scant 4.3 million people scattered over two islands stretching roughly 2,000 kilometres (1,250 miles) north to south, New Zealanders are not only isolated from the nearest major land mass – Australia is a further 2,000 kilometres (1,250 miles) away – they are also to an extent isolated from each other. Under such circumstances, needless to say, amassing a population base sufficient to support a growing brewery can be a challenge.

That isolation is not without its benefits, however. Absent from the influence of foreign strains or diseases, New Zealand's hop industry has thrived in recent years, notably with organic varieties but also with home-grown variants such as the fruity, tangy Nelson Sauvin. It is in these hops that the future of Kiwi craft brewing may well be writ.

Already, local beer aficionados trumpet the rise of a uniquely New Zealand style of pilsner, equal parts malty and hoppy in the Czech fashion but imbued with perfumy

Above: Richard Emerson, MD and brewer at the Emerson Brewing Co. of Dunedin, New Zealand.

tropical fruitiness courtesy of the local hops. It is a track other styles, notably pale ale, appear poised to soon follow.

POT KETTLE BLACK (6%)
Yeastie Boys, Invercargill (Southland)
The two friends behind this quirky contract brewery were advised that they could have dubbed this mahogany gem a "black IPA", but have instead wisely decided to call it a "hoppy porter", in deference to the healthy bitterness they layered over its faintly herbaceous, mocha-ish maltiness.
www.yeastieboys.co.nz

OYSTER STOUT (6.2%)
Three Boys Brewery,
Christchurch (Canterbury)
This twist on the local ingredients trend, brewed only during the oyster season, uses Southland Bluff oysters to add richness to this coffeeish, figgy, and lightly smoky autumnal favourite.
www.threeboysbrewery.co.nz

STONECUTTER SCOTCH ALE (7%)
Renaissance Brewing Company,
Blenheim (Marlborough)
This deep-brown delight adds a waft of smokiness to a remarkably complex mix of stewed fruit, chocolaty caramel, a hint of coffee, and a lingering, soft, roasty finish. A pure, restorative ale.
www.renaissancebrewing.co.nz

THE FAR EAST

Those who promote craft beers and the people responsible for steering international brewing groups have little in common, but they all agree that the Far East, and China in particular, is extremely important to beer, not for what its peoples do now but for how they determine their future.

For those in global business, the mesmerizing numbers that attach to even a minimal rise in Chinese beer consumption offer the easiest solution to the problem of falling beer volumes in most, if not all, of their traditional markets. They see China's emerging professional and merchant classes as seeking the trappings of a Western lifestyle, which includes familiar beer brands.

Meanwhile, those attracted to diversity look at China's many different cultures and their collective culinary inventiveness, and wonder what a few hundred million chefs will do once they learn to brew. They see a population emerging from the era of Maoist conformity and how unlikely it is that they will all choose to drink the same type of beer.

In the rest of the region, the lesson seems to be that clean yet dull beers do well up to a point, but that, as consumers become more sophisticated, they wish to try something with more to it. Just like everywhere else.

With Thailand, Vietnam, and Cambodia on the way to becoming the world's top three exporters of rice, brewers in the region are keen to use this cheap cereal as a major ingredient of their beers. If so, characterfulness will depend far more on flavours and aromas derived from special yeast and creative hopping. Due to the current and, more importantly, potential size of the Chinese market, this will put pressure on the global hops market, both in terms of supply and price.

BEST-SELLING LOCAL LABELS

Anchor	(Heineken)
Beerlao	(Carlsberg)
Bintang	(Heineken)
Cass	(Anheuser-Busch InBev)
Hite	(National – South Korea)
Klang	(Carlsberg)
OB	(Anheuser-Busch InBev)
San Miguel	(National – Philippines)
Tiger	(Heineken)

Right: Traditional junk in Halong Bay, Vietnam.

Below: Workers deliver barrels of "bia hoi" on a street in Hanoi, Vietnam. Delivered fresh from the brewery daily, this low-alcohol beer is enjoyed morning to night, often in ramshackle bars where a wooden crate might serve as seating.

BEER SELECTION

ABC STOUT (8%)
Cambodian Brewing (Heineken),
Sihanoukville, Cambodia
Cambodia retains a tradition of strong export stouts from colonial days, the most impressive of which is this liquorice-laden giant, which is brewed stronger than in its state of origin, Singapore.
www.heinekeninternational.com/
cambodiabrewery-cambodia.aspx

BEERLAO LAGER BEER (5%)
Lao Brewery Company Ltd,
Vientiane (Laos)
Rare in a south-east Asian blond beer, this national treasure remains characterful and obviously beery throughout, despite boasting rice in its mash. Best in large (640ml) bottles.
www.beerlao.la

BUKHANSAN OATMEAL STOUT (4.3%)
Craftworks Brewing Company,
Seoul (South Korea)
Korea's first oatmeal stout from a new craft brewery with huge potential. Intensely dark and slightly sweet with hints of coffee and chocolate, from its creamy start to faintly sour finish it avoids anything lightweight without being heavy.
www.craftworkstaphouse.com

Below: With an already large and still growing brewing industry, and as yet only modest per capita beer consumption, China is sure to have a huge impact on the global beer market in the future.

Above: Table-top beer dispensers that allow patrons to serve their own "draught" are a common sight in some parts of Asia.

Japan

On July 8, 1853, the experienced US naval commander, Commodore (later Rear-Admiral) Matthew C Perry docked four frigates in the port of Uraga, at the entrance to Tokyo Bay, engaged his guns in a little target practice, and then invited the Japanese authorities to open their country for trade.

This perfectly timed act of gunboat diplomacy is credited as the catalyst that provoked Japan to begin its gradual and bumpy transition from being an isolated empire run by local warlords to a modern democratic state engaged in a global community.

There had been Europeans living in Japan since the mid-sixteenth century, although the interaction of cultures was minimal. The gap seemed unbridgeable, even when it came to that most universal of social lubricants, alcohol.

The traditional drink of Japan is sake, made by boiling milled rice and fermenting the extract with pitched yeast. Although often referred to as "rice wine", for its alcohol content and lack of carbonation, being a fermented grain drink it is much closer to beer, a beverage unknown on the Japanese archipelago before the nineteenth century, as neither barley nor wheat grew there.

After 1853, political and economic change progressed rapidly.

The country's first beer brewery, Spring Valley – later to become Kirin – was established at Yokohama in 1869. Around the same time, barley, wheat, and hops were introduced to the northern island of Hokkaido, where in 1876 the government established another brewery, at Sapporo. When the Sapporo brewery was sold to private interests in 1889, the money raised was invested in creating hundreds of smaller breweries in the Kansai region around Osaka and Kyoto, including one called Asahi.

Government-sponsored expansion did not last long, though, and by the end of the century, the state was demanding amalgamation. In 1908, a law was passed stipulating that no new brewery could be licensed unless it sold 1,800 hectolitres in its first year – an unlikely target in a largely agrarian society where beer was drunk mainly by the urban middle classes and foreigners.

FRANKENBEERS

Governments are fond of offering tax breaks to those who earn their living by continuing trades or traditions that are seen as part of the shared cultural heritage. So it is that beer – defined in Japan as fermented from a mash that includes at least two-thirds malted barley – is taxed more heavily than fermented grain drinks made from other cereals, such as sake.

Clever brewery companies began to exploit this loophole by producing drinks called *happoshu* (literally "bubbly alcohol"), fermented typically from, say, 25 per cent malted barley mixed with rice, maize, sorghum, soya beans, and other sugars. A more recent variant, called Third Category or "3C", is made entirely without malt.

These drinks contain the same amount of alcohol as beer but through lower duty are significantly cheaper. Grainy flavours are added by use of aromatizing additives, although these often have a hint of stale flower-vase water. Their names and descriptions suggest that they are beers, in order that supermarkets will stack them among the beer shelves.

Dubbed "Frankenbeers", beer lovers fear that they will have the same impact on respect for brewers that the monster created by the well-intentioned Dr Frankenstein had on the reputation of scientists. In 2010, they took one-third of the market in regular beers.

Above: Beer was a late arrival in the Land of the Rising Sun.

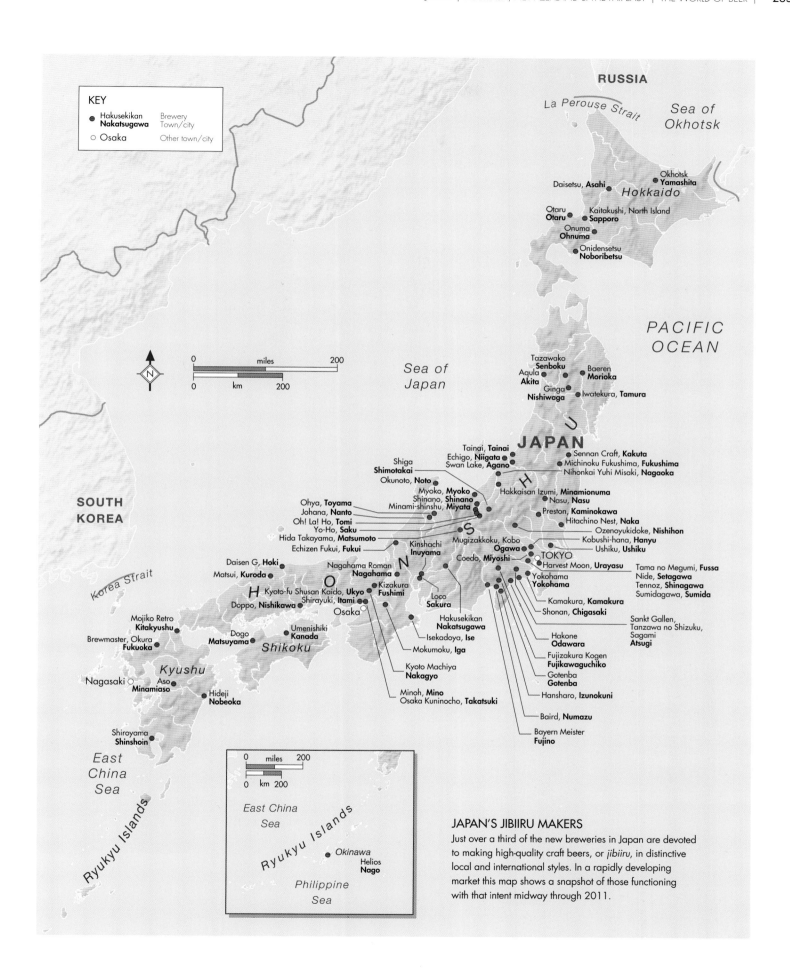

KEY

● Hakusekikan
Nakatsugawa   Brewery
Town/city

○ Osaka   Other town/city

RUSSIA

La Perouse Strait

Sea of Okhotsk

Hokkaido

Okhotsk **Yamashita**
Daisetsu, **Asahi**

Otaru **Otaru**   Kaitakushi, North Island **Sapporo**

Onuma **Ohnuma**

Onidensetsu **Noboribetsu**

PACIFIC OCEAN

Sea of Japan

Tazawako **Senboku**
Aqula **Akita**   Baeren **Morioka**
Ginga **Nishiwaga**
Iwatekura, **Tamura**

JAPAN

Tainai, **Tainai**   Sennan Craft, **Kakuta**
Echigo, **Niigata**   Michinoku Fukushima, **Fukushima**
Swan Lake, **Agano**   Nihonkai Yuhi Misaki, **Nagaoka**
Shiga **Shimotakai**
Okunoto, **Noto**   Hakkaisan Izumi, **Minamionuma**
Myoko, **Myoko**   Nasu, **Nasu**
Shinano, **Shinano**   Preston, **Kaminokawa**
Ohya, **Toyama**   Minami-shinshu, **Miyata**   Hitachino Nest, **Naka**
Johana, **Nanto**   Ozenoyukidoke, **Nishihon**
Oh! La! Ho, **Tomi**   Kobushi-hana, **Hanyu**
Yo-Ho, **Saku**   Mugizakkoku, Kobo   Ushiku, **Ushiku**
Hida Takayama, **Matsumoto**   Kinshachi **Inuyama**   Ogawa, **Ogawa**
Echizen Fukui, **Fukui**   Coedo, **Miyoshi**   Tama no Megumi, **Fussa**
Daisen G, **Hoki**   ○TOKYO   Nide, **Setagawa**
Matsui, **Kuroda**   Nagahama Roman **Nagahama**   Harvest Moon, **Urayasu**   Tennoz, **Shinagawa**
Yokohama **Yokohama**   Sumidagawa, **Sumida**
Kyoto-fu Shusan Kaido, **Ukyo**   Kizakura **Fushimi**   Kamakura, **Kamakura**
Doppo, **Nishikawa**   Shirayuki, **Itami**   Loco **Sakura**   Shonan, **Chigasaki**
Mojiko Retro **Kitakyushu**   Osaka   Sankt Gallen, Tanzawa no Shizuku, Sagami **Atsugi**
Brewmaster, Okura **Fukuoka**   Dogo **Matsuyama**   Umenishiki **Kanada**   Hakusekikan **Nakatsugawa**   Hakone **Odawara**
Shikoku   Isekadoya, **Ise**   Fujizakura Kogen **Fujikawaguchiko**
Kyushu   Mokumoku, **Iga**   Gotenba **Gotenba**
Nagasaki ○   Aso **Minamiaso**   Kyoto Machiya **Nakagyo**   Hansharo, **Izunokuni**
Hideji **Nobeoka**   Minoh, **Mino**   Baird, **Numazu**
Osaka Kuninocho, **Takatsuki**   Bayern Meister **Fujino**
Shiroyama **Shinshoin**

Korea Strait

SOUTH KOREA

East China Sea

Ryukyu Islands

0   miles   200
0   km   200

0   miles   200
0   km   200

East China Sea

Ryukyu Islands

Okinawa
Helios **Nago**

Philippine Sea

JAPAN'S JIBIIRU MAKERS

Just over a third of the new breweries in Japan are devoted to making high-quality craft beers, or *jibiiru*, in distinctive local and international styles. In a rapidly developing market this map shows a snapshot of those functioning with that intent midway through 2011.

By 1940, shortly before Japan attacked the US naval base at Pearl Harbour, beer brewing had condensed to just two companies.

In the period of economic regeneration that followed the war, the two became three (Kirin, Asahi, and Sapporo), but start-up regulations were significantly toughened, ensuring that by 1970 only two further brewers had joined them: Suntory (*see* p.237), adding to its wines and spirits interests, and Orion, created to supply beer to the US bases around Okinawa.

It was only when the Japanese economy began to deflate alarmingly in the early 1990s that legislators removed the regulation that protected the anticompetitiveness. In 1994, companies were allowed into brewing provided that they achieved annual sales of 600 hectolitres within three years.

A few years later, there were 250 new breweries, including at least one in each of the country's 47 prefectures. There were brewpubs

Left: *The Japan Beer Times*, invaluable reading for ex-pats and visitors.

BEST-SELLING LOCAL LABELS

Asahi	(Asahi)
Kirin	(Kirin)
Sapporo	(Sapporo)
Suntory	(National)

WHEN YOU ARE THERE

- Most Japanese craft breweries operate a bar on site.
- In many bars, the glasses are small, so you can share your beer with friends.
- Most *jibiiru* breweries have online stores and will send beer by post.
- Source the bilingual *Japan Beer Times* magazine via www.japanbeertimes.com.

BEER SELECTION

AMBER SWAN ALE (5%)
Swan Lake Beer, Agano (Niigata)
Awash with international awards, this 1997 brewery's most consistent achiever is this ruddy amber, delicately but exquisitely hopped, sweetish ale – the best in a fine range of beers.
www.swanlake.co.jp

BAIRD SURUGA BAY IMPERIAL IPA (7.5%)
Baird Brewing Company, Numazu (Shizuoka)
Deservedly successful husband-and-wife team making reliably tasty beers in a wide variety of styles, such as this double dry hopped, big-tasting, floral bitter IPA.
www.bairdbeer.com

BAEREN CLASSIC (6%)
Baeren Brauerei, Morioka (Iwate)
Having tried faithfully to reproduce German brewing methods, the team here has produced a pretty authentic blond *Helles*, to export quality.
www.baeren.jp

HIDA-TAKAYAMA STOUT (7%)
Hida Takayama Brewing, Matsumoto (Gifu)
Go online and buy the whole range from this crew, spending longest on this complicated chocolaty, upper-middle range stout, with a bit of everything.
www.hidatakayamabeer.co.jp

HITACHINO NEST NIPPONIA (6.5%)
Kiuchi Brewery, Naka (Ibaraki)
Brewing sake since 1823 and beer since 1996, Kiuchi's respected range of Hitachino Nest beers includes this unique blond ale, constructed entirely from revived Japanese barley and hop strains.
www.kodawari.cc

MINAMI SHINSHU DUNKEL WEIZEN (5.2%)
Minami Shinshu Beer, Miyata (Nagano)
A dark, sweet, grainy wheat beer of the Bavarian banana school, from the area sometimes known as the Japanese Alps.
www.ms-beer.co.jp

Above: Speciality craft-beer bars have steadily gained in popularity throughout Japan.

Above: Specialist sake store in Okinawa.

started by some of the larger companies, a few kit breweries to make cheap beer for retail stores, and the odd eccentric set-up to make beers to fit with new health fads.

However, within the group emerged a steadily growing number of top-quality craft brewers dedicated to making *jibiiru* or "local beers", including a few sake makers seeking to increase the use of their brewhouses outside their normal brewing months.

It came as no surprise to those who know Japan that many producers honed their products and their business skills rapidly and at an early stage began exporting to the growing beer markets of North America. More recently, Australasia and Europe have also come into their sights.

Currently, "special beers" account for less than two per cent of the Japanese beer market and much of that is imported, but playing on the love of new and distinctive flavours, their share is growing year on year, despite *jibiiru* being several times the price of ordinary beers and sometimes far more.

At such low volumes, they do not yet threaten the regular beer market dominated by the large domestic brewing groups. That privilege goes to a more ridiculous internal problem (*see* panel, p.234).

MINOH BEER IMPERIAL STOUT (8.5%)
Minoh Brewery, Mino (Osaka)
This big, confident, chocolaty strong stout is one of several world-class beers in a developing range from this prize-winning brewery run by two sisters on the outskirts of the city of Osaka.
www.minoh-beer.jp

FUJIZAKURA WEIZEN (5.5%)
Fujizakura Kogen Mugishu, Fujikawaguchiko (Yamanashi)
This fragrant, sweet, and extreme yet gentle Bavarian-style wheat beer, made with 50 per cent malted wheat, is replaced in the autumn by an even better smoked version called Mori no Weizen.
www.fujizakura-beer.jp

SHIGA KOGEN HOUSE IPA (8.2%)
Shiga Kogen Beer, Shimotakai (Nagano)
This ale and sake brewery produces great porter and five pale ales, of which the strongest is this *grand cru* version of the 6% IPA, brewed with British Maris Otter malt and aromatic hops.
www.tamamura-honten.co.jp

SHONAN RUBY ALE (6%)
Shonan Beer, Chigasaki (Kanagawa)
Highly quaffable, easy-drinking beer of character, probably made with Vienna malt and apparently bottle-conditioned, in a style that is hard to place.
www.kumazawa.jp

THE PREMIUM MALTS (5.5%)
Suntory Liquors Limited, Minato-ku (Tokyo)
As yet, Japan's "Big Four" brewers have not attempted to make craft beers, although each has tried a 100 per cent malt blond lager, of which this is arguably the best.
www.suntory.com

OTARU PILSNER (4.9%)
Otaru Beer, Otaru (Hokkaido)
Made in the north, where the climate resembles that of the European beer belt, this blond lager in the crisper northern German style is lagered for eight weeks (*see* p.22) for extra authenticity.
www.otarubeer.com

Vietnam

The most authentic Vietnamese drinking experience is found most commonly in the north, around the capital Hanoi and along the coast towards Hạ Long Bay. *Bia hoì* refers to freshly made draught blond beers, typically of around 3% ABV, served by gravity dispense from vertical metal kegs that arrive each morning from a local brewery.

<table>
<tr><td colspan="2">BEST-SELLING LOCAL LABELS</td></tr>
<tr><td>33 Export</td><td>(Heineken)</td></tr>
<tr><td>BGI</td><td>(Heineken)</td></tr>
<tr><td>Halida</td><td>(Carlsberg)</td></tr>
<tr><td>Hue</td><td>(Heineken)</td></tr>
</table>

Above: Rice is an obvious and plentiful substitute for malted barley in oriental brewing, but it makes for less full-bodied beers.

From morning till night, small groups of labourers, office workers, students, or travellers squat on upturned plastic crates in shacks or on rough-shaded terraces to share a glass or two of ultra-fresh beer, swap news, and complain about the heat.

In 1995, Vietnam had over 300 small breweries, mostly elderly, ramshackle concerns that had somehow survived from French colonial times to serve local bars with often unlabelled beers.

More recently, countless dozens of new brewpubs have appeared, often serving a small chain of air-conditioned beer halls with large paved gardens. Where polished copper vessels are displayed behind well-staffed bars, beer may or may not be made on the premises, using ingredients from Australasia and expertise from the Czech Republic.

Many South Vietnamese settled in Czechoslovakia after the end of Communist rule there and its start in their own country. Disillusionment with the climate and positive developments back home led many to return, taking with them respect for Bohemian ideas about brewing and a conviction that freshly krausened pale *ležák* (*see* p.98) might go well with an eel and banana flower hotpot.

Above: International beers share shelf space with high-end spirits at this Vietnamese bottle shop.

BEER SELECTION

COI XAY GIO SÈC (4.5%)
Coi Xay Gio, Hanoi
Brewed at the Windmill pub in Đồng Đa but available elsewhere, this reliable Czech-style pilsner – "Yellow" in Vietnamese – is probably the best in the capital.
http://newhanoian.xemzi.com/venue/show/1596/Coi-Xay-Gio-Windmill;
tel: +84 4 38233774

HOA VIÊN SPECIAL (4.8%)
Hoa Viên Brauhaus, Ho Chi Minh City
This brewhouse doubles as the Czech consulate, hence the sound range of Bohemian brews including this "Red" beer, presumably intended as a *polotmavé* (*see* p.104).
www.hoavien.vn

LOUISIANE DARK LAGER (5%)
Louisiane Brewhouse, Nha Trang
Vietnam's foremost resort has several brewpubs, including this beach-side example that brews this "Black" and other draught beers for the restaurant and elsewhere.
www.louisianebrewhouse.com.vn

NHÀ HÀNG NẤU BIA
HOA VIÊN®
BRÄUHAUS
WE RESPECT YOUR TASTE
1A Tăng Bạt Hổ, Hà Nội • 28 Mạc Đĩnh Chi, HCMC • 2A Nguyễn Đình Chiểu, Mũi Né
Đường dây miễn phí: 1800 58 88 69 • Email: hoavienbia@vnn.vn • Website: www.hoavien.vn

Thailand

After China (for quantity) and Japan (for sophistication), a case could be made in favour of Thailand as the beer capital of Asia. Although a rural fondness for domestic whisky means that the country trails Vietnam in total production and limits the national per capita consumption to a modest 31 litres (6.8 gallons) per year (in 2009), urban Thais are nothing if not enthusiastic beer consumers.

Whether at the sprawling and sadly now-defunct Suan Lum Night Bazaar Beer Garden or the newer 1,600-seat Tawandang German Brewery brewpub and concert hall, Bangkok Thais embrace beer as only the residents of a perennially hot and congested city can.

The vast majority of Thai beers are German-influenced golden lagers, with ale-brewing confined to such niche locales as the rather disappointing, expat-populated brewpub, The Londoner. Market leader Singha (*see* below) surprises with a slightly elevated strength and malty, almost *Märzen*-like character, although its reign is being challenged by the simpler, inelegant pretender, Chang.

The craft beer renaissance has yet to have a significant effect on Thai beer, perhaps in part thanks to the government's policy of sheltering the domestic brewing industry from foreign influence via rather steep duties on imported beers.

Above: While tourists may travel to Thailand for its idyllic beaches, the country's best brewing destinations are centred more around the densely populated capital region.

BEER SELECTION

DUNKEL (4.5%)
Tawandang German Brewery, Bangkok
A full-bodied, chocolaty, lightly roasty, and earthy dark lager from a successful, two-decade-old brewpub now operating locations in both Bangkok and Singapore.
www.tawandang.co.th

HOPF BRAUHAUS WEISSE (5.3%)
Hopf Brauhaus, Pattaya
Fruity and sweetish Bavarian-style wheat beer from a brewpub in a resort town south of Bangkok more famous for its beaches and nightlife than its beer.
tel: + 66 (0)38 710 650

MOKU MOKU SMOKED ALE (5%)
Mokumoku Ji-Beer, Iga (Mie)
Highly complex, smoked, light-bodied porter made in a sophisticated brewery based at a showpiece farm museum dedicated to fine, old-style agricultural crafts.
www.moku-moku.com

SINGHA LAGER (6%)
Boon Rawd Brewery, Bangkok
This rich gold, roundly malty, and slightly peppery brew is a Bangkok standard, and a beer tailor-made for complementing the sweet-sour-salty taste of Thai food.
www.boonrawd.co.th

REST OF THE WORLD

Tracking the spread of craft brewing around the globe is like watching the colonization of a new species. In nations where brewers are normally called upon to produce lightly alcoholic, cold and frothy yellow fluids, the first signs of new life are usually brewpubs, which either expand their operations to serve others or else entice new colleagues to join the entrepreneurial wagon train. Few parts of the world remain untouched by ambitious brewing.

In China, the café brewers of Beijing, Shanghai, and Hong Kong can expect to be joined in due course by craft breweries run by graduates from the German-sponsored national brewing academy, founded in 1988 in Wuhan. As in Japan before it, suitable regions will no doubt be found for large-scale hop and barley propagation as the taste for beer evolves beyond the simplistic.

The handful of new small breweries in Cambodia, Taiwan, Mongolia, and South Korea also draw from Germany, although there are early Belgian influences, too. US-style craft beers are found at Storm Brewing (www.stormbrewing.net) on the Indonesian island of Bali, whereas Pivo Praha of Makati in the Philippines is clearly Czech (www.pivopraha.com).

The brewpub culture found in Singapore dates from the late 1990s and is best described as eclectic. The bigger question here, as elsewhere in Southeast Asia, is whether new indigenous styles and preferences will evolve. Is it possible to create beer styles of character that are more attuned to the climate?

At the other end of Asia, in the Middle East, where beer was invented, the green shoots take a different form.

Previous page: Modern India is embracing the global economy as never before, but will it prove as welcoming to a new breed of domestic craft-brewers?

Whether the Arab Spring of 2011 will lead to a less restrictive, some would argue more authentically Qu'ranic, attitude to alcohol across the Islamic world remains to be seen. Meanwhile, the only multinational brewer based in a Muslim country, albeit a secular one, the Turkish group Efes has produced 80 per cent of the beer in its growing home market, including a newish wheat beer and one brewed with coffee. More significantly, it has expanded into the Balkans and the former Soviet Union, and was subject to significant investment from SABMiller in late 2011.

Turkey has four brewpubs, too, including one pioneered by expat US craft brewers, while further south the Palestinian territories and Lebanon boast one determined production brewery apiece.

Israel's nascent brewing revival is more distinctly West-facing, with around a dozen companies testing the water since young Israelis brought a taste for beer back from overseas travel and fell on early imports from the likes of Sam Adams. The country's best-known craft brewer, Dancing Camel, is based in Tel Aviv, with the more experimental Mivshelet Ha'Am a few miles north at Evan Yehuda. In the south of the country, pioneers include Isis of Moshav Dekel, Malka of Yehiam, and the prize-winning Negev from Kiryat Gat (*see* below, opposite).

In North Africa, Tunisia has thus far led the way with three German-style brewpubs, two in the northern beach resort of Hammamet.

BEER SELECTION

ALTSTADT WEISSBIER HEFE (4%)
Drayman's Brewery, Pretoria (South Africa)
Rocky-headed, light, misty wheat beer with a slight sharpness, made by a hands-on brewer of German descent, who also distills.
www.draymans.com

BREWERKZ SCHOLAR RED (5%)
Brewerkz Restaurant & Microbrewery, Riverside Point (Singapore)
Interesting, faintly pinkish ale brewed from a mash containing 15 per cent red Thai sticky rice, which gives it a perfumy quality you can taste. Served at two Singapore beer restaurants.
www.brewerkz.com

CAMELTHORN RED (4.5%)
Camelthorn Brewery, Windhoek (Namibia)
A well-made example of the sort of ruddy amber light ale that is commonplace in North America but unique in Africa, designed to turn heads.
www.camelthornbrewing.com

GUINNESS FOREIGN EXTRA STOUT (7.5%)
Guinness Ghana, Kumasi (Ghana)
This strong, sweet, oddly accented black beer is made from Dublin-brewed stout wort and local sorghum lager, distinguished from the Nigerian version by excluding wheat.

LION STOUT (8%)
Lion Brewery Ceylon, Biyagama (Sri Lanka)
Sri Lankan strong stout, a relic of empire, is preserved in this anomalous, sweet, faintly lactic, liquoriced and chocolaty black monster of a beer, widely exported.
www.lionbeer.com

MITCHELL'S RAVEN STOUT (5%)
Mitchell's Knysna Brewery, Knysna, Western Cape (South Africa)
Somewhere between a porter and a Scotch ale but billed as a milk stout, sweet and burned with allusions to whisky malt, this ale comes from South Africa's longest-surviving small brewer.
www.mitchellsbrewery.com

In other parts of Africa, home-brewing traditions that have continued into the twenty-first century employ cereals such as sorghum in West African *shakparo* and South African *chichi*. Millet appears in Namibian *oshikundu* or *ontaku*, and honeyed in *tella* from the Horn of Africa. Making these ancient brews often falls to the women of the household or community, preserving an authentic line back to ancient traditions elsewhere.

The Kenyan capital Nairobi is home to a couple of confident brewpubs. Its strong base of international visitors may prove to make it the seedbed for craft beer brewing in East Africa at some point, although despite its recent reputation as an area of drought and famine, the normal climate and agriculture of Ethiopia lends itself far better to grain cultivation.

Perhaps the world's most unlikely sited *Hausbrauerei* is just outside the Ethiopian capital Addis Ababa, where the Beer Garden Inn (www.beergardeninn.com) produces the remarkably good Garden Bräu Blondy and Ebony. The country's commercial breweries, along with those in Eritrea, retain a more "local" feel, too.

With Nigeria still stuck in the ways of global business, the country on the African continent most likely to spawn an interesting new beer culture is South Africa. The SAB in SABMiller stands for South African Breweries, and its descendant company still dominates the markets of the sub-Saharan region. However, in the country of its forebears, nearly 20 new firms are advancing gingerly into creative brewing, with others planned or promised (*see* www.beermag.co.za).

Nowadays the country's second-largest brewery is Mitchell's, opened at Knysna in the Western Cape in 1983, which concentrates on making British-style ales (*see* below, opposite). In Cape Town itself, well-equipped Boston makes some restrained own-brand beers effectively enough, but reveals its potential when contracted to brew for new enterprises like Bierwerk, Darling, and Jack Black.

Around Johannesburg and Pretoria, three new breweries have joined Gilroy of Muldersdrift and Drayman of Silverton in making "old-fashioned" beers, while around Durban and KwaZulu-Natal, Robson's beers from Shongweni are setting the pace (*see* below).

Windhoek, the capital of neighbouring Namibia, gave its name to a slightly above-average commercial light lager long before it hosted the pioneering craft brewery Camelthorn, an extraordinary brewpub-based operation that is already exporting its well-made beers to South Africa and beyond, and may well be set to become the region's torchbearer (*see* below, opposite).

Those who seek an island paradise as a suitable backdrop to their beer need to travel to the other side of the globe, to that part of the western Pacific styled locally as Oceania.

The islands of Fiji host a small organic brewery called Savusavu, a boutique lager maker (www.islandbrewing.com.fj), and in the capital Suva the Malt House brewpub. Not far away in Pacific terms, the Cook Islands are enjoying the arrival of two new breweries on Rarotonga, the largest island in the group – Reka Reka brewery concentrating on making a local lager and the craftier Matutu Brewing Company (www.matutubeer.com) beginning with a couple of ales.

Further north on the American dependency of Guam is the appropriately brewpub-style Great Deep Brewing (www.greatdeepbrewing.com), while the Micronesian island of Yap has the more hobby-like Stone Money Brewing.

However, if we were giving awards, the one for the most remote prize-winning brewery on earth would have to go to the Norfolk Island Brewery Company (www.beer.nf), roughly equidistant but still many hundreds of miles from the northern tip of New Zealand, the Queensland coast of Australia, and the islands of New Caledonia to its north.

Whether one is talking about quality, style, or geography, good beer, it would appear, no longer has frontiers.

NEGEV PORTER ALON (5%)
Negev Brewing Co, Kiryat Gat (Israel)
German in its methods but international in style, this light porter earns praise for this southern Israeli brewer, as does its amber ale and summer ale with passion-fruit in the mash.
www.negevbrewery.co.il

ROBSON'S DURBAN PALE ALE (5.7%)
Shongweni Brewery, KwaZulu-Natal (South Africa)
Challenger and Cascade hops, a full malt recipe, and English ale yeast make this re-creation of the IPAs unloaded on route to India in the nineteenth century.
www.shongwenibrewery.com

TAYBEH GOLDEN (5%)
Taybeh Brewing Company, West Bank (Palestine)
Plucky brewing company surviving multiple obstacles, including an intifada, to craft a trio of beers, including this modestly hopped lager with a crisp character.
www.taybehbeer.net

Emerging Markets

There may be some question about when the renaissance in modern brewing began – was it with Fritz Maytag's purchase of the Anchor Brewing Company in San Francisco in 1965 (*see* p.180), Pierre Celis's re-creation of Flemish *witbier* in 1966 (*see* p.72), the formation of CAMRA to protect traditional British beer styles in 1971 (*see* p.108), or perhaps the publication of Michael Jackson's first *The World Guide to Beer* in 1977 (*see* p.34) – but there can be little doubt it has blossomed into a global phenomenon.

From its starting points in Europe and North America in the 1970s and 1980s, craft beer in the 1990s and into the new millennium swept into some most unexpected lands, as witnessed in the pages of this book. Few souls would have wagered in 1980 on Italy becoming a playground for craft brewing (*see* pp.158–65), or on Denmark and Norway evolving into influential beer markets (*see* pp.145–9), but of course that is exactly what has happened.

So what next?

Certainly one place to watch is China, with its booming economy, emerging middle class, and mushrooming beer production. From 2000 to 2010, China more or less doubled its annual brewing output to 448 million hectolitres, making it the world's largest producer, despite sitting far down in the ranks of per capita beer consumption. Global companies hope this indicates a thirst that will be largely quenched by industrial brews, but we suspect it will also allow room for the development of a craft beer market.

India, too, is an immature market that is showing signs of early development, seen most starkly in the emergence of Dr. Vijay Mallya's Bangalore-based UB Group as a global force in both beer and spirits. Mallya has invested heavily in craft beer before, at California's Mendocino Brewing, so should not be averse to seeing such developments in India. New Delhi, Orissa, and Pune already have brewpubs, and cosmopolitan Bangalore is set to spawn many more.

The greatest unknown is Russia. The world's third-largest beer-producing nation (after China and the USA) is still emerging

Above: With beer production almost twice that of the second-largest brewing nation, and a low per capita consumption, China remains the biggest wild card in the emerging beer market deck.

from an era of state control and has allowed Heineken, Carlsberg, and Anheuser-Busch InBev to create subsidiary companies to invest heavily in improving technical standards at existing breweries, without as yet creating beers with stimulating flavours.

Back in imperial times, the best beers found in the Russian capital, Moscow, were imported from Baltic, Scandinavian, and other brewers via St Petersburg. By odd coincidence, it is the same two cities that now see demands for more challenging beers – like those enjoyed by other Europeans.

Probably the single most promising of the emerging beer markets, however, is South America in general and Brazil in particular (*see* pp.220–1). With a rapidly growing middle class, an existing network of as many as 200 craft breweries, and a great degree of enthusiasm for beer in all its many forms, the only factor holding back Brazil's beer revolution is transportation infrastructure – the so-called "cold chain" of refrigerated distribution – an issue destined to be resolved as the country continues its rapid economic growth.

With Argentina and Chile poised to follow Brazil's lead (*see* pp.222–3), it seems likely that we will soon be seeing big things in beer from across the Southern Americas.

Above: Bottling remains very much a hands-on process at the Szot brewery in Santiago, Chile. Along with neighbouring Argentina and Brazil, Chile is poised for great craft-beer growth in the coming years.

Above: Kingfisher Lager remains massively popular in India, but brewpubs are springing up to challenge the status quo in urban areas.

Above: Turkey's Efes brewing group has brought high-tech production to its Moscow plant. But will distinctive flavours follow?

Beer Festivals

Like everything else in the world of brewing, beer festivals vary in their origins, purposes, and traditions. Here is our selection of the best and the most famous. For further suggestions, try www.beerfestivals.org.

GREAT BRITISH BEER FESTIVAL
London, UK; first week in August; www.gbbf.org.uk
The UK's largest celebration of domestic cask-conditioned beers that nowadays includes an impressive Bières Sans Frontières bar of worldwide imports.
TIP Take advantage of the one-third-pint (20cl or 7fl oz) pours to sample the greatest variety.

GREAT AMERICAN BEER FESTIVAL
Denver, Colorado, USA; late September or early October; www.greatamericanbeerfestival.com
Unrivalled variety of close to 2,000 American beers from breweries large and small, served in 1oz (30ml) tasting portions.
TIP All-you-can-sample tickets sell out months in advance; buy early.

OKTOBERFEST
Munich, Germany; 17 days ending the first weekend of October; www.oktoberfest.de
More Bavarian folk fest than beer-tasting event, this 200-year-old celebration features beer from Munich's "Big Six" brewers.
TIP Go for the experience, not the beer, and consider enjoying the city's superb pubs and beer gardens once the crowds grow too thick.

ØL FESTIVAL
Copenhagen, Denmark; last week in May; www.beerfestival.dk
Arguably Europe's best-organized festival, run by the consumer group Danøl and staffed by brewers, featuring over 700 craft beers served in snifter-sized measures.
TIP Plan a tasting strategy to avoid being overwhelmed by the selection (and strength) of many of the best beers.

WEEKEND OF SPONTANEOUS FERMENTATION
Opstal, Belgium; last weekend in May; www.bierpallieters.be
Simple, beautifully civilized celebration featuring every lambic beer available. Held in a Flemish village parish hall.
TIP Plan your transportation in advance, arriving at either Lebbeke, Opwijk, or Buggenhout station, with minibus service available only from the last of these.

FESTIVAL BRASILEIRO DA CERVEJA
Blumenau, Brazil; mid-November; www.festivaldacerveja.com
This young and growing beer festival features the best of an exciting, fast-developing craft beer market.
TIP Book accommodation well in advance, as the city has limited hotel stock.

MONDIAL DE LA BIÈRE
Montréal, Canada; June; also Strasbourg, France; October; www.festivalmondialbiere.qc.ca
Exciting family of beer festivals helmed by organizers with a keen eye on developing beer countries.
TIP Especially in Montréal, plan your tasting early, as crowds can grow daunting in the later hours.

SALON DE GRANDE BIÈRE
Tokyo, Japan; end-April; www.craftbeerassociation.jp
Japan's most prestigious beer event featuring 60 imported and indigenous craft beers in a top venue, served in limitless 5cl (2fl oz) measures.
TIP Book online in advance for at least two sessions so as to sample not gulp.

Above: Few beers to choose from, but mighty volumes at Stuttgart's *Volksfest*, Germany.

Above: Getting a taste for it at Qingdao Beer Festival in Shandong, China.

Above: Pints of persuasion at one of a hundred annual festivals of real ale in Britain.

International Beer Festivals Calendar

JANUARY

Great Alaska Beer & Barley Wine Festival	Anchorage, Alaska, USA;	http://auroraproductions.net/beer-barley.html	American winter beers
National Winter Ales Festival	Manchester, UK	www.alefestival.org.uk	British and foreign winter beers

FEBRUARY

Extreme Beerfest	Omaha, Nebraska, USA	www.beercornerusa.com	300 international extreme beers

MARCH

March Fest	Nelson, New Zealand	www.marchfest.com	Craft beers, food, and wines
London Drinker Beer & Cider Festival	London, UK	www.camranorthlondon.org.uk	Beers and ciders
Festival Brasileiro da Cerveja	Blumenau, Brazil (see opposite)		

APRIL

Helsinki Beer Festival	Helsinki, Finland;	www.helsinkibeerfestival.com	Finnish beers, ciders, and whiskies
Salon de Grande Bière	Tokyo, Japan (see opposite)		

MAY

Český Pivní Festival	Prague, Czech Republic	www.ceskypivnifestival.cz	Czech beers and food
Øl Festival	Copenhagen, Denmark (see opposite)		
Weekend of Spontaneous Fermentation	Opstal, Belgium (see opposite)		

JUNE

Great Japan Beer Festival	Tokyo, Japan; also Osaka, July; Yokohama, September	www.craftbeerassociation.jp	Japanese and imported craft beers
Bestfest Asia	Singapore	www.beerfestasia.com	Commercial and craft brewers
Scottish Real Ale Festival	Edinburgh, Scotland	www.scottishbeerfestival.org.uk	The ultimate Scottish beer experience
American Craft Beer Fest	Boston, Massachusetts, USA	www.beeradvocate.com/acbf/	Part of Boston Beer Week
Mondial de la Bière	Montréal, Canada (see opposite)		

JULY

Annafest	Forchheim, Germany	www.nordbayern.de/events	Two-dozen Franconian brewers
Õlletoober	Lilbi, Saaremaa, Estonia	www.olletoober.ee	Local, international, and homemade beers

AUGUST

Beervana	Wellington, New Zealand	www.beervana.co.nz	200 plus New Zealand and Australian craft beers
Opladener BierBörse	Leverkusen-Opladen, Germany	www.bierboerse.com	1,000 international beers
Great British Beer Festival	London, UK (see opposite)		

SEPTEMBER

Kölner BierBörse	Cologne (Köln), Germany	www.bierboerse.com	International beers
All-Ireland Craft Beerfest	Dublin, Ireland	www.irishcraftbeerfestival.com	Smaller Irish breweries
Great Canadian Beer Festival	Victoria, British Columbia, Canada	www.gcbf.com	50 Canadian craft brewers
Great American Beer Festival	Denver, Colorado, USA (see opposite)		
Oktoberfest	Munich, Germany (see opposite)		

OCTOBER

PINT Bokbierfestival	Amsterdam, Netherlands	www.pint.nl	Dutch bokbier
Brassigaume	Marbehan, Belgium	www.brassigaume.be	Tiny European breweries
Stockholm Beer & Whisky Festival	Stockholm, Sweden	www.stockholmbeer.se	Commercial and craft companies
Mondial de la Bière	Strasbourg, France (see opposite)		

NOVEMBER

Bitter & Twisted International Boutique Beer Festival	East Maitland (New South Wales), Australia	www.bitterandtwisted.com.au	Australian craft beers in a disused jail

DECEMBER

Kerstbierfestival	Essen, Belgium	www.kerstbierfestival.be	All of Belgium's winter beers

Glossary

ABBEY ALE A term used mainly outside Belgium to denote the styles of sweet, heavy ale associated with monastic breweries. *See also* TRAPPIST BEER.

ABV (ALCOHOL BY VOLUME) Amount of alcohol relative to the total volume of a beverage. Multiplied by 0.796, it yields the more rarely used ABW (alcohol by weight).

ADDITIVES Collective term for substances added to beer to help present, preserve, or flavour it artificially.

ADJUNCTS Cereals, sugars, fruits, and syrups used as a substitute for malted barley (*see* MALT) in the MASH.

ALE Beer resulting from warm FERMENTATION by YEAST of the family *Saccharomyces cerevisiae*; sometimes referred to as TOP-FERMENTED.

ALPHA ACIDS Chemical compounds found in HOPS that, when converted to iso-alpha acids in the boil, contribute much of the bitterness to beer.

ALT OR *ALTBIER* Style of warm-fermented, cold-conditioned (*see* SECONDARY FERMENTATION) beer typical of the German city of Düsseldorf and the surrounding region.

BARLEY MALT *See* MALT.

BARLEY WINE Term used historically to denote the strongest beer in a brewer's portfolio, often of low carbonation or even "flat", with the strength of a light wine. Nowadays it is more often a specific style of strong ale, which is hoppier in the American interpretation.

BARREL (BBL) With HECTOLITRE, the most common unit of measure for beer production. In the UK, a barrel is 163.65 litres (36 imperial gallons); in the USA, 117.34 litres (31 US gallons).

BEER ENGINE The correct term for what is known colloquially as a "handpump" or "handpull", the most popular means of dispensing CASK-CONDITIONED ales by drawing beer mechanically from a cask in the pub cellar.

BERLINER WEISSE Low-strength, tart style of WHEAT BEER once common to Berlin, now more frequently brewed elsewhere.

BIÈRE DE GARDE Traditional northern-French style of "stored beer", found most frequently in the Nord, Pas-de-Calais and Picardy regions.

BITTER/BEST BITTER/EXTRA SPECIAL BITTER Today the standard ale of British pubs, pale, mildly to moderately hopped, and increasing in body and strength as it progresses from "ordinary" to "best" and "extra special" bitter (or ESB).

BOCK German style of strong LAGER thought to have originated from the city of Einbeck. Stronger and heartier in the *Doppelbock* or "double" version and usually pale of hue in the *Maibock*, springtime version.

BOK Term used in the Netherlands to describe dark, autumnal beers partially related to German *Bock*, appearing as pale, sweet *lentebok* or *meibok* in April and dark, heavy *eisbok* in midwinter.

BOTTLE-CONDITIONED Beer that undergoes further FERMENTATION in the bottle.

BOTTOM-FERMENTED *See* LAGER.

BROWN ALE Style of dark-coloured ale still most frequently associated with England but widely brewed. It varies in character, sometimes dramatically so.

CASK-CONDITIONED Term first coined in the 1970s to describe beer that has been refermented in the barrel, typically in the pub cellar. *See also* REAL ALE.

CONDITIONING *See* SECONDARY FERMENTATION.

CONTRACT BREWING The process whereby a brewery produces one or more beers for a separate company that owns the brands and markets them as their own. *See also* LICENSED BREWING.

CRAFT BREWING OR CRAFT BEER The opposite of INDUSTRIAL BREWING OR INDUSTRIAL BEER.

CREAM ALE American style of blond beer fermented warm but conditioned more like a LAGER.

DIACETYL The common name for butanedione, a compound that can develop in beer and gives it a butterscotch or buttery flavour and aroma. It is usually considered a flaw when found in high concentration.

DOUBLE Term increasingly used to indicate a stronger, fuller-bodied version of an existing style. *See also* IMPERIAL.

DMS (DIMETHYL SULPHIDE) Sulphurous compound sometimes found in beer that, in high concentrations, yields aromas and flavours of cooked vegetables.

DRY HOPPING The practice of adding hops to a beer during its FERMENTATION or conditioning period.

DUBBEL A term associated with Belgian monastic brewing, originally coined for the use of double the MALT of standard beer, to create a moderately strong, usually dark, predominantly malty ale. *See also* ABBEY ALE.

DUNKEL Dark LAGER of a style once native to Munich and the surrounding area. Sometimes referred to as *Münchener* or *Münchener Dunkel*.

EXTREME BEER Voguish expression referring to beers of high strength or brewed with the use of unusual ingredients or techniques.

FERMENTATION The process through which YEAST converts sugar into CO_2 and alcohol.

FILTERED Term used to denote beer from which YEAST has been physically removed in some fashion.

FININGS Substances used to cause YEAST and proteins to drop as sediment in CASK-CONDITIONED ales.

FRUIT BEERS Wide-ranging classification referring to any beer fermented and/or conditioned with fruits or flavoured by fruit juices, extracts, or syrups.

GRAIN BILL The mix of MALTs and other grains used to make a beer.

GRAVITY DISPENSE Method of serving CASK-CONDITIONED or other beers directly tapped from the barrel.

GRUIT Historically, mixtures of dried herbs and spices for flavouring beer before the use of HOPS (also *grut* or *gruut*), but nowadays a term occasionally used to describe a beer made entirely without the use of hops.

G(U)EUZE A bottled beer made with LAMBIC. When designated *oud(e)* or *vielle*, it must contain 100 per cent lambic beer only.

HECTOLITRE (HL) The commonest unit used to measure the output of a commercial brewery, equal to 100 litres (22 gallons).

HELLES Pale LAGER style originally associated with Munich and the surrounding areas. Sometimes referred to as *Münchener* or *Münchener Helles*.

HIGH-GRAVITY BREWING Production method common to industrial brewing whereby a beer is fermented to a high percentage of alcohol and reduced with water to the desired final strength at the bottling or kegging stage.

HOPS The flowers or cones of the plant *Humulus lupulus*, first introduced to brewing on a grand scale in the Middle Ages and now considered an essential ingredient in all but a very small number of beers.

HOPS – AMERICAN American hop varieties that typically bestow on a beer an aggressive, often citric bitterness. Sometimes known collectively as "C-hops" (including Cascade, Centennial, Chinook, Citra, and Columbus) and "non-C" (Amarillo, Magnum, Simcoe, and others).

HOPS – CZECH The classic Czech hop Saaz, also known as Žatec after the town around which they were originally cultivated, is very floral in character and used for Bohemian-style PILSNER. Now grown in many countries.

HOPS – ENGLISH English hop varieties are characteristically mild to moderate in their bitterness and aroma. East Kent or Kentish Goldings are perhaps best known, along with Styrian Golding, Fuggle, Target, Challenger, Northern Brewer, and others.

HOPS – GERMAN The best-known German hops are referred to as noble hops and include Hallertau, Hersbrucker, Tettnang, and Spalt, each possessing diverse characteristics.

HOPS – NEW ZEALAND Noted for their intensely aromatic qualities and tropical fruit notes, and featuring new varietals, such as Nelson Sauvin, Riwaka, and Motueka.

IMPERIAL Term originally used to denote a strong and intensely flavoured style of STOUT, now haphazardly employed to describe any unusually strong interpretation of a classic style. *See also* DOUBLE.

IPA (INDIA PALE ALE) Style of PALE ALE that derives its name from its popularity in India during the days of the Raj. Originally native to England, it is now widely brewed in American (very hoppy and moderately strong) and British (less assertively hopped and often weaker) versions.

INDUSTRIAL BREWING OR INDUSTRIAL BEER The production of beer on a massive scale, usually by large, multinational companies and often using HIGH-GRAVITY BREWING.

KÖLSCH A style of light blond beer, warm-fermented but cold-conditioned, confined by legislation in the European Union to the city of Cologne (Köln) and its immediate area but still imitated elsewhere.

KRAUSENING The process of adding a small amount of vigorously fermenting WORT to an already fermented beer, typically LAGER, to encourage a SECONDARY FERMENTATION and cause natural carbonation.

KRIEK When designated *oud(e)* or *vielle*, a LAMBIC refermented on draught while whole cherries are steeped within it and subsequently BOTTLE-CONDITIONED. More commonly applied to cherry-flavoured beers made with fruit juices or extracts and often sweetened.

LAGER Beer resulting from cool FERMENTATION by YEAST of the *Saccharomyces uvarum* family, such as the *carlsbergensis* strain, traditionally afforded a long and cool conditioning period; also referred to as bottom-fermented. In Germany, lager is sometimes used to describe beers that have been given extended periods of cool conditioning, regardless of type of fermentation.

LAMBIC Collective name for the family of beers fermented by the action of wild YEAST, and also the name given to the unblended draught form of such beers.

LICENSED BREWING A commercial arrangement whereby a brand or brands from one brewery are produced and then marketed by another company. *See also* CONTRACT BREWING.

LIGHTSTRUCK *See* SKUNKY.

MALT Grain, usually barley, that after germination is kilned or dried to stop the growth.

MÄRZEN Moderately strong style of German LAGER historically brewed in the month of March for cellaring and consumption during the non-brewing summer season. Widely associated with autumn festivals, such as Munich's Oktoberfest.

MASH OR MASHING The mixing of ground malt with hot water, which begins the process of converting grain starch into fermentable sugars, resulting in WORT.

MÉTHODE TRADITIONALE Method of bottle FERMENTATION most famously practised in the Champagne region of France, where it originated. It involves a lengthy SECONDARY FERMENTATION in the bottle followed by the gathering of the spent YEAST cells in the neck of the bottle and removal of same, resulting in a clear liquid. It is also known as *méthode champenoise*.

MICROBREWERY Term from the early 1980s used to distinguish new, small breweries set up to produce older styles of beer against the trend to industrialization. Now becoming meaningless.

MILD OR MILD ALE Traditional British term originally used to describe immature beer but now used as a style term denoting ales light in alcohol, usually dark in colour, and predominantly malty.

MÜNCHENER OR *MÜNCHNER See* HELLES

OKTOBERFESTBIER See MÄRZEN.

ORIGINAL GRAVITY (OG) A measure of the concentration of fermentable sugars found in WORT relative to the density of water, which is given the base value of 1.000. It is usually expressed as a four-digit number without the decimal, for example 1050 rather than 1.050.

OXIDIZED Term used to describe beer that has suffered the usually deleterious effects of overexposure to oxygen, which eventually converts alcohol to vinegar.

PALE ALE Hoppier style of ale that first appeared in Britain in the seventeenth century and classically featured English HOPS.

PASTEURIZATION A means of cleansing microorganisms from beer (or other consumables) by applying heat for a brief period of time, stopping short of sterilization.

PHENOLIC A solvent-like or medicinal quality sometimes found in beer due to the high presence of unappealing volatile compounds known as phenols.

PILSNER Pale LAGER first brewed in the Bohemian, now Czech, city of Plzen (Pilsen).

PLATO OR DEGREES PLATO An alternative way of expressing original gravity, or other specific gravities, measured with a device known as a saccharometer, expressed in degrees (°) Plato and used in some countries on beer labels to denote style and strength.

PORTER A moderately bitter, deep-brown or black style of ale originating in London in the eighteenth century. In modern terms, it is virtually indistinguishable from STOUT.

PRIMARY FERMENTATION First stage of fermentation during which the bulk of fermentable sugars are converted to CO_2 and alcohol. It can last for up to 14 days but more frequently takes between three and seven.

QUADRUPEL The term invented by the Dutch Trappist brewery La Trappe in 1990 to distinguish its then new barley wine, increasingly adopted by craft brewers to denote a strong ABBEY ALE.

RAUCHBIER German style of LAGER made using a portion of MALTs that have been smoked over wood, typical of Bamberg and the surrounding area.

REAL ALE Term coined by the British beer consumer group CAMRA (Campaign for Real Ale) to denote CASK-CONDITIONED and BOTTLE-CONDITIONED ales, although more often taken to mean the former only.

REINHEITSGEBOT Bavarian beer purity law of 1516, ultimately adopted by all Germany until it was ruled a restriction of trade by the European Union.

SAHTI Traditional Finnish style of beer brewed from barley and rye, fermented with bread YEAST and filtered through juniper boughs.

SAISON Belgian style of golden ale formerly brewed in the spring for cellaring and consumption during the non-brewing summer months, now widely interpreted and misinterpreted.

SCHWARZBIER Type of black-hued, dominantly malty LAGER once typical of eastern Germany.

SCOTCH ALE Term used to denote sweet, malty, and strong ales originally widely brewed in Scotland but nowadays more common elsewhere, most notably in Belgium and North America.

SECONDARY FERMENTATION The slower, second stage of FERMENTATION, also known as conditioning, in which residual sugars continue to ferment and flavours are allowed to meld. It can last anywhere from a week to several months.

SKUNKY Description given to beer in which a chemical reaction caused by ultraviolet light has affected flavour chemicals that derive from HOPS, creating a compound said to smell like a skunk.

STEAM BEER Hybrid style of beer developed in California using LAGER YEAST fermented at warm temperatures. In the USA, the term is copyrighted by the Anchor Brewing Company.

STEINBIER Beer produced by the ancient practice of raising the temperature of the WORT through the addition of superheated stones.

STOUT A family of black or near-black ales originally derived from PORTER, including oatmeal, milk, oyster, Irish, dry, sweet, imperial, and others, ranging widely in strength and hoppiness but always featuring some measure of roasty character.

TERTIARY FERMENTATION A protracted period of fermentation by slower YEAST strains, found mainly in old (*oud*) LAMBIC and oak-aged ales, lasting anything up to three years.

TOP-FERMENTED *See* ALE.

TRAPPIST BEER Celebrated ales brewed under the direct supervision of monks at a Trappist monastery. *See also* ABBEY ALE.

TRIPEL The strongest type of beer produced by monastic breweries and their imitators, originally dark and made with triple the MALT of standard beer but nowadays usually golden after the Tripel of the Trappist Abbey at Westmalle, Antwerp.

UNFILTERED Reference to beers left hazy by residual YEAST or grain haze, although not necessarily bottle-fermented (*see* LAGER).

UR- German prefix indicating "original type".

VIENNA LAGER OR *WIENER* Style of amber-red or medium-brown LAGER, once associated with the city of Vienna but now more directly related to the use of a specific type of barley MALT known as Vienna malt.

WEISSBIER, *WEIZENBIER*, AND *HEFEWEIZEN* Titles denoting a style of wheat beer typical to Germany containing a large proportion of malted wheat and properly fermented with one of a family of YEASTs that produce banana and clove aromas and flavours during FERMENTATION.

WEIZENBOCK Strong and usually quite dark *WEIZENBIER*.

WHEAT BEER OR WHEAT ALE General terms used to indicate that a sizeable proportion of wheat has been added to barley in the GRAIN BILL of a beer.

WHITE BEER, *WIT*, OR *BIÈRE BLANCHE* Words meaning "white" usually suggest a beer of a style typical to Belgium made with barley MALT and unmalted wheat, generally spiced with dried orange peel and coriander but sometimes other spices, too.

WORT The sugar-rich liquid that results from the MASH. After the boil but prior to FERMENTATION, it is sometimes referred to as the "hopped wort".

YEAST Microscopic and unicellular organisms of the family *Saccharomyces* that consume sugar and produce CO_2 and alcohol. Yeast are essential to the production of alcohol and, therefore, beer.

Index

Beer names all in *italics*
Page numbers in **bold** indicate major references
Page numbers in *italics* indicate illustrations

1516 Brewing Company 94
3 Monts 130
3 Schténg 76
3F Schaarbeekse Oude Kriek 62
3F Vintage Oude Gueuze 62
5 Barrel Pale Ale 188
8 Wired Brewing: *Hopwired IPA* 230

Aass brewery: *Aass Bock* 148
Abadessa Export 220
Abbaye Notre Dame de Saint-Rémy 55; *Trappistes Rochefort 6 / 8 / 10:* 55
Abbaye Notre Dame de Scourmont 55, 56; *Chimay Triple* 54
Abbaye Notre Dame d'Orval 55, *56*; *Orval* 54
abbey ale **54–9**, 248
ABC Stout 232
Abita Brewing Company: *Restoration Pale Ale* 202
ABV (alcohol by volume) 248
Adam 184
Adam Ravbar Kvasno Svetlo Pivo 168
additives 248
adjuncts 26–8, 248
Adnams Brewery *123*; *Tally Ho!* 122
Aecht Schlenkerla Rauchbier Märzen 84
Ægir Bryggeri: *India Pale Ale* 148
Africa 17, 242–3
ageing 28, 58–9, 158, 178
Agrofirma Tervete: *Tervetes Originalais* 155
Agullons Pura Pale 168
Alaska 184–7
Alaskan Brewing 187; *Smoked Porter* 186, 187
Alaus Darykla Ponoras: *Ponoras Kaimiškas Nefiltruotas Šviesusis Biržietiškas* 154
Alba Weizen 220
Alberta 212–13
Aldaris brewery: *Porteris* 154
Ale Street News 183
ales 248; *see also* individual types
AleSmith Brewing 182; *My Bloody Valentine* 182
Alko (drinks stores) 152
All About Beer 202
Allagash Brewing: *Curieux* 196
Alley Kat Brewing 212, *213*; *Old Deuteronomy Barley Wine* 213
Allsopp, Samuel 110
Almond '22 brewery 162, *163*; *Pink IPA* 161
Alpäide 76
alpha acids 22, 248
Alpha King 190
Altbiers 86–7, 248
Altstadt Weissbier Hefe 242
Amager Bryghus: *Sundby Stout* 147
amber lagers 104–7
Amber Swan Ale 236
Amnesiac Double IPA 212
Anchor Brewing 180, 204; *Steam Beer* 180
Anchorage 187
Andechser Spezial Heil 82
Anderson Valley Brewing 182; *Barney Flats Oatmeal Stout* 181

The Angel's Share 183
Anniversary Beer 180
Anosteké 130
Antares Barley Wine 216
Antica Birreria Theresianer: *Vienna* 163
APA 230
Arbor Ales: *Oyster Stout* 116
Arctic Devil Barley Wine 184
Argentina 224–5
Arioli, Agostino 160–1
Arrogant Bastard Ale 180
Arthur, Tomme 178, 182
Asia 242
Atna Øl brewery: *Stabburøl* 148
Augrenoise 72
Augustiner-Bräu Wagner: *Edelstoff* 82
Australia 228–9; map *229*
Austria 94–5; map *95*
Autumn Maple 180
Avatar Jasmine IPA 184
Avery, Adam 178
Avery Brewing 178; *Collaboration Not Litigation* 172; *Hog Heaven Barley Wine* 188
Ayinger Jahrhundert-Bier 82

Back Hand of God Stout 212
Badische Staatsbrauerei Rothaus: *Rothaus Pils* 83; *Tannenzäpfle* 83
Baeren Brauerei: *Classic* 236
Baird Brewing: *Suruga Bay Imperial IPA* 236
Balling scale 98
Baltic States 144, **154–5**
Bam Bière 190
Bamberg 84
Bamberg Rauchbier 220
Banskobystrický Pivovar: *Urpiner Ležiak VýCapný Tmavý* 171
barley **17**, 92
barley wine 248
Barney Flats Oatmeal Stout 181
Baronen Barley Wine 150
barrels 26, 28, 178, 248
Batemans XXXB 110
Bathams Best Bitter 110
La Bavaisienne Ambrée 131
Bavaria 80, 90–1, 93
Bavik brewery 58; *Petrus Aged Pale* 59
Bayerische Staatsbrauerei Weihenstephan: *Infinium* 172; *Weihenstephaner Hefe Weissbier* 91
Beagle Fuegian Ale 224
Bear Republic Brewing: *Racer 5 IPA* 182
Beau's All Natural Brewing: *Lug Tread Lagered Ale* 210
beer 16–23; buying 35; definition of 11, 13; and food 42–5; ingredients 11, 29; origins 15, 49; pouring 38–9; production 49; production map *24–5*; quality 55, 98; serving 37; storing 36, 130–1; styles 34, 50; tasting 40–1
beer engine 248
Beer Here: *Infantøl* 146
Beerlao Lager 232
Békésszentandrási Sörfozde: *Black Rose* 168
Belgian Pour 38–9
Belgium 50, 52–79; influence of 160–2, 208; map *53*
Bella Mère 76
Bellevaux Black 74
Bell's Brewery 202; *Expedition Stout* 191
Berlina Pub Brewery 224; *India Pale Ale* 224

Berliner Weisse 91, 248
Bernard, Humpolec brewery: *Svátecní Ležák 12°* 100
Bierbrouwerij Emelisse: *Emelisse Rauchbier* 138
bière de blé noir 132–3
bière de garde 130–1, 248
Bierwerkstatt Weitra brewery: *Weitra Bräu Hadmar* 95
Big Rock Brewery 212; *McNally's Extra* 213
La Binchoise Spéciale Noël 78
Bink Blonde 76
Birra Amiata Artisanale: *Vecchia Bastarda* 162
Birra del Borgo: *Reale* 161
Birrificio Baladin: *Xyauyù Etichetta Argento* 163
Birrificio BI-DU: *Confine* 160
Birrificio Brùton: *Brùton Stoner* 160
Birrificio Del Ducato: *Verdi Imperial Stout* 163
Birrificio Grado Plato 163; *Strada San Felice* 162
Birrificio Italiano: *Tipopils* 162
Birrificio Lambrate 163; *Domm* 160
Birrificio Ticinese: *San Martino Gold* 170
Birrificio Torrechiara 163; *Panil Barriquée* 161
Birrificio Troll: *Shangrila* 161
Bishops Farewell 110
Bison Brewing: *Organic Chocolate Stout* 181
Bitburger Braugruppe 80; *Premium Beer* 82
bitter 18, **110–13**, 248
Bjergsø, Jeppe 146
Bjergsø, Mikkel Borg 145, *173*
Black Albert 76
Black Bavarian 191
black beers 118
Black Boss Porter 168
Black Butte Porter 184
Black Creek Historic Brewery: *Porte* 210
Black Label 64
Black Magic Woman 146
Black Oak Brewing: *Nut Brown Ale* 210
Black Raven Brewing: *Tamerlane Brown Porter* 187
Black Rose 168
Blanche de Chambly 208
Blanche des Honelles 72
Blitz-Weinhard Brewery 184–6
blonde ales 76
La Blonde d'Esquelbecq 132
blonde lagers 98, 100–3
Blue Anchor, brewpub *124*; *Spingo Middle* 127
Bluebird Bitter 110
Bock 92–3, 248
Bodebrown Cervejaria & Escola: *Wee Heavy* 221
Bodgers Barley Wine 122
Boelens, Kris 73
Bøgedal Bryghus: *Bøgedal* 146
Bohemia 98, 106
boiling 22
bok 138–9, 248
Boltens Ur-Alt 86
Boon, Frank 62
Boon Oude Geuze Mariage Parfait 62
Boon Oude Kriek 62
Boon Rawd Brewery: *Singha Lager* 239
Boscos Brewing: *Famous Flaming Stone Beer* 200

Boston Beer 196, 198–9; *Infinium* 172; *Samuel Adams Boston Lager* 198; *Utopias* 199
bottle-conditioned 248, 249
bottled beer *31*, 37
bottom-fermented 50, 248, 249
Boulder Beer 188–9; *Mojo India Pale Ale* 188
Boulevard Brewing: *Tank 7 Farmhouse Ale* 192
Brahaus Hartmannsdorf: *Goedecke Döllnitzer Ritterguts Gose* 90
Brandt, Johan 79
Brasserie à Vapeur: *Saison de Pipaix* 69
Brasserie Artisanale de Matzenheim: *Matten La Schwortz* 132
Brasserie Artisanale de Rulles: *Estivale* 77
Brasserie Artisanale Millevertus: *Bella Mère* 76
Brasserie Bailleux: *La Cuvée des Jonquilles* 131
Brasserie Brootcoorens: *La Sambresse Blonde* 78
Brasserie Caracole: *Caracole* 77
Brasserie Coreff: *Coreff Ambrée* 132
Brasserie d'Abbaye des Rocs: *Blanche des Honelles* 72
Brasserie d'Achouffe 208
Brasserie d'Augrenoise: *Augrenoise* 72
Brasserie de Bellevaux: *Bellevaux Black* 74
Brasserie de Cazeau: *Saison Cazeau* 68
Brasserie de Jandrain: *IV Saison* 68
Brasserie de la Senne: *Taras Boulba* 79
Brasserie de Silenrieux: *Sara Brune* 73
Brasserie de Silly: *Scotch Silly* 75
Brasserie de St Sylvestre: *3 Monts* 130
Brasserie d'Ecaussinnes: *Ultra-Frâiche* 69
Brasserie des Franches-Montagnes: *L'Abbaye de Saint Bon-Chien* 170
Brasserie des Garrigues: *Nuit de Goguette* 133
Brasserie des Géants: *Saison Voison* 69
Brasserie du Grain d'Orge: *3 Schténg* 76
Brasserie du Pays Flamand: *Anosteké* 130
Brasserie Dupont: *Saison Dupont* 69
Brasserie Duyck 131; *Jenlain Ambrée* 130
Brasserie Ellezelloise: *Hercule Stout* 74
Brasserie Fantôme: *Fantôme* 77
Brasserie La Binchoise: *La Binchoise Spéciale Noël* 78
Brasserie La Choulette: *La Choulette Brune* 130
Brasserie Lancelot: *Telenn Du* 133
Brasserie Lefebvre: *Hopus* 78
Brasserie McAuslan: *St-Ambroise Oatmeal Stout* 209
Brasserie Meteor: *Meteor Pils* 133
Brasserie Pietra 132–3
Brasserie St Feuillien: *St Feuillien Triple* 56
Brasserie Theillier: *La Bavaisienne Ambrée* 131
Brasserie Thiriez: *La Blonde d'Esquelbecq* 132
Brasserie Trois Dames: *India Pale Ale* 170
Brassiere de Blaugies: *Saison d'Épeautre* 73

Brau Union 94
Brauberger zu Lübeck: *Brauberger Zwickelbie* 82
Brauerei Aying: *Ayinger Jahrhundert-Bier* 82
Brauerei Egg: *Wälder Senn* 95
Brauerei Fässla: *Zwergla* 85
Brauerei Först: *Goldener Löwe Altfränkisches Lager-Bier* 84
Brauerei Friedrich Gutmann: *Gutmann Weizenbock* 90
Brauerei Gebr Maisel: *Maisel's Weisse Kristall* 90
Brauerei Hirt: *Hirter Morchl* 95
Brauerei Hofstetten: *Granitbock* 94
Brauerei Hummel: *Merkendorfer Hummel-Bräu Räucherla* 84
Brauerei im Füchschen: *Füchschen Alt* 86
Brauerei Johann Kneitinger: *Kneitinger Bock* 92
Brauerei Karg: *Karg Weizen-Bock* 90
Brauerei Keesmann: *Keesman Bamberger Herren* 83
Brauerei Locher: *Schwarzer Kristall* 170
Brauerei Päffgen: *Päffgen Kölsch* 89
Brauerei Pinkus Müller: *Original Pinkus Obergärig* 86
Brauerei Roppelt: *Roppelt Kellerbier* 85
Brauerei Schönram: *Schönramer Altbayrisch Dunkel* 93
Brauerei Schumacher: *Schumacher Alt* 87
Brauerei Schwechat: *Schwechater Zwickl* 95
Brauerei Spezial: *Spezial Lagerbier* 85
Brauerei Zehendner: *Mönchsambacher Lager* 84
Brauerei Zur Malzmühle: *Mühlen Kölsch* 89
Brauhaus Gusswerk: *Urban-Keller's Steinbier* 95
Brauhaus Malbu-Bock 168
Brauhaus Stiefl-Jürgens: *Stiefl-Jürgens Ur-Alt Dunkel* 87
Brazil 220–1, 244
Breakfast Stout 191
BrewDog brewery 172, 204; *Hardcore IPA* 111
Brewerkz Microbrewery: *Scholar Red* 242
Brewery Ommegang: *Ommegang Ale* 198
brewing **22–3**, 26, 30; innovation 28–9; large brand names 49, 80
brewpubs 99, 104, 106, 181, **202**; map *117*
brewspapers 183
Bridgeport Brewing: *India Pale Ale* 185
British Columbia 207, 212–13
Brittany 132–3
Brooklyn Brewery: *Lager* 196
Brootcoorens, Alain 78
Broumov brewery: *Opat Medový Kvasnicák 12°* 101
Brouwerij Alvinne: *Melchior* 58
Brouwerij Boelens: *Waase Wolf* 73
Brouwerij Boon: *Boon Oude Geuze Mariage Parfait* 62; *Boon Oude Kriek* 62
Brouwerij Bosteel: *Tonneke* 56
Brouwerij Contreras: *Tonneke* 79
Brouwerij De Dochter van de Korenaar: *Embrasse* 77

Brouwerij De Glazen Toren: *Odineke Oilsjtersen Tripel* 78
Brouwerij De Koningshoeven: *La Trappe Quadrupel* 139
Brouwerij de Molen 137, 140; *De Molen Hel & Verdoemenis* 138
Brouwerij De Ranke: *Cuvée de Ranke* 77
Brouwerij De Ryck: *Special de Ryck* 75
Brouwerij Dilewyns: *Vicaris Generaal* 79
Brouwerij Duvel Moortgat 78–9; *Duvel* 77
Brouwerij Girardin: *Black Label 64*; *Girardin Lambic* 64; *Gueuze Girardin* 64
Brouwerij Het Anker: *Goudon Carolus Classic* 77
Brouwerij Kerkom: *Bink Blonde* 76
Brouwerij Leroy: *Stout Leroy* 75
Brouwerij Lindemans: *Lindemans's Cuvée René Oude Gueuze* 65
Brouwerij Nieuwhuys: *Alpäide* 76
Brouwerij Sint Jozef: *Limburgse Witte* 72
Brouwerij Smisje: *T Smiske* 79
Brouwerij Strubbe: *Strubbe Pils* 79
Brouwerij 't Oude Schooltje: *Black Albert* 77
Brouwerij Vanden Bossche: *Pater Lieven Bruin* 79
Brouwerij Verhaeghe 58; *Duchesse de Bourgogne* 58; *Echte Kriekenbier* 58
Browar Amber: *Grand Imperial Porter* 169
Browar Witnica: *Black Boss Porter* 168
brown ales 52, 58–9, **120–1**, 248
The Bruery 182; *Autumn Maple* 180
Bruggsmidjan Ehf,: *Kaldi Dökkur* 144
Brussels 62–5; map *63*
Brüton Stoner 160
Brynildson, Matt 180
Budejovický Budvar 102–3; *Budvar 99*; *Budvar 12°* 100; *Budvar Kroužkovaný Ležák* 100
Budelse Brouwerij: *Budels Herfstbok* 138
Budvar 99
Budvar 12° 100
Budvar Kroužkovaný Ležák 100
Budweiser 100
Budweiser Budvar 12° 100
Bukhansan Oatmeal Stout 232
Buller Brewing: *Dry Stout* 224
Burton-upon-Trent 110
Bushwakker Brewpub: *Palliser Porter* 211

Ca L'Arenys: *Guineu Montserrat* 169
Cabesas Bier: *Trigo* 225
Café À la Mort Subite *52*
Calagione, Sam 178
California 180–3; map *181*
Camba Bavaria 93
Cambodian Brewing: *ABC Stout* 232
Cambridge Brewing 202; *Cerise Cassée* 196
Camelthorn Brewery: *Red* 242
CAMRA (Campaign for Real Ale) 6, 26, **108**
Camusi, Paul 181
Canada 176, **206–15**; map *207*
cans 30
Cantillon brewery: *Broucsella Grand Cru* 63; *Iris* 63; *Rosé de Gambrinus* 63

Captain Cooker Manuka Beer 230
Caracole 77
caramelising 22, 94
Carib Brewery: *Royal Extra Stout* 203
Caribbean 203
Carlow Brewing 118; *O'Hara's Leann Folláin* 118
Carlsberg 144, 148, 152, 154
Cascade Brewing: *Kriek Ale* 185
cask-conditioned 248, 249
Celis, Pierre 72
cellaring 36
Central America 218–19
Central City Brewing 212; *Red Racer IPA* 213
Cerise Cassée 196
Cerná Hora brewery: *Moravské Sklepní* 100
Cerveceria Beagle: *Beagle Fuegian Ale* 224
Cerveceria Kross: *Kross 5*; 216
Cervecería Primus: *Tempest Doble Malta* 219
Cervejaria Abadessa: *Abadessa Export* 220
Cervejaria Bamberg: *Bamberg Rauchbier* 220
Cervejaria Colorado 221; *Colorado Indica* 216
Cervejaria Coruja: *Alba Weizen* 220
Cervejaria Way: *Way Amburana Lager* 221
Cervesa Artesana Masia Agullons: *Agullons Pura Pale* 168
Cerveza Artesanal Antares: *Antares Barley Wine* 216
Cerveza Beagle 225
Cerveza Jerome: *Grosa* 224
Cerveza Zeppelin: *Pale Ale* 224
Ceské Budejovice 102
chestnuts 162
Chiltern Brewery: *Bodgers Barley Wine* 122
Chimay Triple 54
Chimera Dark Delight 124
China **232–3**, 242, 244
Chocolate Marble 124
Chotebor brewery: *Prémium 12°* 100
La Choulette Brune 130
Christaens, Gert 65
Christoffel Bier 138
Chuckanut Brewery: *Vienna Lager* 187
Cigar City Brewing: *Maduro Brown Ale* 201
Cilurzo, Vinnie 182
Clanconnel brewery 118; *McGrath's Irish Black* 117
Clipper City Brewing: *Heavy Seas Small Craft Warning Über Pils* 201
Coi Xay Gio: *Gio Sèc* 238
collaboration beers 172–3
Collaboration Not Litigation: Imper Ale Chiara 172
Collesi brewery: *Imper Ale Chiara* 160
Cölner Hofbräu P Josef Früh: *Früh Kölsch* 89
Cologne 88–9
Colorado 188–9
Colorado Indica 216
colour 40
Commercial Suicide 200
conditioning 23, 28
Confine 160
Coniston Brewing: *Bluebird Bitter* 110
contract brewing 248
convenience beers 30

Coop Ale Works: *Horny Toad Cerveza* 201
Coopers Brewery 228; *Extra Strong Vintage Ale* 228
Copenhagen 145, *146*
Copper Coast Red Ale 111
Coreff Ambrée 132
Corfiot Microbrewery: *Corfu Beer Real Ale Special* 168
Costa Rica's Craft Brewing: *Segura Red Ale* 219
craft brewing 9, 17, **26–9**, 248; collaboration beers 172–3; the future 244–5; growth of 8, 49
Craftworks Brewing: *Bukhansan Oatmeal Stout* 232
Crannóg Ales: *Back Hand of God Stout* 212
cream ale 248
Croatia 168
Curieux 196
Cuvée de Ranke 77
Cuvée des Fleurs 196
La Cuvée des Jonquilles 131
Czech Republic 98–107; map *99*

D L Geary Brewing: *Geary's Hampshire Special Ale* 197
Dale's Pale Ale 188
Dancing Camel brewery 242
Daniel Batham Brewers: *Bathams Best Bitter* 110
Dark Arts Porter 116
dark beers 92–3, 104–7
dark lagers 104–7
dark mild 120–1
Dark Ruby 120
Dark Star Brewing *126*; *Original* 125
De Cam Oude Geuze 63
De Dolle Brouwers: *Oerbier Reserva* 59
De Hemel Godelief 138
De Molen Hel & Verdoemenis 138
De Prael Johnny 138
De Schans brewery: *Van Vollenhoven's Extra Stout* 140
De Splenter, Annick 77
DeBakker Brewery 181
DeBakker, Ted 181
Debelder, Armand 62
decoction mashing 98, 102
degrees Plato 98, 249
Denison's Brewing: *Weissbier* 210
Denmark 145–7; map *145*
Deschutes Brewery: *Black Butte Porter* 184
Desnoes & Geddes: *Dragon Stout* 203
Det Lille Bryggeri: *Indian Pale Ale* 146
diacetyl 248
Die Weisse Hell 94
Dieu du Ciel: *Route des Épices* 209
Dits, Jean Louis *68*, 69
DMS (dimethyl sulphide) 248
Dogfish Head Craft Brewery 178, 202; *Palo Santo Marron* 198; *Portamarillo* 172
Dominus Vobiscum Brut 208
Domm 160
Doppelbock 92–3
doppio malto 160
Dorothy Goodbody's Wholesome *Stout* 117
Dortmund 82
Dortmunder Gold Lager 191
double 248
Double Maxim 120

Downton Brewery: *Chimera Dark Delight* 124
Dragon Stout 203
Drayman's Brewery: *Altstadt Weissbier Hefe* 242
Dreher, Anton 94
Drie Fonteinen brewery: *3F Schaarbeekse Oude Kriek* 62; *3F Vintage Oude Geuze* 62
Dry Stout 224
dubbel 248
Duchesse de Bourgogne 58
Duck-Rabbit Craft Brewery: *Duck-Rabbit Milk Stout* 200
Dugges Ale- & Porterbryggeri: *Bollox!* 150
Dulcis Succubus 208
Dungarvan Brewing 118; *Copper Coast Red Ale* 111
Dunkel 92
Dunkel 239
Dunkel 248
Düsseldorf 86–7
Duvel 77
Duyck family 131
Dvur Kralove nad Labem: *Tambor Tmavý Speciál 13°* 106

Eastern Europe 170–1
Echte Kriekenbier 58
Eggenberg Urbock 23° 94
Einbecker Brauhaus: *Dunkel* 92
El Toro Brewing: *Poppy Jasper Amber Ale* 181
Elysian Brewing: *Avatar Jasmine IPA* 184
Embrasse 77
Emelisse Rauchbier 138
Emerson Brewing 231; *Pilsner* 230
Emerson, Richard 231
Epic Brewing 172; *Mayhem* 230; *Portamarillo* 172
Estivale 77
Estonia 154
Estrella Damm Inedit 169
Ettaler Curator 92
Europe 50, 166–73; map 51, *167; see also* individual countries
Evil Twin Brewing: *Istedgade Hipster Ale* 146
Exit 4 American Trippel 197
Exmoor Ales brewery: *Gold* 111
Expedition Stout 191
extreme beers 204–5, 248

Falke Bier: *Tripel Monasterium* 221; *Vivre pour Vivre* 221
Fancy Lawnmower 200
Fantôme 77
Far East 232–9, 242
farmhouse ale 68–9
farmhouse brewing 154
faro 65
Feral Brewing: *Hop Hog India Pale Ale* 229
Ferdinand brewery: *Sedm Kulí Polotmavý Ležák 13°* 104
fermentation 20–1, 23, 248; cold 86, 102; primary 249; refermentation 23, 111; secondary 23, 249; tertiary 249
festivals 80, 93, 160, 162, 177, 189, **246–7**
Fiji 243
filtered 23, 248
finings 23, 248
Finkel, Charles 187
Finland 152–3
Firestone Walker: *Anniversary Beer* 180

Five 186
flavouring 29; chestnuts 162; fruit 59, 65, 76, 158; spices 72, 76
Flekovský Tmavý Ležák 13° 104
Flemish beers 52, **62–5**
Flying Fish: *Exit 4 American Trippel* 197
food and beer 42, 44–5
Forstner Biere Handbrauerei: *Styrian Ale* 94
Founders: *Breakfast Stout* 191
framboise 65
France 128–33; map *129*
Franconia 84–5; map 85
Frankenbeers 234
Fraøch Heather Ale 125
Frederic Robinson brewery: *Robinson's Old Tom* 122
freeze-distillation 204
Früh Kölsch 89
Früh, P Josef 89
fruit beers 59, 65, 76, 158, 248
Füchschen Alt 86
Fujizakura Kogen Mugishu: *Weizen* 237
Full Sail Brewing: *Session Lager* 186
Fuller Smith & Turner: *Golden Pride* 122
Fynsk Forår 146

Gaffel Kölsch 89
The Gahan House: *Island Red* 208
Gale's Prize Old Ale 122
Galway Hooker Irish Pale Ale 111
Garrison Brewing: *Imperial IPA* 208
Geary's Hampshire Special Ale 197
Gentse Stadsbrouwerij Gruut: *Gruut Amber* 77
George Bateman & Son: *Batemans XXXB* 110
Geuzestekerij De Cam: *De Cam Oude Geuze* 63
'gipsy' brewers 172
Girardin Lambic 64
glasses 37, 88–9
Goddeau, Karel 63
Goedecke Döllnitzer Ritterguts Gose 90
Goetelen, Jef 74
Golden Pride 122
Goldener Löwe Altfränkisches Lager-Bier 84
Goose Island Beer: *Matilda* 192
Gose beers 91
Goudon Carolus Classic 77
grains **17**, 22, 26, 248
Grand Imperial Porter 169
Grand Ridge: *Moonshine* 228
Grand Teton *187; Trout Hop Black IPA* 189
Granitbock 94
Granite Brewery *210; Best Bitter* 211
Grant, Bert 181, 184, 202
Granville Island Brewery *212*
Gravel, Jean-Francois 209
gravity dispense 248
Great Britain & Ireland 50, **108–27**; map *108*
Great British Beer Festival *125*, **246**
Great Divide Brewing: *Oak Aged Yeti Imperial Stout* 188
Great Lakes 190–3
Great Lakes Brewing: *Dortmunder Gold Lager* 191
Great Northern Brewing: *Snow Ghost* 189
Greece 168, 171
Green Flash Brewing: *Trippel Belgian Style Ale* 183

Green Man Brewing: *IPA* 200
Greene King brewery 122; *Strong Suffolk Vintage Ale* 123
grist 22
Grosa 224
Grossman, Ken 181
gruit 248
Grupo Damm: *Estrella Damm Inedit* 169
Gruut Amber 77
gueuze **65**, 66, 248
Gueuze Girardin 64
Gueuzerie Tilquin: *Tilquin Gueuze à L'Àncienne* 65
Guineu Montserrat 169
Guinness, Arthur 118
Guinness Ghana: *Foreign Extra Stout* 242
Gulden Draak 77
Gulpener Bierbrouwerij: *Lente Bock* 139
Gutmann Weizenbock 90

Haand Bryggeriet: *Norwegian Wood* 148
Hair of the Dog Brewing: *Adam* 184
Half Pints Brewing: *Humulus Ludicrous* 211
Hambleton Ales: *Nightmare* 118
Hanssen, Sidi 64
Hanssens Artisanaal: *Oudbeitje* 64; *Oude Gueuze* 64
Hantverksbryggeriet: *Baronen Barley Wine* 150
Hardcore IPA 111
Hart & Thistle Brewery: *Kryptonite* 209
Harvey and Son brewery: *Imperial Extra Double Stout* 117
Harviestoun brewery: *Ola Dubh* 126
Hausbrauerei Zum Schlüssel: *Original Schlüssel* 86
Havran Tmavý Ležák 12° 104
Hawaii 184–7
Hazelnut Brown Nectar 186
Heavy Seas Small Craft Warning Über Pils 201
Hebrew Origin Pomegranate Ale 197
hectolitre (HL) 248
Hefeweizen 249
Hefeweizen Pour 38–9
Heineken 94, **136–7**, 148, 152
Heineken, Freddie 136
Hell 150
Heller-Bräu Trum: *Aecht Schlenkerla Rauchbier Märzen* 84
Helles 82–3, 248
hemp beer 212
Herbst, Neil 212
Hercule Stout 74
Hida Takayama Brewing: *Stout* 236
high-gravity brewing 26, 30, 248
Hilden brewery 118
Hirter Morchl 95
Hitachino Nest Nipponia 236
Hoa Viên Brauhaus: *Special* 238
Hobsons Brewery: *Mild* 120
Hoegaarden 72
Hofblues 74
Hofbräu Munich: *Oktoberfestbier* 82
Hofbrouwerij brewery: *Hofblues* 74
Hog Heaven Barley Wine 188
Hog's Back Brewery: *OTT Old Tongham Tasty* 121
Holgate Brewhouse: *Mt Macedon Ale* 228
Holy Heart of Westmalle 56; *Westmalle Dubbel* 57; *Westmalle Tripel* 57
Hooker Brewery: *Galway Hooker Irish Pale Ale* 111

Hop Hog India Pale Ale 229
Hopf Brauhaus: *Weisse* 239
Hopfen 192
Hopfenstark, L'Assomption: *Postcolonial IPA* 209
Hopitoulas IPA 201
Hoppit Classic Bitter 112
hops 15, **18**, *19*, **22–3**, 248; American 18, 28; dry hopping 23, 248; harvesting 113; Saaz 18, 98, 100; Styrian 94, 112
Hopus 78
Hopwired IPA 230
Hornbeer brewery: *Black Magic Woman* 146
Horny Toad Cerveza 201
Howe Sound Brewing: *King Heffy Imperial Hefeweizen* 212
Huisbrouwerij Klein Duimpie: *Klein Duimpje Hillegoms Tarwe Bier* 139
Huisbryggeriet Jacobsen: *Jacobsen Extra* 146
Human Fish Pale Ale 169
Humulus Ludicrous 211

ice beers 30
Iceland 144
Ich Bin Ein Berliner Weisse 197
Imper Ale Chiara 160
Imperial 248
Imperial Brown Stout 125
Imperial Extra Double Stout 117
India 244
India Pale Ale (Ægir Bryggeri) 148
India Pale Ale (Berlina Pub) 224
India Pale Ale (Brasserie Trois Dames) 170
India Pale Ale (Marble) 188
India Pale Ales (IPAs) 104, 110, 248
Indslev Bryggeri: *Sort Hvede* 147
industrial brewing 248
Infantøl 146
International Bitterness Units (IBU) 18
invalid stout 118
Ireland 116–19; map *117*
Island Bere 125
Island Hoppin' IPA 203
Island Red 208
Islenskur Úrvals Stout 144
Israel 242
Istedgade Hipster Ale 146
Italy 158–65; map *159*
IV Saison 68

Jackson, Michael 6, 34
Jacobsen Extra 146
Jaipur IPA 112
Jämtlands Bryggeri: *Hell* 150
Japan 234–7; map *235*
Jenlain Ambrée 130
Jester King Craft Brewery: *Commercial Suicide* 200
Jevner Pilsener 83
jibiiru 237
Johnson, George Maw 74
Jolly Pumpkin Artisan Ales: *Bam Bière* 190
jong 65
Jopen brewery: *Extra Stout* 139

Kaggen! Stormakts Porter 150
Kaldi Dökkur 144
Kapittel Prior 54
Kauno Alus brewery: *Biržiecᵢiu* 154
Keesman Bamberger Herren 83
Keisari Elowehnä 152
Kelham Island Brewery: *Pale Rider* 112

Keller Bier 83
Kemper, Will 187
Keptinis 154
Kernel brewery: *Imperial Brown Stout* 125
King Brewery 210; *Pilsner* 211
King Heffy Imperial Hefeweizen 212
King Pilsner 211
Kinn Bryggeri: *Sjelefred* 149
Kiuchi Brewery: *Hitachino Nest Nipponia* 236
Klášter brewery: *Ležák 11°* 101
Klein Duimpje Hillegoms Tarwe Bier 139
Klosterbrauerei Andechs: *Andechser Spezial Heil* 82
Klosterbrauerei Ettal: *Ettaler Curator* 92
Klosterbrauerei Weltenburg,: *Weltenburger Kloster Asam Bock* 93
Kneitinger Bock 92
Kneitinger, Johann 92
Koch, Jim 196, 198–9
Kocour brewery: *Tmavý Ležák* 104
Koko Brown 186
Kölsch **88–9**, 249
Kona Brewing: *Brown* 186
König Ludwig Schlossbrauerei Kaltenberg: *Dunkel* 92
Koskipanimo Plevna: *Severin Extra IPA* 153
Köstritzer Schwarzbierbrauerei: *Schwarzbier* 93
Kout na Šumave brewery: *Tmavý Speciál 14°* 105
Krakonoš brewery: *Svetlý Ležák Kvasnicové 12°* 101
krausening 23, 100, 249
kriek **65**, 249
Krombacher Pils 80
Kross 5 216
Kryptonite 209
Kulmbacher Brauerei: *Mönchshof Schwarzbier* 93
Kupiškio Alus: *Keptinis* 154

L'Abbaye de Saint Bon-Chien 170
lager 20, 50, 249
lagering 23
L'Agrivoise La Commun'Ale 132
Lagunitas Brewing: *Pils* 181
Laitilan Wirvoitusjuomatehdas: *Kukko Tumma* 152
Lake Michigan: map *191*
lambic beers **62–5**, 249
Lammin Sahti Oy: *Lammin Sahti* 152
Landlord 112
Lao Brewery: *Beerlao Lager* 232
Latvia 154
Lava 144
Le-Brewery: *Odo* 133
Le Trou du Diable: *Dulcis Succubus* 208
Lead Dog Ale 212
Leeds Brewery: *Midnight Bell* 120
Lervig Aktiebryggeri: *Lucky Jack* 149
Les Trois Mousquetaires: *Porter Baltique* 209
Ležia k Tatran 12° Export Lager 170
licensed brewing 249
Lichtenstein 171
Liechtensteiner Brauhaus: *Brauhaus Malbu-Bock* 168
light beers 30, 76
Limburgse Witte 72
Limet, Marc 76
Limfjords Porter 146
Lindemans Cuvée René Oude Gueuze 65

Lion Brewery: *Stout* 242
Lithuania 154
Litovel brewery: *Svátecní Speciál 13°* 101
Little Creatures Brewery: *Pale Ale* 229
Live Oak Brewing: *Pilz* 201
Loddon Brewery: *Hoppit Classic Bitter* 112
Lohin, Gary 212
London 116
The Lost Abbey 178, 182, 202; *The Angel's Share* 183
Louisiane Brewhouse: *Dark Lager* 238
Lucky Jack 149
Luther, Martin 92
Luxembourg 171

Macedonian Thrace Brewery: *Vergina Weiss* 171
Macks Ølbryggeri: *Juleøl* 149
The Mad Elf Ale 199
Mad Hatter India Pale Ale 192
Maduro Brown Ale 201
Mahr's Bräu brewery: *Ungespundet-hefetrüb* 85
Maisel's Weisse Kristall 90
maize 28
Malheur Bieren: *Dark Brut* 78
Malmgårdin Panimo Oy: *X-Porter* 152
malt 15, **17**, 22, 30, 249
Malta 171
Marble Brewery: *Chocolate Marble* 124; *India Pale Ale* 188
Marcus Aurelius 126
Märzen 82–3, 249
Märzen (Staffelberg-Bräu) 83
mashing 12, **22**, 249; decoction mashing 98, 102
Matilda 192
Matten La Schwortz 132
Matthy, John 64
Matuska, Adam *105*
Matuška brewery 105, 106; *Raptor IPA 15°* 105
Maudite 209
Maxim Brewery: *Double Maxim* 120
Maytag, Fritz 180
McAuliffe, Jack 178, 181
McGrath's Irish Black 117
McMenamin, Brian & Mike 186–7
McNally's Extra 213
Meantime Brewing Company *116*; *London Porter* 117
Mehringer Altb ayerisches Weissbier Dunkel 90
Meibok 138–9
Melchior 58
Merkendorfer Hummel-Bräu Räucherla 84
Merlin Cerný Tmavé Ležák 105
Meteor Pils 133
méthode traditionale 249
Mexico 177, 218–19
Micro Brasserie L'Agrivoise: *L'Agrivoise La Commun'Ale* 132
Micro Brasserie "Le Paradis: *La P'tite Sylvie* 131
MicroBrasserie Charlevoix: *Dominus Vobiscum Brut* 208
microbrewery 99, 249
Middle East 242
Midnight Bell 120
Midnight Sun Brewing: *Arctic Devil Barley Wine* 184
Midtfyns Bryghus: *Ale* 146
Midwest America 190–3
Mighty Oak Brewing: *Oscar Wilde* 121
Mikkeller brewery 145, 172; *Beer Geek Breakfast* 147

mild ale 249
Milton Brewery: *Marcus Aurelius* 126
Minami Shinshu Beer: *Dunkel Weizen* 236
Minoh Brewery: *Imperial Stout* 237
Mitchell's Extra Special Bitter 213
Mitchell's Knysna Brewery: *Raven Stout* 242
Moa Brewing: *Five Hop* 230
Mojo India Pale Ale 188
Mokumoku Ji-Beer: *Smoked Ale* 239
MolsonCoors 207
Mommeriete brewery: *Blond* 140
Monaco 171
Mönchsambacher Lager 84
Montréal *209*
Moorhouse's Brewery: *Pendle Witches Brew* 112
Moorilla Estate: *Moo Brew Dark Ale* 229
Moosehead Brewing 208
Mordue Brewery: *Workie Ticket* 113
Mühlen Kölsch 89
Münchener 17, 92, 154, 155
Murray's Craft Brewing: *Pilsner* 228
museums: Budvar Museum and Brewery 106; Cantillon Brewery/Museum 63; National Brewing Centre, Burton-upon-Trent 111
Mussel Inn,: *Captain Cooker Manuka Beer* 230
Musso, Teo 160, 163
My Bloody Valentine 182

Náchod Primátor Weizenbier 105
Närke Kulturbryggeri: Kaggen! Stormakts Porter 150
Naudts, Dirk 76–7
Negev Brewing: *Porter Alon* 243
Netherlands 136–41; map *137*
New Albion Brewing 178, 181
New Belgium Brewing: *Ranger India Pale Pale* 189
New England: map *198*
New Holland Brewing: *Mad Hatter India Pale Ale* 192
New York City 199; map *197*
New Zealand 172, 230–1; map *230*
Nickels, Bret 183
Nightmare 118
Nils Oscar Company: *Rökporter* 151
Nodding Head Brewery 202; *Ich Bin Ein Berliner Weisse* 197
Nøgne Ø brewery 148, 172; *Imperial Stout* 149
Nokian Panimo Oy: *Keisari Elowehnä* 152
NOLA Brewing: *Hopitoulas IPA* 201
Norfolk Island Brewery 243
Nørrebro Bryghus: *Pacific Summer Ale* 147
North America 176–7
North Coast Brewing: *Pranqster* 182
North Rhine Westphalia 86–7
Northeast America 196–9
Norway 148–9
Nuit de Goguette 133
Nynäshamns Ångbryggeri: *Smörpundet Porter* 151

O8 126
oak-aged ales 58–9
Oak Aged Yeti Imperial Stout 188
Oakham Ales brewery: *Bishops Farewell* 110
oast houses *111*
oats 17
Oberfranken 84
Obolon: *Pshenichne* 170

Ocean Bryggeriet: *Julöl* 151
Odell Brewing: 5 Barrel Pale Ale 188
Odineke Oilsjtersen Tripel 78
Odo 133
Oerbier Reserva 59
O'Hara's Leann Folláin 118
Okkara brewery: *Portari* 147
Oktoberfest 80, **246**
Ola Dubh 126
Old Brown Dog Ale 198
Old Deuteronomy Barley Wine 213
Olivier, Mennon 140
Ölvisholt Brugghús: *Lava* 144
Ommegang Ale 198
Ontario 206, 210–11
Opat Medový Kvasnicák 12° 101
Oppigårds Bryggeri: *Amarillo* 151
Ørbæk Bryggeri: *Fynsk Forår* 146
Organic Chocolate Stout 181
original gravity (OG) 249
Original Pinkus Obergärig 86
Original Schlüssel 86
Orkney Brewery: *Dark Island Reserve* 126
Orval 54
Oscar Wilde 121
Oskar Blues Brewery: *Dale's Pale Ale* 188
Otaru Beer: *Pilsner* 237
Otley Brewing: *O8* 126
OTT Old Tongham Tasty 121
Otter Brewery: *Mild* 121
Oud Beersel: *Oude Kriek* 65
Ourdaller Brauerei: *Wëllen Ourdaller* 171
oxidation 15, 18, 158, 249
Oyster Stout 231

Pacific Islands 243
Pacific Northwest 184–7
Päffgen Beer Hall *88*
Päffgen Kölsch 89
pale ale 28, 29, 34, **110–13**
Pale Ale 224
pale ale 249
pale lagered beers 82–3
pale lagers 98, 100–3
pale malts 82
Pale Rider 112
Palliser Porter 211
Palm Breweries: *Dobbel* 78
Palmers brewery 113
Palo Santo Marron 198
Panil Barriquée 161
Papazian, Charlie 188
pasteurization 15, 23, 112, 249
Pater Lieven Bruin 79
Paulaner Brauerei: *Salvator* 93
Pausa Cafe: *Tosta* 162
Payottenland 63, 65
Penlon Cottage Brewery: *Twin Ram* 127
Pernštejn brewery: *Pardubický Porter 19°* 106
Petrus Aged Pale 59
phenolic 249
Philadelphia: map *197*
Phillips Brewing: *Amnesiac Double IPA* 212
Phillips, Matt 212
Pike Brewing: *XXXXX Extra Stout* 187
Pikeland Pils 198
Pilsen 102
Pilsner Urquell: *Unpasteurized Tank Beer* 102
pilsners *8*, 82–3, 100–3, 249
Pink IPA 161
PINT (Promotie Informatie Traditioneel Bier) 137, 138–9

Pitburger Premium Beer 82
Pitfield Brewery: *1850 London Porter* 118
Pivovar Pilsberg: *Ležia k Tatran 12° Export Lager* 170
Pivovara Licanka: *Tamno Velebitsko Pivo* 171
Pivovarna Adam Ravbar: *Human Fish Pale Ale* 168
Pivovarna Cloveška Ribica: *Human Fish Pale Ale* 169
Pivovarna Zagorka: *Stolichno Temno* 171
Platan brewery: *Merlin Cerný Tmavé Ležák* 105
Plato 249
Pliny the Younger 204
Poirot, Hercule 74
Poland 168
Polygamy Porter 189
Ponoras Kaimiškas Nefiltruotas Šviesusis Biržietiškas 154
Poppy Jasper Amber Ale 181
Portamarillo 172
Porter Baltique 209
Porterhouse Brewing 118; *Wrasslers XXXX* 119
porters **116–19**, 249
Portland 186–7; map *186*
Postcolonial IPA 209
Pot Kettle Black 231
The Prairies 210–11, *214–15*
Pranqster 182
The Premium Malts 237
pressure groups: *see* PINT; CAMRA
Prignon, Dany 77
Primátor brewery: *Náchod Primátor Weizenbier* 105
Privatbrauerei Bolten: *Boltens Ur-Alt* 86
Privatbrauerei Gaffel Becker: *Gaffel Kölsch* 89
Privatbrauerei Specht: *Schwarzer Specht* 93
Proefbrouwerij, Lochristi 76–8; *Viven Porter* 79
Prohibition 6, 176
Provo Girl Pilsner 189
Prykmestar Savu Kataja 153
La P'tite Sylvie 131
Purity Order **80**, 90, 94, 171

quadrupel 249
quality 55, 98
Québec 206, 208–9, 213

Raasted Bryghus: *Trippel Nelson* 147
Racer 5 IPA 182
racking 23
Radeberger Gruppe: *Jevner Pilsener* 83
Rail Yard Ale 189
Ranger India Pale Pale 189
Rauchbiers 84, 249
real ales 113, 249
Reale 161
Rebel brewery: *Cerný 11°* 106
Red Hook Brewery 184
Red Racer IPA 213
Reinheitsgebot **80**, 90, 94, 171, 249
Renaissance Brewing *173*; *Stonecutter Scotch Ale* 231
Restoration Pale Ale 202
Robinson's Old Tom 122
Robson's Durban Pale Ale 243
Rocky Mountains 188–9
Rodenbach brewery 58; *Grand Cru* 59
Rogue Brewery: *Hazelnut Brown Nectar* 186
Roppelt Kellerbier 85

Rothaus Pils 83
Route des Épices 209
Royal Extra Stout 203
Rudgate Brewery: *Ruby Mild* 121
Rudge, David 211
Russia 170–1, 244
Russian River Brewing 182, 204; *Collaboration Not Litigation* 172; *Pliny the Younger* 204; *Temptation* 183
Rychtár brewery: *Natur 12°* 102
Rye Squared 202
Ryman, Roger 113

sahti **152**, 154, 249
Saint Arnold Brewing: *Fancy Lawnmower* 200
saison beers **68–9**, 130, 249
Saison Cazeau 68
Saison de Pipaix 69
Saison d'Épeautre 73
Saison Dupont 69
Saison Voison 69
Salzburger Weissbierbrauerei: *Die Weisse Hell* 94
La Sambresse Blonde 78
Sambrook, Duncan 127
Sambrook's Brewery: *Wandle* 127
Samuel Adams Boston Lager 198
San Diego 182; map *182*
San Francisco Bay: map *181*
San Martino Gold 170
Sapporo brewery 208
Sara Brune 73
Sarah Hughes Brewery: *Dark Ruby* 120
Saskatchewan 206, *211*
Saxony 93
Scandinavia 142–53; map *143*
Schneider & Sohn: *Weisse* 91
Schneider, Georg 90–1
Schneider Weisse 91
Schönramer Altbayrisch Dunkel 93
Schorschbräu brewery 204
Schumacher *Alt* 87
Schuwer, Will 74
Schwarzbier 92–3, 249
Schwarzer Kristall 170
Schwarzer Specht 93
Schwechater Zwickl 95
Scotch ales 74–5, 95, 122, 249
Scotch Silly 75
Scotland 108; map *108*
Seattle: map *185*
Segura Red Ale 219
Session Lager 186
Severin Extra IPA 153
Shangrila 161
Shelta brewery 118
Shiga Kogen Beer: *House IPA* 237
Shiner Dortmunder 202
Shmaltz Brewing: *Hebrew Origin Pomegranate Ale* 197
Shonan Beer: *Ruby Ale* 237
Shongweni Brewery: *Robson's Durban Pale Ale* 243
Sia Zaksi: *Užavas Tumšais Nefiltretais* 155
Sierra Nevada Brewing 181; *Pale Ale* 182
Sigtuna Brygghus: *Extra Bitter* 151
Sillamäe Õlletehas: *München Vaskne* 155
Sinebrychoff 152
Singapore 242
Singha Lager 239
Sint Christoffel Bier 140; *Christoffel Bier* 138
skunky 249

Slaghmuylder brewery: *Witkap Pater Dubbel* 57
Slottskällans Bryggeri: *Red Ale* 151
Slovenia 168
Sly Fox Brewing: *Pikeland Pils* 198
smell 40
smoke beers 84
Smoked Porter 186, 187
Smörpundet Porter 151
Smuttynose Brewing: *Old Brown Dog Ale* 198
Snow Ghost 189
Somnambulator Doppelbock 186
Sort Hvede 147, 186
South Africa 243
South America 177, 216–25, 244–5; map *217*
South Australian Brewing: *Southwark Old Stout* 229
Southampton Publick House: *Cuvée des Fleurs* 196
Southern States (USA) 200–2
Southwark Old Stout 229
Spain 166
sparging 22
special beers 50, 74
Special de Ryck 75
Spezial Lagerbier 85
spices 72, 76
Spingo Middle 127
Spinnakers Gastro Brewpub: *Mitchell's Extra Special Bitter* 213
Spoetzl Brewery 200; *Shiner Dortmunder* 202
Sprecher Brewing: *Black Bavarian* 191
Squatters Pubs & Beers: *Provo Girl Pilsner* 189
St-Ambroise Oatmeal Stout 209
St Austell Brewery Co: *Tribute* 113
St Benedictus 55; *Trappist Achel Extra Bruin* 55
St Bernard, Watou: *St Bernadus* 55
St Boisterous Hellerbock 199
St Feuillien Triple 56
St Georgen Bräu brewery: *Keller Bier* 83
St Giles 127
St. John Brewers: *Island Hoppin' IPA* 203
St John's Stout 209
St Peter's Brewery: *Old-Style Porter* 118
St Sixtus 55, 57; *Trappist Westvleteren* 56; *Trappist Westvleteren Blond* 56
Stadsbrouwerij De Hemel: *De Hemel Godelief* 138
Staffelberg-Bräu brewery: *Märzen* 83
Stafford, Nick 118
steam beer 249
Steinbier 94, 249
Stewart Brewing: *St Giles* 127
Stichting Brouwerij de Prael: *De Prael Johnny* 138
Stiefl-Jürgens Ur-Alt Dunkel 87
stock ale 122
Stöhr GmbH & Co. brewery: *Eggenberg Urbock 23°* 94
Stolichno Temno 171
Stone Brewing 182; *Arrogant Bastard Ale* 180
Stonecutter Scotch Ale 231
storing 36, 130–1
Storm Brewing 242
Stout Leroy 75
stouts 74–5, **116–19**, 249
Strada San Felice 162
Strong Ale 225
strong ales 122–3

Strong Suffolk Vintage Ale 123
Strubbe Pils 79
styles 34, 50
sugars 26–8
Sun King Brewing: *Wee Mac Scottish Ale* 193
Sundby Stout 147
Sunshine Coast Brewery: *Summer Ale* 229
Suntory Liquors: *The Premium Malts* 237
Surrogate Prohibition (Germany) 80
Svaneke Bryghus: *Mørk Guld* 147
Svijany brewery: *Rytír 12°* 102
Swan Lake Beer: *Amber Swan Ale* 236
Sweden 150–1
Switzerland 166–8, 170
Systembolaget (drinks stores) 150
Szot Microbrewery: *Strong Ale* 225

T Smiske 79
Tambor Tmavý Speciál 13° 106
Tamerlane Brown Porter 187
Tamno Velebitsko Pivo 171
Tampa Bay Brewing 202
Tank 7 Farmhouse Ale 192
Tannenzäpfle 83
Taras Boulba 79
taste 28–9, 40–1
tasting 40–1
Tawandang German Brewery: *Dunkel* 239
Taybeh Brewing: *Golden* 243
Telenn Du 133
Temperance Movement 6, 111–12, 118, 120, *121*
Tempest Doble Malta 219
Temptation 183
Terrapin Beer Company: *Rye Squared* 202
Tervetes Originalais 155
Thailand 239
Theakston brewery: *Old Peculier* 121
Thiriez, Daniel 132
Thisted Bryghus: *Limfjords Porter* 146
Thornbridge Brewery 113; *Jaipur IPA* 112
Three Boys Brewery: *Oyster Stout* 231
Three Floyds Brewing: *Alpha King* 190
Three Tuns Brewery: *Three Tuns XXX* 112
Tilquin Gueuze à L'Àncienne 65
Tilquin, Pierre 65
Timothy Taylor brewery: *Landlord* 112
Tipopils 162
Titanic Brewery: *Stout* 119
Tonneke 79
top-fermented beers 20, 82, 91
Tosta 162
La Trappe 55, 172
La Trappe Quadrupel 139
Trappist Achel Extra Bruin 55
Trappist breweries **54–9**, 139–40, 249
Trappist Westvleteren 56
Trappist Westvleteren Blond 56
Trappistes Rochefort 6 / 8 / 10 55
Traquair House brewery: *Ale* 123
Tribute 113
Trigo 225
Tripel 249
Tripel Karmeliet 56
Trippel Belgian Style Ale 183
Tröegs Brewing: *The Mad Elf Ale* 199
Trouble Brewing 118; *Dark Arts Porter* 116
Trout Hop Black IPA 189
Trumer Privatbrauerei: *Pils* 95
Tuatara Brewing: *APA* 230

Tübinger Microbrews: *Brown Ale* 225
Turkey 242
Tuscany 160, 162
Twin Ram 127

U Fleku (brewpub) *104*, 106; *Flekovský Tmavý Ležák 13°* 104
U Medvídku brewery: *X Beer 33:* 106
Uerige Obergärige Hausbrauerei: *Alt* 87
Ukraine 171
Ultra-Fraîche 69
Unertl Weissbier brewery: *Ursud* 91
unfiltered 249
Ungespundet-hefetrüb 85
Unibroue 208; *Blanche de Chambly* 208; *Maudite* 209
United States 26, 34, 172, **178–202**; map *179*
unpasteurized beer 102
unstoppered beer 84
Upright Brewing: *Five* 186
Ur 249
Urban Chestnut Brewing: *Hopfen* 192
Urban-Keller's Steinbier 95
Urpiner Ležiak VýCapný Tmavý 171
Utopias 199
Užavas Tumšais Nefiltretais 155

Vakka-Suomen Panimo Oy: *Prykmestar Savu Kataja* 153

Valhalla Brewery: *Island Bere* 125
Van Eecke, Watou: *Kapittel Prior* 54
Van Roy, Jean *29*, 63
Van Steenberge brewery: *Gulden Draak* 77
VandenBerghe, Matt 36
VCBW Cascadian Dark Ale 172
Vecchia Bastarda 162
Verdi Imperial Stout 163
Vergina Weiss 171
Verhelst, Grégory 77
Vicaris Generaal 79
Victory Brewing: *St Boisterous Hellerbock* 199
Vienna 163
Vienna Lager 187
Vienna lager 249
Vietnam 238
Viking Ölgerd: *Islenskur Úrvals Stout* 144
Vilnius 154, *156–7*
Viven Porter 79
Vivre pour Vivre 221
Vollbier 84
Vyškov brewery: *Havran Tmavý Ležák 12°* 104

Waase Wolf 73
Wagner-Bräu brewery: *Pils* 83
Wälder Senn 95

Wales: map *108*
Walking Man Brewing: *Somnambulator Doppelbock* 186
Wallonian beers 68–9
Wandle 127
Wasatch Brew: *Polygamy Porter* 189
water content 30
Way Amburana Lager 221
Wee Mac Scottish Ale 193
Weihenstephaner Hefe Weissbier 91
Weissbier 249
Weisses Brauhaus Wolfgang Mehringer brewery: *Mehringer Alth ayerisches Weissbier Dunkel* 91
Weitra Bräu Hadmar 95
Weizenbier 249
Weizenbock beers 91
Wëllen Ourdaller 171
Weltenburger Kloster Asam Bock 93
Westmalle Dubbel 57
Westmalle Tripel 57
Westphalia 86–7; map 87
wheat **17**
wheat beers 62–5, **72–3**, 90–1, 106, **132–3**, 249
white beers **72–3**, 249
Wiener 249
William Worthington's Brewery: *White Shield* 113

Williams Bros Brewing: *Fraøch Heather Ale* 125
Wisconsin Belgian Red 193
Witkap Pater Dubbel 57
Woodforde's Broadland Brewery: *Wherry* 113
Workie Ticket 113
worts 20, 22, *23*, 94, 249
Wrasslers XXXX 119
Wye Valley Brewery: *Dorothy Goodbody's Wholesome Stout* 117
Wynkoop Brewing: *Rail Yard Ale* 189

XX / XXX 55
XXXXX Extra Stout 187
Xyauyù Etichetta Argento 163

Yakima Brewing 181, 202
Yakima Valley 184
yeast 15, **20–1**, 249; Hefeweizen 20, 90–1; saccharomyces 65; skimming *91*; wild 20, 28, 65
yeast beer 100
Yeastie Boys: *Pot Kettle Black* 231
YellowBelly Brewery: *St John's Stout* 209
Yukon Brewing 212; *Lead Dog Ale* 212
Žatecký brewery: *Baronka Premium 13°* 102

Zwergla 85

Picture Credits

Abbaye Rochefort www.abbaye-rochefort.be 55 a; **Adnams Brewery** www.admans.co.uk 123; **Alamy** Arterra Picture Library 60–1, 70–1, 73; Aurora Photos 7; BigTom 66–7; Blickwinkel 94; Bon Appetit 19; Cephas 54 bc, 55 br, 56 bl & br, 59 bc, 69 bl; Chris Frederiksson 8 r, 245 ar; Danita Delimont 200, 244; Darren Baker 92; David Jones 133; David Noton Photography 46; Eddie Gerald 104, 106; F1online 168; Gareth Dobson 82; guichaoua 134–5; H Mark Weidman Photography 177 br; ilpo musto 78 a; Imagebroker 96–7; ITAR-TASS Photo Agency 245 b; John Woodworth 233 b; Jonny Cochrane 153 ar; Julia Gavin 156–7; Kari Niemeläinen 153 al; Lonely Planet Images 37 ar, 170 l, 203; Lordprice Collection 162; M&N 113 al; Mary Evans Picture Library 6 b; Mireille Vautier 219; Neil McAllister 112; Niall McDiarmid 35; Oliver Knight 52; Om Images 166 a; Peter Adams Photography 151; Picture Contact BV 140, 141; praguepix 101; Prisma Archivo 14; Prisma Bildagentur AG 194–5; Robert Estall Photography 111 r; Robert Gilhooly 237 l; Robert Harding World Imagery 103, 130, 142; Stephen Roberts Photography 56 a; Tegestology 59 br; Universal Images Group/Lake County Discovery Museum 218; Werner Dieterich 88 a; Yadid Levy 128, 177 a; **Aldaris Brewery** www.aldaris.lv 154; **Alesmith Brewing Company** StudioSchulz.com 12; **Alley Kat Brewing Company** www.alleykatbeer.com 213; **Anderson Valley Brewing Company** www.avbc.com 183 l; **Beergenie.co.uk** Warminster Maltings 17; **Bernt Rostad** www.flickr.com/people/brostad 138; **Birra Almond '22** www.birraalmond.com 163; **Birrificio Italiano** www.birrificio.it 161; **Brouwerij Boon** www.boon.be 62; **The Boston Beer Co Inc/Weihenstephan** www.bostonbeer.com 172 l, 199; **Brasserie de Silly SA** 74, Jimmy Tanghe 75 l; **La Brasserie à Vapeur** www.vapeur.com 68; **The Brewers Association** www.brewersassociation.org 189 l; **Bridgeman Art Library** Hermitage, St. Petersburg/Peter Willi 65; **Camba Bavaria** www.braukon.de 93 r; **CAMRA** www.gbbf.org.uk 125 r; **Carlsberg** www.carlsberggroup.com 15; **Cephas** Joris Luyten 59; **Cerveza Berlina** www.cervezaberlina.com 224; **Cerveza Blest** www.cervezablest.com 225; **Charles D Cook** 29 a, 77; **Corbis** Atlantide Phototravel 164–5, 169, 209; C J Blanchard/National Geographic Society 184 a; Chris Sattlberger 166 b; Darwin Wiggett/All Canada Photos 214–15; David Yoder/National Geographic Society 48–9; Gaetan Bally/Keystone 31; Image Source 240–1; Imaginechina 246 c; John Short/Design Pics 114–15; Knaup/photocuisine 43; Larry Mulvehill 83; Luke MacGregor/Reuters 125 l; Michael Nicholson 113 ar; Monty Rakusen/cultura 20, 28 b; Moodboard 226–7; Niall MacLeod 11; Owen Franken 57; Pecanic, Maja Danica/the food passionate 45 r; Philip Gould 201; Radius Images 174–5; Robert Simoni/Robert Harding World Imagery 222–3; Stephanie Maze 220; Steve Raymer 238 r; Swim Ink 2/LLC 131 l; Tim Thompson 212; Wayne Barrett & Anne MacKay/All Canada Photos 211; **Craft Beer** www.craftbeer.com 177 b l; **Dark Star Brewery** www.darkstarbrewing.co.uk 126 & 7;

Brouwerij De Ryck, Herzele www.brouwerijderyck.be 75 a & b; **Duvel Moortgat** www.duvel.be 79; **Emerson's** www.emersons.co.nz 231; **Fotolia** Beboy 233 al; BesitosClaudis 158; David Kelly 37 a4; euregiophoto 88 b; Gradt 37 b5; Iuliia Sokolovska 239; John Photon 69 a; Jules Kitano 234 b; Richard Majlinder 147; sonne07 84; spinetta 37 a5, 37 b2; WoGi 37 b3; **Fullers** www.fullers.co.uk 122 r; **Getty Images** 6 a, 50 b, 120 r, 111 l, 121; AFP 16 a; 245 al; Altrendo 16 b, 27, 91; Beth Perkins 32–3; Buyenlarge 207; Christian Kober 237 r; Darren McCollester 28 a; De Agostini 155; Gamma-Keystone 176; Hoang Dinh Nam/AFP 232; Hunstock 21; Justin Sullivan 26; Martin Poole 42; Matthias Trentsensky/Bridgeman Art Library 18; Michal Cizek/AFP 105; Miroslav Kucej/isifa 8 l; Monty Rakusen/cultura 23; Peter Macdiarmid 246 r; Rachel Weill 34; Sean Gallup 98 a, 100; Thomas Winz 246 l; **Grand Teton Brewing Co.** www.grandtetonbrewing.com 187; **Great American Beer Festival**/Jason E Kaplan www.greatamericanbeerfestival.com 189 r; **Brauerei Gutmann** www.brauerei-gutmann.de 90; **Heineken** www.heineken.com 136 b; **Japan Beer Times** www.japanbeertimes.com 236; **Jed Soane** www.thebeerproject.com 173 bl, bc & br; **Jenlain** www.jenlain.fr 131 r; **Jose Gabriel Marcelino** www.flickr.com/photos/gkpics 233 ar; **Kirin Brewery Company Limited** 234 r; **The Lost Abbey** StudioSchulz.com 22; **Mary Evans Picture Library** 110; INTERFOTO/Sammlung Rauch 80 a; **Meantime Brewery** www.meantimebrewery.com 118; **Mike McColl** 38–40; **Mikkeller** www.mikkeller.dk 173 a; **NewBrewThursday.com** 36; **Nøgne Ø Brewery** www.nogne-o.com 148, 149; **Octopus Publishing Group** Adrian Pope 2; **Photolibrary Group** 50 a, 93 l, 122 l, 159, 170 r; **R & B Brewing Co** www.r-and-b.com 172 r; courtesy **Renee De Luca** www.brewersdaughter.com 178; **Rex Features** Business Collection 136 a, Liba Taylor/Robert Harding World Imagery 216; **Robert Harding World Imagery** James Strachan 102, Yadid Levy/age footstock 89; **Rodenbach** www.palmbreweries.com 58; **Russian River Brewing Company** www.russianriverbrewing.com 172c, 204 l, 205; **Schafly Brewery** Troika Brodsky, www.schlafly.com 193; **Schorschbräu** www.benz-weltweit.de 204 r; **Shawn Parker** www.flickr.com/photos/shawnparkerphoto 192, 210; **Shutterstock** Steve Heap 37 b6; **Stone Brewing Co** StudioSchulz.com 9, 45 l; **SuperStock** age fotostock 124, Nordic Photos 107; Courtesy of **Synebrychoff** 30; **Systembolaget AB** Magnus Skoglöf 150; **Thinkstock** Brand X 158 br3; George Doyle 37 a2, 180; Hemera 72 cr & r, 98 b, 119, 158 ar3 & br2, 221; Ingram Publishing 120 l, 188; iStockphoto 37 a3, 37b4, 53, 72 l, c & cl, 80 b, 137, 158 ar1 & 2, cr 1& 2, br1,184 b, 190, 196, 206, 208, 238 l; Stockbyte 158 cr3; **Thornbridge** www.thornbridgebrewery.co.uk 113 b; **Tina Westphal** 29b, all 139; **TopFoto** Ria Novosti 171; **Brouwerij der Trappisten van Westmalle** 54 a; **Villaggio della Birra** www.villaggiodellabirra.com 160; **Brewery Zum Schlüssel** www.zumschluessel.de 86

Finally, Mitchell Beazley would like to thank all the breweries and their agents, credited on the page, who have so kindly supplied images for the Beer Selection features in this book.

Bibliography & Acknowledgements

The authors wish above all else to acknowledge the leadership and indispensible contributions of the late Michael Jackson (1942–2007), beer writing pioneer and friend. You remain in our thoughts.

We further wish to thank the following for their insight and generously offered advice, counsel and knowledge over the years, with apologies to the countless souls, here unnamed, who have abetted our research with everything from a hastily drawn map to a convivially shared pint:

Jason and Todd Alström, Mirella Amato, Bia Amorin, David Anderson, Rodolfo Andreu, Max Bahnson, Marcelo Franck Barboza, Séan Billings, Martín Boan, Matt Bonney and Matt Vandenberghe, Frank Boon, Daniel Bradford, Jay Brooks, Pete Brown and Liz Vater, Adam Brož, Lew Bryson, José Felipe Pedras Carneiro, Vinnie Cilurzo, Greg Clow, Steve Collis, John Conen, Chuck Cook, Joanna Copestick, Martyn Cornell, Jim Cornish, Peter Crombecq, Andy Crouch, Lorenzo Dabove, Erik Dahl, Tom Dalldorf, Charles Darby, Yvan De Baets, Des De Moore, Armand Debelder, Mario D'Eer, the late Ray Deter, Horst Dornbusch, Mark Dredge, Ken Ellingwood, Casimir Elsen, Tim Eustace, Jeff Evans, Don Feinberg and Wendy Littlefield, Charles and Rose Ann Finkel, Christoph Flaskamp, Theo Flissebaalje, Tony Forder, David Frost, Sara Gardner, Brian Glover, Joe Goldsworthy, Jeremy Gray, Geoff Griggs, Hubert Hanghöfer, John Hansell and Amy Westlake, Stan Hieronymus, Paul Holgate, Bo Jensen, Julie Johnson, Heikki Kähkönen, Dave Keene, Dominic Kelly, Roger Kerrison, Matt Kirkegaard, Fernanda Lazzari, Marie-Josée Lefebvre, Kari Likovuori, Marc Limet, Iain Loe, Tom Maderos, Jeannine Marois, Ben McFarland, Mark Meli, Juliano Borges Mendes, Ralph Morana, Lisa Morrison, Laurent Mousson, Matthias Neidhart, Luke Nicholas, Thomas Nilsson, Eamonn O'Dowd, Peter Olesen, Menno Olivier, Garrett Oliver, Andzrej Olkowski, Charlie Papazian, Amilcar Parada, Edu Passarelli, Ron Pattinson, Joris Pattyn, Anne-Mette Meyer Pedersen, Clare Pelino, Tom Peters, Cassio Piccolo, Chris Pollard and Siobhan McGinn, Roger Protz, Evan Rail, Scott Robertson, Marcelo Carneiro da Rocha, Roger Ryman, Rie Sasaki, Lucy Saunders, Jaan Schaer, Keith Schlabs, Chris Schryer, Conrad Seidl, Dan Shelton, Tim and Amanda Skelton, Joe Stange, Torben Steenberg, Peter Sutcliffe and Pauline Doyle, "Dr." Bill Sysak, Mike and Bo Tessier, Steve Thomas, Adrian Tierney-Jones, Rob Titley, Matthias Trum, Joe Tucker, Kerry Tyack, Fred Waltman, Polly Watts, and the late John White.

Thank you to the Barth-Haas Group for permission to use data from *The Barth Report: Hops 2010/2011*.

Beer-friendly networks and finding your way about:

International:	www.ratebeer.com; www.beeradvocate.com; www.beerme.com; www.beermapping.com; www.beerfestivals.org
Europe:	www.europeanbeerguide.net
Australia:	*The Beer Lover's Guide to Australia*, Matt Kirkegaard (Scribal Publishing, 978-0977565610); *The Australian Beer Companion*, Willie Simpson (Explore Australia, 978-1741173697); www.pint.au.com
Austria:	*Bier Guide* Conrad Seidl (www.bier-guide.net); consumer group Bier IG (www.BierIG.org)
Belgium:	*Good Beer Guide Belgium*, Tim Webb (CAMRA Books, 978-1852492618); *LambicLand*, Tim Webb, Chris Pollard and Siobhan McGinn (Cogan and Mater, 978-0954778972); consumer group Zythos (www.zythos.be); www.babblebelt.com
Brazil:	www.brejas.com.br
Canada:	www.canadianbeernews.com; *TAPS The Beer Magazine*; www.bartowel.com
Czech Republic:	Consumer group SPP (www.pratelepiva.cz); www.pivni.info
Denmark:	Danske Ølentusiaster (www.ale.dk)
Finland:	Consumer group Olutliitto (www.olutliitto.fi)
France:	www.brasseries-france.info
Germany:	*Good Beer Guide Germany*, Steve Thomas (CAMRA Books, 978-1852492199); www.german-breweries.com; www.bierfranken.eu; www.franconiabeerguide.com
Ireland:	Consumer group Beoir (www.beoir.org)
Italy:	*Guida alle Birre d'Italia 2011*, L. Giaccone (Slow Food, 978-8884992093); consumer group Unionbirrai (www.unionbirrai.com); www.microbirrifici.org
Latvia:	*Beer Guide Latvia* (pdf file at http://labsalus.lv/beer-guide/)
Lithuania:	www.alutis.lt/aludariai
Netherlands:	Consumer group PINT (www.pint.nl); www.cambrinus.nl
New Zealand:	www.beertourist.co.nz; www.brewersguild.org.nz
Norway:	Consumer group Norøl (www.nor-ale.org)
Poland:	Consumer group Bractwo Piwni (www.bractwopiwni.pl)
Sweden:	Consumer group SÖ (www.svenskaolframjandet.se)
Switzerland:	Consumer group ABO (www.abo-ch.org); www.bov.ch/beer/swissbeers.htm
UK:	Consumer group CAMRA (www.camra.org.uk); *Good Beer Guide*, Roger Protz (CAMRA Books, annual); *Good Bottled Beer Guide: The CAMRA Guide to Real Ale in a Bottle*, Jeff Evans (CAMRA Books, 978-1852492625)
US:	Beer magazines include *All About Beer*; *Beer Advocate*; *Celebrator*; *DRAFT*; *Imbibe*; *Ale Street News*. For general brewery information, www.brewersassociation.com and www.craftbeer.com, plus innumerable regional guidebooks and websites.

Further reading:

Brewers Publications in the United States maintains a catalogue of numerous books covering topics from homebrewing and beer styles to how to open a craft brewery. While a few of our favourites are listed below, the rest may be reviewed at www.brewerspublications.com.

The Best of American Beer and Food: Pairing & Cooking with Craft Beer, Lucy Saunders (Brewers Publications, 978-0937381915)

Brew Like a Monk: Trappist, Abbey and Strong Belgian Ales and How to Brew Them, Stan Hieronymus (Brewers Publications, 978-0937381878)

Dictionary of Beer and Brewing (Second Edition), Dan Rabin and Carl Forget (Brewers Publications, 978-0937381618)

The beer historian and blogger Ron Pattinson has built a treasure trove of research and insight at his blog "Shut Up About Barclay Perkins", much of which he has subsequently compiled in themed books he self-publishes. Browse the complete selection at http://barclayperkins.blogspot.com

Scotland! The Truth About Scottish Beer, Ronald Pattison (Kilderkin)

Brown Beer Ronald Pattison (Kilderkin)

Peace! Beer in the 1920s and 1930s, Ronald Pattison (Kilderkin)

One of us (Tim) publishes a series of city beer guides that the other (Stephen) frankly thinks are quite clever. A few are listed below, but the entire up-to-date catalogue may be discovered at www.booksaboutbeer.com.

Around Berlin in 80 Beers, Peter Sutcliffe (Cogan and Mater, 978-0954778989)

Around Bruges in 80 Beers, Chris Pollard and Siobhan McGinn (Cogan and Mater, 978-0954778941)

Around Amsterdam in 80 Beers, Tim Skelton (Cogan and Mater, 978-0954778965)

Uncorking the Past, Patrick E McGovern (University of California Press, 978-0520267985): for the rationale of how man's thirst for beer and wine shaped our world.

We also like:

Hops & Glory: One Man's Search for the Beer that Built the British Empire, Pete Brown (Macmillan, 978-0330511865)

Amber Gold & Black: The History of Britain's Great Beers, Martyn Cornell (The History Press, 978-0752455679)

Cheers! An Intemperate History of Beer in Canada, Nicholas Pashley (Collins, 978-1554682577)

America Walks into a Bar: A Spirited History of Taverns and Saloons, Speakeasies and Grog Shops, Christine Sismondo (Oxford University Press, 978-0199734955)